Sport, Culture & Society, Vol. 12
Karin A. E. Volkwein-Caplan
SPORT | FITNESS | CULTURE

## ABOUT THE SERIES — SPORT, CULTURE & SOCIETY

The "Sport, Culture & Society" series deals with issues intersecting sport, physical activity and cultural concerns. The focus of the book series is interdisciplinary, groundbreaking work that draws on different disciplines and theoretical approaches, such as sociology, philosophy, cultural anthropology, history, cultural studies, feminist studies, postmodernism, or critical theory. The "Sport, Culture & Society" series seeks to reflect both, the variety of research concerns from a multi-disciplinary perspective and discussions of current topics in sport and physical activity and their relationship to culture.

## The Editors:

Karin Volkwein-Caplan (USA), Jasmin Tahmaseb McConatha (USA), and Keith Gilbert (UK)

**For further information about the book series or the submission of proposals please contact:**

Karin Volkwein-Caplan, West Chester University, Department of Kinesiology, West Chester,PA 19383, USA, e-mail: *kvolkwein@wcupa.edu*

Jasmin Tahmaseb McConatha, West Chester University, Department of Kinesiology, West Chester, PA 19383, USA, e-mail: *jtahmaseb mcconatha@wcupa.edu*

Keith Gilbert, University of East London, School of Health, Sport and Bioscience; Water Lane, Stratford, London E145 4LZ, e-mail: *k.gilbert@uel.ac.uk*

Sport, Culture & Society, Vol. 12
Karin A. E. Volkwein-Caplan

# SPORT | FITNESS | CULTURE

Meyer & Meyer Sport

British Library Cataloguing in Publication Data
A catalogue record for this book is available from the British Library

Karin A. E. Volkwein-Caplan
Sport | Fitness | Culture
1st edition 2014
Maidenhead: Meyer & Meyer Sport (UK) Ltd., 2014
(Sport, Culture & Society; Vol. 12)
ISBN 978-1-78255-041-9

© 2017 by Meyer & Meyer Sport (UK) Ltd.
1st reprint 2017 of the 1st edition 2014
Aachen, Auckland, Beirut, Budapest, Cairo, Cape Town, Dubai, Hägendorf,
Indianapolis, Maidenhead, Singapore, Sydney, Tehran, Vienna

 Member of the World Sport Publishers' Association (WSPA)
www.w-s-p-a.org

Printed by: Color House Graphics, Grand Rapids, MI, USA
ISBN: 978-1-78255-041-9
E-Mail: info@m-m-sports.com
www.m-m-sports.com

# CONTENTS

# **DEDICATION**

To the people I love and who inspire me, – most of all James and Benjamin, and my parents. And to the many students at West Chester University who will not stop being inquisitive, and thus, keep me going...

# FOREWORD

Universally, in the world throughout the years, sport and all its associated facets are part of daily and weekly communication media in every country on Earth. Historically, it has been principally a major part of male life. The 20th century provided for the emergence of women into this "sacrosanct" men's world. Associated with the phenomenal development was the creative need for it to encroach upon education for all women.

The cultural impact along with the differentiated anatomical and physiological variations between the sexes has expanded into medical, psychological, and social complications that increased the total complexity of athletics/sport for all females. Thus, Dr. Karin A. E. Volkwein-Caplan and her professional associates have, like Jason and the Argonauts, built a ship to invade the technical and controversial field.

Dr. Volkwein-Caplan's professional life coupled with her extensive experience in the educational field has provided the rather unique qualifications required to successfully captain this project. To completely enhance and magnify her reputation, drive, and dedication, she has fearlessly proceeded with not only her education in a number of universities in several major countries but has been a principal investigator and participant in professional international conferences with many successful presentations and subsequent publications. Like the success of Jason and the Argonauts, I predict Karin and her "educational crew," though the production of texts like this, will bring back the "golden fleece of Colchis!"

*Russell L. Sturzebecker, Ph.D.*
*Professor Emeritus*
*West Chester University*
*September 2004*

# INTRODUCTION

## SPORT | FITNESS | CULTURE

*Sport for every person, all through life, and an intensification of international efforts in physical training, could have decisive impact on solving the problems of today's world. (UNESCO Declaration)*

*Contemporary sport is an important part of social, political, cultural and economic engagement, action and struggle in the global age. (Marjoribanks & Farquharson, 2012)*

Millions of people around the globe participate in a vast array of sport, fitness, and physical activities on a daily basis. They span from young to old and come from all walks of life – whether they engage in play, coaching, sporting competition, fitness and health activities, or even as spectators; and they talk about sports, even if they are not actively involved. Sport has become an integral part of the lives of many people in the 21st century, not only in highly industrialized societies. Thus, physical activities, fitness, and sports can be considered cultural practices reflecting multiple meanings. Sometimes these activities are trivilized as being separate from the real world. However, the book series *Sport, Culture & Society* deals with issues intersecting sport, fitness, and physical activity with cultural and societal concerns; and thus, interpreting sport as a microcosm of society. Indeed, sport, fitness, and physical activities are also phenomena for social change, since they have a profound influence on social life for many people of all ages in all parts of the world.

The focus of the book series is interdisciplinary and multicultural, drawing from various disciplines and theoretical approaches, such as sociology, psychology, cultural anthropology, history, philosophy, feminist/gender/race studies, political science, all of which are applied to this text, *Sport – Fitness – Culture*. Thus, the perspectives represented in this book reflect a variety of research concerns from a multidisciplinary perspective, as well as discussions of current topics in sport, fitness, and physical activity and their relationship to culture. *Sport – Fitness – Culture* is the culmination of research and teachings undertaken during the tenure of my academic life, including the work of various faculty members and graduate students from institutions I have worked at in the United States and Germany. Thus, this work reflects various cultural understandings and interpretations of sport, fitness, and physical activity in the 21st century. It is my hope that this volume, *Sport – Fitness – Culture,* will aid in improving the understanding between different cultures, various theoretical backgrounds, and the plentiful interpretations of the field of kinesiology, encompassing all forms of physical activity undertaken by human beings.

This book starts out with laying the theoretical foundations for the sociology and psychology of sport, fitness, and physical activity (Chapters 1 and 2), as well as culture and values in the 21st century (Chapter 3). Then the health aspects (Chapter 4) and youth involvement in sport, fitness, and physical activity (Chapter 5) are discussed. Major concerns of interpretations of race/ethnicity, gender, (dis)ability, and body image issues as applied to human movement are analyzed in Chapters 6, 7, 8 and 9. Lastly, the influences of politics on sport - fitness - physical activity and vice versa, as well as the relationship between sport and religion, conclude this text (Chapter 10).

In order to better facilitate discussions about the role of sport, fitness, and physical activity in the 21st century, it is necessary to first lay out the definitions and key concepts used throughout this book. While Chapter 3 focuses on culture and values and their effects on human movement, this introduction will establish working definitions for the terms "sport," "fitness," and "health" as they will be used throughout this text.

## Definition of Terms

### Fitness and Health

The scientific literature in kinesiology (performance and human movement related sciences) distinguishes between two forms of physical fitness: one related to health, including rehabilitation; and the other related to performance. Fitness is often described as an integral part of health and self-realization:

> Physical fitness is considered a multifaceted continuum which measures the quality of health ranging from death and disease that severely limit activity to the optimal functional abilities of various physical aspects of life. (AAHPER Research Council, 1996)

The concept of fitness not only refers to exercise and its effects, but also to the general state of a person's psychophysical well-being (Glassner, 1990, 216). Although some fitness enthusiasts distinguish between fitness and health, in everyday usage, the two words have become generally synonymous. Both terms incorporate exercise, diet, lifestyle, and more (Volkwein, 1998).

> The International Consensus Conference on Physical Activity, Physical Fitness, and Health (Bouchard, et al., 1990) defined health as a 'human condition with physical, social, and psychological dimensions, each characterized on a continuum with positive and negative poles. Positive health is associated with a capacity to enjoy life and withstand challenges; it is not merely the absence of disease. Negative health is associated with morbidity and, in the

extreme, with premature mortality.' (U.S. Department of Health and Human Services, 1996).

Fitness and health also reflect the underlying concept that both are essential to the development of individuals, for the body as well as the mind. *"Mens sana in corpore sano"* – a sound mind in a sound body. Fitness is "stabilized health," achieved through training. Indeed, both are associated with the quality of life, with life satisfaction and fulfillment, as well as the ecological and social parameters of each individual. That is, fitness and health are major determinants of how well people master their lives and adapt to new situations and requirements.

Numerous researchers have evaluated the benefits associated with regular participation in fitness activities. Uhlenbruck (1992, 1996), for example, in his immunological research on cancer and sport found that the effects of a well-balanced engagement in movement, sport, or fitness activities have led to a sense of subjective psychological well-being. He also found an increase in cognitive ability and creativity. Other researchers have noted that as a consequence of greater physical endurance, people are better able to master the daily routines of the job and the home. Furthermore, when engagement in sport and fitness activities results in enjoyment, the subjective quality of life is also positively influenced regardless of age (Volkwein-Caplan & Tahmaseb McConatha, 2012; see also Chapter 4 in this text).

### Cultural Variations of the Term Sport

The term "sport" has many definitions around the globe and multiple meanings, which can only be fully understood within its historical, social, and cultural contexts. The origin of the word "sport" is derived from the Latin *deportare*, which means "to divert." In most European languages, the term "sport" has an all-inclusive meaning, incorporating a variety of human movements, including sport, recreation and leisure activities, as well as exercise and physical fitness. The German language, for example, distinguishes between different forms of sporting engagement depending on the major focus of the activity. For example, a physical activity with the orientation toward fitness is called *Fitness-Sport*; an orientation toward health is called *Gesundheits-Sport* (health sport); an orientation toward achievement and competition is called *Leistungs-Sport* (athletics or top-level sport); an orientation toward rehabilitation is called *Reha-Sport* (Volkwein, 1998). A focus on (dis)abled body sport as well as Paralympics has exploded over the past ten years (see Chapter 8). Recently, terms such as *Geronto-Fitness* (fitness activities for older adults) and *Prestige-Sport* (e.g., golf and yachting) have been added to the sporting vocabulary, which is expanding as the diversity of sporting activities increases. Hence, the term sport is used in the broadest sense of human movement and exercise.

Modern sport has been defined by the Council of Europe as a free, spontaneous physical activity, which is conducted as leisure pursuit for enjoyment, recreation, and relaxation. Proper sport is executed with physical effort and encompasses several categories, which include competitive games and athletics, outdoor pursuits, aesthetic movement (e.g., dance) and conditioning activity.

In North America, on the other hand, the term "sport" is generally used in reference to competitive sporting endeavors, which limits sports to activities that occur only in formal structures. "This definition would include officially organized running races, but not casually racing a friend" (Majoribanks & Farquharson, 2012, 4). However, any physical activity that is called a sport in North America has evolved historically from individual or team exercises. Thus, sport can be better understood as an evolving process. While certain activities might be considered sport in a given time period, they might not always be defined as such. Changes over time also shape our thinking and whether we consider an activity as a sport or not. For example, football/soccer has not always been a sport; but no one would debate that it is a sport today. In addition, new activities are emerging and taking claim of being a sport, such as the rise of extreme games or online gaming, which results in struggles over whether they are real sports. Is an activity only a real sport once it has made it to the Olympic level? What about skateboarding or e-gaming? People involved in these activities spend hours practicing and perfecting their skills. These examples demonstrate that sport is a highly contested terrain, which changes over time.

In North America, various forms of physical activity have their specific terminology depending on the focus of the activity, much like the German differentiation. However, those forms of human movement are labeled as fitness or health exercise, leisure and recreational activities, dance, play, games, and more. The term sport is not attached here, as it is in the German language, thus the concept of sport in the North American context is essentially much more narrow and only used when the main objective is competition.

> Although definitions of *sports* vary, those who offer definitions tend to emphasize that *sports* are *institutionalized competitive activities that involve rigorous physical exertion or the use of relatively complex physical skills by participants motivated by internal and external rewards.* (Coakley, 2004, 21)

Readers of this book should be aware of the historical, social, and cultural differences in the usage of the term sport, nationally and internationally. "Sport is a social and political construction. That is, how sport is constituted and what is defined as sport are the outcomes of struggles, contests and decisions that occur within particular societies at particular moments" (Majoribanks &

Farquharson, 2012, 6). However, since the *international understanding* of sport captures all aspects of human movement and physical activity, and it embraces the health aspect of regular engagement in exercise as well as functional fitness, this interpretation of *sport* seems to be more suitable for the issues discussed in this text.

## Conclusion

Social and cultural changes in the 21st century, as well as the effects of the globalization process, impact the curricular development of sport and physical education programs, health and wellness education, as well as our body culture in general. Thus, it is important to understand the impact of these changes on peoples' lives and their needs, especially in regard to physical activity. The "old" rather traditional "sport for all" concept, with its focus on competition and achievement, may not satisfy these changed physical, psychological, and spiritual needs of individuals in modern societies any longer. Rather, the "new" fitness and exercise development in the 21st century with its emphasis on health, relaxation, and general life fulfillment may be more appropriate to the contribution of the overall psychophysical well-being of modern individuals. And, as the process of globalization continues, it is likely that this understanding of fitness and exercise will spread to non-Western cultures as well. Eventually, it might become the global "sport for all" concept in the future.

# References

AAHPER Research Council (1996). *Health Related Physical Fitness Test Manual.*

Coakley, J. (2004). *Sport in Society.* 8th Edition. Boston: McGraw-Hill.

Glassner, B. (1990). "Fit for Postmodern Selfhood." In: H. Becker, M. Call (Eds.) *Symbolic Interaction and Cultural Studies.* Chicago: The University of Chicago Press. Pp. 215-243.

Marjoribanks, T. & Farquharson, K. (2012). *Sport and Society in the Global Age.* Great Britain: Palgrave Macmillan.

Uhlenbruck, G. (1992). Sport und Fitness – ein Leib-Seele- "Problem." *Natur- und Ganzheitsmedizin, 5,* 50-52.

Uhlenbruck, G. (1996). *Bewegungstraining verbessert Lebensqualität.* TW Gynäkologie, 9, 345-351.

US Department of Health and Human Services (1996). *Physical Activity and Health: A Report of the Surgeon General.* Pittsburgh, PA: Superintendent of Documents.

Volkwein, K. (Ed.) (1998). *Fitness as Cultural Phenomenon.* Münster, New York: Waxmann Verlag.

Volkwein-Caplan, K. & J. Tahmaseb McConatha (2012). *The Social Geography of Healthy Aging.* Aachen/Germany: Meyer & Meyer Publishers.

## CHAPTER 1:

# SOCIOLOGY OF SPORT – FITNESS – PHYSICAL ACTIVITY

*What does sociology have to do with sport? "Sociologists study social behavior of all kinds, from interpersonal social relations to group formations to formal social organizations. Sport is fundamentally a social phenomenon that encompasses all of these social forms of human activity. ... Sport is an extraordinarily popular and pervasive worldwide social endeavor, and therefore a suitable subject for study and analysis. ... Newspapers in North America devote more space to sports than any other topics, including business news, which would seem more important in a capitalist economy."* (Sage & Eitzen, 2013, 2)

*The sociological imagination requires that we consider people in their social contexts. This means considering how historical, cultural and structural factors relate to and connect with each other. (Marjoribanks & Farquharson, 2012, 3)*

Sport has become a major institution in the North American society, as well as in other highly industrialized nations. However, our understanding of it remains limited. There are many statements people make about sport that are either overstated, understated, misinterpreted or simply mythical. Can sport truly contribute to the improvement of modern society? It is certainly true that sport is a tremendous force for the status quo, and it distracts millions of people from more serious thoughts or painful existences. Does sport hold society together and does it empower women as much as it has men?

The question a sociologist might ask is: *Why is social life organized in particular ways?* Most people agree that the field of sport sociology "is the sub-discipline of sociology that studies sports as part of social and cultural life" (Coakley, 2004, 6). More recently, sport sociologists have also investigated the phenomenon of physical activity, fitness and health, and not only competitive, organized sports. In doing this research, people theorize about social life and the meaning of sport, fitness, and physical activity in it. Theorizing includes a combination of description, reflection, and analysis of social phenomena. This is based on the assumption that humans could make the world better; that is, more efficient, just and harmonious, as well as more controllable through the use of knowledge and science and technological advancements. Thus, sociologists first try to dissect what society is all about and what its various components are. It is assumed that social institutions, such as politics, education, media, and religion, are the general foundation and building blocks of a society.

The sociology of sport as an organized field of study is about 50 years old; it emerged around the same time that sport psychology, sport history, and sport philosophy arose as systematic academic disciplines of study applied to sport and most recently exercise and fitness as well. Sport sociologists are mainly employed at colleges and universities, teaching and publishing in this area, but they are also thought after "experts" and consultants by newspapers and sports television broadcasting when a story has sociological relevance. The field of sport sociology is organized nationally through the *North American Society for the Sociology of Sport* (NASSS) with about 400 members, and internationally through the *International Sociology of Sport Association* (ISSA), which was founded in 1965. These organizations hold annual conferences and sponsor scholarly publications and research journals, such as the *Sociology of Sport Journal, the Journal of Sport and Social Issues, and the International Review for the Sociology of Sport.*

"Sociology is the systematic study of social behavior, in groups, and in organizations. Sociologists are especially interested in the social patterns that emerge whenever people interact over periods of time" (Sage & Eitzen, 2013, 4). They study human groups that could be as small as a couple, a family, a business, a community or a nation. Similarities and differences exist in any of these groups, big or small, which are analyzed through a sport focus in the field of sport sociology. The human interactions in and through sport center on values, rules, hierarchical structure of ranks, power, prestige, criteria for evaluating people's behaviors, reward and punishment, and more. All social scientists are interested in the underlying order of social life, whether it is from a political perspective, historical, psychological, economic or anthropological venue. Each of these social sciences is useful to aid sport sociology research, since they are important indicators of the general social conditions people live under in a given period of time and place. Issues might include leisure time, inflation, unemployment, restricted opportunities for minority groups, and more. Furthermore, the meaning people attach to these external influences are important indicators of what constitutes culture (see Chapter 3).

Sociologists in general bring with them different viewpoints of the world, which then leads to several different interpretations and theories. Societies are complex phenomena; they have their own histories, dynamics and cultures, and they can be viewed from many different perspectives. It is recognized that no single perspective can tell us all we need to know about social life. Thus, we have a multitude of theories today. For example, feminist scholars have made very convincing arguments that theories based on men's experience of the world do not tell us all about social life, because 50% of the population is left out of this equation. Global social changes have shown us that we are operating from a Euro-centric viewpoint that is irrelevant to other parts of the world.

New communication technologies, computer-based and media-generated, have altered our sense of what is real and what is not. Thus, new dimensions of social life have been created. For example, you can meet someone over the internet and think you know them, but you really do not. This is a different kind of reality that has been created that is not "real" anymore. Furthermore, scientists have come to understand that science itself is part of culture; thus, the system is reflected in the theories and not free from them. That is, only certain views are present and represented, which reflect the world experienced by the powerful and the educated; many other voices are not expressed or not heard. Worst yet, they are not acknowledged, and therefore do not exist.

In this chapter, the theoretical framework of sport sociology will be discussed as well as the various theories about sport, fitness, physical activity and society. The pros and cons of these theories help us to understand the strengths and weaknesses of each one. It will become obvious that there is not one best theory that can explain the complexity of social life; rather a multiplicity of approaches helps to form a better understanding of the social phenomena of sport and physical activity in the modern world.

## Theoretical Frameworks

Sport sociologists uncover and discover "things are not as they seem" (Bryant & McElroy, 1997, 4). They try to debunk existing myths and misconceptions about sport, fitness, and physical activity. One very widely held belief is that sport is free from racism and discrimination, which we will see is not true (see Chapters 6, 7 and 8). Other myths are that everyone has access to sport, fitness, and physical activities or that women's sport is inferior to men's sport. Social scientists challenge these popular misconceptions; they hold that each event in sport, fitness, and physical activity affects various social groups differently, which then produces a multitude of causes and effects.

However, all sport sociologists agree on the following assumptions that sport is used in several ways: as a social, political, and/or economic agenda. These purposes are recurring themes throughout this book. For example:

(1) *Social Agenda:* Analyzing sport and physical activity in the social context will reveal that not everyone has equal access to these societal goods. In fact, inequalities in social conditions are reflected in the participation patterns of exercise and sports. For example, "advocates of women's issues have used sport situations to highlight practices that discriminate against women" (Bryant & McElroy, 1997, 5). Other minority groups in society, e.g., African-

Americans, Native Americans, gays and lesbians, or disabled people are also not receiving the same tolerant attitude as the dominant group in society, which is white men (see Chapters 6,7 and 8).

(2) *Political Agenda:* Sport is used to advance certain political views, i.e., during various Olympic Games, World Cup soccer matches, or even Super Bowl events. In Chapter 10, the governmental involvement in the former communist East Germany and the democratic West Germany is spelled out to illustrate the importance of government in advancing certain political views and the influence of exercise and sport practices of individuals.

(3) *Economic Agenda:* Economics is an underlying force in sport and exercise. At the international level, for example, Olympic competitions would not be possible without the sponsorship of big corporations. "Perhaps the single best illustration is corporate America's partnership with the city of Atlanta in the 1996 Olympic Games" (Bryant & McElroy, 1997, 5). Private business is helping every day to finance sporting events, whether they are held locally or nationally (e.g., building sport stadiums, underwriting youth competitions, and more).

When doing research in sociology, we also need to be aware that there are different levels of thinking, dominant culture vs. subculture. The dominant thought processes reflect the viewpoints of the majority in a given culture, while the subculture thinking is the thinking of a smaller group that is different. Because dominant thinking has evolved over a longer period of time, it is usually difficult to change. It requires a lot more effort to challenge the focus of sport as being male-dominated, competitive and profit driven. Not all groups in society identify with the dominant culture; for example, the all-male sports clubs that are still prevalent in parts of the country are not necessarily receiving support by women, minorities and members of disadvantaged groups (such as low income, low education). The thinking of these various groups or subcultures reflects values that are opposite to those of the dominant culture. "Differences between the dominant culture and subcultures make their point of interaction a place of social struggle" (Bryant & McElroy, 1997, 7). Several of these social groups' struggles will be examined throughout this book.

Sport sociology research takes place on the macro as well as the micro level. Macro-level studies examine social life and social structures on a larger scale. They use categories, such as social class or social institutions (family, education, politics, etc.) and social systems (war, unemployment, or divorce), to explain social existence. Micro-level studies, on the other hand, analyze the immediate social environment, such as an individual's experience or the interpretations of an event. They attach personal meaning to engagements in sport and physical activity. Both sides are correct.

Sociologists are interested in making a positive change in social life; sport sociologists are particularly interested in social action pertaining to sport and physical activity. Questions they would ask are regarding the social environment (i.e., *Why don't women play football?*), regarding social relationships (i.e., *It is not what you know but who you know*), regarding social dynamism (i.e., *Does sport provide grounds for upward social mobility?*), and in the cultural context (i.e., *Are the dominant American values reflected in sports?*).

## Theories about Sport, Fitness, Physical Activity, and Society

Each author writing a textbook on sociology groups theories differently. Theories are useful tools to describe, explain and predict behavior of people and events. There are a great number of theories and theoretical paradigms, which are based on a set of fundamental assumptions about society that guides sociological thinking. However, there is great disagreement on what the important questions are in the field, as well as which theory is the best approach to use when studying sport, fitness, and physical activity. The array of currently existing theories include (see Coakley 2004 or Sage & Eitzen, 2013):

- Functionalist Theory (asking what sports can contribute to society)
- Conflict Theory (asking whether sports are all about money and economic power)
- Critical Theory (asking how sports are involved in creating and changing culture and social relations)
- Interactionist Theory (asking how people experience sports)
- Feminist and Race Theories (asking what the connections are between gender, race, and sports)

Although there are tremendous differences between the various theoretical approaches, there are also points where they overlap. These six theories will be explained and analyzed separately, but they are fluid and often have similar frameworks. However, each theory gives us a unique perspective for imagining and studying the complexity of the relationships between sport - fitness - physical activity, culture, and society.

### (1) Functionalist Theory

Social science researchers who are functionalists assume that the driving force behind all social life is to continue to operate and function efficiently; that is to support the status quo of a given society. They believe that social change is dysfunctional unless it occurs in a gradual, evolutionary manner. It is believed that society and the social institutions in it function efficiently when the following needs are met by:

- Teaching people the system's basic values and rules they have to live by.
- Establishing cohesive social relationships and bringing people together (i.e., through sport).
- Teaching what goals in life and society are important and how to achieve these goals.
- Responding to social and environmental changes that are occurring outside the system/society while maintaining equilibrium within the system.

The research questions that functionalists seek to answer are affirmative in nature. Examples include: What is the relationship between sports participation and the development of good moral character? Can sport and physical activity foster social integration of various groups? What is the relationship between sport participation and achievement motivation? Can sport participation build character? Most people would answer these questions with a resounding YES.

*Weaknesses:* Functionalist theory has several limitations. First, theorists exaggerate about the positive effects sport, fitness, and physical activity have on people who are involved, while the dysfunctional parts of sport and the social system are eliminated or not acknowledged. For example, the statement that "sports builds character" is used in the promotion of sporting activities. A failure of character building (e.g., an athlete taking performance-enhancing drugs) is solely attributed to the athlete's personal failure rather than a combination of internal and external pressures.

Another weakness of the functionalist thinking is the assumption that the needs of all individuals in society are the same; differences are not accounted for. The assumption that everyone has equal access to sports, fitness, and physical activity is simply a myth. It ignores the sociocultural reality where research has clearly shown differences when it comes to gender, race/ethnicity, socioeconomic backgrounds, age, religious beliefs, sexual orientation, (dis-) ability, the environment, and more.

The third major limitation of the functionalist theory is the ignorance of the fact that sport - fitness - physical activity are the creation of people, and thus, they can be changed. However, since functionalists believe that there are no major downsides to sport - fitness - physical activity and how they are organized, they insist that no change is needed and that the system works well for everyone involved. "This causes us to underestimate the existence of differences and conflicts of interest within a society and to ignore cases in which sport benefits some groups more than others" (Coakley, 2004, 40). Chapters 6, 7, and 8 in this book will speak to these inequalities existing not only in the North American society but in the global world of sport, fitness, and physical activity.

## (2) Conflict Theory

The general assumption of the conflict theorists is that sport is a reflection of the exploitative and unequal practices of capitalist society. Society is viewed as an ever-changing set of relationships characterized by inherent differences of interest and disagreements of various groups. The focus of conflict theorists is on processes of change and the consequences of inequality in society rather than on what is required to keep a society running. Based on Karl Marx' idea that "religion is an opiate," conflict theorists see sport as being the opiate for people in capitalist society. This means that the capitalist system is inherently based on the exploitation of workers; while sports are organized to benefit the owners of sport teams, the athletes are exploited. Furthermore, sport is seen as a perfect distraction for people, which occupies their free time and leaves little room for critical thoughts or any formation of rebellion against the inequalities in society. Thus, organized sports are a distorted form of physical exercise shaped by those possessing power and resources in capitalist systems.

Conflict theoretical researchers focus on issues that question the status quo and widely held beliefs. Questions they try to answer include: Does sport contribute to the alienation of people in capitalist society? What coercion and social control is executed in sports and organized forms of physical activity? Is sport reflecting destructive capitalist phenomena, such as commercialism, nationalism, and militarism? Are racism and sexism part of sport and organized physical activity, just as they are in society in general?

**Weaknesses:** The limitations of the conflict theory are threefold. First, these theorists exclude any factors other than the capitalist system in explaining the relationship between physical activity, sport, and society. "They see sport as a site where people learn to define their bodies as tools of production and then become alienated from their bodies in the process" (Coakley, 2004, 42). The focus here is that the people in power organize sport for their own benefits and the maximization of their wealth, while the possibility of sport being a force of empowerment for women (see Chapter 7) are totally ignored. Thus, we have an overemphasis on the extent to which sport is controlled by people in positions of power in capitalist society. And lastly, conflict theorists ignore the fact that sport and physical activity, even in a capitalist society, can still be personally creative, expressive, and liberating experiences for individuals.

Functionalist and conflict theorists analyze sports and physical activity in society from its social structure. They do not provide a picture of the meaning of sport, fitness, and physical activity in the life of a person and the different needs of various groups in society. Through sport and physical activity, people do not only experience their world, they also form and create it and are formed in return.

These theories also ignore the complexity of social life and the struggles of what is important for different people in their lives. The theories that will pay attention to these facts are: critical, interactionist, as well as feminist and race theories.

## (3) Critical Theory

Critical theories see sport as more than a reflection of society. They encompass a variety of theoretical approaches, such as functionalism, conflict, feminist, race, and cultural studies. With this broader focus, they can avoid the major problems of the functionalist and conflict theories when trying to explain the relationship between sport, physical activity, and society. The general assumption is that historical and economic forces are crucial for the understanding of the role of sport and physical activity in society, because these influences govern and shape how people experience and define exercise and sport in their everyday lives. Furthermore, critical theory recognizes that sport - fitness - physical activity in society must be explained in terms of something more than simply the needs of the social system (as done by functionalism) or the production needs of a capitalist system (as done by conflict theorists). Critical theory is based on the idea that both shared values and conflicts of interests exist simultaneously in society; people are not simply puppets following other persons' order. The relationship between sport and society is never set for all time. It changes as history and economic forces change. Thus, the social structure changes from time to time as well and reflects the way things are in the rest of society. And critical theorists assume that sport - fitness - physical activity can also become a source of protest, opposition, and change.

**Weaknesses:** General weaknesses of critical theories are that they do not provide a tight, clearly understood framework on how to conduct research in sport sociology that will actually lead to social action; that is, to change society so that everyone will have equal access to the goods of sport - fitness - physical activity. Furthermore, critical theorists do not provide explicit guidelines for determining when sport reaffirms or opposes the status quo of society. In other words, when does sport participation result in the affirmation of societal expectation (i.e., How can sports participation build good character?) or the negation of social values (i.e., *Why do some athletes take illegal drugs to enhance their performance?*). These issues cannot be answered easily.

Furthermore, critical theory has seldom led to a consideration of the experiences of actual people in everyday life settings. "However, it is clear that dominant norms are not always unfair or oppressive, and that the voices and perspectives of some marginalized and disadvantaged groups are not based on concerns about fairness, liberation, and tolerance of differences. It is important to respect the voices and creative potential of marginalized and oppressive groups, but it is not politically or morally wise to assume that the contributions made by all groups have equal value when it comes to transforming social life" (Coakley, 2004, 50). Thus, criteria to prioritize ideas and interventions that impact people's lives need to be established, and how they will impact sport - fitness - physical activity and vice versa.

### (4) Interactionist Theory

Interactionist theorists see sports as *meaningful interaction* between people. This view is based on the assumption that human behavior involves choices, and that choices are based on "meaningful definitions of the situation" that people create as they interact with others. Human beings choose to behave in certain ways, and our identities are formed through the interaction with people. They are never set. In fact, interactions can change over time. That is the reason, for example, why so many couples get divorced when a partner goes back to school. The interactions between partners change, one is advancing and the other is remaining the same, which then leads to different patterns of interactions.

Interactionist theorists research what meaning people give to things and events in their world, which tells us a lot about a person. They do not believe in the cause-effect model, as is used a lot in animal research and then applied to human beings. In many situations, people might react similarly, but they think independently which leads to numerous behavioral variations. Research methods include: ethnographic studies, observational methods, interviews, and more. Questions interactionists try to answer include: *Why do some people get involved in sport and physical activity and others do not? How do people see their social worlds and their connections to those worlds?*

**Weaknesses:** Interactionist theories almost solely focus on the interactions and personal relations of people in sport and physical activity. Thus, any explanation on how sport and physical activity partake in the construction of social reality and material conditions in society is missing. The connection between the personal experiences and the sport cultures or the systems of power and inequality that exist in societies, communities, organizations, families, and small groups are not addressed (Coakley, 2004). Issues of power, for example, are of central concern to people who use feminist and race theories.

### (5) Feminist and Race Theories

Feminist and race theories are critical theories based on the experiences of women and minorities and the evidence that these groups have been systematically devalued, exploited, and oppressed in many societies. All feminist and race theories recognize that the values and experiences of men and people in power have shaped science and the production of scientific knowledge. Although all feminists and race theorists are committed to changing the way social life is organized in order to achieve greater equality to all, they do not necessarily agree on what changes are needed. While liberal thinkers identify discrimination and unequal opportunities, radical theorists believe that problems go much deeper since many activities and organizations promote the power of men and the white majority race. Organized popularized sport, for example, reflects male traits, such as physical strength, aggression, and competition that are dominant in sports such as football, ice hockey, boxing, and more. The question of feminist researchers then is how does sport promote the power of women in sport and physical activity? And the question for race theorists is how is racism still entrenched in social life and what are the effects on the world of sport - fitness - physical activity?

"Race theory's primary mission is to analyze, deconstruct, and socially transform society to improve relationships among race, racism, and power" (Sage & Eitzen, 2013). Historical research of North American sport reveals that sport has been a powerful institution reinforcing stereotypes of women, as well as prejudice and racist thinking about people of color. Since African Americans play such an important role in the world of sports, researchers have incorporated race theory in their analyses of sport, culture, and society. The role of racial and ethnic minorities in sport - fitness - physical activity is examined in greater details in Chapter 6.

Regarding feminist research, in the gendered world of sport, being supportive, kind, caring, and responsive to others – typical so-called female traits – does not count for much; and it certainly does not make one qualified to do anything more important than being a volunteer on the hospitality committee. This is not to say that only women display these behaviors. However, without these voluntary activities, organized sports in our society would fail, especially for children and youth. Here, typically mothers take on the role of "taxi drivers" to the various sporting events, while fathers become the coaches of their children.

Critical feminists have asked uncomfortable questions, such as: *Why have many men in the U.S. resisted the spirit of Title IX for over 20 years?* This question offends the status quo of sport and society; thus, there have been concerted efforts over the past 10-15 years to portray feminists as social demons. Feminist theorists also assert that sport is more than a mere reflection of society; it takes on a life at its own, which can shape, influence, and change society.

Generally, feminist theories are based on a holistic approach. Stereotypical assumptions about feminists are that these women are not very attractive and are constantly challenging the status quo in society, demanding abandonment of family, as well as abortion. However, feminists communicate issues regarding women's role in the family, relationships, sport, and society as a whole. In order to develop the needed knowledge, it is important to look at diverse fields of study, including philosophy, sociology, anthropology, biology, political science, history, economics, religion, and more. There is not just one entity known as feminist theory; there are all kinds of views ranging from the conservative, liberal, radical, psychoanalytical, Marxist/socialist to postmodern feminist thought. The social meaning of feminism is constructed as the range of choices for women. Each perspective offers a challenging and compelling point of view. They all agree on the issue of oppression of women in society, but no coherent answer on how to solve this problem is provided.

The common bond of these various feminist views and race theories is the commitment to gender and racial equality, and an understanding that we are far from having reached that goal. Such equality is intertwined in issues such as Equal Rights Amendments, equal pay for equal work, Title IX, reproduction rights, quality child care facilities, violence against women, and so on. There is considerable disagreement as to the sources of sexism and inequality, and the actions that should be taken to fight the oppressive state. Some believe we need a radical change, some talk about a revolution, and others state that only minor changes have to occur. However, it is important to understand what these various theories all have in common – that they further communication rather than separatism. A common thread might be the identity concept: women and minorities share similar experiences; they face the same external situations, such as economic oppression, commercial exploitation, legal discrimination, and internal responses, such as feelings of inadequacy and the realization of a limited future.

*Weaknesses:* Feminist and race theories have most of the same weaknesses as critical theories. Additionally, because of their exclusive focus on gender or race, they have sometimes given too little attention to other influences that are related to gender in important ways, such as age, social class, (dis)ability, religion, race and nationality.

### Is there a best theoretical approach to use when studying sport and physical activity?

Every theory serves a certain function. We might think that we do not need theory to make certain decisions in sport - fitness - physical activity, but in effect, everyone bases their choices on some kind of theory they believe in, even subconsciously. Every theory takes us in a different direction. If we do not want to go in that direction, then other decisions are needed, based on a different theory. Functionalism focuses on the positive sides of sport/physical activity and sport involvement, while conflict theory emphasizes the problematic side. Critical theory suggests that sports are connected to social relations in complex and diverse ways, and that changes are needed in social, political, and economic relations. Interactionist theory focuses on the interpersonal relations of people in sports and physical activity and the subsequent meaning and identities that are formed thereof. Feminist and race theories point out how sport really is supporting the dominant white male culture. All theories have strengths and weaknesses, and no theory explains the complexity of social life. Some theories allow for more social change than others, thus leading to more choices and alternatives for people in sports. Creating alternative ways of doing sports and physical activity requires an awareness of the values underlying dominant forms of sport. This will be discussed in Chapter 3.

## References

Bryant, J. & McElroy, M. (1997). *Sociological Dynamics of Sport and Exercise.* Englewood, CO: Morton Publishing Company.

Coakley, J. (2004). *Sport in Society – Issues and Controversies.* [8th Edition]. Boston, MA: McGrawHill Higher Education.

Sage, G. & S. Eitzen (2013). *Sociology of North American Sport.* [Ninth Edition]. New York, Oxford: Oxford University Press.

## CHAPTER 2:

# PSYCHOLOGY OF SPORT – FITNESS – PHYSICAL ACTIVITY

*(with Margaret Ottley)*

> *Sport and exercise psychology is the scientific study of people and their behavior in sport and exercise activities. Sport and exercise psychologists seek to understand and help elite athletes, children, the physically and mentally disabled, seniors, and average participants achieve peak performance, personal satisfaction, and development through participation (Weinberg & Gould, 1995).*

During the past three decades, sport and exercise psychology has emerged as a legitimate field of scientific inquiry (Silva & Weinberg, 1984; Wiggins, 1984). This is evident in the growing number of sport psychology researchers and consultants who have studied numerous topics and worked with athletes, coaches, and sport teams (Gordon, 1990; Halliwell, 1990; Loehr, 1990; Martin, Wrisberg, Beitel & Lounsbury, 1997; Murphy & Ferrante, 1989; Ravizza, 1988). The emergence of a number of professional organizations and numerous publications that promote the study of sport and exercise psychology nationally and internationally is further indication of the growth of the field (Salmela, 1984).

Internationally, academic training and research has developed in the field of exercise and sport psychology in over 40 countries. Outside of North America, some countries with documented utilization of sport psychology consultation are Australia, China, the Czech Republic, England, France, Germany, and Japan (Cox, Qui, & Lin, 1993; Salmela, 1984). Salmela (1994) describes the global perspectives of sport psychology as emerging, diversified, and enthusiastic. The values and attitudes toward sport and psychology of each country significantly shape the respective structures and functions of sport psychology to conform to societal contexts.

Sport psychology has been defined as the science of the application of psychological theories to sport performance (Cox, et al., 1993). There are three major aspects to the discipline of sport psychology: (1) research; (2) educational; and (3) clinical sport and exercise psychology. First, research development focuses on the investigation of psychological theories and the development of new knowledge in the field. Second, educational sport psychology or applied sport psychology involves the dissemination of overall knowledge to achieve optimal performance level (Cox, et al., 1993). Educational sport psychology consultants utilize research findings to develop psychological skills training (PST) programs. PST is sometimes referred to as performance enhancement, mental training, or mental toughness training. Some frequently implemented skills in PST are goal setting, concentration, arousal control, stress management, motivation, imagery, and visualization (Bull, 1995; Martens, 1987; Partington & Orlick, 1991). The third aspect of sport psychology is clinical or counseling sport/exercise psychology. Clinical sport psychologists diagnose and treat athletes with emotional problems associated with such conditions as eating disorders, substance abuse, drug dependency, anxiety, and interpersonal conflict (Cox, et al., 1993).

In this chapter, the development of sport and exercise psychology will be traced back to its roots; cross-cultural perceptions of sport psychology consulting will be analyzed; and the development of knowledge in this field will be examined. Lastly, the perceptions and attitudes of athletes and coaches toward sport psychology consultation are described, which gives us a glimpse into future developments of the field.

## Development of Sport and Exercise Psychology

In most countries, the evolution of sport psychology (and later exercise psychology, as well) occurred almost exclusively within departments of physical education, kinesiology, or leisure studies. Earliest research done by physical educators, not psychologists, were theoretical attempts to understand the psychological benefits derived from physical activity (Wiggins, 1986). In North America, for example, in 1895, Reverend William Augustus Stearn, president of Amherst College, wrote that a moderate amount of daily physical exercise would preserve lives and health, promote animation and cheerfulness, and secure intellectual life (Leonard & Affleck, 1947). In 1898, Kellor wrote that playing games directed women's minds into new channels, produced enthusiasm, activity, and energy, and generally, a person reflected, reasoned, observed, and engaged in various mental processes (Kellor, 1898).

As sport psychology evolved, it underwent changes in terms of research interests and approaches to study behavior. Beyond the psychological advantages from vigorous physical training programs, it explored other benefits. It promoted the idea that mental and moral culture was not an end in itself (Hall, 1908). Especially after the 1960s, sport psychology integrated components of motor learning research. The pioneers, whose contributions may be traced back to the 1920s, were Carl Diem of Germany, Coleman Griffith of the United States, and A.Z. Puni of the Soviet Union (Salmela, 1984). In North America, the move from laboratory research to fieldwork was the beginning of the area of applied sport psychology. In Eastern Europe, the focus was initially on performance enhancement, especially for elite athletes.

The first sport psychology organizations in North America were the *North American Society for the Psychology of Sport and Physical Activity* (NASPSPA), and the *Canadian Society for Psychomotor Learning and Sport Psychology* (CSPLSP), which were formed in 1967 and 1977 respectively (Wiggins, 1984). Further developments in the field brought about other organizations, such as the *Association for the Advancement of Applied Sport Psychology* (AAASP) in 1985, and *Division 47* (Exercise and Sport Psychology) within the *American Psychological Association* (APA) in 1986.

In recent years, sport psychology has become broader by including exercise and fitness into its research, education, and consultancy. Consulting with individual athletes or athletic teams to develop psychological skills for enhancing competitive performance and training are no longer the only tasks sport psychology consultants engage in. Many sport psychologists also work with coaches, and most recently, sport and exercise psychologists now work in the fitness industry, as well (Weinberg & Gould, 1995). Here, they help individuals design exercise programs that maximize participation and promote physical, as well as mental, health and well-being. And sometimes, consultants support a sports medicine or physical therapy program, providing psychological services to injured athletes.

## Sport and Exercise Psychology Around the World

Simultaneous to the development of sport psychology in North America, is its development around the world; which will be highlighted here for several highly industrialist countries. In *Japan*, for example, sport psychology began to progress in the 1960s. Research activities in the field were promoted by the Japanese Society for Physical Education (JSPE) (Fujita & Ichimura, 1993). Research in sport psychology developed through physical education departments in colleges and universities. Most institutions offered the psychology of physical education or sport psychology as compulsory subjects. Additionally, researchers suggested that institutions published research bulletins, which were important sources of information in sport psychology. After the 1964 Olympic Games in Tokyo, research in sport psychology developed as a science independent of physical education. The formation of the *Japan Society of Sport Psychology* (JSSP) in 1973 was established to oversee the direction and promotion of sport psychology. Interests for research focused on areas such as developmental studies, achievement motivation, perceptual motor behavior, biofeedback for motor control, anxiety and anxiety control. The main problems reported in Japan were the training of counselors to bridge the gap in the application of physical knowledge in elite competition and the recreation setting, since most of the research in Japan still focuses on top-level sports. The lack in social-psychology research is evident.

In *China*, research in sport psychology emerged from the needs determined in physical education and sport. Research programs were established in consideration of sport practice and development of specialties (Qiu & Qiu, 1993). Since 1978, nationwide projects were completed in the areas of psychological selection of athletes and the investigation of personality characteristics and psychological traits of elite athletes. Other areas of research include the formulation of a psychomotor ability test for youngsters, psychological diagnosis and selection of athletes, and psychological counseling and training of Chinese fencing athletes. Generally, the main focus of sport psychology in China remains on the issues related to top-level performance while the exercise and fitness realms are not of concern.

Sport psychology in *France* had a modest beginning until the early research in the 1980s. Research was initiated by the *Institut National du Sport et de l'Education Physique of Paris* (INSEP). At the INSEP, upper graduate level programs created specialization in Science and Technique in Physical and Sport Activities (STPSA), which included sport psychology research. Traditionally, sport psychology has focused on the use of applied psychology in order to provide assistance to athletes and coaches. Sport federations were concerned with the detection of talent and training of young people in sport specialized schools. Other interest areas for psychological skills training (PST) in France included experimental and clinical interventions. Research development evolved from the study of surface, overt aspects of behavior to more in-depth psychology factors involved in performance. Assessment of psychological factors affecting athletic performances was conducted with elite athletes and children. However, recent studies have also included issues on personality and motivation, psychological evaluation and intervention, as well as motor learning and its application to the fields of pedagogy and cognitive neuroscience.

In *Germany*, sport psychologists unified in 1990 to form the *German Association of Sport Psychology* (ASP) (Hackfort, 1993). The diversification of interests by its members has led to a variety of research investigations, which include methodological and theoretical approaches. The first published journal, *Sport Psychologie*, reported on basic problems and applied contributions in the field. Today, the main interests of sport psychologists are identified as basic research and application to sport performance in areas such as holistic orientation, assessment with elaboration of action theory, focusing on integration of psychobiological, and psychosocial factors. Other areas include cognition, emotional, and kinesthetic factors essential in analyzing psychomotor or sensorimotor processes and the functional meaning of cognitive emotional motivation. Applied research was designated for elite sport, top-level sports for children, career counseling, and participation of the elderly in high level sports.

Today, investigations span from conceptual and methodological development to the meaning of sport-specific instruments, such as the measuring of flow experiences, as well as a focus on exercise, fitness and recreational engagements through the lifespan.

The sport psychology research in *Australia* has been maintained by various universities' departments of Psychology, Human Movement Studies, and Sport Science (Glencross, 1993). Glencross found that the Australian Institute of Sport (AIS), and to a lesser extent, individuals working with sport bodies, made invaluable contributions to the body of research. In recent years, the impetus and encouragement for research development has been made by funding agencies. Research represents a broad spectrum of pure and applied interests. However, limited research monies from universities and the federal government typically support areas such as motor control and motor learning. The major role of the AIS has been the assessment and profiling of elite, sport psychology protocols and procedure, stress management, and relaxation and flotation (Glencross, 1993). In recent years, the focus of Australian sport psychology research has also included topics of recreational pursuits, as well as health and healthy aging.

## Sport and Exercise Psychology Orientations

The future of sport psychology has been viewed as dependent upon the development of a continuous knowledge base. Knowledge is seen to increase the understanding of factors influencing attitudes and perception. Understanding the determinants of attitudes and perceptions is the initial step in developing successful interventions to change behavior (Theodorakis, 1994). The more knowledge that is acquired about factors underlying a decision to perform a given behavior, the greater the probability of influencing that behavior becomes (Fishbein & Middlestadt, 1987). A strong knowledge base helps practitioners become better able to learn from experience and determine which rules apply when. And it enables athletes to rely on an increasing internal symbolic performance standard and devise strategies from this knowledge. Sport and exercise psychologists differ in how they view the application of knowledge into practice. There are generally three different approaches: a behavioral, a psychophysiological, and a cognitive-behavioral approach (Weinberg & Gould, 1995).

### (1) Behavioral Orientation

Psychologists with a behavioral orientation view the primary determinants of the behavior of athletes or exercisers as coming from the environment. Other factors that influence behavior, such as thoughts, personality, and individual perceptions, are not emphasized in this approach. The main focus here is the analysis of reinforcement and punishment, as coming from the environment, from the outside. Famous behaviorists in the development of this psychological theory are: John Watson, Ivan Pavlov, and B.F. Skinner.

## (2) Psychophysiological Orientation

Sport and exercise psychologists who apply the psychophysiological orientation to their analyses believe that the best way to study behavior during sport and exercise is to examine the physiological processes of the brain and their influences on the physical activity. "They typically assess heart rate, brain wave activity, and muscle action potentials, drawing relationships between these psychophysiological measures and sport and exercise behavior" (Weinberg & Gould, 1995, 19). Typically, biofeedback techniques are used to train elite athletes. For example, in archery, one must learn how to shoot between heartbeats in order to improve accuracy.

## (3) Cognitive-Behavioral Orientation

Psychologists using this orientation assume that behavior is determined both by environment and cognition. They believe that athletes and exercisers can train their focus and thoughts while participating in physical activity, which will then positively influence the outcome of their participation. Techniques used by cognitive-behavioral psychologists include assessment of self-confidence, anxiety, goal orientations, imagery, and intrinsic motivation. These assessments can be used to rate the sources of stress in competition, for example. It has been found that losing wrestlers turned out to worry more often about coach evaluation, losing, and making mistakes than the ones winning (Gould &Weinberg, 1985). This might be true in general, that a higher level of anxiety is counterproductive to the goal of winning in sports; while a low level of performance concern may be beneficial.

Social learning theories, for example by Albert Bandura (observational learning) or Julian Rotter (internal vs. external observations), are representative of the cognitive-behavioral orientation. Observational learning theory, according to Bandura, includes the following: observing others behaving in certain ways; observing others being rewarded, reinforced, or punished for certain behaviors; engaging in those behaviors themselves and being rewarded or punished. The social conditions that affect sport participation include economic support/ money, opportunity, social values, political support, social support, education, need, the environment, and socialization in general. Socialization is defined as the process by which a person learns to be a participating member in his/her culture, that is to behave in socially appropriate ways and to meet one's needs (Murphy, 1995). If people, and especially children, have positive experiences with sport and exercise, they are more likely to stay active throughout their lives. Furthermore, personal attributes, such as perceived competence and abilities, also influence a person's social learning paradigm for sport and exercise participation; just as parents, peers, and the availability of coaches and equipment are of major importance.

## Attitudes in Regard to Sport Psychology Consultation

Closely related to research in the development of knowledge is the exploration of attitudes in regard to sport psychology. Attitudes are defined as feelings, thoughts, and behavior tendencies toward other people, objects, and ideas. They are learned dispositions that actively guide individuals toward specific behaviors (Pettijohn, 1989). Attitudes consist of long lasting, general evaluations of people, objects, and issues (Petty & Cacioppo, 1985). Attitudes are sometimes irrationally formed cognitively, emotionally, or behaviorally. For example, attitudes may be formed by factual or unfounded ideas from others. They may also be formed due to direct personal experiences or definite feelings with or without personal experience. The formation of attitudes may be a result of early childhood experiences resulting through direct contact, indirect contact with others, or inadvertent conditioning. Inadvertent conditioning is described as the adoption of attitudes toward people or events because they are associated with pleasant or unpleasant memories (Pettijohn, 1989).

Information and knowledge are important variables that mediate attitude-behavior consistency (Theodorakis, 1994). Theodorakis argues that attitudes can affect behavior directly, rather than intentionally. Other variables involved in the attitude-behavior consistency are personal experience, attitude importance, accessibility, confidence, and affective-cognitive consistency. Liska (1984) believes that attitude strength involves three aspects: direction, confidence, and strength. Direction involves that which was good/bad, positive/negative. Confidence is derived from self-efficacy and the ability to perform a given behavior. Strength refers to the increased behavior versus how weak was the behavior. The use of conceptually relevant social psychology theories may yield a more complete understanding of behavior. Social learning theories, such as developmental learning approach, locus of control and theoretical construct, identify ones' generalized expectancy to perceived reinforcement as being dependent on ones' internal control and contingent upon forces external to ones' control (McCready & Bonita, 1985). McCready & Bonita note that sport psychology adherence should be greatest among those who highly value one or more psychological advantages, such as stress release, goal setting, time management, discipline, and/or motivation.

## Cross-Cultural Issues in Sport Psychology Consultation

Researchers found that one of the barriers facing successful sport psychology consultations is a lack of sport specific knowledge (Martin, et al., 1997). Also, more cross-cultural investigations are needed in the field (Duda & Alison, 1990). The development of knowledge would enhance the credibility and practice of sport psychology, identify trends in knowledge development, and establish a scientific basis for mental training (Vealey, 1994). Suinn (1985) believes that the visibility and recognition of the field of sport psychology by coaches and athletes are important factors in the success of athletes' performance. Coaches and athletes would then have a better understanding of and become more receptive to sport psychology consultation. In turn, this may then encourage coaches to more readily relinquish the responsibility of psychological consultations to qualified professionals.

Research in sport psychology focuses on consultations with athletes and coaches of various performance levels and cultural backgrounds. Some researchers have specifically been directed to the needs of minorities, particularly African-American athletes (Anshel, 1990). Despite the growth of sport psychology consultations, many athletes remain reluctant to utilize the services of sport psychology consultants. Ravizza (1988) found that sport psychology consultants were faced with major hurdles, such as being viewed as "a shrink," a lack of sport specific knowledge, and insufficient knowledge of experiences and policies related to the sport environment.

Barriers to sport psychology consultations within a cultural framework may initially be examined through the relationship between coaches and athletes. Most coaches are strongly influential and view themselves as fully capable of filling the role of mental preparation (Schell, et al., 1984). Most sport psychology consultants understand that coaches exert a major impact upon the sport context, as well as athlete behavior and development (Vealey, 1994). Potential conflict between coaches and sport psychology consultants may occur when psychological interventions are not accepted by coaches. Many coaches may feel compelled to maintain complete control over their athletes. As a result, they may become over-protective and fear that interventions will undermine interpersonal skills.

Additionally, research on white and black players' perception of their coaches indicated that black athletes are less trusting and more distant compared to white players (Anshel & Sailes, 1990). The mistrust may be in response to white coaches' misinterpretation of black athletes' behavioral tendencies (Cashmore, 1982). For example, college football coaches have been found to describe black players in terms of physical speed, quickness, and high achievement motivation. White players were stereotyped as being high on reliability and having quick thinking skills (Anshel, 1990).

Studies found racial differences between blacks and whites in areas of intervention, psychological preparation, and needs or styles in the competitive environment. For example, African-American athletes' perceptions of sport psychology consultation showed perceived racism, as well as a lack of sensitivity to the individual and sociocultural needs of black players (Anshel, 1990). Hall (1996) found that African-Americans were more cognizant of their ethnicity than white athletes. Failure to take into account the historical, cultural, and personal characteristics of minority participants hindered the effectiveness of the intervention (Partington & Orlick, 1991). Studies suggest that in relation to cultural differences, sport psychology consultants should take time to speak the athletes' language in order to gain acceptance of the players (Ravizza, 1988). Ravizza also found that there are two obstacles white consultants must overcome: their role as a consultant and their own race-based perceptions.

Sport psychology literature that examined social-psychology differences between black and white athletes included little empirical work at the causal or explanatory level (McPherson, 1976; Wiggins, 1986). As a result, findings offered limited evidence of the effectiveness of white sport psychology consultants who consult with black athletes. In effect, understanding of the function of race and cultural differences in sport psychology consultation was limited.

In conclusion, the field of sport and exercise psychology is still changing as new knowledge in the applied areas is acquired. "Sport involvement can be a positive experience for all participants, but only if the experience is properly structured with the physical and psychological needs of the participants in mind" (Murphy, 1995, 13).

# References

Anshel, M. H. (1990). Perceptions of Black Intercollegiate Football Players: Implications for the sport psychology consultant. *The Sport Psychologist, 4,* 235-248.

Anshel, M. H., & Sailes, G. (1990). Discrepant Attitudes of Intercollegiate Football Players: Implications for sport psychology consultants. *The Sport Psychologist, 13,* 68-77.

Bull, S. J. (1995). Reflections on a 5-year Consultancy Program with the England Women's Cricket Team. *The Sport Psychologist, 9,* 148-163.

Bunker, L. K., & McGuire, R. T. (1985). Give Sport Psychology to Sport. In: L. K. Bunker, R. J. Rotella. A. S. Reilly, & R. T. McGuire (Eds.). *Sport Psychology: Psychological Considerations in Maximizing Sport Performance.* Pp. 3-14. Ann Arbor, MI: McMaughton & Gunn.

Cashmore, E. (1982). Black Sportsmen. Boston, MA: Routledge & Kegan Paul.

Cox, R. H., Qui, Y., & Lin, Z. (1993). Overview of Sport Psychology. In: R. N. Singer, M. Murphey, & L. K. Tennant (Eds.). *Handbook of Research on Sport Psychology.* Pp. 3-5. New York, NY: Macmillan.

Duda, J. L., & Allison, M. T. (1990). Cross-cultural Analysis in Exercise and Sport Psychology: A Void in the Field. *Journal of Sport & Exercise Psychology, 12,* 114-131.

Fishbein, M., & Middlestadt, S. (1987). Using the Theory of Reasoned Action to Develop Educational Interventions: Applications to Illicit Drug Use. *Health Education Research, 2,* 361-371.

French, K. E., & Thomas, J. R. (1987). The Relation of Knowledge Development to Children's Basketball Performance. *Journal of Sport Psychology, 9,* 15-32.

Fujita, A. H., & Ichimura, S. (1993). Contemporary Areas of Research in Sport Psychology in Japan. In: R. N. Singer, M. Murphey, & L.K. Tennant (Eds.). *Handbook of Research on Sport Psychology.* Pp. 52-53. New York, NY: Macmillan.

Glencross, D. (1993). Sport Psychology in Australia: Current Research. In: R.N. Singer, M. Murphey, & L.K. Tennant (Eds.). *Handbook of Research on Sport Psychology.* P. 44. New York, NY: Macmillan.

Gould, D. & Weinberg, R.S. (1985). Sources of Worry in Successful and Less Successful Intercollegiate Wrestlers. *Journal of Sport Behavior, 8,* 115-127.

Gordon, S. (1990). A Mental Skills Training Program for the Western Australia State Cricket Team. *The Sport Psychologist, 4,* 386-399.

Hackfort, D. (1993). Contemporary Areas of Research in Sport Psychology in Germany. In: R. N. Singer, M. Murphey, & L. K. Tennant (Eds.). *Handbook of Research on Sport Psychology.* Pp. 40-41. New York, NY: Macmillan.

Hall, G. S. (1908). *Physical Education in Colleges: Report of the National Association.* Chicago, IL: University of Chicago Press.

Hall, R. L. (1996). *Ethnic Identity and Cross Racial Experiences of College Athletes.* Unpublished Master's Thesis. Temple University, Philadelphia, PA.

Halliwell, W. (1990). Providing Sport Psychology Consulting Services in Professional Hockey. *The Sport Psychologist, 4,* 56-68.

Hart, M. M. (1972). *Sport in the Socio-Cultural Process.* Dubuque, IA: Wm. C. Brown.

Kellor, F. A. (1998). A Psychological Basis for Physical Culture. In: J. M. Silva, III & R. A. Weinberg (Eds.). *Psychological Foundations of Sport.* Pp. 23-24. Champaign, IL: Human Kinetics.

Leonard, F. E., & Affleck, G. B. (1947). *A Guide to the History of Physical Education.* Philadelphia, PA: Lea & Febiger.

Liska, A. E. (1984). A Critical Examination of the Causal Structure of the Fishbein/Ajzen Attitude-Behavior Relation. *Social Psychology Quarterly, 47,* 61-74.

Loehr, J. E. (1990). Providing Sport Psychology Consulting Services to Professional Tennis Players. *The Sport Psychologist, 4,* 400-408.

Martens, R. (1987). *Coaches Guide to Sport Psychology.* Champaign, IL: Human Kinetics.

Martin, S. B. (1998). *Sport Psychology Attitudes-Revised Form.* Unpublished Test Manual. Denton, TX: University of North Texas, Department of Kinesiology, Health Promotion, and Recreation.

Martin, S. B., Wrisberg, C. A., Beitel, P. A., & Lounsbury, J. (1997). Athletes' Attitudes Towards Seeking Sport Psychology Consultation: The Development of an Objective Instrument. *The Sport Psychologist, 11,* 201-218.

Matlin, M. W. (1988). *Sensation and Perception.* Boston, MA: Allyn-Bacon.

McCready, M. L., & Bonita, C. L. (1985). Locus of Control, Attitudes Toward Physical Activity and Exercise Adherence. *Journal of Sport Psychology, 7,* 346-359.

McPherson, B. D. (1976). The Black Athlete: An Overview and Analysis. In: D. M. Landers (Ed.). *Social Problems in Athletics.* Pp. 122-150. Urbana: University of Illinois Press.

Murphy, S., & Ferrante, A. P. (1989). Provision of Sport Psychology Services to the U.S. Team at the 1988 Summer Olympic Games. *The Sport Psychologist, 3,* 374-387.

Murphy, S. (1995). *Sport Psychology Interventions.* Champaign, IL: Human Kinetics.

Orlick, T. (1989). Reflections on Sportpsych Consulting with Individual and Team Sport Athletes at Summer and Winter Olympic Games. *The Sport Psychologist, 3,* 354-365.

Partington, J., & Orlick, T. (1987). The Sport Psychology Consultant: Analysis of Critical Components as Viewed by Canadian Olympic Athletes. *The Sport Psychologist, 1,* 4-17.

Partington, J., & Orlick, T. (1991). An Analysis of Olympic Sport Psychology Consultants' Best-Ever Consulting Experiences. *The Sport Psychologist, 5,* 183-193.

Pettijohn, T. F. (1989). *Psychology: Concise Introduction*. Guilford, CT: Dushkin.

Petty, R. E., & Cacioppo, J. T. (1985). The Elaboration Livelihood Model of Persuasion. In: L. Berkowitz (Ed.). *Advances in Experimental Social Psychology*, (Vol. 19). New York, NY: Academic Press.

Polyani, M. (1966). *The Tacit Dimension*. Garden City, NY: Doubleday.

Qui, Y., & Qui, Z. (1993). Contemporary Areas of Research in Sport Psychology in the People's Republic of China. In: R. N. Singer, M. Murphey, & L. K. Tennant (Eds.). *Handbook of Research on Sport Psychology*. Pp. 3-5. New York, NY: Macmillan.

Ravizza, K. (1988). Gaining Entry with Athletic Personnel for Season-Long Consulting. *The Sport Psychologist, 4,* 330-340.

Ripoll, H., & Thill, E. (1993). Contemporary Areas of Research in Sport Psychology in France: Overview and Perspectives. In: R. N. Singer, M. Murphey, & L. K. Tennant (Eds.). *Handbook of Research on Sport Psychology*. Pp. 34-35. New York, NY: Macmillan.

Salmela, J. H. (1984). Comparative Sport Psychology. In: J. M. Silva, III & R. A. Weinberg (Eds.). *Psychological Foundations of Sport*. Pp. 23-24. Champaign, IL: Human Kinetics.

Scanlan, T. K. (1985). Social Psychological Aspects of Competition for Male Youth Sport Participation: Determinants of Personal Performance Expectancies. *Journal of Sport Psychology, 7,* 380-399.

Schell, B., Hunt, J., & Lloyd, C. (1984). An Investigation of Future Market Opportunities for Sport Psychologists. *Journal of Sport Psychology, 6,* 335-350.

Silva, J. M., & Weinberg, R. S. (1984). *Psychological Foundations of Sport*. Champaign, IL: Human Kinetics.

Suinn, R. M. (1985). The 1984 Olympics and Sport Psychology. *Journal of Sport Psychology, 7,* 321-329.

Theodorakis, Y. (1994). Planned Behavior, Attitude Strength, Role Identity and the Prediction of Exercise Behavior. *The Sport Psychologist, 8,* 149-165.

Thomas, J. R., French, K. E., & Humphries, C. A. (1988). Knowledge Development and Sport Performance: Directions for Motor Behavior Research. *Journal of Sport Psychology, 8,* 259-272.

Vealey, R. S. (1994). Knowledge Development and Implementation in Sport Psychology. *The Sport Psychologist, 8,* 331-348.

Weinberg, R.S. & D. Gould (1995). *Foundations of Sport and Exercise Psychology*. Champaign, IL: Human Kinetics.

Wiggins, D. K. (1984). The History of Sport Psychology in North America. In: J. M. Silva & R. S. Weinberg (Eds.) *Psychological Foundations of Sport*. Pp. 9-22. Champaign, IL: Human Kinetics.

Wiggins, D. K. (1986). From Plantation to Playing Field: Historical Writings on the Black Athlete in American Sport. *Research Quarterly for Exercise and Sport, 57,* 101-116.

## Chapter 3:

# Culture and Values in the 21st Century

> *Cultures and traditions are simply the forms of social interaction accepted by particular communities at particular times, and according to their world view and historical experiences, such that there are several alternatives and systems of values selected for their usefulness. ... Cultures are not static. They change over time in accordance with the interpretive values, beliefs, norms, and practices of the group, whose members define and live by the ideals of those practices and values. (Airhihenbuwa, 1995, xiii-xiv)*

> *It has been argued that spectator sports represent all that is bad in American culture, that classism, racism, sexism, substance abuse, and violence in society are reinforced by the sports that fans love. Others point to the good in sports – how they exemplify concepts of community, teamwork, and striving for excellence. Both points of view are valid. (Quinn in Sage & Eitzen, 2012, 47)*

Culture is an ever-changing process, which crosses national boundaries. Individual differences within each culture are reflected by race, ethnicity, gender, social class, education, and personality. Furthermore, various regions in one country have their own differences, and represent so-called mini-cultures. As a result of migration and globalization (or more specifically Westernization), cultural values and traditions are shared, exchanged, changed, and transformed. Thus, within a given country, numerous cultures can be represented and exist simultaneously (Volkwein, 1998).

At the beginning of the 21st century, globalization was introduced as a new, universal language. Globalization appears to be a-cultural, where individual distinctions are no longer considered. This process is problematic because it threatens to marginalize individual cultural differences. Every culture holds its own set of values; these can overlap depending on the socio-historical development of each particular culture. Highly industrialized societies or (post) modern cultures hold similar values; however, each country and nationality is determined by its own tradition and set of values that have been passed on by generations.

Research on changes in values in middle class adults (20-50 years of age) asserts that the public's emphasis has shifted from more socially oriented values, e.g., equality or national security, to personal values, such as freedom, comfort, and excitement (Inglehart, 1985). This shift indicates a change from materialistic to post-materialistic values. Klages, et al., (1992) state that the value change is characterized by processes of individualization; they acclaim value changes due to the process of "functional differentiation of modern industrialized societies." That is, Klages, et al., explain value change not as a shift but rather as an expansion, as "value pluralism" (see also Tetlock, 1986).

Thus, the traditional value orientation does not vanish, it is extended. The "old" achievement ethic is losing its significance. "Post-industrialized society" is described by Klages, et al., as one with decreasing achievement ethics, increasing expectations of the state, and an increased orientation and interest in leisure activities. Value changes can be attributed to the increasing process of secularization that occurred after WW II: the rise in the standard of living, the resulting increase in consumption, the relative freedom of choice of behavior, increased mobility, the expansion of the educational system, ecological problems, changes in family structures, the extended use and influence of mass media, and a number of other factors (see Digel, 1986, 25-29). Politics, economics, and personal values are all inextricably linked.

A definition of values implies that values, unlike attitudes, encompass a notion of what is *desirable*. These are "stable higher-order constructs," and they have a direct and/or indirect causal influence on attitudes as well as behavior (Bryant & McElroy, 1997). In the United States, general values held up in society coincide directly with the values promoted in the sport and fitness domain. These are mainly a means to achieve success, progress, achievement and recognition. Fitness and sport related activities perpetuate certain positive values, such as building character, discipline, hard work, competitions, and more. These American core values are a direct reflection of the dominant thinking in American society (Byant & McElroy, 1997, 52).

| American Core Values | Values in Sport |
|---|---|
| Achievement | Achievement |
| Hard work | Hard work |
| Material comfort | Success |
| Equality | Competition |
| Freedom | Recognition |
| Democracy | Progress |
| Patriotism | Patriotism |

The so-called *American Dream* embodies a belief that those who work hard and take advantage of the opportunities presented will be rewarded with a good life of material comfort. This does not necessarily work for everyone; for example, an overemphasis on competition can lead to dishonesty, cheating, too much control or even eating disorders (see Chapter 9). Further examples of how values might have a negative impact in people's lives is that they might perpetuate biases and stereotypes about certain people in regard to race/ethnicity, gender, age, sexual orientation, and religious beliefs. These overgeneralizations often lead to erroneous beliefs that are based on fiction but not facts. And they are a very powerful force in the treatment of others. It is not easy to uncover some of these deeply held beliefs that have been passed on from generation to generation, and every young person takes them for granted.

Values and social development influence each other. That is, when society changes its goals, then institutions and values are changing as well. This development directs the behavior and action of individuals and groups. Values are related to the needs of people, which vary from culture to culture and also within culture. Even if different cultures share the same values, they might have a different position in the hierarchy according to their importance in that society. Values can be in harmony or in conflict with each other. This does not necessarily depend on the position they hold in the hierarchy, as Ingelhart (1985) suggests, but rather on the given situation and context in which an action takes place. In the case of value conflict, the individual has to engage in a weighting procedure in which s/he has to trade between sometimes equally important and relevant values. Thus, values and their ranking are culturally and situationally determined, based on the time and place of the action taking place.

Changes in the ways in which sport, physical fitness, and health are perceived are a reflection of changes in society – in a microscopic dimension. New offerings in the movement culture are described as a reflection of dramatic value changes (Heinemann, 1989). Changing values in sport are identified by Digel (1986) as part of the general process of value change in society, especially in the area of leisure. Society and the subsystem sport have an interrelationship: society influences the world of sport, for example, through an increase in leisure time, and sport influences society through body worship, fitness, and new body ideals.

Traditional values associated with contemporary society are also inherent in the sporting process. Values such as the means to achieve success, progress, external conformity, patriotism and individualism are reinforced through images associated with highly visible athletes and specific sports. It provides an outlet and escape for those who face a world of conflict and turmoil. The growing cynicism and disillusionment in modern societies is reflected in sport and exercise. Individualism has been transformed from an admirable value to a different value of self-focus. Corruption of the amateur ideal, eroding religious values of morality and ethics, the disappearing work ethic, and distrust in traditional social institutions have contributed to concern and debate.

This chapter will explore the topic of value change as it pertains to human movement in the 21st century across the lifespan. The first issue examines changing values in highly industrialized societies and its impact on human movement. Issue two explores the impact of the fitness movement on people moving in the 21st century. The third issue addresses how culture and values influence the aging process and well-being of people from different nations. And the fourth issue talks about the paradoxes of values and how they are portrayed in top-level sports.

## Issue 1

# *Changing Values and their Impact on Movement Culture*

During the last two decades, the influence of sport and the quest for fitness has grown tremendously in the USA, as well as in other highly industrialized societies across the globe. The enormously popular success of televised sports and the ever-increasing participation of both men and women of all ages in organized and unorganized sport and fitness activities attest to this importance. This development has led to a change in the understanding and structure of the relationship between sport/human movement and society, body and culture. There are many indications that changes in the area of sport/physical culture, including fundamental forms of human movement and diverse forms of physical activity, go hand in hand with the changes of the ethos of life in highly industrialized societies. Hence, these changes are reflected in the values and behavior of the individuals (Coakley, 1990). Along with the changes in society goes a change of the role of the body, which today is becoming a source for happiness and a provider for meaning in people's lives. It is of vital importance to understand these changes in society in order to adequately serve and address the needs of people as they will impact, for example, the curriculum development of sport and physical education programs, health and wellness education, as well as our body culture in general. The following analysis will, first, address the changing values in highly industrialized societies and their impact on the movement culture, with a focus on North America and Germany. Secondly, a meta-theoretical framework will provide the basis for a sociological interpretation of these changes in the 21st century.

## Changing Values in Highly Industrialized Societies

According to Schulze (1992), people in modern societies direct their actions toward the potentially challenging experiences or "thrilling" feedback an action may provide. That is, the decision for or against a certain action is not simply determined by its pragmatic character or durability, but rather by the adventure that goes with the action. Modern society is increasingly characterized by the process of secularization, wherein traditional religious values are losing their significance. In this process, religion no longer provides significant meaning in people's lives. The place and function of religion increasingly becomes replaced by worldly endeavors, such as the focus on the body: "the body as heaven."

People's daily striving and acting is focused on the experience of happiness here and now, the satisfaction through adventure, and the maximization of excitement and exhilaration. In and through sport, people seem to find a promise of such experiences; and thus, sport has gained importance as a meaningful provider in people's lives. When people are longing for the experiences of adventure in and through sport, their focus is on the body; that is, the body is central to the sporting experience. The question arises as to how people in modern societies solve their existential problems. Problem solving seems to take place in conjunction with the body, through which satisfaction and happiness can be gained. Researchers have characterized this phenomenon as "happiness through and from the body" (also known as *Glück aus dem Körper*, see Rittner/Mrazek, 1986).

One of the most important issues facing people in contemporary societies is their concern for health. Since the focus is not on the afterlife any longer, but rather on the here and now, people are striving to live a comfortable and fulfilling life. Reasons for this development are also related to increasing automation and technological advancement, which has had a particular impact, not only on the workplace but on life in general. One result of this development is a decrease in bodily labor and human movement in general. Thus, people need some kind of physical compensation in order to balance their rather inactive lifestyles in advanced societies. If they fail to do so, they are more likely to develop health problems, such as obesity, heart and bone structure diseases, and more. In modern societies, health has become a precious commodity, which is no longer seen as simply provided by God; rather, people have to actively be concerned about their health. They turn to various forms of exercise in order to take care of themselves. Programs offered in health and fitness studios have become extremely popular since the 1970s.

Although, the positive relationship between an active lifestyle and healthy living has been known for quite some time, exercise has just recently experienced a tremendous boom in the areas of health promotion and illness prevention. Today, health seems to be sold in various forms, not only in health/fitness studios, but also in drug stores, hospitals, health and grocery stores, and more. Exercise has become a catapult for health. The development of sport and exercise in highly industrialized societies goes hand in hand with the quest for health prevention. That is, sport has lost its unity and primary focus on competition. Rather, the general social processes of differentiation have also influenced the world of sport leading to a variety of diverse sport offerings. The motto in sport is no longer just competition; the focus in sport now also includes: sport for fun and happiness, sport for fitness and health, adventure sport, sport for all, sport for the disabled, sport for rehabilitation, sport for prevention, and more. However, counting the number of people involved in some form of sport or another, fitness and health activities are clearly leading. Studies investigating the reasons for people's involvement in physical activity clearly reflect this tendency (Volkwein-Caplan &

Tahmaseb McConatha, 2012; Rittner, 1994). Subsequently, in the area of fitness and health activities there also has been a great increase in sport novelties.

The changes in human movement culture in modern societies are reflected in greater differentiation including new dimensions (new activities in the areas of rehabilitation, leisure, adventure, fitness, relaxation, etc.), added choices (new sports such as jogging, aerobics, walking, bungee jumping, hang gliding, surfing, body building, etc.), and sport serving as a meaningful provider through bodily engagements in people's lives. The traditional achievement principle, governing mainly top-level sport, is substituted for the fun, fitness, health, and happiness people seek through their involvement in the various sporting activities.

Lifestyle changes are also directly connected with a different understanding of health and the body. New body ideals have been formed. An example of the dramatic changes is the shift in the body ideal in conjunction with the fitness movement. Since the '50s, the ideal body image is one of being fit, sporty, young, dynamic, and so on. Before that time, the ideal body image was characterized as being "static"; that is, the body was determined by status and dignity (Elias, 1978). This radical shift needs explanation. The sense of shame and agony of the body becomes more differentiated in the process of social differentiation. In highly industrialized societies, where physical labor becomes more and more obsolete, the values are changing, too: the body becomes suppressed and the mind becomes elevated. By the same token, almost paradoxical, bodily behavior becomes more important. In this regard, Goffmann (1974) speaks of the "best self" people aspire to become, which includes having the perfect body. For example, one should have no bodily odors, no dandruff, no hair on female legs, and more. This movement can even be characterized as a clinical fight against the body – "the self without a body." What is interesting about this shift in the body ideal is that now people are using their body as representation of the self rather than physical labor: "You are how you look." The ideal of the fit, slim, dynamic body represents a revolution in dealing with the body, which is directly connected with the general change and shift of social norms and values in advanced societies.

How can these value changes in advanced societies be explained? A theoretical and methodological reflection in regard to the development of movement culture in postmodern societies will shed some light on this question.

## Theoretical/Methodological Considerations

The history of research in sport and human movement sciences has had a narrow understanding of the concepts of body and movement, which in the past has mainly focused on performance. Thus, most research has been geared toward empirical data analyses. However, various other theoretical approaches need to be discussed in order to accommodate complex societal phenomena. Changes and aspects of differentiation in highly industrialized societies are confronting the field of sociology; sport sociologists in particular are faced with the problem of searching for new models of interpretation. Various theorists have come up with diverse explanations of modernization, such as critical theory, postmodern theory, systems theory, and others.

A theoretical approach, such as critical theory, plays an important role here in that it helps to focus our attention toward the understanding of sport and human movement within its social and cultural context. It aims to explain the role sport has played in society; how the opportunities in terms of sport vary from one group to another; how sport reflects the interests of participants; and when and how sport can be used as a catalyst for change in society as a whole. A phenomenon such as the fitness movement cannot be explained using empirical data analysis, rather it first has to be understood as a socio-historical and cultural phenomenon, which has to be analyzed from within this context. Critical theory has taught us to look at society with a more critical eye and not to take common explanations for granted. Every social development has its function and ways that people adapt to it, e.g., new meaning attached to the body. However, these changes in the new fitness movement are not free from repression and alienation either. This movement can be explained in positive and negative ways at the same time. On one hand, one could argue that the increased participation of women in sport has had a positive correlation to the emancipation of women in the still male-dominated society. On the other, one could argue that the female role has not changed at all because women mainly exercise for beauty reasons; hence, women are still bound to the idea of being the beauty object for men. The latter analysis supports the alienation and repression argument of the critical theory; however, this theory cannot explain the apparent juxtapositions in society.

Markula (1991) has shown that not one single interpretation of this phenomenon is correct. On one hand, there is an increased participation of women in fitness activities and exercise, which fosters further emancipation; and, on the other hand, women are exposed to even more objectification, which still confines them to the traditional female role. Thus, this paradox can best be explained as embodying both: emancipation and objectification at the same time. Markula's (1991) analysis goes beyond that of critical theory, which among most European researchers/theorists today is considered outdated, by adopting a postmodernist approach. Postmodernism helps to explain even juxtaposed situations in society explaining social phenomena from a pluralistic perspective: the meaning is contingent on the context and the specific situation. This approach seems to be very suitable for researching the fitness movement in complex societies because it focuses on the interaction of the various social systems, especially health, body, and movement culture. Representatives of the postmodern theory claim that modernizing capitalism creates the condition of social and cultural pluralism, wherein historically marginalized groups come to demand changes in the system, and thus disrupt the traditional claims of power and status; which is especially true for females and blacks (Dunn, 1991). This theory has high validity by providing an accurate account explaining, for example, the role of women in the fitness movement.

Postmodern theory explains the process of modernization as a paradox, meaning that modern societies incorporate apparently juxtaposed trends. Attention is paid to these opposing movements. For example, modern societies can be characterized, on one hand, by a neglect of the body in highly industrialized societies because the body is no longer needed for the production process due to technological advancements and automation at work. At the same time, there is an increased awareness of the body "as the embodiment of individual accomplishments and personal success: beauty, fitness, health, pleasure, sexuality, vitality, and youthfulness" (Loy, et al., 1993, p. 81). This body boom finds its manifestation in the fitness movement, the increased focus on beauty for both, women and men, as well as the extensive beauty industry, including cosmetic surgery. It is a paradox phenomenon indeed: there is the creation of the body (people create, form, and style their own bodies), and juxtaposed to this movement there is the creation through the body (people create something else through so-called "physical" labor, which is not very physical in many cases). *Ein Zeichen unserer Zeit* is a symbol of postmodern societies that develops its own dynamics and cannot be explained by one set of logical principles. Rather, high-tech mass communication has led to a new "reality logic" based on subjective experiences – a result of the circulation of televised images. Indeed, Loy, et al., speak about "reality transmitted by the media" (1993, 82).

Finally, systems theorists are also concerned with the social and value changes in modern times. They try to explain these phenomena systematically, that is through reflection and rational thought processes. The major interest of the systems theorist is not the value change per se, but rather how the individual systems of society react to these changes and what the consequences are for the system and the subjects in the system. That is, how the process of change occurs and lies at the heart of the system's analysis. The subject becomes important for the system theorist only when a collective behavior of several individuals is apparent. General tendencies, characteristic for advanced societies, such as an increasing individualization processes or differentiation in lifestyles, are identified as a collective phenomenon, in which the individual becomes more and more dependent upon oneself. However, many people collectively find themselves in the same situation.

Social change takes place in conjunction with value changes in society. According to Schulze, "these processes manifest themselves in the formation, disintegration, and rearrangement of social groups; in the new interpretation of tradition and the emergence of new meaning providers; in the formation of new reality types and subsequent behavior strategies; in the submerging of old and the development of new forms of general social processes" (1992, p. 15). These value changes, then lead to personality changes in the individuals; that is, greater differentiation, individualization, subjectivation, and a new understanding/awareness of the body are resulting consequences. The effects of these processes affect all institutions or systems in society, e.g., economy, state, jurisdiction, politics, church, etc., including sport (Cachay, 1988).

Critical theory, postmodernism, and systems theory all have their place within the social sciences, and so has empirical research. Once hypotheses are formulated, they can be checked taking empirical research into account, in order to check the validity of the theory. Although, it could be argued against an empirical research approach that it does not allow for any critical perspective of the status quo in society, this can be considered when interpreting the data. Every empirical analysis depends on theoretical guidance. For example, a survey has shown that 60% of German, as well as American, people say that they are engaged in sport and exercise in some form or another on a regular basis. This information cannot be taken out of its sociocultural context. We need to understand that because being fit and active represents the current desired lifestyle, people aspire to it so much that they tend to claim an active involvement in sporting and fitness activities, even if that takes place only once a month. Hence, without social, historical, philosophical, political, and psychological analyses, empirical data cannot be interpreted in an adequate fashion, because the data by itself does not explain correlations between culture and society, social systems and body culture. Thus, the epistemology suggested here can best be described as a meta-scientific, interdisciplinary, pluralistic approach.

## Conclusion

An analysis of value changes in advanced societies and its impact on movement culture in highly industrialized societies is only possible when the different social systems (health system, body culture, sport system, etc.) are taken into account with their various changing values and norms. This can only be achieved with a meta-theoretical interdisciplinary research approach. Since the social problems are interdisciplinary, analyzing movement culture through body culture makes sense. People, both men and women, try to solve problems through their bodies. This approach might also lead to better solutions in health education and questions in gerontology. It will provide guidance for adequate curriculum development in postmodern societies in the 21st century. This is not solely focused on the education of Physical Education teachers, but it includes the preparation of fitness specialists or "lifestyle specialists," focusing on issues such as health care, prevention and rehabilitation rather than "ill care."

## References

Airhihenbuwa, C. (1995). *Health and Culture: Beyond the Western Paradigm.* Thousand Oaks, CA: Sage Publications.

Bette, K.-H. (1989). *Körperspuren – Zur Semantik und Paradoxie moderner Körperlichkeit.* Berlin, New York: Walter DeGruyter.

Bryant, J. & McElroy, M. (1997). *Sociological Dynamics of Sport and Exercise.* Englewood, Colorado: Morton Publishing Company.

Cachay, K. (1988). *Sport und Gesellschaft.* Schorndorf: Hofmann.

Coakley, J. (1990). *Sport in Society.* St. Louis/Toronto/ Boston/ Los Altos: Times Mirror/Mosby College Publishing.

Digel, H. (1986). Über den Wandel der Werte in Gesellschaft, Freizeit und Sport. In: K. Heinemann, H. Becker (Eds.). *Die Zukunft des Sports.* Schorndorf: Hofmann. Featherstone, M. (1982). The Body in Consumer Culture. *Theory, Culture, and Society, 8,* 18-33.

Dunn, R. (1991). Postmodernism and Gender Relations in Feminist Theory. *Signs, 12* (4), 621-643.

Elias, N. (1978). *The Civilizing Process.* Oxford: Blackwell.

Flax, J. (1987). Postmodernism: Populism, Mass Culture, and Avant-Garde. *Theory, Culture and Society, 8,* 111-135.

Gergen, K. (1994). Exploring the Postmodern – Perils or Potentials? *American Psychologist,* May, 412-415.

Heinemann, K. (1989). Der "nicht-sportliche" Sport. In: K. Dietrich, K. Heinemann (Eds.). *Der nicht-sportliche Sport: Beiträge zum Wandel im Sport.* Schorndorf: Hofmann.

Inglehart, R. (1977). *The Silent Revolution. Changing Values and Political Styles among Western Publics.* Princeton: Princeton University Press.

Inglehart, R. (1985). Aggregate Stability and Individual Level Flux in Mass Belief Systems: The level of analysis paradox. *American Political Science Review 79,* 97-116.

Klages, H., Hippler, H.-J. & Herbert , W. (1992). *Werte und Wandel. Ergebnisse und Methoden einer Forschungstradition.* Frankfurt, New York: Campus Verlag.

Loy, J., Andrews, D. & Rinehart, R. (1993). The Body in Culture and Sport. *Sport Science Review, 2* (1), 69-91.

Lyotard, J.-F. (1986). *Das postmoderne Wissen. Tranlated from French* (original 1979) by Peter Engelmann. Wien: Ernst Becvar.

Markula, P. (1991). "Firm but Shapely, Fit but Sexy, Strong but Thin: The Postmodern Aerobicizing Bodies." Paper presented at the NASSS Conference, Milwaukee, Wisconsin.

Rittner, V. & Mrazek, J. (1986). Neues Glück aus dem Körper. *Psychologie Heute*, November, 54-63.

Rittner, V. (1994). Die 'success-story' des modernen Sports und seine Metamorphose: Fitneß, Ästhetik und individuelle Selbstdarstellung. *Das Parlament*, May, 3-11.

Schulze, G. (1992). *Die Erlebnisgesellschaft – Kultursoziologie der Gegenwart.* Frankfurt/New York: Campus Verlag.

Tetlock, P. (1986). A Value Pluralism Model of Ideological Reasoning. *Journal of Personality and Social Psychology, 50* (4), 819-827.

Volkwein, K. (1998). *Fitness as Cultural Phenomenon.* Münster, Germany: Waxmann Verlag.

Volkwein-Caplan, K. & Tahmaseb McConatha, J. (2012). *The Social Geography of Healthy Aging.* Maidenhead/UK: Meyer & Meyer Publisher.

## Issue 2

# Fitness – The Global Sport-for-All?

During the last two decades, the influence of sport and the quest for physical fitness has grown tremendously in the Western world. According to a recent survey, Americans annually spend more than $100 billion on health, wellness goods and fitness products. "And as boomers get older, more are turning to wellness products as an antidote to the signs of aging" (Merriman, et al., 2008). The fitness industry has greatly expanded over the last two decades. The number of gyms has steadily increased with memberships totaling 41.5 million in 2007. And this growth is still on the rise. Furthermore, new developments in exercise equipment are attracting members and opening novel markets. Commercial equipment manufacturers are benefiting from the domestic growth in gyms and now are focusing on the international and vertical markets (hotels and spas) as excellent opportunities.

The proliferation of exercise equipment and fitness facilities and the emergence of personal trainer and home gym have generated a new vocabulary of fitness terms and greater public awareness of the importance of exercise (Bryant & McElroy, 1997). The popular success of televised sports and the ever-increasing participation of men and women of all ages in organized and unorganized sport and fitness activities attest to this importance. This development has led to changes in the relationship between sport, fitness and society; it has also brought into focus the relationship of body and culture. There are many indications that changes in the area of sport or physical culture, including fundamental forms of human movement and physical activity, go hand in hand with changes in the way of life in highly industrialized societies (Sage & Eitzen, 2012).

The roots of the ongoing fitness movement go back to the 1970s in the USA; at the end of the 20th century, this movement had successfully spread to other highly industrialized nations in the world. It is not simply a response to the current crisis in modern societies; rather fitness has become an integral part of modern lifestyle. Reasons for the rise of the fitness movement are culture specific as well as global or transnational.

Although culture is experienced personally, it represents a shared system, "a program for behavior" (Hall & Hall, 1990). Traditions, values, and worldviews differ from culture to culture. Culture is an ever-changing process that crosses national boundaries. Individual differences within each culture are reflected in race, ethnicity, gender, social class, education, and personality. Additionally, regional differences have their own "mini-cultures." As a result of migration and globalization (or more specifically Westernization), cultural values and traditions are shared, exchanged, changed, and transformed. Thus, within a given country, numerous cultures can be represented and exist simultaneously.

At the end of the 20th century, globalization has been introduced as a new, universal language. Globalization appears to be "a-cultural," where individual cultural distinctions are no longer considered. This process is problematic because it highlights and marginalizes cultural differences. However, although a globalized phenomenon, the fitness movement is still rooted in the context of specific cultural codes and meaning. It can be described as a cultural phenomenon that is experienced primarily by a select group of people from a particular social class, the middle and upper middle class. Income, gender, age, race and ethnicity have also been identified as variables that determine who is participating in fitness activities and why they are participating (Volkwein, 1998). Thus, although it seems that the fitness movement is becoming the "sport for all," not everyone in the world and not everyone in a given culture has access to it. Sport and also fitness activities seem to be mainly reserved for those countries and people within these societies who have sufficient access to economic and recreational resources.

In order to answer the question of whether fitness has indeed become a global sport-for-all concept, it is necessary to first investigate the historical roots of the fitness phenomenon. Secondly, the changing role of sport and fitness in the (post)modern era will be analyzed, which sheds light on the world wide rise of the fitness movement.

## Historical Roots of the Fitness Phenomenon

To understand the fitness movement, one needs to examine its historical roots. Originally, *fitness* – although the term was created much later – was regarded as being "fit for fighting." In different time periods, as well as different countries, physical fitness has been an important component for the military. In order to provide national security and to fight in wars, young men (today, women also) had to be strong and fit to defend their countries. Thus, fitness was seen as a useful tool for serving political purposes.

In the 18th century, an important fitness movement was started by "Turnvater Jahn" (Friedrich Ludwig Jahn 1778-1852) in Germany. This movement later spread to other European countries and the USA. "From the movement's origin in the latter half of the 1840s, the Turnverein phenomenon rose to become the most vivid centerpiece in the tapestry of German culture transplanted to

America" (Barney, 1991, 3). Although Jahn's ideas of *turnen* and fitness were still connected to the physical fitness ideals of the military, fun and enjoyment were new components added – as exemplified in the slogan *"frisch, fromm, froehlich, frei"* (fresh, pious, happy, free). Also, for the first time, women had access to these sporting activities called *turnen* and were able to improve their physical fitness levels.

A new understanding of fitness became associated with industrialization. This perspective connected physical fitness with work and an increase in productivity. Workers were expected to keep in shape so that they could perform better and stay healthy. Employers began to support worker's sports clubs much like the military incorporated fitness training at the workplace.
Another shift in the meaning associated with fitness developed after World War II. Physical fitness now was believed to positively enhance the quality of life for the individual. The focus was to derive pleasure and enjoyment from engaging in fitness and other sporting activities, which in return will benefit not only the physical aspects of a person, such as a more pleasurable sex life, but also social and psychological well-being.

While the previous fitness movements were dictated and supported from the outside, e.g., the military, national leaders, and employers, it can be argued that this new fitness development is driven by the individuals from within. This might be a major reason why this latest fitness movement has been much more influential than its predecessors and is on the brink of becoming a global cultural phenomenon.

Today, individuals themselves assume responsibility for their health and well-being. They engage in various activities to enhance the quality of life, to stay healthy, fit, youthful and attractive. Fitness now is marketed as a means of achieving these goals and aspirations. As can be expected, the social and personal pressures to stay fit, healthy, beautiful, and thin (that go along with this fitness ideology) have had some detrimental effects as well. An increase in eating disorders and the rise of dangerous and unnecessary cosmetic surgery are only some of the consequences affecting both men and women. However, women have disproportionately been distressed more than men, as women have traditionally faced more pressure to adhere to certain beauty standards and body ideals (see Chapter 9).

These changes in the way of life are directly related to the socioeconomic developments of the latter part of the 20th century. For example, the enormous progress in the medical sciences has affected large segments of the population. However, not everyone has been able to benefit from these advancements.

National leaders again are interested in the health and well-being of their people. In the 21st century, fitness has become a vital part in keeping overall health care expenditures down (Volkwein-Caplan & Tahmaseb McConatha, 2012). Consequently, this latest fitness movement may be characterized by an overlapping of national and personal interests.

The development of the various meanings of fitness accumulated during the period of the Third Reich, wherein military power, labor power and "power through joy" *(Kraft durch Freude)* reflected the fatal hegemony of the Third Reich. Today's fitness ideology is characterized by "joy through power" (e.g., in body building, see Klein and Bolin, in Volkwein, 1998). People who do not fit the current body and fitness ideals, that is being fit, beautiful, and muscular (muscular *and* thin for females), become marginalized. They become second-class citizens, whose accomplishments do not get the same recognition (e.g. being selected for a job), much like Jessie Owens when his accomplishments during the 1936 Olympics in Berlin were not recognized by Hitler because Owens did not represent the Arian ideal. Thus, one could argue that an overemphasis on fitness to these extremes cannot represent a *global sport-for-all concept* but rather stands for "anti-culture," where the non-fit are discriminated against.

The current fitness movement with its positive and negative contributions represents the ethos of life in highly industrialized societies. Like other social phenomena in the post-modern world, fitness is characterized by contradictions, as the various contributions to the book *Fitness as Cultural Phenomenon* (Volkwein, 1998) reveal. For example, on one hand, one could argue that fitness can pave the way to emancipation, as music, oral and written language, as well as cinema, have done in the past, and on the other hand, fitness is simply another form of hegemonic social practice.

The cross-cultural analysis of the fitness movement, as it has been described for Germany and North America in the 1990s (Volkwein, 1998), reveals the complex development of the human movement culture, as well as its export and import during the time of global expansion of Western values and traditions. However, it is important to acknowledge that the contemporary fitness movement is not a world-wide phenomenon – not yet – and not everyone is participating – only a select class of people. The fitness phenomenon is a product of the so-called Western world, unique to industrialized societies. The fitness phenomenon, as we know it today, has its roots in the USA. Many people associate Kenneth Cooper as the "father of the modern fitness movement" that started in the USA in the late '60s. One could argue that from there, it has been imported into other highly industrialized nations.

It is important to analyze the fitness movement in its country of origin with its specific values and cultural dimensions. This movement has not only been imported to other parts of the world but rather has also undergone a specific process of adaptation, which reflects cultural variations and differences in value systems. The movement has demonstrated significant similarities and differences with each cultural adaptation; however, there is no doubt that fitness has established itself as an important cultural phenomenon in the 21st century.

## Conditions of the (Post)Modern

Over a hundred years ago, social critic Max Weber characterized modernity as the collapse of religious authority and the rise of a rationalized, bureaucratic social order with increased specialization. In *The Protestant Ethic and the Spirit of Capitalism* (1904), Weber observed that the whole "mighty cosmos of the modern economic order" is seen as "an iron cage." Marx, Nietzsche, Kierkegaard, Tocqueville, Mill and other great thinkers have further extrapolated on the forces that modern technology and social organizations exert over humankind. "But they all believed that modern individuals had the capacity both to understand this fate and, once they understood it, to fight it" (Berman, 1988, 27).

Twentieth century social scientists, on the other hand, seem to lack this empathy and faith in a better tomorrow. For example, Herbert Marcuse writes in *The One-Dimensional Man* (1964) that the masses have no egos, no ids, their souls are devoid of inner tension or dynamism: their ideas, their needs, even their dreams, are "not their own"; their inner lives are "totally administered" from the outside, programmed to produce exactly those desires that the social system and capitalism can satisfy. Marcuse criticized that "the people recognize themselves in their commodities; they find their soul in their automobiles, hi-fi sets, split-level homes, kitchen equipment" (Marcuse, 1964, 9). He described modern men and women as objects, as "beings without spirit, without heart, without sexual and personal identity ... without being" (Berman, 27). This lost hope of people is characterized as the postmodern condition.2 "Post-modernist social thought pours scorn on all the collective hopes for moral and social progress, for personal freedom and public happiness. ... These hopes ... have been shown to be bankrupt, at best be vain and futile fantasies, at worst engines of domination and monstrous enslavements" (Berman, 1988, 9-10).

The result of modernity, the so-called "post-modern condition," is not necessarily leading to achieving more happiness for people but rather to a loss of control over nature, which is characterized by the occurrence and increase of health problems such as heart disease, obesity, cancer, AIDS, and more. The advances of the technological age have a dark side. Postman remarks cynically that "...the uncontrolled growth of technology destroys the vital sources of our humanity. It creates a culture without a moral foundation. It undermines certain mental processes and social relations that make human life worth living" (1992, xii).

The disappointments associated with modern culture started to be expressed in America in the '60s, in the arts and leftist politics. The fitness movement that followed in the '70s is described by Glassner as a reaction by the general public "to disengage the negative effects of life in modern culture" (1990, 219). This reaction is described as an attempt by individuals, mainly people from the middle and upper class, to counterbalance the deficiencies of the modern era. An interpretation of this trend may be that given the fact that people have lost the hope to change the social conditions, they are focusing *inward* to change themselves and their bodies.

As societies change so does the role of the body, which today has become a source for happiness and a provider of meaning in people's lives. We are bombarded daily with countless images of idealized bodies on television, in newspapers, magazines, and billboards. These images "channel capital and serve as a common resource for judging the adequacy of self and others"(Glassner, 1990, 215). Cultural economy critics state that the economy can simply not afford the increase in health expenditure due to sedentary lifestyle (Featherstone, et al., 1991). When bodies are simply described as commodities, this will not sufficiently explain the heart of the fitness furor. "In addition to the commercial and consumerist interest in the body, there is a new emphasis on keeping fit, the body beautiful and the postponement of aging by sport" (Featherstone, 1982, 18). It is true that a general commodification of society and the bodies within it has taken place; but the question, *why fitness*, still remains to be answered.

The end of the 20th century is characterized by the decolonization and de-Europeanization of the world; the complex process of post-traditional and post-national identification has given rise to the modern fitness movement. Traditional hierarchies and status based on income and education has been extended to the body. We are living in a world of body culture, where the body and taking care of one's body make a social statement (see Gebauer, in Volkwein, 1998). As major determinants for shaping the body, exercise and fitness activities have become means to acquire social status.

The concept of fitness is "sold" to people in many ways, not only in relation to improving the health status and lowering the health care costs of the population. Fitness promises range from general health improvement, to relief of stress and depression, to the achievement of happiness in life. Fitness is also said to offer an intimate and holistic marriage between the self and the body. Since the body is experienced as an important dimension of the self, the physique and how someone looks become signs of the self in a way that fashion and cosmetics no longer can (see Chapter 9). Fitness enthusiasts turn inward and avoid social problems (Glassner, 1990, 225). They focus on themselves and their bodies. The fitness movement can be described as a personal response to the aspirations and failings of modernist culture. Values and value changes are an important part of this development in the global age.

## Conclusion

Social and cultural changes, as well as the effects of the globalization process, will also impact curricular development of sport and physical education programs, health and wellness education, as well as our body culture in general. Thus, it is important to understand the impact of these changes on peoples' lives and their needs, especially in regard to human movement. The "old" traditional sport-for-all concept, with its focus on competition and achievement, may not satisfy these changed needs of individuals in modern societies any longer. Rather, the "new" fitness development with its emphasis on health, relaxation, and general life fulfillment may be more appropriate to the contribution of the general psychophysical well-being of modern individuals. As the process of globalization continues, it is likely that this fitness movement will spread to non-Western cultures and become the *global sport-for-all concept* in the future.

## References

AAHPER Research Council (1996). *Health Related Physical Fitness Test Manual.*

Barney, R. (1991). The German-American Turnverein Movement: Its Historiography. In: Naul, R. *Turnen and Sport – The Cross-Cultural Exchange.* Münster/New York: Waxmann Verlag.

Beckers, E. (1988). Körperfassaden und Fitness-Ideologie – Wiederkehr des Körpers in der Fitness-Bewegung? In: Schulz, N.; Allmer, H. (Eds.) *Fitness-Studios. Anspruch und Wirklichkeit.* Brennpunkte der Sportwissenschaft, 2, 153-175.

Berman, M. (1988). *All That is Solid Melts in the Air. The Experience of Modernity.* Harmondsworth, England: Penguin Books.

Bryant, J. & McElsroy, M. (1997). S*ociological Dynamics of Sport and Exercise.* Englewood, CO: Morton Publishing Company.

Bouchard, C.; Shepard, R.; Stephens, T.; Sutton, J.; McPherson, B. (Eds.) (1990). *Exercise, Fitness, and Health.* Champaign, IL: Human Kinetics.

Council of Europe (no year). European Sport for All Charter.

Featherstone, M., Hepworth, M. & B. Turner (1991). *The Body – Social Process and Cultural Theory.* London: Sage Publications.

Glassner, B (1990). Fit for Postmodern Selfhood. In: H. Becker, M. Call (Eds.) *Symbolic Interaction and Cultural Studies.* Chicago: The University of Chicago Press. Pp. 215-243.

Lellness, A. & Nation, J. (1996). *Sport Psychology.* Chicago: Nelson-Hall Publisher.

Marcuse, H. (1964). *One-Dimensional Man: Studies in the Ideology of Advanced Industrial Society.* Boston: Beacon Press.

Merriman Curham Ford (2008). Fitness and Wellness Industry. Consumer/ Internet/Media Industry Report. www.physicventures.com

Postman, N. (1992). *Technopoly – The Surrender of Culture to Technology.* New York: Vintage Books.

Rittner, V. & Mrazek, J. (1986). "Neues Glück aus dem Körper." *Psychologie Heute,* November, 54-63.

Sage, G. & Eitzen, S. (2012). *Sociology of North American Sport.* New York/ Oxford: Oxford University Press.

Schulze, G. (1992). *Die Erlebnisgesellschaft – Kultursoziologie der Gegenwart.* Frankfurt/New York: Campus Verlag.

Turner, B. (1984). *The Body and Society.* London: Blackwell.

Uhlenbruck, G. (1996). Bewegungstraining verbessert Lebensqualität. *TW Gynäkologie, 9,* 345-351.

U.S. Department of Health and Human Services (1996). *Physical Activity and Health: A Report of the Surgeon General.* Pittsburgh, PA: Superintendent of Documents.

Volkwein, K. (1995). Fitness in the Context of the North American Health and Sport System. In: Mester, J. (Ed.). *Images of Sport in the World – Congress Proceedings.* Köln, Germany.

Volkwein, K. (1997). Living Faith: Sport – The New Religion in the "New World". In: Mahlke, R., Pitzer-Reyl, R., Süss, J. (Eds.) *Living Faith – Lebendige religiöse Wirklichkeit – Festschrift für Hans-Jürgen Greschat.* Frankfurt: Peter Lang. 461-470.

Volkwein, K. (Ed.) (1998). *Fitness as Cultural Phenomenon.* Münster, New York: Waxmann Verlag.

Volkwein-Caplan, K. & Tahmaseb McConatha, J. (2012). *The Social Geography of Healthy Aging.* Maidenhead/UK: Meyer & Meyer Publishers.

Weber, M. (1904). *The Protestant Ethic and the Spirit of Capitalism.* Translated by Taslcott Parsons in1930.

## Issue 3

## Culture, Aging and Well-Being:
## The Importance of Place and Space[1]

*(with Jasmin Tahmaseb McConatha)*

### Introduction

In the near future, there will be an exponential growth of older adults in the world. The growing population of older adults in Europe and North America has put a strain on the health care systems of the industrialized world. Older adults sometimes need specialized and long-term care for such pernicious disorders as cancer, heart disease, stroke, and Alzheimer's disease. These conditions also create social and economic strains on friends, partners, and other family members, often young and middle-aged adults, who become economic and social caregivers for their aging parents.

The specter of "old age" also has a cultural dimension. We often associate "old age" with physical and mental decline. Old people are often seen as physically and mentally incapable of looking after themselves. They are depicted in stereotypical ways, walking with canes, shuffling in walkers and moving along in wheelchairs. They are perceived as cognitively impaired, unable to competently function in the contemporary technological world. These images are, of course, cultural stereotypes based on prejudice. They form the bedrock of what many commentators have called "ageism," a body of attitudes and practices that discriminate against older adults (Butler, 1989). A review of several decades of research in gerontology, of course, presents a fuller and more nuanced account of the social and economic lives of older adults. Advances in medical care have not only extended the lifespans of contemporary men and women but have increased the emotional and physical quality of later life. In fact, research results indicate that in the past several decades, an increasing percentage of men and women lead active and healthy lives well into later life.

In this issue, we consider how older adults pursue well-being in later life. We are especially interested in how physical activity – fitness – is related to both physical and emotional health. Fitness and emotional health, of course, cannot be considered in isolation. We therefore consider the social, cultural, and economic parameters associated with aging, health and well-being. Using this

---

1 Parts of this manuscript have been previously published in *The International Journal of Sport & Society, 2(2),* 41-48.

macro-context, we analyze the interview results of our recent research with a specific group of people – women in the Russian Diaspora.

## An Aging World and Health Challenges

As mentioned at the outset, the population of older adults is expanding in every region of the world. Although life expectancy varies from region to region, most people are not only living longer but also having fewer children. This trend means that the average age of the world population is increasing. One hundred years ago, average life expectancy in the United States was 47.3 years, today it is 77 (Hoyer & Roodin, 2009). Although people are living longer in most places, there are still great variations in life expectancy. People tend to live longest in Japan with a life expectancy of 82.9 years; the United States is number 19 in life expectancy.

Considerable ethnic and cultural differences exist in the domains of life expectancy and health and well-being. Studies in the United States have found, for example, that African Americans and Hispanics tend to have a higher rate of chronic illness and lower life expectancy than European Americans. Substantial gender differences have also been documented: white women tend to live an average of 6 years longer than other older adults, but these women tend to struggle with a greater number of health concerns. Those with the lowest income are more likely to struggle with poor health and have a lower life expectancy.

In the past, people tended to live longer in the industrial societies of Europe and North America. In those societies, technological sophistication, which provided better nutrition, sanitation and health care, produced populations with high percentages of people over the age of 65. By the year 2050, in fact, one-third of the world's population is expected to be over sixty. Along with increasing age, we will face specific health challenges. Although prevention methods and improved treatments have helped to prolong life, we are also faced with an increase in chronic disease and debilitating illness, as well as a wide range of disabilities.

The exponential increase in obesity – among all age groups – is another important health challenge in the 21st century. Obesity is a widespread epidemic, especially in the USA. According to the 2007 National Health and Nutrition Examination Survey, more than 64% of US adults are overweight or obese (www.cdc.gov/nchs). Although women and men share similar percentages of obesity, women are more often socially sanctioned for their weight. They are subjected to age, gender, and weight bias (Fontane, 1996).

So, the world is graying at a faster rate than previously anticipated. Given this tectonic change, what social and psychological challenges will older adults face in the coming years? What will it take to help these elders maintain a positive quality of life? One way to maintain well-being as we age is to be physically and socially active. Indeed, later adulthood can be, according to a variety of studies, an active and productive time of life (Baltes & Carstensen, 1996; Diener, Diener & Diener, 1995). Accordingly, it seems that an increasing number of older men and women are living healthy and productive lives – often well into their eighties. Ironically, advances in life expectancy have led to a dramatic decrease in social appreciation of older adults. The various sources of the media are flooded with negative images of aging and older men and women.

## Ageism and Physical Activity

Cross-cultural studies have found that older adults today are subjected to multiple sources of discrimination. Among the most prominent of these is ageism, which is widespread around the world. It may seem surprising, but studies in the United States have found that the majority of older adults say that they have been subjected to some form of ageism (Palmore, 2001). Ageism is a process of systematic stereotyping and prejudice against older men and women (Butler, 1963). This form of prejudice results from a widespread and deep-seated fear of the aging process, which also compels younger people to distance themselves from older men and women (Palmore, 2001). Scholars have called this distancing, "aging anxiety," which centers on the anticipation of loss as we age. Fear about aging usually begins early in life and continues throughout one's life. Concomitantly, ageism has a negative impact on the self-images of older men and women.

Older women especially, are often subjected to what Susan Sontag (1972) called "double jeopardy" – the double whammy of ageism and sexism combined. With the increase in the number of elders with various needs, many of the positive attitudes about age have eroded and ageism has spread from the industrialized world, especially the global reach of the Internet and television programs from the West. Images on the Internet and television tend to value youth and denigrate age and aging.

Indeed, social theorists have linked modernization to the loss of elder power. Atchley (1994) contends that modernization theory helps to understand social change and aging. In this early theory of modernity, much attention is focused on the status of elders. In more traditional societies, older men and women play an active and vital role. In societies in which the processes of modernization have unfolded, older adults have experienced losses of position, status and power. In other words, there tends to be an inverse relationship between the status of elders and the processes of modernization and technological advancement.

Films, commercials, books, and magazines depict older adults as depressed, unattractive, ill, disabled, lonely, decrepit, and even ready to die (Haught, et al., 1999). These images reinforce social attitudes that "old age" is the time of life when one loses physical and mental competence. The reality of what it means to be older in the 21st century, of course, presents a very different picture. Changes in patterns of activity, robust lifestyles, improved health care, and increased life expectancy mean that greater numbers of older adults present living and breathing challenges to the traditional images of old age – as a sedentary period of life, as a time to sit on a rocking chair and relax, as a time to shrivel up and die. Older men and women are staying physically, socially and sometimes sexually active well into their nineties. They are healthier, happier, and more economically potent than ever before.

Clearly perceptions of age and older adults are not connected to the reality of what it means to be an elder in contemporary societies. Younger people may think older people are old and decaying. The economic, social, cultural and political processes that constitute globalization will play an increasingly important role in how "society" perceives older adults. Indeed technological innovations triggered by the flows of the global economy will help define new processes of aging as well as the positive and negative attitudes society holds toward older men and women. Changes in roles and attitudes about aging will influence the entire developmental process and extend to the arenas of employment, health care, lifelong learning, and social services in developing countries as well as in developed nations (Weaver, 1999; McConatha, 2002).

As the population of older adults expands exponentially, one wonders how this will impact the spread of ageism. By the year 2050, demographers estimate that nearly one third of the world's population will be over 60 years old (www.ilcusa. org). Western Europe, Italy, Greece, Germany, Spain, France, and other countries in Europe currently have populations in which least 16% of the people are over 65 years of age (www.ilcusa.org). With nearly 38 million Americans currently older than 65 years old, health promotion for this population is an important area of social and political consideration (www.census.gov). Numerous studies have found that staying active leads to increased well-being and happiness in older adulthood. People who are physically and socially active seem to be most likely to maintain their physical and psychological health (Atchley, 1989). Thus, it is of critical importance that older adults have access to places and spaces in which they can be active, an access that would ensure a more graceful and healthy aging process.

## Health Promotion and Physical Activity

The Healthy People 2010 campaign in the United States seeks to increase life expectancy and quality of life. The campaign promotes information so that every individual can have the opportunity to make informed decisions about their health. This program encourages educators, politicians, and social leaders to increase access to health care for all American. It is particularly interested in promoting healthy environments, vital neighborhoods, and vibrant communities that can foster well-being regardless of age, gender, ethnicity, and social class.

Through their health outreach programs, non-profit organizations around the country have begun to urge older adults, especially immigrants – such as our group of interviewees from the Russian Diaspora – to increase their physical activity, eat healthier foods, manage their stress, and engage in preventive health care. In order for a health promotion program to be successful, outreach activities need to be designed in a sensitive and culturally appropriate fashion. Such activities need to incorporate an understanding of the values, religion, diet, and beliefs about health and illness of the populations they are attempting to reach.

In a recent study of health and well-being among women in the Russian Diaspora, we asked about health promotion and access to physical activities in the greater Philadelphia area. We utilized a qualitative research methodology and conducted extensive semi-structured interviews. This case study approach focused on 20 older women (65-85 years old). Questions asked included: How are their health needs met? What sources of support are available to them? What are their existential struggles in a country that is socially, culturally and linguistically alien to them? The majority of women indicated that there was support from various governmental agencies as well as social workers, including translators, to help them cope not only with the transition to start a new life in a different culture, but also with information regarding health promotion availability and fitness programs offered in the sponsored housing complex they resided. However, it was evident that their well-being at large depends on their adaptive success; that is, how well they were able to maintain social, physical and spiritual engagement.

As our study of Russian immigrant women suggests, globalization has put an increasing number of older men and women into situations of economic, social and cultural marginalization. These older adults may be ill or disabled, live in rural or underserved areas, lack education, or suffer from the impact of poverty. They may also hold different set of beliefs about health and illness and culturally varied thoughts about how to manage health and well-being. These divergent beliefs regarding health promotion present a considerable challenge to health promotion researchers and practitioners, who at any given moment may be faced with the challenge of confronting a culture of resistance to health promoting behavior change.

Health promotion is the art and science of helping people discover the synergies between their core passions and optimal health. In so doing, they become motivated to strive for optimal health, a dynamic balance of physical, emotional, social, spiritual and intellectual health. Such lifestyle changes can be facilitated through a combination of learning experiences that enhance awareness, increase motivation, build skills and most importantly create supportive environments that provide opportunities for positive health practices (O'Donnell, 2009). In our study, our subjects had access to healthy breakfast and lunch options in their building, as well as daily exercise programs in a near-by fitness center. They also had ample opportunity to walk outside on the large residential property as well as in near-by shopping centers. This availability encourages walking rather than driving to do errands.

Health promotion strategies are not limited to a specific health problem or to a specific set of behaviors. Recognizing the difficulties of outreach, the World Health Organization (WHO) has addressed the problem of health promotion. WHO suggests that the principles of and strategies for health promotion should be fine-tuned for a variety of population groups, risk factors, diseases, and in various settings. Health promotion outreach, WHO suggests, should be sponsored in schools, community development organizations and highlighted in health policy, legislation and regulation. Such outreach efforts should be also applied equally to the prevention of communicable diseases, injury, acts of violence, and mental health.

In the research study, we found that the well-being of the Russian women results from their ability to maintain social, physical, and spiritual engagement. We suggested that their ability to maintain this engagement is, to a large extent, dependent on their sense of cultural competence, a state that results from their participation in communities of like-minded people who share their sociopolitical history, language, and culture. We argued that, on the one hand, this shared experience provided them with a sense of connection in an alien and alienating world. On the other hand, we also found that shared experience may also hinder their adaptability to the larger social and cultural environment.

The key to successful aging, following the results of gerontological research, is a sense of well-being, a process involving a person's physical, mental, spiritual, and social dimensions. The difference between a successful and unsuccessful aging experience depends, to a large extent, on how people are able to successfully engage in health promoting behaviors that maintain a sense of well-being. In other words, health care providers believe that health promotion, or outreach, should be holistic – an ecological approach that focuses on understanding the person in the context of his or her environment (Stokol, 1992). From this perspective, each person's health and well-being can be best understood by considering the interaction of an individual's genetic predispositions, personality, along with his/her social and cultural circumstances. Indeed, the social and cultural environment plays an important role that helps or hinders a person's ability to age with energy and grace. When an environmental context deteriorates into unstable political situations, unsafe streets, or poverty-stricken neighborhoods, the atmosphere not only increases individual stress but also hinders an aging person's ability to engage in health promoting activities.

## Aging Well through Physical Activity

Regular physical activity can be an important moderating variable that influences the detrimental effects of aging. Regular physical activity can lower the risks for various chronic illnesses. Physical activity is one among several preventative behaviors that health care professionals promote. Others include consuming a healthy diet, avoiding excessive use of alcohol, not smoking, reducing stress, as well as sustaining satisfying relationships and accessible social support. They also include having a personality that is optimistic and resilient. Regular physical activity seems to create a positive context that reinforces these health-promoting behaviors. Physical activity can increase social interaction, improve stress management, and even increase cognitive functions, such as memory and problem solving (Lemme, 2006).

Studies have found that social and cultural environments that enable older adults to remain physically active can significantly influence the overall quality of life. Among the most important supports for physical activity is a safe walking trail. Statistics indicate that by the age 75, one in three men and one in two women do not engage in any regular physical activity. Research has indicated that knowledge, attitudes, beliefs about health and fitness and perceived barriers to physical well-being influence to what extent older adults exercise (Dishman, 1994). For example, if an older man or woman feels unsafe in their neighborhood, they are less likely to walk. If they do not have the resources to join an exercise facility, they are less likely to maintain physical activity. If they feel anxious about possible injury, they may be more likely to be sedentary. There are currently 38 million Americans who are over the age of sixty-five. Although the benefits of physical activity have been proven, more than half of this older population is still inactive. More specifically, it is estimated that 47% of adults 65 to 74 years of age are sedentary. Educational information and program planning can be beneficial in increasing the number of older men and women who incorporate physical activity into their routines. Participation in regular physical activity helps to slow the gradual decline in physical functioning associated with age (Centers for Disease Control and Prevention, 2005). For those who do maintain a level of activity, walking and gardening are the most popular physical activities.

The benefits of regular physical exercise have been widely known for years. In 1959, WHO defined the health of older adults in terms of fitness rather than pathology. The Duke University Center for the Study of Aging and Human Development has concluded that regular exercise appears to reverse some of the physical and psychological changes associate with aging (Fontane, 1996). Clearly, there is overwhelming evidence that physical activity is key to successful aging (Sawatzky, Liu-Ambrose, Miller, & Marra, 2007; Tahmaseb McConatha & Volkwein-Caplan, 2010).

Medical advances have enabled people to live longer, healthier, and happier lives. Despite medical advances, though, older adults require more medical and long-term care services than any other segment of the population. With the growing number of older adults, it becomes increasingly important to address health behaviors and lifestyles that can improve the quality of life in later adulthood and help decrease the millions of dollars spent each year on medical care. Indeed, one of the great social and cultural issues of our time is how society will adapt to the expenses of an increasingly aging and interconnected population.

## Conclusion

Well-being in later adulthood is greatly dependent on community support – the place and space people live in. Our study indicated that support from a cohort of like-minded individuals is an important factor that concomitantly increases feelings of competence and self-worth and diminishes feelings of loneliness and isolation. Supportive communities can enable people to solve their problems and buffer their feelings of cultural isolation and dislocation – especially for older immigrants. A sense of control, feelings of competence, subjective health, spirituality, and the availability of and satisfaction with social and emotional support are important factors that promote well-being. The maintenance of a regular exercise or fitness program is an important resource that ensures an active and healthy aging process. Whether the physical activity is simply based on functional activities, such as gardening or household chores or walking to the store or in a park, the research results of the last 30 years have significantly suggested "use it or lose it." In the end, we strongly suggest that scholars and policy-makers concentrate on the availability of and access to health promoting behaviors. It is important for communities to provide places and spaces that ensure healthy aging. Keep moving!

## References

Atchley, R. C. (1989). A Continuity Theory of Normal Aging. *The Gerontologist, 29,* 183- 190.

Atchley, R.C. (1994). *Social Forces and Aging: An Introduction to Social Gerontology.* Belmont, CA: Wadsworth Publishing Company.

Baltes, M., & Carstensen, L. (1996). The Process of Successful Ageing. *Ageing and Society, 16,* 397-422.

Butler, R.N. (1963). The Life Review: An Interpretation of Reminiscence in the Aged. *Psychiatry, 26,* 65-76.

Butler, R. N. (1989). Dispelling Ageism: The Cross-Cutting Intervention. *Annals of the American Academy of Political and Social Science, 503,* 138-147.

Diener, E., Diener, M., & Diener, C. (1995). Factors Predicting the Subjective Well-Being of Nations. *Journal of Personality and Social Psychology, 64,* 851-864.

Dishman, R.K. (1994). Motivating Older Adults to Exercise. *Southern Medical Journal, 87*(5), 75-83.

Fontane, P.E. (1996). Exercise, Fitness, and Feeling Well. *American Behavioral Scientist, 39*(3), 288-305.

Haught, P., Walls, R., Laney, J., Leavell, A. & Stuzen, S. (1999). Child and Adolescent Knowledge and Attitudes about Older Adults across Time and States. *Educational Gerontology, 25* (6), 501-518.

Hoyer, W.J., & Roodin, P.A. (2009). *Adult development and aging.* (Eds.). McGraw Hill: Boston.

Lang, J. E., Moore, M. J., Harris, A. C., & Anderson, L. A. (2005). Healthy Aging: Priorities and Programs of the Centers for Disease Control and Prevention. *Generations, 29*(2), 24-29.

Lemme, B. H. (2006) *Development in Adulthood.* Boston: Allyn and Bacon Publishing.

McConatha, D. (2002). The e-Quality Theory of Aging: Using the Internet to Improve the Lives of the Elderly. In: Roger Morrell (Ed). *The Older Adult and the World Wide Web.* Lawrence Earlbaum Co., New Jersey.

O'Donell, M.P. (2009). Integrating Health Promotion into National Health Policy. *Journal of Health Promotion, 23*(6), 3-9.

Palmore, E. (2001). The Ageism Survey: First Findings. *The Gerontologist, 41*(5), 572-575.

Tahmaseb McConatha, J. & Volkwein-Caplan, K. (2010). *Cultural Contours of the Body: Aging and Fitness.* Kendall/Hunt.

Sawatzky, R., Liu-Ambrose, T., Miller, W.C., & Marra, C.A. (2007). Physical Activity as a Mediator of the Impact of Chronic Conditions on Quality of Life in Older Adults. *Health Quality Life Outcomes, 5*, 68-77.

Sontag, S. (1972). The Double Standard of Aging. *Saturday Review of the Society, 1*(1), 29-38.

Stokol, D. (1992). Establishing and Maintaining Healthy Environments: Toward a Social Ecology of Health Promotion. *American Psychologist, 47*(1), 6-22.

Weaver, J. (1999). Special issue: Aging education: Preparing for the 21st Century. *Educational Gerontology; 25*, (6), 475-478. (2007). www.cdc.gov/nchs. Retrived April 30, 2009 National Health and Nutrition Examination Survey (2009). www.ilcusa.org. Global Aging Report: Threats to Longevity. Retrieved April 29, 2009. (2004) www.census.gov. Expectation of life at birth, 1970 to 2004, and projections, 2010 and 2015. Retrieved April 29, 2009.

## Issue 4

# The Paradox of Top-level Sports

The crisis of modern sport is all too apparent and presented to us almost daily by the media. Especially at the top level, professionalization and industrialization have become the major characteristics of sport and seem to have pushed the notion of sport as play out the door. Top-level sport has become a "big business," an important branch of modern industry. The purpose of sport has shifted; it does not lie in itself (intrinsically) any longer, but rather top-level sport is mainly determined by extrinsic motivations, such as rewards, salary contracts, media representation. Hence, we are facing so-called "unethical" practices in top-level sport, such as violence, cheating, gambling, doping, and more. In the view of many, these problems result from a morally distorted sport world "where moral values have become confused with dollar values" (Eitzen, 1988, 17). The notion of "winning at all costs" has taken over the so-called "sport spirit," which is playing by the rules.

*"The prevailing form of sport – the corporate level – has corrupted the original intentions of sport. Instead of player-oriented physical competition, sport has become a spectacle, a big business, and an extension of power politics. Play has become work. Spontaneity has been superseded by bureaucracy. The goals of pleasure in physical activity have been replaced by extrinsic rewards, especially money." (Sage & Eitzen, 2012, 19)*

This apparent crisis directs our attention toward the question about the meaning of (top-level) sport, and thus points to a moral dilemma. A potential moral dilemma exists whenever an action is involved. Every action is based on and within a given social context. In order to understand the apparent "moral dilemma" of top-level sport, we have to inquire about the social structures underlying top-level sport in modern societies. The socio-structural context of top-level sport seems to be based on three notions: (1) winning at all costs, (2) the overemphasis of success, and (3) the body as an element of uncertainty (Bette/Schimank, 1993). The last notion refers to the athletes being dependent upon their bodies for the sporting performance. Because they cannot totally rely on their body to "deliver" that desired performance, there is always the risk of failure confronting the athletes. I herein argue that there is a strong linkage between these (un)written rules and laws of top-level sport, and the actions taken by athletes, trainers, coaches, administrators, and others involved. Hence, it is not surprising that under the constraints of success athletes use whatever resources are available to them, such as drugs, cheating, gambling, or under-the-table-payments, in order to reach these goals. The question then arises as to whether moral appeals, such as *"play fair," "don't cheat"* or *"don't take drugs"* are the appropriate reactions in order to combat these widespread unethical practices amongst people involved in top-level sport.

Below, I will critically examine – with a sport philosophy approach – what sport ethics is and whether it can help us to change some of the apparent unethical practices we are facing in modern top-level sport. The following questions will be addressed: (1) what constitutes ethical and moral behavior in sport; (2) are ethics and top-level sport incompatible; (3) are the current practices and proposals for solving the "crisis" adequate to combat the problems?

## What is Ethical, Moral Behavior in Sport?

Before I elaborate on the ethics of sport, a clarification of the terms "ethics" and "morality" has to be established. In general usage, the terms "ethics" and "morality" are often used interchangeably. Meinberg (1991), however, makes the following significant distinction between ethics and morals: moral behavior includes actions that are based on certain basic values and norms of society, while ethics represent the reflection of such behavior. That is, ethics are the reflection of moral behavior (Meinberg, p. 21). In regard to sport, ethics are the theory of the moral behavior in sport. Thus, the task of sport ethics is to critically reflect on the phenomenon of sport within its social and cultural setting.

Sport receives much of its meaning from the social and cultural context within which it is performed. Sport ethics then become valid only within general ethics that incorporate the whole of the human being and of life as such. Thus, the autonomy of sport ethics is only relative in that it depends on ethics and moral values in society in general. What might be right in one society might be considered wrong in another. For example, doping in former East Germany used to be legal, while in former West Germany, it was considered a crime. Ethical theories can describe, analyze, and be used to understand the current situation of sport. The ethicist can also propose betterment for sport by describing what good sport (morally right) is independently of social and cultural factors. The critical function of sport ethics is to correct the apparent problems of sport, in order to make it better for the future. Sport ethics then need to work out proposals for a "clean" sport.

Sport philosophers Loland (1991) and Gerhardt (1991), for example, constructed such proposals: a moral norm system for fair play in sports contexts. However, their appeals fall short in combating the existing problems in top-level sport. Let me explain why: the two basic norms Loland cites are fairness and equality.

The fairness norm requires that "contestants voluntarily engaged in sports contests ought to act according to the rules if the contests are just." The equality norm demands that in sport contests "all contestants ought to be given equal opportunity to perform athletic skills" (1991, 150). Loland realizes that no institutionalized sport contests will ever be completely just, meaning that everyone will have an equal and fair start, but the people involved have an obligation to try to make the process as just as it can reasonably be. Good sport contests, then, are based on one major principle, which is play. Loland claims that the act of contesting ought to be focused on play and fun as its highest obligation in order to realize the intentional goals of the actors involved. This statement assumes that an athlete's main focus is on intrinsic rewards, e.g., having fun. Fame and fortune or political prestige ought to be of secondary interest, Loland argues, if the focus of the involvement in the sporting activity is to achieve the best for the most, according to the utilitarian principle. What is missing in Loland's very well-established argument is the critical application to the actual situation in top-level sport as we face it today in modern societies. There is a distinct gap between these norms that he constructed from "outside the real" and the reality of modern sport as such.

The same criticism can be stated for Gerhardt, who also requests that the play spirit and the spirit of competition ought to be the governing moral principles for everybody involved in sport. I would counter-argue with Meier (1988) that there is no necessary connection between the "play spirit" and sport; that is, the essential nature of sport is not compromised if there is no play in evidence (Meier, 1988). Gerhardt's argument overlooks also that top-level sport is not an isolated, distinct phenomenon in modern societies anymore, but rather it has become an integral part of economics and an important and very profitable part of modern industry. Hence, the actions in top-level sport do not solely depend on the idealistic/ normative moral norms Loland and Gerhardt established for it, but rather they are oriented toward forces controlling and manipulating sport. Thus, in order to develop sport ethics that address the current crisis of top-level sport accurately, the socioeconomic forces of that given society have to be taken into consideration.

Loland and Gerhardt might want to counter-argue that sport ethics differ from ethics in other spheres of life, such as environmental ethics, in that they are not critical for survival. Usually, people engage in sport freely. Since sport is not existentially necessary, sport ethics are not necessary for survival either. But this argument overlooks that top-level sport has indeed become a survival tool for those involved, such as athletes, coaches, trainers, sport administrators, empires, etc. For them, sport is of great practical value.

Loland's and Gerhardt's arguments might also suggest that sport ethics is tied to a specific ethos, the sport ethos. This means that the ethos refers only to the specific sport situation and has no consequences for other spheres of life. The athlete, who acts morally correctly within the sportive situation, may not necessarily act similarly in other situations of life. Hence, sport ethics are special ethics. However, I wish to forward a counter argument, namely, that athletes' actions within sport are indeed dependent on ethics in general, in that they apply general cultural norms, values, ideals, and imperatives to the specific situation of and within sport.

Furthermore, the key word to ethical and moral behavior is responsibility. In the literature, responsibility is regarded as the characteristic of ethical considerations, for any particular action. Such engagement can only be undertaken in a free and voluntary manner and is the prerequisite for any ethical actions (Schulz, 1972). In regard to ethics, responsibility for other human beings has expanded in the last 10-20 years to the responsibility for the world, nature and cosmos as such, since we have become aware that not only human beings are vulnerable, but the environment is as well (Jonas, 1987; Birnbacher, 1980; Auer, 1985). This understanding of ethics is an expanded version of Kant's approach in that it calls for actions whose effects should promote the permanence of a truly humane life on earth (Jonas, p. 36). Kant's ethics are based on the idea that there are moral norms valid for every person, to which everybody must adhere to freely. While Kant's categorical imperative is directed toward the individual, I argue that ethics, including sport ethics, refer to the public life in general, including politics (Jonas, 1979).

Sport officials and administrators demand precise norms and strict controls for athletes and harsh punishment for those who do not obey the rules. Athletes are confronted with this demand that comes from the "outside." Like Kant's categorical imperative, this moral demand seems like a foreign authority to the ones involved in top-level sport because it comes from other people (from the outside) not involved in sport. The gap between these outside demands and the ones that come from within the socioeconomic constraints of top-level sport (e.g., success, winning at all costs) often seems worlds apart. It is difficult to follow these idealistic requests because the "laws" of top-level sport may stay in contrast to these outside demands.

Meinberg (1991) explains, in accordance with Franke (1987), that historically sport ethics have solely been applied to the individual athlete as such (see Aristotle, Plato, Rousseau, Gutsmuths, Diem – just to name a few). These ethical theories did not acknowledge that people live in rather complex societies, which might require a variety of different moral behaviors according to each specific situation. In our pluralistic society, there is not just one moral principle or ethos that is ultimately right or valid for every situation. Thus, the old saying that "sport teaches character and morals" cannot simply be transferred to other spheres of life in general. Meinberg requests pluralism for the realm of sport ethics, which he calls "meta-ethics." The object of ethics is moral behavior; the object of meta-ethics is ethics. Thus, meta-ethics is a highly theoretical construct that acknowledges that sport, as a complex phenomenon, needs to be analyzed theoretically in its structure and within its social system. Meta-ethics does not come up with any proposals for right or wrong behavior in sport. A critical analysis of the ethics of the current sport system and its structure is the object of meta-ethics in sport.

## Are Ethics and Top-level Sport Incompatible?

From a meta-ethical viewpoint, then, the question arises: is competitive top-level sport a paradox in itself or are ethics and top-level sport incompatible? The answer is twofold. First, in top-level sport, the athlete's actions do not display individual, isolated moral behavior. Franke points out that the individual top-level athlete is at the same time a sport idol (1987, 36), produced by politics in the East and by the media in the West. Ethical considerations usually assume that the person, whose actions are morally judged and valued, is identical with the person who is acting. As in the doping case of Ben Johnson, he was stripped of his gold medal because he broke explicit rules prohibiting this behavior. Thus, his steroid use was unethical behavior in the context of sport. He "failed" as an athlete; but does that make him a failure as a person, too? This incident was not morally looked at within the context of top-level sport. It is not acknowledged here that athletes have dual-personalities – the athlete as the individual person and the athlete as the sport idol, produced by the media.

Gebauer (1983, 1987) has also elaborated on the dilemma of the media producing a reality of competition, which is fictional, and thus, it is not identical with the reality of life as such. For sport ethics, it is important to distinguish between these two different realities, as it is usually done in other spheres of our cultural life, for example in theater and film. We know that the actors in theater, film and other artistic productions are playing a role, which is not identical with who the actors are as individual persons. But within the sphere of sport, we tend to believe that the athletic achievements are identical with the athletes as persons (Franke, 1987, 38), while in reality the athlete is reduced to the achievement principle: faster, higher, farther. And thus, through the athletic achievement, the athlete receives an imaginary personality, which is not necessarily identical with the athlete as a person. The athlete then is transformed into an idol, and when the idol does not live up to moral expectations, such as in the Ben Johnson case, the hero becomes a bad person.

In the case of former East German athletes: after unification, people started to turn their backs on the formerly glorified athletes who were used by their system. The widespread doping practices among former East German athletes fit here very well because they just did what they were asked to do; there was no base for freely making any decisions. This represents an extreme case of the manipulation of the athletes, but are we so much better in the West? Athletes here are also not self-determined individuals anymore. At the high school and university levels in the USA, athletes follow the orders of coaches and administrators, and the schools and universities also use them as political tools to promote their schools. The public seems to be in need of sport idols, and the media covers this need. But, when the athletes fail to live up to these falsely set high moral standards, they are ridiculed and/or rejected.

Second, another argument showing the inconsistency between what is (rules of top-level sport) and what ought to be (so-called ethical standards) is demonstrated well by the sociological analysis of Bette & Schimank (1993). They argue in this context that every action has to be seen in light of its specific context and the experience of the people making the decisions on how to act. Bette & Schimank are referring to "biographical fixation," meaning that persons can only make certain choices according to their sociocultural background and experience. Thus, an action can never be made totally freely. That does not mean that humans are not able or capable of making decisions that are not necessarily dependent on their "path," but that the opportunity to decisions independently of their path is highly unlikely. This is called the "biographic trap" (Bette & Schimank). Athletes are in danger of being trapped biographically; that is, they will most likely act according to what they have learned to be most important in top-level sport: winning and success by any means. Whether this is achieved in a fair manner and morally correct is often of secondary consideration. Only those who are successful will be rewarded in top-level sport; whether or not they achieved this in a fair manner is not rewarded. Hence, the lesson learned is that the outcome is most important and not how the outcome has been achieved. When coaches, for example, only get contract renewals when they have had a winning season, they receive the message: you must win at any cost. This principle will then be indoctrinated into the athletes as well. Hence, any actions will always have to be evaluated in light of the specific situational constraints, which cannot be overlooked when formulating timely ethics for sport.

From an ethical viewpoint, we have to conclude that top-level sport is a paradox (Franke 1989) because on one hand, competitive sports call for actions leading to disadvantages for others; on the other hand, it cries out for fairness and equal chances for all competitors. The two rules of top-level sport, to overcome the opponent by any means that are legal or appear to be legal and to act fairly and morally sound at the same time, contradict each other. Hence, taking drugs in order to gain an advantage over your opponent conforms to the first norm set out by competitive sport (to overcome the opponent), but it conflicts with the second rule of equal chances and fairness. The top-level athlete has to juggle between these two requests, which are presented to him/her by the structure of the sport system. What are the athletes supposed to do, how should they act? "Play fair" is the rather simplistic answer of traditional sport moralists.

## Why do the "Fair Play Initiatives" and Other Moral Appeals not Work in the Combat of the Moral Crisis of Top-level Sport?

Representatives of the "old" sport ethics assume that the norms of sportive competition are valid in general. Problems arise when it is argued that sport, as an isolated phenomenon in society, has educational values. For instance, when it teaches character and sportsmanship, and when – as in the case of Ben Johnson – this thesis or norm is disproven, the athlete becomes declared the sinner (or "der Sündenbock", Gebauer,1987) in order to justify the traditionally created normative structure of sport. Sport ethics today seem to use two different approaches in argumentation. First, appeals are made, such as "be fair," "stay fit," or "don't take drugs." Here, it is falsely assumed that these appeals will lead to the establishment of appropriate action or that in and of themselves they change behavior. Second, in the argumentation of sport ethics, it is assumed that general values such as health, humanity, and self-determination will influence the actions within the realm of sport. It is often overlooked that general norms do not necessarily lead to "right actions." Since the world we live in is ever-changing and becoming more complex, ethical norms are changing, too. The conditions and structure of sport have changed over this century. Thus, engagement in sport does not necessarily lead to self-development or self-determination of the athletes, as once was assumed, especially not in top-level sport, because the sole focus here has become the principle of success/achievement rather than the physical, social, and psychological development of the persons.

Bette & Schimank in their argument about the "biographical fixation" of the athletes in top-level sport also come to conclude that the actions in top-level sport will not change simply because of moral appeals. Hence, in the case of doping, these appeals have not worked, as we all know too well. On the contrary, athletes who have been banned for drug abuse in top-level sport have been found not to stop these practices even after severe punishment (e.g., Ben Johnson, Katrin Krabbe, Lance Armstrong, and many others). It is apparent that the principle of achievement and success at all costs in top-level sport dominates their actions. Hence, from the point of view of "biographical fixation," it was to be expected that the athletes will not (and cannot) change their doping practices as long as they are determined to produce records. The "sane sports world" is nonexistent. The principle of winning at all costs also produces fear and uncertainty, and in order to combat these emotions, the psyche is tricked by taking performance-enhancing drugs, which are even suggested by coaches and prescribed by trainers and doctors. We have to conclude that the extrinsic logic of top-level sport is more prevalent than any moral or pedagogical appeals.

In the case of doping, the question arises here, as to whether more and stricter controls will be able to combat the problem. This question points to even greater problems such as the internationalization of those controls (financial difficulties) as well as the privacy issue of the athletes. But besides these points, we know that athletes often are sheltered from and warned about doping controls by their coaches and trainers (examples: former East Germany and China today). Thus, these controls often only appear to be accurate, and they are used as a buffer for the athletes in order to avoid exposure of their positive results. If the controls had any positive effects then they should help to establish a basis for trust amongst athletes and coaches. But on the contrary, they seem to present to everybody involved that the doping practices are prevailing in top-level sport. Hence, the solution, then, for the other athletes involved can only be to dope as well in order to ensure equity.

This observation shows clearly that the "fair play initiatives" and other moral appeals do not work in order to combat the moral crisis of top-level sport. We need to start analyzing the problems from a philosophical/socio-economical point of view, taking into consideration the various paradoxical rules and norms that everybody involved in the actions of top-level sport is facing. Top-level sport is not an isolated phenomenon in society that simply can be explained by analyzing its normative value structure. It is a complex, rather pluralistic phenomenon that has to be treated as such in order to find adequate answers as to its apparent crisis.

## Conclusion

We are in need of a new ethics, which provides grounds for an ethical evaluation of specific actions within a concrete situation. Lenk (1985), in the context of sport ethics, points to the utilitarianism of behavior *(Handlungsutilitarismus).*

Utilitarian ethics requires that the moral judgment of an action should be based on the consequences of the action rather than on the disposition of the mind (as Kant argues) or the individual and social motives. The principle of these ethics is simply to gain "the greatest good for most people." Lenk elaborates that in regard to sport ethics the moral judgment of an action should not be based on the ethical motive of the action, but rather on the reconstruction of the alternative possibilities for the action. These actual possibilities determine the intentional action decision. Lenk names four criteria for the ethical judgment of actions: the consequences of the action; the usefulness of the action (which has to be good in itself); the acceptance of ethical theories (here utilitarianism); and the greatest good for most people (which opposes egocentric actions).

I would go further – beyond Lenk – requiring that sport ethics must reflect on the presuppositions of concrete moral actions before it can propose a betterment for moral actions in sport. A structural analysis of sport in society has to be the starting point of a new sport ethics. If the structure of top-level sport, with its overemphasis on winning and its "ends-justifies-the-means" approach, does not change, there is little hope for changing the unethical practices in top-level sport. As long as we continue to blame the individual athlete for his/her actions, we are only justifying the system's needs, that is, we cover up the real problems in sport. Hence, philosophers, sociologists, pedagogues, and sport scientists from all areas need to work together in order to propose a new charter of sport ethics.

## References

Auer, A. (1985). *Umweltethik. Ein theoretischer Beitrag zur ökologischen Diskussion.* Düsseldorf.

Bette, K.-H. & Schimank, U. (1993). *Doping: Hochleistungssport am Scheideweg.* Unpublished manuscript.

Birnbacher, D. (Ed.) (1980). *Ökologie und Ethik.* Stuttgart.

Deutsche Vereinigung für Sportwissenschaft – Informationen. 2 (1990).

Eitzen, S. (1988). Ethical Problems in American Sport. *Journal of Sport and Social Issues, 12* (1), 17-20.

Franke, E. (1989). Sportler-Ethik als 'Character-Ethik' oder 'Handlungs-Folgen-Ethik'? Eine programmatische Skizze für den medienrelevanten Hochleistungssport. In: Allmer, H. & Schulz, N. (Eds.) *Sport und Ethik: Grundpositionen. Brennpunkte der Sportwissenschaft* 1, 3. Jhg., St. Augustin.

Gebauer, G. (1983). Geschichten, Rezepte, Mythen. Über das Erzählen von Sportereignissen. In: *Der Satz "Der Ball ist rund" hat eine gewisse philosophische Tiefe.* Sport-Kultur-Zivilisation. Berlin: Transit. Pg. 128-145.

Gebauer, G. (1987). Die Masken und das Glück. Über Idole des Sport. In: Becker,P. (Ed.) *Sport und Höchstleistung.* Reinbek: Rowohlt. Pg. 105-122.

Gerhardt, V. (1991). Die Moral des Sports. *Sportwissenschaft, 21* (2), 125-145.

Herms, E. (1986). Ist Sportethik möglich? *Die Zukunft des Sports* – Materialien zum Kongreß "Menschen im Sport 2000." Schorndorf: Hofmann. Pg. 84-110.

Jonas, H. (1979). *Das Prinzip Verantwortung.* Frankfurt/Main.

Jonas, H. (1987). Warum die Technik ein Gegenstand für die Ethik ist: Fünf Gründe. In: Lenk, H./Rohpohl, G. (Eds.) *Technik und Ethik.* Stuttgart.

Lenk, H. (1975). Pragmatische Philosophie. Hamburg.

Lenk, H. (1985). Aspekte einer Pragmatisierung der Ethik – auch für die Sportethik. In: Cahey, K. et al. (Eds.) *Sport und Ethik.* dvs-Protokolle 16, Claus-Zellerfeld: DVS. Pp. 1-20.

Lenk, H. & Pilz,G. (1989). *Das Prinzip Fairness.* Osnabrück: Verlag A. Fromm.

Loland, S. (1991). Fair Play in Sports Contests – a Moral Norm System. *Sportwissenschaft, 21* (2), 146-162.

Meier, K. (1988). Triad, Trickery: Playing with Sport and Games. *Journal of the Philosophy of Sport, 15.*

Meinberg, E. (1991). *Die Moral im Sport – Bausteine einer neuen Sportethik.* Aachen: Meyer & Meyer Verlag.

Schulz, W. (1972). *Philosophie in der veränderten Welt.* Pfullingen.

Sage, G. & Eitzen, S. (2013). *Sociology of North American Sport.* New York, Oxford: Oxford University Press.

## Chapter 4:

# Health and Sport – Fitness – Physical Activity

- *Sport, fitness, and physical activity can help prevent ill health and assist those recovering from illness or injury. Adults who are physically active have a 20-30% lower mortality risk than those who are inactive. (World Health Organization, 2010)*
- *The benefits of exercise training for fatigue, dyspnoea, pain, nausea, anxiety, depression and quality of life have all been examined in the scientific literature ... and has done so across a range of healthy and diseased populations.*
- *With regard to anxiety and depression, exercise has shown to be a useful treatment for a wide range of chronic disease populations.*
- *Multiple studies have shown mild to moderate exercise to be a highly effective strategy to reduce fatigue and in some cases pain in cancer patients, as well as in those suffering from cardiovascular disease, fibromyalgia and chronic-fatigue syndrome.*
- *Aerobic exercise is sufficient to reduce fatigue and increase vigor in healthy individuals. This is an effect that has been shown to occur with as little as a 10-minute brisk walk.*
- *Exercise has consistently been listed as one of the most popular self-care therapies. Exercise has the potential to be a beneficial treatment across the range of symptoms and adverse effects experienced by HIV-infected individuals. (see Ciccolo, et al., 2004)*
- *The country is beginning to recognize childhood obesity as a major public health epidemic that will incur substantial costs to the nation. We need to promote healthy lifestyles through government, industry, schools, community, and home, emphasizing the benefits of sport, fitness, and exercise activities, as well as nutrition. (Institute of Medicine, 2006)*

Sport, fitness, and physical activities have been correlated to positively effect peoples' health for a long time. During the 20th century, especially since 1960, an overwhelming amount of research has focused on scientifically proving some of these long held assumptions. This research was mainly conducted in the biological and medical sciences, but soon the social sciences, such as psychology, sociology, anthropology, and cultural studies, embraced the topics of health, sport and physical activity.

## Summary of Research Studies on Physical Activity and Health

Physical activity is recognized as a key determinant of health, but most people in North America (as well as other highly industrialized nations) lead a mainly sedentary lifestyle and do not participate in physical activity and sport regularly enough to obtain health benefits. The lowest participation levels are among people living in disadvantaged areas and from certain sections of the community, including older people, people from black and ethnic minorities and with disabilities. Encouraging people who live in renewal areas to participate in sport and be active regularly to achieve health benefits takes time and resources to address unmet needs, change attitudes amongst those who are sedentary, identify appropriate solutions and build sustainable local infrastructure.

To achieve health benefits, recommended levels of physical activity for adults is at least 30 minutes of moderate intensity physical activity (similar to brisk walking) on three to five days per week. Activity can be taken in bouts of 10-15 minutes, allowing for accumulation of activity throughout the day. Young people should engage at least one hour per day of moderate intensity activity. This hour can be made up of a variety of activities, including organized sport, play, walking to school, physical education or planned exercise. At least twice a week, young people should participate in physical activity of at least moderate intensity to enhance and maintain muscular strength and flexibility and bone health (US Department of Health, 2010).

There are opportunities for physical activity in four major areas of day-to-day life:
- method of transportation (walking, biking, to school or work or leisure activities)
- work (e.g., manual labor on the job)
- household activities, such as gardening or housework ("functional fitness")
- leisure time, in sports, exercise, and recreational activities

Most people's activity will involve a combination of these areas, but sport, fitness, exercise and recreational activities can make a significant contribution. Despite the many opportunities to be active, most people in North America and other highly industrialized nations, such as the UK or Germany, do little or no physical activity. The percentage of the US population not achieving the recommended physical activity levels are about 75-78%, in the UK about 68-70%, and in Germany 65-70%. Various studies show differences in participation between different groups. Older people, women and girls, those in lower socioeconomic groups and in deprived areas, ethnic minority groups and people with disabilities all show below average participation levels (www.renewal.net overview, 2010).

The changes in lifestyles and the nature of work in recent years have affected the amount of physical activity that people engage in. These changes include a reduction of physical labor, improvement in technology reducing the amount of time and physical effort required to do chores, as well as less travel on foot or by bicycle due to increased car ownership, expectations of convenient travel and parking, as well as time pressure and safety fear. Furthermore, there are additional barriers to engagement in physical activities if there is limited or no access to appropriate facilities for physical activity and affordability, lack of access to appropriate activities, coaching or instruction, limited time availability, community and personal attitudes, beliefs, and knowledge about sport, fitness, and physical activity. In addition, people with medical conditions may face additional barriers, such as fear of injury, embarrassment or failure, and concerns over the impact on current lifestyle. All of these factors have to be considered in the development of appropriate intervention programs and strategies.

A number of different approaches have been tried to address the barriers to regular participation in physical activity and sport and increase its contribution to health improvement (see Department of Health, 2010, www.renewal.net). They include:

- providing activities to meet the needs of specific user groups
- exercise referrals by physicians to local facilities
- providing low cost or free activities or equipment
- improving the range of facilities and activities, including non-traditional locations
- mentoring and motivational support (i.e., buddying with someone in a similar situation)
- education and awareness-raising campaigns
- developing a sport and health plan for the nation down to the local areas

In this chapter, a selection from various areas of research on the impact of physical activity on health will be presented. In the first issue, medical experts demonstrate that the immune system of a person can be positively influenced when one engages in regular physical activity, which also includes brain development as well as the aging process. The second issue focuses on the psychological and social well-being of people, especially as they get older, which is greatly enhanced when people engage in regular physical activity. The third issue deals with one of the most severe health threats we are facing in the 21st century, obesity, which is analyzed from a sports medicine perspective. The fourth issue focuses on people with infectious diseases, such as HIV/AIDS, where no cure has been found yet, but where people are experiencing health-enhancing stimuli through active participation in sport and physical activity.

## Issue 1

# Exercise, Health and Life Satisfaction

*(with Christiane Jennen & Gerhard Uhlenbruck)*

*Sport has made*
*A few healthy people ill,*
*But sport has also made*
*A few ill people healthy!*
*(Gerhard Uhlenbruck, aphorism)*

It has been found that the influence of exercise on one's sense of well-being and perceived fitness in various groups of people over age 50 is significant. The frequency of exercise greatly influences the perceived wellness of older adults (Uhlenbruck, 1993a). In addition, other psychological parameters, such as one's relationship to children and grandchildren, are also important variables for mental health which, in return, may stabilize the immune system. Research over the last twenty years has shown that exercise seems to be the most efficient strategy for healthy aging. Maintaining or adopting a moderate or high degree of physical activity is associated with a lower risk of death across a wide range of ages in both sexes (Schnohr, Scharling, Jensen 2003). Psychosocial factors also greatly influence the immune system; they are a vital source for the feeling of well-being and life satisfaction throughout one's lifespan (Abele & Becker, 1991). Another important factor associated with wellness and life satisfaction in older adults is social participation (McConatha & McConatha, 1989). Participation in social groups has a direct influence on one's happiness. This research in activity theory (Diener, 1984) can be applied to group activity, physical activity, hobbies, artistic, and cultural activities. Numerous studies have demonstrated that social support greatly impacts health related behavior (e.g., Lin, 1979).

This study focuses on the analysis of the influence of exercise and fitness in regards to satisfaction in health and leisure time activities. Furthermore, the relationship to other cultural activities and the family situation in modern society will be analyzed for older adults. The measurement of life satisfaction involves an attempt to understand the processes by which an individual views his/her past, as well as feelings about present lifestyle and future expectations (McConatha & McConatha, 1989). Research dealing with life satisfaction in older adults has been approached from several perspectives. Developmental theorists have focused on the identification of positive characteristics and challenges of adults with a major focus on the growth processes that go along with aging. The challenges that people face during adulthood have been identified by Erikson

(1959) as emotional relationships, performance of tasks, and assessment of life. He connects adulthood with the development of the sense of family and the established vocational role. In later adulthood, retirement causes people to detach from people and activities with which they have been a part for many years. Acquiring and maintaining life satisfaction have been viewed as the most enduring of life's tasks (McConatha & McConatha, 1989).

The best method of evaluating life satisfaction is the subjective responses individuals give (Havighurst, 1973). Thus, this socioeconomic study on exercise, fitness, and life satisfaction investigates the various relationships between perceived health, life contentment, and enjoyment during leisure time of the older adult population in Germany, with special focus on physical activity. Figure 1 shows that mental distress is mainly induced by lost life expectations and major disappointments that may lead to depression and resignation. This, in turn, results in inactivity. Regular exercise seems to be an effective antidote, if it is practiced correctly. Too little exercise, e.g., once a week, has no physical training effect. Extreme and overly ambitious exercise in the long run may cause induced stress overloading syndrome as well as injuries, to which older adults are more susceptible. Regular aerobic endurance training, e.g., three times a week for about 20-30 minutes, has the best training effect, and thus can positively counteract mental distress.

## Methods and Results

The social-economic study (SOEP) delivers reliable facts about persons and households in Germany. The SOEP is a panel that gives representative data about people over 16 years of age (households and families) based on a questionnaire designed by the Universities of Frankfurt and Mannheim in collaboration with the German Institute for Economic Research in Berlin (DIW). The first interviews were conducted in 1984 in about 6,000 households; since then these studies were continued with a different number of households every year. For our study, interviews from 1995 and 1996 were analyzed. The samples were selected with the random-route (Aaron, et al., 1995).

The findings of the study were grouped into three areas: (1) the influence of exercise and physical activity on life satisfaction; (2) cultural and artistic engagement during the aging process; and (3) life satisfaction of people over 50 in their relationship with grandchildren.

### 1. Exercise and Physical Activity

In general, 44.7% of the German population assessed perform no exercise at all, whereas 27.4% exercise occasionally (seldom and minimally 1 time a month) and 27.3% perform regular exercise daily or at least once a week (Mielke, 1997). The percentage of people over 50, who perform daily exercise, is between 2.2% and 2.7%. With increasing age, the engagement in exercise activities decreases rapidly (see Table 1).

Table 1: Age versus Frequency of Sports Activity/Exercise

Frequency of sports activity  n= 3248

Table 2: Frequency of Sports Activity/Exercise

Frequency of sports activity  $n_{Welle7}$ = 9457

[$n_{daily}$ = 392; $n_{min.1x/week}$ = 2207; $n_{min.1x/month}$ = 805; $n_{seldom}$ = 1799; $n_{never}$ = 4254]

83

Table 2 shows the different frequency of participation in sport and physical activities between women and men. Men generally participate more than women. Two thirds of the people who participate on a daily level are men (64.8%), while the people who are not physically active are two-thirds women (57.0%).

Life satisfaction changes with age as well; people in their sixties seem to have greater life satisfaction. From the sixth decade on, life satisfaction is about 6.5% higher than in the age groups before, which amounts to 50.7% (Mielke, 1997). Table 3 shows the relationship between the frequency of sports and physical activity and life satisfaction. Life satisfaction reaches the highest level for those performing exercise and sport activities on a daily basis. Life satisfaction is diminished when people are not as physically active. Regular exercise obviously leads to increased fitness, which apparently has a positive influence on the immune system and, therefore, is greatly related to enjoyment of other life activities.

*Table 3: Frequency of Sports Activity versus Life Satisfaction*

Frequency of sports activity          $n_{Welle7} = 9421$

$[n_{daily} = 389; n_{min.1x/week} = 2197; n_{min.1x/month} = 803; n_{seldom} = 1789; n_{never} = 4243]$

When comparing men and women with respect to the frequency of exercise activity versus life satisfaction, we obtained the following results: the share of woman satisfied with their life in the group of the daily exercisers is 3% higher than in the male population (64.7% vs 67.9%). That applies also to the women and men performing exercise minimally, one time per month or never (60.5% vs 57.9% and 49.6% vs 46.2%). The share of the satisfied people performing minimally, one time a week, is 4% higher in the male group. The tendency is the same for both sexes: when sport is performed rarely, the sense of life satisfaction decreases (Mielke, 1997).

Contentment with health decreases from one age group to the next. Among people under 50 years of age, 56.4% are content with their health. This feeling decreases to only 20% in the age group 80 and older. On the average, health satisfaction rates 24.7% among the older adults (Mielke, 1997).

The next table (4) shows the influence of sports and exercise on health satisfaction:

Table 4: Frequency of Sports Activity versus Health-Satisfaction

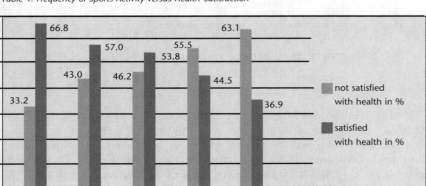

Frequency of sports activity        nWelle7 = 9450

$[n_{daily} = 392; n_{min.1x/week} = 2205; n_{min.1x/month} = 805; n_{seldom} = 1796; n_{never} = 4252]$

Comparing this table with Table 3 one can see that frequent exercise and sports activities show a positive correlation to perceived health satisfaction. Satisfaction with health rates higher among people who are physically active, which is true for all ages. People who are physically active on a daily basis are the most satisfied with their health; only 36.9% people who do not exercise at all are satisfied with their health. The share of people satisfied with their health increases from 36.9% to 66.8%, the more often they exercise. Therefore, exercise has a positive influence on health satisfaction when it is fully integrated into one's lifestyle. Comparing men and women, men are more often satisfied with their health when performing sport/exercise daily, minimally one time per week, minimally one time per month, or never is 4.8% higher woman (Mielke, 1997).

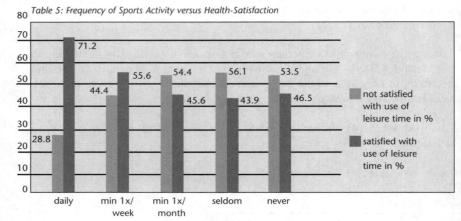

Table 5: Frequency of Sports Activity versus Health-Satisfaction

Frequency of sports activity     $n_{Welle7}$ = 9429

$[n_{daily}$ = 389; $n_{min.1x/week}$ = 2202; $n_{min.1x/month}$ = 803; $n_{seldom}$ = 1794; $n_{never}$ = 4241]

The participants in this study who perform sports and exercise daily are 71.2% satisfied with the use of their leisure time. This part is 55.6% for the minimally one time per week exercising people, 45.5% for those exercising minimally one time per month, and 43.9% for those exercising seldom. People who never exercise are only 46.5% satisfied with the use of their leisure time.

A difference between men and women is found in the groups of people performing sports minimally one time per month or less: the share of those satisfied with the use of leisure time is 7.3% higher in men than in women (48.6% vs. 41.3%).

## Summary and Discussion

In order to determine the influence of physical and mental exercise on fitness and wellness in the older adult population, polls were taken with about 9,400 people in 1990 and with about 13,600 people in 1991. These socioeconomic panel polls were analyzed with respect to contentment of life, health, and leisure time. Men and women were equally satisfied with life; it increased for both at age 60 and higher. However, during a time of unemployment, in general, people's satisfaction with life drastically decreases. It is important to note that contentment with life is positively linked to contentment with labor. Being employed or having a good job seems to be a stabilizing health factor. Satisfaction with leisure time activities is closely connected to general life satisfaction. Contentment with life improves the more people are engaged in artistic and cultural activities, which is also true for those doing handicrafts or house repair (Mielke, 1997).

There is a significant positive link between contentment with life and health. Men and women who have an optimistic outlook on life live, on average, up to seven years longer than pessimists (Volkwein-Caplan & Tahmaseb McConatha, 2012).

Women, however, are, in general, less satisfied with their health than men. Regarding sport and exercise participation, 47.7% of the interviewees were not active during the time of the investigation in 1995/1996. Only 4.1% performed daily exercise, which decreased among the over fifty population (2.2-2.7%). Also, the share of the non-active persons rises linearly, which might be due to orthopedic or other health problems. However, limitations during the aging process with respect to exercise do not exist. On the contrary, over the last several years, more and more older people are engaging in sport and exercise in order to prevent or combat heart disease, obesity, diabetes, high blood pressure, osteoporosis, cancer, and depression. Accordingly, the percentage of people over 59 years of age exercising has risen to 21%.

Nearly half of the people interviewed in this study in the 1990s never engaged in exercise or sport activities. The percentage of those engaging in daily sport and exercise activities was nearly the same in every age category, whereas the percentage of those exercising only occasionally (once a week, once a month, or seldom) declines with increasing age. Men engage in sport/exercise more often than women. Generally, the more often people exercise the more satisfied they are with their life, regardless of age.

It was expected that men would engage in sport/exercise more often than women, and consequently the number of daily active men was 64.8% compared to 57% women, who perform no exercise at all. It can be assumed that professional and family stress does contribute to this negative picture. However, older people who exercise for the prevention of getting sick show women participating to fight off osteoporosis and to rehabilitate after breast cancer, while men fight off coronary and heart disease. The general public needs to be educated to the fact that the number one killer for women is heart disease, as it is as for men.

Life satisfaction is extremely dependent on the frequency of exercise. It is lower (from 65.8% down to 48.1%), the less exercise is performed. The number of men who are content with their health is significantly higher in the exercise group versus those who never exercise. This is also true for women. Satisfaction with one's health is also positively correlated to the engagement in leisure pursuits. Among those engaging in handicrafts or house repair, health satisfaction is the highest when done "at least once a month" (Mielke, 1997). Furthermore, there is a significant relationship between contentment and the frequency of participating in sports and exercise. The more often people exercise, the more content they are with their health.

An important aspect of aging nowadays is that people need to keep fit in order to avoid premature incapacitation. The ability to take care of oneself becomes a critical aspect for one's social, medical, and financial well-being. Thus, strategies for good health and general fitness need to be developed and realized. An interesting by-product of this study was the contentment with life in relation to the existence of grandchildren and the closeness to them. Summarizing the results of this study, the following suggestions can be postulated in order to ensure physical and psychological well-being throughout one's life:

1. Regular daily exercise routines should be performed in order to ensure general well-being and the ability to look after oneself (Volkwein-Caplan & Tahmaseb McConatha, 2012; see also Booth & Tseng, 1995; Macera, et al., 1995; Paffenberger, et al., 1993).

2. It is suggested to perform exercise three to four times a week by burning 2000-2500 kcal per week (1 minute of jogging burns about 10 kcal). In addition, lifestyle changes should also include dietary awareness and a change in nutritional behavior.

3. Daily mental training, not by passively watching TV, but rather by participation in cultural events or personal hobbies, such as arts and crafts, should be engaged in. This stimulates and strengthens the immune system, which is controlled through the brain and the general nervous system.

It is assumed that these suggestions stabilize the psychoneuroimmunological network, slow down physical and mental aging processes, and prevent premature disabilities. As the costs of clinical and geriatric care are becoming more expensive, regular exercise, mental fitness, and psychosocial interests are increasingly important for coping with the "stress" of belonging to the "old or useless people."

# References

Aaron, D. J., Kriska, A. M., Dearwater, S. R., Cauley, J. A., Metz, K. F. & LaPorte, R. E. (1995). Reproducibility and Validity of an Epidemiologic Questionnaire to Assess Past Year Physical Activity in Adolescents. *American Journal of Epidemiology, 142*, (2), 191-201 (Jul 15).

Ader, R.; Felten, D. L.; Cohen, N. (1991). *Psychoneuroimmunology*. 2. Edition. San Diego, CA: Academic Press Inc.

Abele, A. & P. Becker (Eds.) (1991). *Wohlbefinden: Theorie, Empirie, Diagnostik*. Weinheim, München: Juventa-Verlag.

Booth, F. W. & B.S. Tseng (1995). America Needs to Exercise For Health. *Medical Science Sports Exercise*, 462-465.

Ciccolo, J., Jowers, E. & Bartholomew, J. (2004). The Benefits of Exercise Training for Quality of Life in HIV/AIDS in the Post-HAART Era. *Sports Medicine, 34*(8), 487-499.

Department of Health (2010). *Sport, Physical Activity and Health*. www.renewal. net Overview, 1-21.

Deutsches Institut für Wirtschaftsforschung (Ed.) (1993). *Das Sozio-ökonomische Panel (SOEP), Benutzerhandbuch Version 7*. Berlin, November.

Diener, E. (1984). Subjective Well-being. *Psychological Bulletin, 95*, 542-545.

Havighurst, R. (1973). Social Roles, Work Leisure, and Evaluation. In: C.Eisdörfer & M.Lawton (Eds.) *The Psychology of Adult Development and Aging*. Washington, DC: American Psychological Association.

Hollmann, W.; Fischer, H. G.; Meirleir, K.; Holzgraefe, M. (1993). Über neuere Aspekte von Gehirn, Muskelarbeit, Sport und Psyche. *Deutsche Zeitschrift für Sportmedizin, 44*, 478-490.

Institute of Medicine of the National Academies (2006). *Progress in Preventing Childhood Obesity: How Do We Measure Up?* Report Brief, September.

Jennen, C. (née Mielke) (1997). *Wohlbefinden und Fitness: Eine empirische Analyse zur Lebens-, Gesundheits- und Freizeitzufriedenheit Älterer Menschen*. Dissertation, Medical Faculty, University of Cologne, Germany.

Lin, E. (1979). Social Support, Stressful Life-events, and Illness: A model and An Empirical Test. *Journal of Health and Social Behavior, 20*, 108-119.

Lötzerich, H.; Uhlenbruck, G. Präventive Wirkung von Sport im Hinblick auf die Entstehung maligner Tumore? *Dtsch Z Sportmedizin 46* (1): 86-94 (1995)

Macera, C. A.; Croft, J. B.; Brown, D. R.; Ferguson, J. E.; Lane, M. J. (1995). Predictors of Adopting Leisure-Time Physical Activity Among a Biracial Community Cohort. *American Journal of Epidemiology, 142* (6), 1-7.

McConatha, J. & McConatha, D. (1989). The Study of the Relationship Between Wellness and Life Satisfaction of Older Adults. *Activities, Adaptation & Aging, 13* (1/2), 129-140.

Paffenbarger, R. S.; Hyde, R. T.; Wing, A. L.; Lee, I.-M.; Jung, D. L.; Kramper (1993). The Association of Changes in Physical Activity Level and Other Lifestyle Characteristics with Mortality. *New England Journal of Medicine, 328,* 538-545.

Proceedings of the *Congress Healthy Aging, Activity and Sports*, Heidelberg, August 1996, Verlag für Gesundheitsförderung (Health Promotion Publications), Hamburg, Germany (1997).

Schnohr, P.; Scharling,H.; Jensen, J. S. (2003). Changes in Leisure-time Physical Activity and Risk of Death: An Observational Study of 7000 Men and Women. *American Journal of Epidemiology, 158,* 639-644.

Shephard, R. J. (1993). Exercise and the Prevention and Treatment of Cancer. *Sport Medicine, 15,* 258-280.

Uhlenbruck, G. (2003). Sport, Alter und Immunsystem. *Medizinische Welt, 44,* 303-308.

Uhlenbruck, G. (1993). Wie Sporttreiben psychische Funktionen beeinflusst. *TW Sport + Medizin, (5-6),* 395-398.

Volkwein-Caplan, K. & Tahmaseb McConatha, J. (2012). *The Social Geography of Healthy Aging.* Maidenhead/UK: Meyer & Meyer Publishing.

World Health Organization (2010). *The World Health Report: Reducing Risks, Promoting Healthy Life.* www.who.int/whr

## Issue 2

# Physical Activity and the Perceptions of Aging

(with Jennifer Sutera & Judith Ray)

There is no doubt that physiological and psychological benefits can be derived from regular physical activity. Some of the physiological benefits consist of the regulation of blood glucose levels, improvement of sleep quantity and quality, aerobic/cardiovascular endurance, muscle strengthening, and increased flexibility, balance, and coordination. Exercise has also been shown to combat diseases such as colon cancer, Type 2 diabetes, arthritis, and osteoporosis. In addition, physically active people are less likely to become obese, which is affecting increasing numbers of Americans today. Psychological benefits consist of enhanced relaxation, stress and anxiety reduction, and enhanced elevations of a positive mood state. It improves the general well-being and mental health of a person in cognition and motor control and performance, as well as new skill acquisition and learning. In addition, exercise has a calming effect by reducing anxiety or providing a break from a mental task.

People of any gender, race, socioeconomic status, and age can experience the benefits of exercise. Research over the past 10 years or so has shown how physical activity can actually delay the effects of aging or slow down the aging process (Schilke, 1991). The cardiovascular system changes as one ages, primarily in regard to maximal oxygen consumption and respiratory exchange. With increasing age, there is a decline in how efficiently the cardiovascular system transports oxygen to the tissues. However, the negative effects in the capacity of oxygen exchange can be retarded by maintaining regular exercise (Blumenthal & Gullete, 2002). Endurance training has shown to counteract the effects of and reduce mean blood pressure as well as systemic vascular resistance in aging individuals (Schilke, 1991). The musculoskeletal system also undergoes many changes as an individual ages. Muscle mass and tone decreases and adipose tissue increases with age. To offset these changes, exercise has been shown to maintain or even increase muscle mass and reduce bone resorption in the elderly (Arnaud, 2000). Regular exercise may offset the declines in the psychological realm. Physical activity has a positive effect on both meaning in life and self-rated health and functioning (Takkinen, et al., 2001). Studies have also found that lower levels of physical activity are associated with more severe depressive symptoms. There has been evidence that those who exercise regularly viewed themselves at a younger cognitive age or self-perceived age than those who did not exercise (Moore, et al., 1999; Clark, et al., 1999).

These findings suggest that no matter what age, it is never too late to begin an exercise program. However, how do older adults perceive physical activity and aging? In one study, American adults over the age of 60 were asked to provide information regarding their perceptions of the benefits of physical activity and their stage of readiness to participate in the activity. Results indicated that although the majority of the subjects were aware of the benefits, over half did not participate in physical activity (Gogin & Morrow, 2001). This is a public health concern because according to the United States 2001 Census, the older adult population is increasing; older adults (65+) represented 35 million in 2000, roughly 12.4% of the U.S. population (Administration on Aging, 2001). This chapter will analyze the current perceptions of aging in the United States and the effects of physical activity in this process.

## Perceptions of Aging

Aging is an expected physiological degenerative process. Older adults may develop negative attributes about themselves due to this process. Society also portrays less positive images of older adults through media, as seen in magazine advertisements and in country music (McConatha, Schnell, & McKenna, 1999; Aday & Austin, 2000). These images also may foster negative attitudes. With all of these negative influences, how do older adults perceive the aging process? A study by Loomis & Thomas (1991) assessed elderly women who lived in nursing homes and those who lived independently. Health problems, body attitudes, self-esteem and life satisfaction were reported for both groups. Results showed that although women in the nursing homes were older and reported more health problems, negative body attitudes and less life satisfaction, both groups scored low on questionnaires relating to all three aspects with age. The results are consistent with previous research that physical health is the most important correlate of life satisfaction in the elderly. Milligan, et al., (1985) asked elderly men to assess attitudes toward aging and physical health. Specifically, three groups of elderly men (aged 65-85) were asked to rate a hypothetical "old man" and a "young man" as well as themselves. As found in previous studies, the "older man" appeared to receive more negative ratings on each dimension than the "younger man." This study confirmed previous studies the negative stereotypes associated with the elderly. However, a study by Levy, et al., (2002) found that older individuals with more positive self-perceptions of aging lived longer than those with less positive self-perceptions of aging. These findings suggest that self-perceptions can influence longevity of life.

Perceptions of aging have also been studied among young and middle-aged adults. One study by Milligan, et al., (1989) gave participants a hypothetical profile of an individual, which ranged from old-healthy and old-sick to young-healthy and young-sick, and asked them to rate the individual on different scales. It was found that regardless of the participant's age, the profiles describing a person in poor health or sick were rated more negatively than the healthy person, whether young or old. This supports the hypothesis that poor health results in negative perceptions about one's health. Interestingly enough, the young-sick profile was rated the most negative, which sheds light on the concept that it is accepted that older people may be sick but that is not expected for younger people.

The purpose of this study is to evaluate perceptions of aging in relation to regular exercise participation. Considering the increasing elderly population, it is beneficial to explore the young adults' and middle adults' perceptions of aging to see whether regular physical activity leads to more positive perceptions of aging. Therefore, this study will examine the responses of US young and middle-aged adults who exercised regularly, at least three times a week. First, the relationship between regular exercise and perceptions of aging will be measured by four dimensions associated with aging: fear of old people; fear of losses associated with aging; physical appearance changes; and psychological concerns. Second, the relationship between regular exercise and subjective health and life satisfaction will be evaluated. Furthermore, this study will analyze at which age participants consider themselves to be "old" and will gather descriptive information on ideals and fears of getting older. It is hypothesized that participants who belong to a fitness center and regularly exercise will exhibit positive perceptions of aging, as well as positive life and health satisfaction.

## Methodology

The participants in this study included 100 young and middle-age adults, ranging from 17-63 years of age. They responded to a questionnaire relating to age anxieties and perceptions of life and health satisfaction. The participants were men and women, mainly Caucasians, who were available and volunteered their time to complete the questionnaire. Volunteers belonged to a fitness center and racquet club in a suburb of Philadelphia, Pennsylvania.

Participants were administered the questionnaire "Questions on Age and Aging." The three-part questionnaire focused on (1) perceptions of aging, (2) perceptions of health and life, and (3) exercise questions. Anxiety about Aging, part one of this questionnaire, consisted of 20 items (Lasher & Faulkender, 1993). It was designed to measure fear and anxiety about aging. The 20 items were divided into four subscales: Fear of Older People, Fear of Loss Associated with Aging, Anxiety about Physical Appearance, and Psychological Concerns about Aging. Respondents indicated their disagreement or agreement with each item on a four-point Likert scale, ranging from strongly disagree to strongly agree.

Participants responded to demographic questions regarding gender, age, income, religion, educational goals, nationality, and ethnicity. Additional questions included items evaluating life and health satisfaction, and one question asked participants "At what age will you consider yourself to be 'old'?" Lastly, the participants were asked to indicate whether they exercised on a regular basis and to rate their current level of fitness.

## Results

The findings of the *Anxiety about Aging* scale indicated more positive responses by the participants regarding *Fear of Old People* and Psychological Concerns About Aging, and more negative responses regarding *Fear of Losses* and *Physical Appearance Related to Aging* (see Table 6). The first subscale, *Fear of Old People*, revealed a mean of 1.85 on a scale of 1-4. Since a lower score indicated a more positive response in these five statements, the majority of these regular exercisers do not have negative perceptions in regard to fear of old people. Instead, most respondents indicated that they enjoy being around older people, doing things for the older population, and have a positive comfort level in general with older people. This correlates with previous research of a growing trend that more young people have positive attitudes toward the elderly (Milligan, et al., 1989).

The second subscale, *Fear of Losses*, revealed a mean of 2.21 on a scale of 1-4. Most participants disagreed with the statement expressing fear of not having a meaningful life when they get old. However, participants agreed more with worrying about their health and getting nervous thinking about someone else making decisions for them when they are old. This was interesting as these participants are regular exercisers; therefore, it might be assumed that worrying about health would not be as much of a concern. On the other hand, it could be argued that people who are concerned with their health will exercise more often.

The third subscale, *Physical Appearance,* contained the highest mean score of 2.31 on a scale of 1-4; the most anxiety on all the subscales. On a positive note, participants disagreed to never lying about their age in order to appear younger. However, every other statement responded on the more negative side indicating more concerns with physical appearance than any other subscale, including the most negative response of dreading looking old. Although this study did not compare regular exercisers with inactive people, this is a somewhat surprising finding. A recent study by Loland (2000) indicated that physically active people tend to be more satisfied with personal appearance than inactive people. It could be argued that people who are regular exercisers are more aware and concerned about their body image. As a result, they may be more critical or less satisfied with their physical appearance.

The subscales of *Physical Appearance* and *Fear of Losses* revealed the highest scores, indicating there was more anxiety associated with these two areas of concern. The statement contained in the subscale Physical Appearance, "I have never dreaded looking old," received the highest score (M = 2.71), and the second highest negative response was contained in the subscale Fear of Losses. Evidently, participants appear to be the most concerned about someone making decisions for them when they are old (M = 2.65), which implies the greatest fear of losing control over one's life decisions. Ironically, the most positive responses were noted in the same two subscales. Fear of Losses contained the statement dealing with the "fear of no meaning in life when old." This statement received the lowest score overall indicating there was less anxiety (M = 1.58). The subscale of Physical Appearance contained the second most positive response, which was "never lying about your age in order to appear younger" (M = 1.62). Both the subscales of Fear of Old People and Psychological Concerns revealed the lower scores of the 4 subscales, indicating less anxiety or more positive responses.

The mean scores for the fourth and last subscale, *Psychological Concerns,* revealed a mean of 1.80 on a scale of 1-4. This subscale showed the least anxiety compared to the other subscales. This includes such statements as "having plenty to occupy my time when I am old" and "feeling good about life when I am old." These findings can also be related to previous research indicating that psychological well-being improves with regular exercise, which includes mood improvements and less depressive symptoms (Wantanabe, et al., 2000; Moore, et al., 1999).

Table 6

| Mean Scores Obtained for the Anxiety about Aging Scales | |
| --- | --- |
| Scales | Mean Scores |
| | |
| *Fear of Old People:* | |
| I enjoy being around old people. | 1.92 |
| I like to go visit my older relatives. | 1.94 |
| I enjoy talking with old people. | 1.78 |
| I feel very comfortable when I am around an old person. | 1.89 |
| I enjoy doing things for old people. | 1.70 |
| | |
| *Fear of Losses:* | |
| I fear that when I am old, all my friends will be gone. | 2.12 |
| The older I become, the more I worry about my health. | 2.53 |
| I get nervous when I think about someone else making decisions for me when I am old. | 2.65 |
| I worry that people will ignore me when I am old. | 2.17 |
| I am afraid that there will be no meaning in my life when I am old. | 1.58 |

*Physical Appearance:*

| | |
|---|---|
| I have never lied about my age in order to appear younger. | 1.62 |
| It doesn't bother me at all to imagine myself as being old. | 2.63 |
| I have never dreaded the day | |
| I would look in the mirror and see gray hairs. | 2.33 |
| I have never dreaded looking old. | 2.71 |
| When I look in the mirror, it bothers me to see how my | |
| looks have changed with age. | 2.26 |

*Psychological Concerns:*

| | |
|---|---|
| I fear it will be very hard for me to find contentment in old age. | 1.80 |
| I will have plenty to occupy my time when I am old. | 1.74 |
| I expect to feel good about life when I am old. | 1.84 |
| I believe that I will still be able to do most things for myself when I am old. | 1.87 |
| I expect to feel good about myself when I am old. | 1.73 |

Analysis of variance results (see Table 7) also indicated significant age and gender interactions with regard to Fear of Old People. Males scored higher (indicating more negativity) on Fear of Old People, while females scored higher on Fear of Losses, Physical Appearance, and Psychological Concerns. Physical Appearances contained the highest score of all subscales, with a score of 2.45 for the females as compared to 2.14 for the males. Females' scores were slightly higher overall, indicating more negative perceptions regarding aging anxieties. Previous literature (Cummings, et al., 2000) has shown that males score higher than females in knowledge of aging or understanding the aging process, and females score higher than males in anxiety of aging.

Lasher and Faulkender (1993) found being male correlated with higher scores of fear of old people when developing their anxiety about aging scale. In this study, females have more anxiety about losses associated with aging as well as physical and psychological declines. These results, however, contradict Lasher & Faulkender's (1993) finding where males once again had higher anxiety scores, specifically regarding fear of losses. McConatha, et al., (2003) found that females from both the United States and Germany scored higher on the Physical Appearance subscale than the males from both countries. Once again, this supports females' higher anxieties regarding aging perceptions, especially physical appearance.

Table 7

| Mean Scores Obtained for Anxiety about Aging Scale by Subscale and Gender | | |
|---|---|---|
| Scales | Mean Scales – Males | Mean Scales – Females |
| Fear of Old People | 1.96 | 1.76 |
| Fear of Losses | 2.14 | 2.29 |
| Physical Appearance | 2.14 | 2.45 |
| Psychological Concerns | 1.73 | 1.88 |

No significant differences were found when comparing Caucasian and African-American responses. Caucasian scores were slightly higher than African-Americans' indicating Caucasians had more negative perceptions on the Anxiety about Aging scale than did African-Americans. Specifically, Caucasians' responses were more negative regarding physical appearances and psychological concerns, while African-Americans' responses were more negative regarding fear of old people and fear of losses. This contradicts a previous finding that shows Caucasian subjects scored higher on knowledge of aging and lower on anxiety of aging (Cummings, et al., 2000). However, this may be largely due to the unequal number of subjects in each group; there were 69 Caucasian participants and only 5 African-American participants.

Part 2 of the questionnaire focused on evaluating life and subjective health satisfaction. Almost all of the participants, 95%, responded "very satisfied," "somewhat satisfied," or "satisfied." Only 5% responded "somewhat unsatisfied" or "not satisfied." In conjunction, when asked to rate life satisfaction, 96% of the participants responded "very satisfied," "somewhat satisfied," or "satisfied." Only 4% responded "somewhat unsatisfied" or "not satisfied." This response directly correlates with previous findings that physical activity has a positive effect on both meaning in life and self-rated health and functioning (Takkinen, et al., 2001; Miehlke, et al., 1999). It was concluded that greater levels of endurance exercise participation were significantly associated with a better rating of physical health (Stewart, et al., 1993).

Part 3 of the questionnaire asked open-ended questions such as what do you do for exercise. Most participants (68%) reported performing some type of cardiovascular training combined with weight training when they exercise. The remainder combined either cardiovascular or weight training with another form of exercise, such as yoga/Pilates or sports. All participants exercised on a regular basis with 96% exercising more than 30 minutes at a time, and only 4% exercising less than 30 minutes at a time. All participants reported exercising 3 or more times a week.

When asked what positives they were looking forward to in old age, most participants said they looked forward to doing things they enjoy, such as spending time with loved ones and participating in exercise and hobbies. On the other hand, when asked about fears associated with getting older, the responses consisted of being alone and having poor health. The most frequently reported word describing an ideal older man and older women was "healthy." Most participants consider themselves old around 73-74 years of age. The most frequently reported age was 70, followed closely by 80, then 60. The youngest reported age of participants feeling "old" was 50, while the oldest age reported was 110.

## Conclusion

It has become apparent that the perception of aging anxieties is greatly reduced amongst people who exercise on a regular basis; that is at least 3 times a week. Thus, those who engage in regular exercise exhibit positive perceptions of aging and show satisfaction with life and health as well as subjective health ratings. The results of this study show positive perceptions toward aging. Thus, exercise should be encouraged to all ages, in hopes to offset physical, physiological, and psychological declines, and give greater satisfaction and meaning to overall life and health. This is clearly supported in this study.

The benefits of this study support the ongoing effort to educate young and middle-aged adults about the effects of regular exercise. Research has shown physiological and psychological effects with regular exercise, and this study has added another benefit to the psychological arena; regular exercisers may perceive the anxieties of aging with a more positive outlook. If positive perceptions of aging can be attained, as well as positive life and subjective health satisfaction, people at any age may have one more additional reason to be encouraged to participate in regular exercise.

# References

Aday, R.H. & Austin, B.S. (2000). Images of Aging in the Lyrics of American Country Music. *Educational Gerontology, 26* (2),135-155.

Administration on Aging (2001). *Profile of Older Americans: 2001* (on-line). Available: http://aoa.gov/aoa/stats/profile/2001/1.html.

Arnaud, M.J. (2000). Physical Exercise, Aging and Hydration. *Science and Sports* (Paris), 15 (4), 177-179.

Blumenthal, J.A. & Gullete, E.C.D. (2002). Exercise Interventions and Aging: Psychological and Physical Health Benefits in Older Adults. Pp. 155-157. In: Schaie, K.; Warner; Leventhal, Howard, et al. (Eds.) *Effective Health Behavior in Older Adults. Societal Impact on Aging.* New York, NY: Springer.

Clark, S.D., Long, M.M., & Schiffman, L.G. (1999). The Mind-Body Connection: the Relationship among Physical Activity Level, Life Satisfaction, and Cognitive Age Among Mature Females. *Journal of Social Behavior & Personality, 14* (2), 221-241.

Cummings, S.M., Kropf, N.P., & DeWeaver, K.L. (2000). Knowledge of and Attitudes toward Aging among Non-Elders: Gender and Race Differences. *Journal of Women & Aging, 12* (1/2), 77-91.

Goggin, N.L., & Morrow, J.R., Jr. (2001). Physical Activity Behaviors of Older Adults. *Journal of Aging and Physical Activity, 9,* 58-66.

Lasher, K.P., & Faulkender, P.J. (1993). Measurement of Aging Anxiety: Development of the Anxiety About Aging Scale. *International Journal of Aging and Human Development, 37* (4), 247-259.

Levy, B.R., Slade, M.D., Kunkel, S.R., & Kasl, S.V. (2002). Longevity Increased by Positive Self-Perceptions of Aging. *Journal of Personality and Social Psychology, 83* (2), 261-270.

Loland, N.W. (2000). The Aging Body: Attitudes toward Bodily Appearance among Physically Active and Inactive Women and Men of Different Ages. *Journal of Aging and Physical Activity, 8,* 197-213.

Loomis, R.A., & Thomas, C.D. (1991). Elderly Women in Nursing Home and Independent Residence: Health, Body Attitudes, Self-Esteem and Life Satisfaction. *Canadian Journal on Aging, 10* (3), 224-231.

McConatha, J.T., Schnell, F., & McKenna (1999). Description of Older Adults as Depicted in Magazine Advertisements. *Psychological Reports, 85,* (3), 1051-1057.

McConatha, J.T., Schnell, F., Volkwein, K., Riley, L., & Leach, E. (In Press). Attitudes towards Aging: A Comparative Analysis of Young Adults from the United States and Germany. *The International Journal of Aging and Human Development.*

Miehlke, C., Uhlenbruck, G., & Volkwein, K. (1999). Exercise, Fitness, and Life Satisfaction in Older Adults. In: Volkwein, K. (Ed.). *Fitness as Cultural Phenomenon.* Münster/Germany: Waxmann Verlag.

Milligan, W. L., Powell, D.A., Harly, C., & Furchtgott, E. (1985.) Physical Health Correlates of Attitudes toward Aging in the Elderly. *Experimental Aging Research, 11* (2), 75-80.

Milligan, W.L., Prescott, L., Powell, D.A., & Furchtgott, E. (1989). Attitudes towards Aging and Physical Health. *Experimental Aging Research, 15* (1), 33-41.

Moore, K.A., Babyak, M.A., Wood, C.E., Napolitano, M.A., Khatir, P., Craighead, W.E., Herman, S., Krishnan, R., & Blumenthal, J.A. (1999). The Association between Physical Activity and Depression in Older Depressed Adults. *Journal of Aging and Physical Activity, 7*, 55-61.

Schilke, J.M. (1991). Slowing the Aging Process with Physical Activity. *Journal of Gerontological Nursing,17* (6), 4-7.

Stewart, A.L., King, A.C., & Haskell, W.L. (1993). Endurance Exercise and Health-Related Quality of Life in 50-65 Year-Old Adults. *The Gerontologist, 33* (6), 782-789.

Takkinen, S., Suutama, T., & Ruoppila, I. (2001). More Meaning by Exercising? Physical Activity as a Predictor of a Sense of Meaning in Life and of Self-Rated Health and Functioning in Old Age. *Journal of Aging and Physical Activity, 9*, 128-141.

Watanabe, E., Takeshima, N., Okada, A., & Inomata, K. (2001). Effects of Increasing Expenditure of Energy during Exercise on Psychological Well-Being in Older Adults. *Perceptual and Motor Skills, 92*, 288-298.

World Health Organization. (1997). The Heidelberg Guidelines for Promoting Physical Activity among Older Persons. *Journal of Aging and Physical Activity, 5* (1), 2-8.

## Issue 3

# Obesity – The Pandemic

*(by Christine Williams)*

## Introduction

Obesity is a relatively new health concern. Through evolution, the past few million years consisted of ancestors eating as much food as was available in order to survive scarce periods (Power & Schulkin, 2009). Today, in industrialized nations, food is abundant, easily accessible and a wide array of choices exists. On average, today's humans carry more body fat than in any other time in history. The result is an obesity pandemic. From 1980 to 2008, global obesity doubled among adults twenty years of age and older to an obesity rate of 11% (WHO, 2011). The most obese industrialized nation in the world is the United States of America. Thus, this issue will mainly focus on the obesity pandemic on the rise in the U.S. However, the information presented will be valuable for any nation battling the same health crisis.

The term "obesity" refers to body weight that is considered unhealthy for a specific height due to an excessive amount of body fat. Excess fat deposits accumulate viscerally and subcutaneously due to energy consumption being greater than energy expenditure. Obesity is most commonly measured by body mass index (BMI), which is weight (kg) divided by height2 (m). Adults are considered obese when BMI is 30 or greater, while children are considered obese if BMI is at or above the 95th percentile for children of the same age and sex (Barlow, et al., 2007). Between 2009- 2010, 35% (78 million) of adults were obese in the USA, and approximately 17% (12.5 million) of children ages 2-19 were obese (Ogden, Carroll, Kit & Flegal, 2012).

As obesity increased through the years, various levels of obesity developed. Adults with a BMI of 35-39.9 are considered class 2 obesity, and adults with a BMI of 40 or greater are in a third obesity class. The greatest risk for health problems is in the obese class 3 category, which is considered morbid obesity. Children are identified as morbidly obese in the > 120% of the 95th percentile of BMI (Flegal, et al., 2009).

## Historical Perspective

Obesity is less than a century old. Throughout history, obesity was once considered a sign of affluence and health due to the scarcity of food (Eknoyan, 2006). During the 19th century, medical experts concurred that an extra 20-50 pounds of excess weight was healthy and provided extra energy when run down (Eknoyan, 2006). However, obesity became undesirable for aesthetic reasons in the late 19th century (Eknoyan, 2006). In the 1920s, insurance companies began to see the correlation between excess fat and health problems (Dublin & Lotka, 1937), and by the1930s, medical doctors started recognizing that extra fat presented negative health consequences (Guerrini, 2000). Despite the negative social and medical perception of obesity, in the late 1970s and early 1980s, a major shift in body fat occurred (refer to Table 8).

Table 8

| U.S. Overweight and obesity by age, 1971-2004 | Obese adults 20-70 years of age by BMI |
|---|---|
| 1971-1974 | 14.6 |
| 1976-1980 | 15.1 |
| 1988-1994 | 23.3 |
| 1999-2000 | 31.0 |
| 2001-2002 | 32.1 |
| 2003-2004 | 33.9 |

(U.S. Department of Health & Human Services, 2006)

Table 8 refers to the rates of obesity from 1971- 2004 in the United States. In the 1980s, obesity rates began to rise substantially. Ironically, BMI was originally proposed in the 1980s to measure severely underweight individuals in underserved populations (Delpeuch, Maire, Monnier & Holdsworth, 2009). Instead, BMI became the most popular measure for overweight people and obesity. Obesity rates rose to such high rates in the 1980s, that according to the Centers for Disease Control and Prevention, the obesity epidemic emerged in the US (Ogden, et al., 2006). By 2000, obesity rates doubled from 1980, and today are continuing to rise.

The obesity epidemic poses a great risk to individuals because of serious, negative health effects. Obesity increases the risk of morbidities and early mortality. The plethora of morbidities linked with obesity range from leading causes of death, including coronary heart disease and cancer, to less threatening health problems, such as psoriasis (Yosipovitch, DeVore & Dawn, 2007).

Conditions such as Type 2 diabetes, hypertension, stroke, liver and gallbladder disease, sleep apnea, respiratory problems, dyslipidemia, gynecological problems, and osteoarthritis are among the many health problems that surface as weight (fat) increases (Centers for Disease Control and Prevention, 2011). Obesity contributes to a plethora of other health disorders including, but not limited to, mental health problems such as depression.

While obesity leads to many health conditions, genetic factors can also contribute to obesity. Some individuals carry the fat mass and obesity associated gene (FTO), also known as the obesity gene. The obesity gene causes cells to accumulate more fat. People who inherit the obesity gene weigh, on average, 7 pounds more than individuals who do not carry the gene (Frayling, et al., 2007). Carrying the FTO gene increases the odds of becoming obese by 1.67-fold. However, more research is needed because it is still unclear which role exactly the obesity gene plays, since many people who carry this gene do not become obese.

Other genetic conditions also contribute to obesity. Mutations in single genes, called monogenic mutations can result in rare forms of obesity. Monogenic mutations impact one's food intake, appetite control, and energy homeostasis (Hu, 2008). There are several other genetic syndromes that trigger obesity. The most common multi-system genetic syndromes are Prader-Willi and Bardet-Biedl, which are caused by genetic mutations or chromosomal abnormalities (Goldstone & Beales, 2008). Other genetic obesity syndromes include MOMO syndrome, Alstrom syndrome, Cohen syndrome, Rubinstein-Taybi syndrome, Carpenter syndrome and Albright's hereditary osteodystrophy (Goldstone & Beales, 2008). While all of the aforementioned genetic and chromosomal abnormalities are associated with obesity, research indicates that 60% of a person's weight may be determined by genetics, but at least 40% of weight is dependent upon the environment (Moll, Burns & Lauer, 1991).

In addition to genetics, certain medications and other health conditions can contribute to obesity. Medications such as corticosteroids, antidepressants and seizure medication can cause weight gain by slowing metabolic rate, increasing water retention and/or increasing appetite (National Heart, Lung and Blood Institute, 2012a). Other health conditions can cause obesity such as hypothyroidism, Cushing's syndrome, and polycystic ovarian syndrome. While certain health conditions contribute to weight gain, it is important to consider how human behavior may cause weight gain, and how to modify behavior for healthier weight management.

## Etiology

The root cause of increased energy consumption among humans is associated with a myriad of influencing factors including technology, social and cultural changes, and economics (Chou, et al., 2008; Cutler, et al., 2003; Lakdawalla & Philipson, 2009). In 2009, the Centers for Disease Control and Prevention (CDC) reported 2.4 million more adults were obese compared to 2007 (2010). The obesity epidemic is so profound that, to date, nine states in the USA have reached obesity rates of 30% or greater. This continual rise in obesity is a serious threat to the longevity of humans and also the health care system. The health care costs related to treating morbidities as a result of obesity are staggering. In the US, costs totaled $147 billion in 2008 (CDC, 2010). Because obesity is on the rise, health problems will continue to escalate as populations increase in obesity, and the onset of obesity begins at earlier ages. To understand the etiology of obesity and consider solutions, one must consider the change in serving sizes, food selection, inactivity, and other environmental cues.

### Serving Size

Food consumption has changed. A myriad of environmental factors have altered consumption norms leading to the positive energy intake balance in society. The average size of an American dinner plate increased 23%, almost two inches since 1900 (Van Ittersum & Wansink, 2012). The larger the dinner plate, the more likely one is to increase the portion size and thus, more food is consumed (Van Ittersum & Wansink, 2012). A larger plate encourages overeating despite feelings of satiation. Not only have plates increased in size, but overall consumption norms have increased. Larger-sized restaurant portions and larger food packages suggest to individuals that it is normal, appropriate, typical and reasonable to consume large portions (Schwartz, 1996). The result of these consumption norms causes adults and children to ignore internal cues of satiation and intake caloric overabundance.

As early as ages 3-5, children begin to override self-regulation of food intake and overeat based on large portions (Wansnink, Payne & Chandon, 2007). Food retailers are not naive to the effects of these consumption norms. In 1955, McDonald's offered one size of soda consisting of 7 ounces. Today, a children's soda is 12 ounces, the smallest adult soda is 16 ounces, and when supersize existed, it contained 42 ounces (Young, Nestle, 2003). Even the straw used to consume beverages has increased in size at McDonald's. These food portions have drastically altered perceived norms.

Another environmental cue impacting portion control includes stockpiling. While bulk discounts provide financial savings, research indicates consumers pay a high caloric price. Buying in bulk at wholesale clubs may be a risk factor for some. Consumption rates increase when food is purchased in bulk or stockpiled. In a study by Chandon and Wansnick (2002), ready-to-eat stockpiled food was eaten at two times the rate of non-stockpiled food. The increased rate of shopping at wholesale clubs is ultimately contributing to obesity levels. Buying food in smaller amounts decreases consumption rates.

### Food Selection

Another contributor of the obesity epidemic is an increase in low-nutrient, energy-dense food consumption (Briefel, Wilson & Gleason, 2009). Low-nutrient, energy-dense foods contain little nutrients but are high in calories, such as high-fat baked goods, French fries and snack foods such as chips. These foods often have a pleasing taste or flavor, are easily obtainable and may be cheaper than some healthier food options.

Sodas and sugary drinks are no exception to low-nutrient, energy-dense foods. A meta-analysis concluded there is an association between soft drink intake and weight gain (Vartanian, Schwartz & Brownell, 2007). Soft drinks offer no nutritional benefit and contain high amounts of carbohydrates by way of sugar and corn syrup. Several studies indicate that soda and sugary beverage consumption is related to obesity among adults and children (Giammattei, Blix, Marshak, Wollitzer & Pettitt, 2003; Ludwig, Peterson & Gortmaker, 2001; Malik, Schulz & Hu, 2006). Among adults, individuals who drink one or more sodas per day are 27% more likely to be overweight or obese compared to those adults who do not drink soda (Babey, Jones, Yu & Goldstein, 2009). The consumption of high caloric beverages has a profound effect on weight control and carrying extra body fat. One study reported that drinking soda is associated with an increased risk for Type 2 diabetes (Schulze, Manson, Ludwig, Colditz, Stampfer, Willett & Hu, 2004).

Increased caloric consumption may also be due to the processing of foods. While obesity is prevalent among all groups of society, obesity tends to impact lower income groups at a higher rate than compared to higher socioeconomic status groups (Drenowski & Darmon, 2005). This is partly due to processed foods. More prepackaged goods are sold today than previously. Chemicals are used to extend shelf life, and the general composition of processed food compared to fresh food varies. Processed food contains less fiber and water and more sugar, fat, and sodium. This causes processed food to be more fattening, less filling and more energy dense. An inverse relationship exists between price and energy dense of foods (Drenowski & Darmon, 2005). Lower income households are more likely to buy products that have concentrated energy from fat, sugar, and meat products but lack vegetables, whole grains, and fruit (Quan, Salomon, Nitzke, & Reicks, 2000).

Energy dense foods are not only packaged foods but are foods sold in restaurants. Due to busier schedules, people are in search for quick and easy meals. As a result, Americans have decreased in-home cooking and replaced it with meals bought or eaten at restaurants. Eating restaurant meals is associated with higher caloric intake (Powell & Nguyen, 2013). Americans are eating away from the home more than ever in history. In 2010, Americans ate almost half, 47.9%, of their meals away from home compared to 39% of meals eaten away from home in 1980 (USDA, 2013).

While parents with children may find it convenient to eat away from home due to busy schedules, eating restaurant food can be problematic. Parents who ate restaurant food with their children reported that their children consumed more sugary beverages, more savory and sweet snacks, and less water compared to families who did not eat at restaurants as frequently (Ayala, Rogers, Arredondo, Campbell, Baquero, Duerksen, Elder, 2008). A study among teenagers determined that on days when teens ate at fast food restaurants, 309 more calories were consumed (Powell & Nguyen, 2013). Teens eating at fast food restaurants also consumed more soda and less milk.

In addition, individuals from lower socioeconomic backgrounds are more likely to eat fast food than dine in a restaurant. Fast food restaurants tend to offer fewer options for healthier foods in comparison to dine-in restaurants. In poorer neighborhoods, there are twice as many fast food restaurants and convenience stores compared to wealthier neighborhoods (Lee, 2012). The easy access, low price, faster and busy lifestyle makes fast food a convenient choice. While the instant gratification of fast food flavor appeals to many people due to the sugary, salt, and fried food combination, the body fat resulting from continuous unhealthy meals is a high price to pay.

In sum, sodas, processed food and junk food result in people becoming satiated on less nourishing, poorer food selections and this replaces more substantive food options, such as fruits and vegetables. In 2008, individuals consumed 300 more calories compared to 1985 caloric consumption rates (U.S.D.A., 2011). Lower-nutrient, energy-dense foods are a primary cause of increased weight gain (U.S.D.A., 2011).

### Pricing
Over several years, pricing of lower-nutrient, energy-dense foods and drinks has declined, even after adjusting for inflation. Junk food items such as soda and candy are inexpensive. Conversely, the pricing of healthier foods has increased. One study reports a price increase of 19.5% from 2004- 2006 on healthier food selections such as beans, vegetables, lean meats, fruits and low-fat dairy products (Monsivais & Drewnowski, 2007).

The higher cost of healthier food can be a deterrent for better eating habits while low price and easy accessibility promotes people to consume junk foods. For example, local convenience stores have low-nutrient, energy-dense foods permeating the store while one has to search carefully to find a healthy, nutrient-dense snack food. In low socioeconomic areas and rural areas, there is not equivalent access to healthy, fresh, affordable foods compared to more populated and wealthier neighborhoods (Brug, Oenema & Ferreira, 2005). However, some researchers indicate there is a sufficient number of grocery stores in poorer areas compared to high socioeconomic areas (Macintyre, 2007; Lee, 2012). It is simply the food selection that one chooses to eat that is influenced by price.

### Inactivity

Physical activity and exercise are the ways to expend the extra calories that Americans are consuming and are essential for good health. Some experts consider physical inactivity as one of the largest public health problems in the 21st century (Blair, 2009). It is well documented that lack of physical activity and a sedentary lifestyle contribute to obesity. Sedentary behaviors are low in energy expenditure, such as prolonged periods of sitting/lounging including watching television, working on computers, and more (Tremblay, Colley, Saunders, Healy & Owen, 2010).

Research indicates that physical activity levels have decreased and sedentary behaviors are increasing. According to the CDC, physical activity in the USA dropped from 30.5% in 1988 to 25.1% in 2008 (2010). Sedentary levels have increased among both adults and children. Inactivity has increased in K-12 schools due to decreased or eliminated physical education requirements and a reduction in recess or other physical activity.

One main culprit causing an increase in sedentary activity among all age groups is the increased use of technology. Media consumption is a large culprit, including but not limited to tablets, smartphones, games, computers, and televisions. From 1950-2000, ownership of televisions greatly increased in the US. By 2000, over half of the households, 61%, owned 2-3 televisions and 36% of the population owned four or more televisions, according to Nielsen (2011). An abundance of TV ownership has led viewing time to increase from 4.5 hours per day to eight hours per day (Brownson, Boehmer & Luke, 2005). In one study, the health of a group of women was followed for a six-year period. All women participating were less than obese at the beginning of the study but by year six, a two-hour increase in television viewing was associated with a 23% increase in obesity (Hu, Li, Colditz, Williett & Manson, 2003). Doubling sedentary behavior can cause obesity, mutually exclusive of any other factors due to decreased energy output. To worsen matters, many people enjoy eating snack foods while using media. Typical snack foods include foods that can be eaten with the hands, such as chips or candy and are energy-dense, low-nutrient foods.

Not only has media consumption increased over the years but the age of television consumption begins in earlier years. In 1971, children began to watch television by 4 years of age; today, children begin TV viewing as early as three months of age (Zimmerman, Christakis & Meltzoff, 2007). Early television viewing and prolonged periods of TV consumption have contributed to obesity among children.

### The Environment

There are a myriad of other environmental cues contributing to obesity. There are fewer possibilities for people to walk or bicycle safely in communities. More families have dual household income earners, and therefore have less time to prepare in-home meals. People graze and snack rather than limiting eating to mealtime. Snacking typically consists of energy-dense, low-nutrient foods. Also, Americans may snack and eat mindlessly while multitasking. Eating mindlessly can cause overeating and lack of awareness of caloric consumption. Emotions such as stress and depression can also contribute to one eating mindlessly instead of mindfully (National Heart, Lung and Blood Institute, 2012b).

Lastly, poor sleep can contribute to weight gain. Lack of sleep affects the hormone balance and can increase hunger by causing leptin levels to rise and ghrelin levels to decrease (National Heart, Lung and Blood Institute, 2012b). Leptin contributes to feeling satiated while ghrelin influences feeling hungry. With busy schedules, people are challenged in obtaining a healthy 7-9 hours of sleep per night.

## The Future and the Solution

At present, over one-third of the adult population is obese in the USA. Obesity prevalence has steadily risen. In 1999-2000, 27% of men were obese and 33% of women were obese (Ogden, Carroll, Kit & Flegal, 2012). By 2010, both sexes reached an obesity rate of 35%. If future trends remain consistent with past obesity growth rates, obesity will continue to escalate. By 2030, it is projected that 86.5% of the US population will be overweight or obese; specifically 51.1% will be obese (Wang, et al., 2008). By 2048, all American adults will become overweight or obese. With such astonishing projections, it is imperative to implement major programs and timely policies to decrease health outcomes.

Public health programs are needed for all sexes, ethnicities, and ages – even expectant mothers. Overweight expectant mothers and fathers double the risk of obesity in their offspring (Whitaker, Wrights, Pepe, Seidel, & Dietz, 1997). Obesity in childhood predicts obesity in young adulthood (Whitaker, et al., 1997). Young adults who are obese are more likely to remain obese (Guo, Wu, Chumlea & Roche, 2002). In order to make a significant dent in the obesity crisis, all age groups need to be addressed and included in the education and outreach programs.

There is no simple solution to eradicate the obesity epidemic, but there are answers at varying levels to create change. A revolution is possible, but it will take time, resources, and commitments. Treatment programs for existing obese and overweight populations are necessary as well as prevention programs. Effective programs recognize all influential layers. Emphasis must be placed on increasing awareness, knowledge, and motivation for change. Programs must address major obesity causes such as physical inactivity, nutrient-dense foods, and behavioral patterns.

Programs targeting obesity can be expensive and complex. Public health programs must consider various influences such as cultural norms, environmental barriers, and personal attitudes and beliefs. Individuals must possess the willingness, ability, and stability to make healthy lifestyle choices over the long term. This is not an easy task. Some public health programs have achieved success while others have not been as successful in altering obesity rates. For example, the Minnesota Heart Health Program had a disappointing upward trend in weight gain among participants by year seven (Jeffrey, 2012). Despite enormous efforts and financial resources to improve health among 400,000 Midwesterners, the project results were statistically insignificant. Researchers considered that a large population, slightly less than half a million, is perhaps too challenging to create long-term behavior change (Murray, 1995).

On the other hand, some public health programs have achieved success in obesity reduction. The likelihood of programs being successful increases when participants can self-select into a program and when programs target only weight management as opposed to other health behaviors (e.g., smoking) (Stice, Shaw & Marti, 2006). For example, one program using an anti-depression medication, Fluoxetine, was very successful in achieving long-term weight loss among adults (Goldstein, Rampey, Wilson, Hamilton, Sayler & Tollefson, 2012). The underlying root of success is targeting the individual needs of a population. Based on the needs, programs can be tailored to meet the needs of the individual and what is causing obesity. More research is needed to determine the most effective and efficient programs to reduce obesity among adults.

Among children, school-based health programs are ideal due to the cost effectiveness, and the settings provide ample opportunity for exercise and nutrition interventions. School-based programs target children K-12. The success of school-based programs varies by sex (Kropski, Keckley & Jensen, 2012). Research indicates that, for girls, programs that were short in duration were effective (Stice, Shaw & Marti, 2006), and programs including educational components based on the social learning theory have been successful (Kropski, Keckley & Jensen, 2012). Social learning theory posits that people are influenced by observing and modeling the attitudes, emotions, and behaviors of others.

For boys, programs focusing on physical activity have been more successful (Kropski, Keckley & Jensen, 2012).

When targeting obesity public health programs for children, it is also important to include education for parents. Children and adolescent obesity programs are more effective when parents are included (Hinkle, Kirschenbaum, Pecora & Germann, 2011). Parents must have the education and knowledge to recognize obesity in a child and how to seek prevention/treatment. In one obesity prevention program at Head Start, parents were included in creating and participating in the program. The program focused on children 2-5 years of age and included BMI education for parents, family nutritional counseling, parental communication, and conflict resolution skills training and lifestyle education (Davison, Jurkowski, Li, Kranz & Lawson, 2013). After two years, children had significant improvements in weight, physical activity, healthy food intake, and media consumption. By working with the family as a unit, the children have a greater outcome of success because the parents are not only making healthy choices for their children but teaching children to make healthy choices (Davison, et al., 2013).

### Program Content

Programs for adults and children should include education on nutrition, physical activity, and other behavioral factors. Americans must increase the consumption of healthier food choices including vegetables, fruits, lean meats, and whole grains; and decrease eating low-nutrient, energy-dense food choices such as processed, sugary and fried foods. Studies indicate that by reducing sugar-sweetened beverage and soda intake, weight loss reduction will result (Ebbeling, Feldman, Osganian, Chomitz, Ellenbogen & Ludwig, 2006; James, Thomas, Cavan & Kerr, 2004).

As mentioned earlier, soda can be the culprit of consuming excess calories and is a drink of choice for many children. Due to lack of nutrients in soda, some school districts have opted to replace soda machines with alternative options such as water. Additionally, studies measuring states that have detailed nutritional standards among schools report children are less likely to remain overweight or obese (Taber, Chriqui, Perna, Power & Chaloupka, 2012). For children, it is not only important to offer nutritional education in school but also offer healthy foods that are easily accessible. Experts conclude that the most effective school policies on food are the ones that restrict specific food and beverages sold in vending machines, at campus stores, or à la carte cafeteria items. Fortunately, 21 states have enacted nutritional guidance in schools, but all states need to improve school nutrition (Kropski, Keckley & Jensen, 2012).

Additionally, continued education on healthy portion sizes is essential for all ages. Consumers must acknowledge oversized portions at restaurants and instead eat appropriate portions. Customers may choose to split a meal or take leftover food home. Americans must tune in to cues for satiation and hunger. Making a conscious choice to be aware of hunger and satiation is necessary to prevent overeating and unnecessary snacking. Mindful eating also helps people plan better food choices.

Americans may need to spend more on food to stay healthier. Every decade, Americans are spending less money on food. In 2010, Americans spent 9.4% of their disposable income on food (USDA, 2013). In 1960, 17.3% of disposable income was spent on food. While energy-dense, low-nutrient foods such as fast foods and processed foods are inexpensive, whole foods such as vegetables and fruits are essential to a diet. Americans need to allocate more disposable income on high-quality, nutrient-dense foods such as whole grains and lean meats. By investing less in computers and television sets and more on higher quality foods, Americans may be more apt to eat better and reduce sedentary behaviors.

Programs encouraging physical activity are increasing and Americans must make exercise a priority. Some employers are offering fitness centers at the job site or reduced gym memberships. Certain insurance companies offer an incentive for participants who exercise regularly. Schools must retain exercise outlets, such as physical education class, for children. Local governments and communities can support active living. Communities need to create walking paths and biking paths and promote safe methods for increased physical activity. Greater education and awareness must be placed on reducing sedentary activities such as media consumption. More strides through public health programs are needed to help motivate people on how to become more active.

## Conclusion

Obesity is an ever-growing epidemic in Western countries that must change in order to stop the human lifespan from decreasing; it is the first time in human history that humans may be decreasing their longevity (Olshansky, et al., 2005; Wang, Beydoun, Liang, Cabellero & Kumanyika, 2008). Obesity can affect everyone, women and men, children and adults, wealthy and poor, and all ethnicities. The health condition has gained the attention of US health agencies and world health organizations. Billions of dollars are being spent on the treatment and prevention of obesity on the individual and public level. Despite such great efforts, obesity is not decreasing; it continues to grow. We all must make healthy choices for ourselves and our children by having an active lifestyle and selecting healthy foods. We must be advocates within our communities to improve quality of life and longevity.

# References

Ayala, G.X., Rogers, M., Arredondo, E.M., Campbell, N.R., Baquero, B., Duerksen, S.C, Elder, J.P. (2008). Away-from-home food intake and risk for obesity: examining the influence of context. *Obesity, 16,* 1002-1008.

Babey, S.H., Jones, M., Yu, H., Goldstein,H. (2009). Bubbling over: soda consumption and its link to obesity in California. UCLA Center for Health Policy Research. Retrieved on Jan. 10, 2012, from http://escholarship.org/uc/item/1fj3h5cj.

Barlow, S.E., and the Expert Committee (2007). Expert committee recommendations regarding the prevention, assessment, and treatment of child and adolescent overweight and obesity: summary report. *Pediatrics 2007, 120,*164-S192.

Blair, S.N. (2009). Physical inactivity: the biggest public health problem of the 21st century. *British Journal of Sports Medicine, 43,*1-2.

Briefel, R.R., Wilson, A., Gleason, P.M. (2009). Consumption of low-nutrient, energy-dense foods and beverages at school, home, and other locations among school lunch participants and nonparticipants. *Journal of the American Dietetic Association,109* (2), 79-90.

Brownson, R.C., Boehmer, T.K., Luke, D.A. (2005). Declining rates of physical activity in the United States: What are contributors? *Annual Review of Public Health, 26,* 421- 443.

Brug, J. Oenema. A., Ferreira, I. (2005). Theory, evidence and intervention mapping to improve behavior nutrition and physical activity interventions. *International Journal of Behavioral Nutrition and Physical Activity, 2,*

Centers for Disease Control and Prevention (2010). Adult obesity: adult obesity rises among adults. Retrieved on Jan. 10, 2012, from http://www.cdc.gov/vitalsigns/AdultObesity/index.html

Centers for Disease Control and Prevention (2010). 1988- 2008 No leisure-time physical activity trend chart. Retrieved on Jan. 10, 2012, http://www.cdc.gov/nccdphp/dnpa/physical/stats/leisure_time.htm

Centers for Disease Control and Prevention (2011). The health effects of overweight and obesity. Retrieved on Jan. 10, 2012, from http://www.cdc.gov/healthyweight/effects/index.html

Chandon, P., Wansnisk, B. (2002). When are stockpiled food products consumed faster? A convenience- salience framework of post- purchase consumption incidence and quantity. *Journal of Marketing Research, 20,* 467- 477.

Chou, S.Y., Rashad, I.,Grossman, M. (2008), "Fast-Food Restaurant Advertising on Television and Its Influence on Childhood Obesity", *Journal of Law and Economics, 51*:599-618.

Christian, T., Rashad, I. (2009). Trends in U.S. Food Prices, 1950–2007. *Economics and Human Biology, 7,* 113–120.

Cutler, D.M., Glaeser, E.L., Shapiro, J.M. (2003). Why Have Americans Become More Obese? *Journal of Economic Perspectives, 17,* 93-118.

Delpeuch ,F., Maire, B., Monnier, E., Holdsworth, M. (2009). *Globesity: A planet out of control*. Sterling, VA: Earthscan.

Drenowski, A., Darmon, N. (2005). The economics of obesity: dietary energy density and energy cost. *The American Journal of Clinical Nutrition, 82,* 265S-273S.

Dublin, L.I., Lotka, A.J. (1937). Twenty-five years of health progress: A study of the mortality experience among industrial policyholders of the metropolitan life insurance company 1911- 1935. New York, NY: Metropolitan Life Insurance Company.

Ebbeling, C.B., Feldman, H.A., Osganian, S.K., Chomitz, V.R., Ellenbogen, S.J., Ludwig, D. S.(2006). Effects of decreasing sugar-sweetened beverage consumption on body weight in adolescents: a randomized, controlled pilot study. *Pediatrics, 117,* 673-680.

Eknoyan, G.(2006). A history of obesity, or what was good became ugly and then bad. *Advances in Chronic Kidney Disease, 13,* 421- 427.

Flegal, K.M., Wei, R., Ogden, C.L., Freedman, D.S., Johnson, C.L., Curtin, L.R. (2009). Characterizing extreme values of body mass index-for-age by using the 2000 Centers for Disease Control and Prevention growth charts. *American Journal of Clinical Nutrition, 90 ,*1314- 1320.

Frayling, T.M., Timpson, N.J., Weedon, M.N., Zeggini, E., Freathy, R.M., Lindgren, C.M., McCarthy, M.I. (2007). A common variant in the FtO gene is associated with body mass index and predisposes to childhood and adult obesity. *Science, 316,* 889- 894.

Giammattei, J., Blix, G., Marshak, H.H., Wollitzer, A.O., Pettitt, D.J. (2003). Television watching and soft drink consumption: associations with obesity in 11- to 13-year old schoolchildren. *Archives of Pediatric and Adolescent Medicine, 157,*882-886.

Goldstein, D.J., Rampey, A.H., Wilson, P.J., Hamiton, S.H., Sayler, M.E., Tollefson, G.D. (2012). Efficacy and safety of long term Fluoxetine treatment of obesity- maximizing success. *Obesity, 3* (S4), 481s- 490s.

Goldstone, A.P., Beales, P.L. (2008). Genetic obesity syndromes. *Frontiers of hormone research, 36,* 37- 60.

Guerrini, A (2000). *Obesity and depression in the enlightenment: The life and times of George Cheyne.* Norman, OK: University of Oklahoma Press.

Guo, S.S., Wu, W., Chumlea, W.C., Roche, A.F. (2002). Predicting overweight and obesity in adulthood from body mass index values in childhood and adolescence. *The American Journal of Clinical Nutrition, 76,* 653- 658.

Hinkle, K.A., Kirschenbaum, D.S., Pecora, K.M., Germann, J.N. (2011). Parents may hold the keys to success in immersion treatment of adolescent obesity. *Child & Family Behavior Therapy, 22,* 273- 288.

Hu F. (2008). Genetic predictors of obesity. In: Hu F, ed. *Obesity Epidemiology.* New York City: Oxford University Press, 437–460.

Hu, F.B., Li, T.Y., Colditz, G.A., Williett, W.C., Manson, J.E. (2003). Television watching and other sedentary behaviors in relation to risk of obesity and type 2 diabetes mellitus in women. *Journal of American Medical Association, 289,* 1785- 1791.

James, J., Thomas, P., Cavan, D., Kerr, D. (2004). Preventing childhood obesity by reducing consumption of carbonated drinks: cluster randomised controlled trial. *British Medical Journal, 328,* 1237.

Jeffrey, R.W. (2012). Community programs for obesity prevention: the Minnesota Heart Health Program. *Obesity, 3* (S2), 283s-288s.

Kropski, J.A., Keckley, P.H., Jensen, G.L. (2012). School-based obesity prevention programs: an evidence-based review. *Obesity, 16,* 1009- 1018.

Lakdwalla, D., Philipson, T. (2009). The growth of obesity and technological change. *Economics and Human Biology,7,* 283-293.

Lee, H. (2012). The role of local food availability in explaining obesity risk among young school-aged children. *Social Science and Medicine, 74,* 1193- 1203.

Ludwig, D.S., Peterson, K.E., Gortmaker, S.L. (2001). Relation between consumption of sugar-sweetened drinks and childhood obesity: a prospective, observational analysis. *The Lancet, 357,* 505-508.

Macintyire, S. (2007). Deprivation amplification revisited; or is it always true that poorer places have poorer access to resources for healthy diets and physical activity? *International Journal of Behavioral and Nutrition and Physical Activity, 4,* 32.

Malik, V.S., Schulze, M.B., Hu, F.B. (2006). Intake of sugar sweetened beverages and weight gain: a systematic review. *American Journal of Clinical Nutrition, 84,* 274-288.

Moll, P.P., Burns, T.L., Lauer, R.M. (1991). The genetic and environmental sources of body mass index variability: the Muscatine Ponderosity Family Study. *The American Journal of Human Genetics, 49,* 1243-1255.

Monsivais, P., Drewnowski, A. (2007). The Rising Cost of Low-Energy-Density Foods. *Journal of the American Dietetic Association, 107,* 2071-2076.

Murray D.M. (1995). Design and analysis of community trials: lessons from the Minnesota Heart Health Program. *American Journal of Epidemiology, 142,* 569-75.

National Heart, Lung and Blood Institute (2012a). What are overweight and obesity? Retrieved Dec. 29, 2012, from http://www.nhlbi.nih.gov/health/health-topics/topics/obe/.

National Heart, Lung and Blood Institute (2012b). What causes overweight and obesity? Retrieved Dec. 30, 2012, from http://www.nhlbi.nih.gov/health/health-topics/topics/obe/causes.html.

Nielsen Company (2013). Consumer media usage across TV, online, mobile and social. Retrieved Dec. 29, 2012, from http://blog.nielsen.com/nielsenwire/online_mobile/report-consumer-media-usage-across-tv-online-mobile-and-social.

Ogden, C.L., Carroll, M.D., Kit, B.K., Flegal, K.M. (2012). Prevalence of obesity in the United States, 2009- 2010. Retrieved on Jan 2, 2013, from http://www.cdc.gov/nchs/data/databriefs/db82.pdf.

Ogden, C.L., Carroll, M.D., Curtin, L.R., McDowell, M.A., Tabak, C.J., Flegal, K.M. (2006). Prevalence of overweight and obesity in the US, 1999-2004. *Journal of the American Medical Association, 295:*1549-1555.

Olshansky, S.J., Passaro, D.J., Hershow, R.C., Layden, J., Carnes, B.A., Brody, J., Hayflick, L., Butler, R.N., Allison, D.B., Ludwig, D.S. (2005). A potential decline in life expectancy in the United States in the 21st century. *New England Journal of Medicine, 352,* 1138–1145.

Quan, T., Salomon, J., Nitzke, S., Reicks, M. (2000). Behaviors of low-income mothers related to fruit and vegetables consumption. *Journal of American Dietetic Association, 100,* 567- 570.

Powell, L.M., Nguyen, B.T. (2013). Fast-food and full service restaurant consumption among children and adolescents. *Journal of American Medical Association Pediatrics, 167,* 14-20.

Power, M.L., Schulkin, J. (2009). *The evolution of obesity.* Baltimore, MD: Johns Hopkins University Press.

Schwartz, N. (1996). *Cognition and communication: Judgmental biases, Research Methods and The Logic of Conversation.* Mahwah, NJ: Erlbaum.

Schulze, M.B., Manson, J.E., Ludwig, D.S., Colditz, G.A., Stampfer, M.J., Willett, W.C., Hu, F.B. (2004). Sugar-sweetened beverages, weight gain, and incidence of type 2 diabetes in young and middle- aged women. *Journal of American Medical Association: 292,* 927-934.

Stice, E., Shaw, H., Marti, C.N. (2006). A meta-analytic review of obesity prevention programs for children and adolescents: the skinny in interventions that work. *Psychological Bulletin, 132,* 667-691.

Taber, D.R., Chriqui, J.F., Perna, F.M., Power, L.M., Chaloupka, F.J. (2012). Weight status among adolescents in states that govern competitive food nutrition content. *Pediatrics,120,* 437- 444.

Tremblay, M.S., Colley, R.C., Saunders, T.J., Healy, G.N., Owen, N (2010). Physiological and health implications of a sedentary lifestyle. *Applied Physiology, Nutrition, Metabolism, 35,* 725- 740.

U.S. Department of Agriculture, Economic Research Service (2011). Loss-Adjusted Food Availability: Spreadsheets— Calories. Retrieved on Dec. 30, 2012, from http://www.ers.usda.gov/Data/foodconsumption/spreadsheets/foodloss/Calories.xls#Totals!a.

U.S. Department of Agriculture, Economic Research Service (2013). Food expenditures. Retrieved on Dec. 30, 2012, from http://www.ers.usda.gov/data-products/food-expenditures.aspx#26636.

U.S. Department of Health & Human Services (2006). *Health, United States, 2006.* Retrieved on Jan 12, 2013, from http://www.cdc.gov/nchs/data/hus/hus06.pdf.

Van Ittersum, K., Wansink, B. (2012). Plate size and color suggestibility: The Delboeuf Illusion's Bias on serving and eating behavior. *Journal of Consumer Research, 38.* Retrieved on Jan. 10, 2013, from http://scheller.gatech.edu/directory/faculty/van_ittersum/pubs/JCR_11-0251_FINAL_SSRN.pdf.

Vartanian, L.R., Schwartz, M.B., Brownell, K.D. (2007). Effects of soft drink consumption on nutrition and health: a systematic review and meta-analysis. *American Journal of Public Health, 97,* 667-675.

Wang, Y., Beydoun, M.A., Liang, L., Cabellero, B., Kumanyika, S.K. (2008). Will all Americans become overweight or obese? Estimating the progression and cost of the US obesity epidemic. *Obesity, 16* (10), 2323- 2330.

Wansnick, B., Painter, J.E., Lee, Y.K. (20006). The office candy dish: proximity's influence on estimate and actual consumption. *International Journal of Obesity, 30,* 871- 875.

Wansnink, B., Payne, C.R., Chandon,P. (2007). Internal and external cues of meal cessation: the French paradox redux? *Obesity, 15,* 2920-2924.

Whitaker, R.C., Wright, J.A., Pepe, M.S., Seidel, K.D., Dietz, W.H. (1997). Predicting obesity in young adulthood from childhood and parental obesity. *New England Journal of Medicine, 337,* 869- 873.

Yosipovitch, G., DeVore, A., Dawn, A. (2007). Obesity and the skin: skin physiology and skin manifestations of obesity. *Journal of American Academy of Dermatology, 56* (6), 901-916.

Young, L.R., Nestle, M. (2003). Expanding portion sizes in the US marketplace: implications for nutrition counseling. *Journal of the American Dietetic Association, 103,* 231–234.

Zimmerman, F.J., Christakis, D.A., and Meltzoff, A.N. (2007). Television and DVD/video viewing in children younger than 2 years. *Archives of Pediatric & Adolescent Medicine, 161,* 473–479

## Issue 4

# The Threat of HIV to the World of Sport?

HIV/AIDS is still at work. More people are living and working with HIV than ever before. HIV has not gone away. Neither have the complex issues it raises. Has the world of sport responded appropriately and employed moral issues? For example, should an athlete infected with the human immunodeficiency virus (HIV) be allowed to continue to participate in sport, especially contact sports? Two recent situations illustrate the opposing viewpoints. One view is that the infected athlete poses a health risk to other athletes, coaches and trainers with whom he or she may come in direct physical contact and, as a result, must be banned from further competition. This was the mode of thinking in the banning of HIV-positive boxer Tommy Morrison by the Nevada Boxing Commission. Another viewpoint claims that the risk of spread of the infection is so minimal that other athletes are not placed in danger when competing with an HIV-positive athlete. This position resulted in the return of Earvin "Magic" Johnson to the National Basketball Association. In order to come to a just moral and ethical conclusion to this debate, it is imperative that the most prominent facts about HIV first be considered. The final decision should be based on what is best for most individuals. Directly related to this discussion is the question whether or not athletes should undergo mandatory testing for HIV. Before any policy is enacted, it is necessary to decide who is at potential risk and who is risk free.

In order to clarify issues raised, a clear understanding about the medical facts associated with HIV is critical. Furthermore, the probability of contracting HIV through sporting competition needs to be examined. These facts will provide the basis to combat the myths associated with HIV infection and enable subsequent analysis of moral reasoning about HIV and sport participation. Central to the analysis is the question requiring mandatory testing for HIV of all athletes participating in sports, particularly contact sports.

## Facts about HIV/AIDS

HIV and the resultant acquired immunodeficiency syndrome (AIDS) has become a worldwide problem affecting over 190 nations across the globe. The disease has been termed the "modern plague." Unfortunately, there is neither a vaccine to prevent its occurrence nor a cure once a person is infected with HIV. While in developed nations modern-day treatment with multiple medications (cocktail therapy) has resulted in adding years to the life of those infected with HIV, the condition has a high death rate in developing nations with inadequate resources. Added to this medical issue is the widely prevalent social stigma and phobia associated with HIV, which further complicates the lives of those who are infected and those who care for them.

---

**What is the HIV/AIDS Burden? (Centers for Disease Control and Prevention, 2010)**

*Globally*
- 34 million people are estimated to be living with HIV/AIDS in the world
- 50% of the infected people are women
- 3.4 million of the infected are children
- 1.8 million deaths per year due to AIDS
- 2.7 million newly infected in 2010

*In the United States*
- 1.2 million are infected with HIV/AIDS
- 16% is the largest group, age 20-24
- 14% age 25-29

---

In the United States, the first cases of AIDS, a terminal illness resulting from infection by HIV, were reported in 1981. In 1996, the cumulative number of AIDS cases in the US reported to the Centers for Disease Control and Prevention (CDC) had increased to 513,486 (Philadelphia Department of Health, 1996). Today there are about 1.2 million people infected with HIV and AIDS in the US, and 34 million worldwide (CDC, 2010). Among American college students, it is estimated that one student per 1,000 are presently infected with HIV, with the 20-24 age group seeing the highest percentage of infections in the US (16%). The dilemma that confronts athletes, coaches, trainers, athletic administrators and others involved in sports is the fact that still no vaccine or cure is yet available to prevent or combat HIV infection.

The absence of an effective cure is underscored by the high number of deaths among those diagnosed with AIDS, which worldwide comes to 1.8 million deaths per year (CDC, 2010). While AIDS depicts the terminal stage of HIV disease, it does not indicate the magnitude of the burden of HIV infection in the population.

> The term 'HIV disease' describes all manifestations of infection prior to the development of AIDS, whereas AIDS is the final, fatal stage of HIV infection. The majority of people who are infected with HIV appear healthy, lead normal lives, and are unaware that they are infected. Most authorities believe that all patients who are infected with HIV will eventually develop AIDS and that the HIV infection is ultimately 100% fatal. (Seltzer, 1993, p. 111)

HIV targets the cells of the immune system and destroys the body's ability to fight infections and certain types of cancers. Persons diagnosed with AIDS are particularly susceptible to many organisms that are harmless to persons with strong and intact immune systems. These organisms are known to cause opportunistic infections in those living with AIDS and such infections further damage the already malfunctioning immune system (National Institute of Allergy and Infectious Diseases, 1994).

## Modes of Transmission

While HIV is found in almost all body fluids (such as blood, semen, vaginal and cervical secretions, breast milk, saliva, tears, urine, feces, cerebrospinal fluid, and sweat), transmission is known to readily occur specifically through exchange of blood, semen, or vaginal and cervical secretions (National Institute of Allergy and Infectious Diseases, 1994). The following three modes of transmission account for most cases of HIV infection in the United States: sexual transmission; blood-to-blood transmission; and perinatal transmission (mother to fetus/infant transmission).

## Transmission of HIV in Sports

Often the possibility of HIV transmission in sport settings is raised, especially when the media focus is on a celebrity athlete with HIV infection. An analysis of the wealth of currently available epidemiological data on transmission of HIV clearly indicates the absence of a documented case of HIV transmission occurring within the sport setting (World Health Organization, 2010). Athletes who have been infected with HIV to date have contracted the virus outside the sport setting, mostly as a result of their lifestyles. Yet this issue has raised considerable concerns among athletes, coaches, sports organizations and the general public.

The US Olympic Committee released a detailed report on the transmission of infectious agents during athletic competition. The report reiterated that no case of HIV transmission through sports has ever been documented. The riskiest sports for transmission of HIV and other blood-borne agents are clearly the bloodiest: boxing, wrestling, and tae-kwon-do (McGrew, et al., 1993). Also, other collision sports such as football and ice hockey, and contact sports such as basketball and soccer, provide opportunities for open bleeding wounds to occur with a theoretical possibility of transmission of HIV. It is important to note that though there is a theoretical risk of transmission of HIV in certain sports, no documented case of such transmission has presently occurred thus far.

Nevertheless, several studies have been conducted in the past analyzing the potential theoretical risk that HIV-positive athletes may pose when participating in sports, mainly contact sport. A study in the 1990s conducted by the National Football League (NFL), estimated that the risk of transmitting HIV through football, particularly for the linebacker position, would be estimated as one transmission for 85 million games (Brown, et al., 1994). The current NFL policy does not require bleeding football players to leave the field. Another study, conducted in 1992, of 548 responding National Collegiate Athletic Association institutions (out of 860 surveyed) revealed that 35 (6%) had established policies on the participation of HIV-positive athletes, and 15 others restricted participation in some way. Six of the institutions banned HIV-positive athletes from participating in any sport, while nine banned them only from selected sports such as ice hockey or wrestling (McGrew, et al., 1993). These studies clearly reflect the concerns that the public and people in the sporting world still have, nearly twenty years later, regarding HIV transmission, particularly in contact sports.

## Diagnosis of HIV Infection

An individual may not show any signs and symptoms when initially infected with HIV. A flu-like illness within 4-8 weeks after infection with HIV is noted in some individuals. Signs and symptoms in those individuals are usually non-specific and include fever, malaise, headache, and bilateral lymphadenopathy (enlarged lymph nodes, particularly those in the neck and groin on both sides). These non-specific symptoms and signs are easily mistaken for those of another viral infection and usually disappear within 1-4 weeks of onset. The infected person then enters the asymptomatic period, which may last for several months to several years (estimated to be 10-11 years; Leary, 1993). Though the HIV-infected individual may be symptomless during this phase, the immune system is being damaged by the HIV, which targets and kills the CD4+ T cells (also known as T4 cells), which are the key cells for fighting infections (National Institute of Allergy and Infectious Diseases, 1994).

Over a duration of time (several months to several years), as the immune system continues to be further damaged, a variety of complications occur. Persistent generalized lymphadenopathy, frequent fevers and sweats, weight loss, lack of energy, persistent or frequent yeast infections, recurrent herpes infection (with sores in mouth, genital and anal regions), and shingles are some commonly noted conditions at this stage of HIV disease (National Institute of Allergy and Infectious Diseases, 1994).

The next stage of the disease process leads to occurrence of one or more of the multitude of opportunistic infections (such as Pneumocystis carinii pneumonia) and rare forms of cancer (such as Kaposi's sarcoma). A diagnosis of AIDS, indicating an advanced stage of HIV disease, is based on clinical and laboratory findings, including CD4+ cell counts.

## Testing for HIV Infection

Since an individual infected with HIV in the early stages of the disease may be asymptomatic, the diagnosis is made primarily by testing the individual's blood for the presence of antibodies (proteins produced by the body specific to each infectious agent) to the virus. The antibodies to HIV in blood reach detectable levels in about 1-3 months following infection and at times may take as long as 6 months. The period from the time of contact with HIV to the detection of antibodies to HIV in the blood is known as the "window period." When an individual is in the window period, the HIV antibody test result will be negative, while the person (if truly infected) can continue to transmit the virus to others through practice of risky behaviors. The window period accounts for one of the most common causes for the HIV antibody test result to be falsely negative (National Institute of Allergy and Infectious Diseases, 1994; Valentin, 1992).

Individuals can undergo anonymous testing (where an individual's personal identity is not made known to the testing personnel and test site) or confidential testing (where the individual's personal identity is known to the health care provider). Some NCAA affiliated institutions and state sports organizations (such as the Nevada Boxing Association) have instituted mandatory testing (where an individual has to undergo HIV antibody testing if he or she wishes to participate in sports) as a pre-condition for participation in their institutional sports activities.

The HIV testing process involves submitting one's blood sample to two different types of tests, enzyme-linked immunosorbent assay (ELISA) and western blot. Only when an ELISA test has been repeated (twice with the same sample of blood) and a confirmatory test such as western blot has yielded positive results the individual is considered to be infected with HIV (CDC, 2010).

## Treatment

Since the understanding of the disease process induced by HIV is becoming more and more clear, numerous medications to combat HIV infection and other associated illnesses (such as opportunistic infections) have been developed and made available. Many medications are directed toward the prevention of replication of HIV inside the host CD4+ cell by blocking the action of key enzymes necessary for viral replication. The Food and Drug Administration (FDA) approved medications include reverse transcriptase inhibitors (such as AZT, ddI, ddC, and d4T) and protease inhibitors (such as Saquinavir, Rironavir, Indinavir) (Davey, Goldschmidt and Sande, 1996). While these medications and other supportive measures cannot cure a person with AIDS, they have been documented to increase the median survival time after diagnosis and improve the quality of life for these individuals.

## Prevention

Since no vaccine is yet available for the prevention of infection with HIV, the focus of prevention has been to avoid risky behaviors, such as unprotected sexual intercourse and sharing contaminated needles and syringes, which place an individual at risk of infection. The CDC has outlined a set of guidelines called "Universal Precautions" to reduce the risk of transmission of HIV through exposure to body fluids. Organizations such as the *National Athletic Trainers' Association* have developed guidelines for dealing with blood-borne pathogens for use by their members to reduce the risk of transmission of HIV (National Athletic Trainers Association, 1995).2

However, the question regarding participation of HIV-positive athletes in sports is far from being resolved. For a rational decision making process, one must adhere to basic ethical principles, such as non-maleficence (do no harm, avoid causing harm) and beneficence (prevent harm, promote welfare). These principles will be applied in the following moral reasoning about HIV and sport participation.3 Two lines of reasoning will be presented, one calls for mandatory testing of HIV before and during participation in sports, the other allows for participation of HIV positive athletes with strict adherence to "universal precautions."

## Moral Reasoning

Moral reasoning involves the reflection about what is the right thing to do and why is it correct. It can be defined as a "systematic process of evaluating personal values and developing a consistent and impartial set of moral principles to live by" (Lumpkin, Stoll & Beller, 1994,1). This problem-solving activity involves offering reasons for and against moral beliefs. Any such reflection must be consistent with past and present decisions and must be free of emotional biases.

While morals refers to people's motives, intentions, and actions in dealing with one another, ethics is the study of morality. Ethics studies the underlying issues and questions the values people hold. Moral values are based on universal principles, not on monetary rewards, such as fame, fortune, power, and winning. Universal principles should be true regardless of people's beliefs, cultural backgrounds, and the times in which they live. The "Golden Rule" (do unto others as you would have them done unto you) is a classic example of a universal principle.

The following moral values are universally recognized: justice, fairness, honesty, responsibility, right to privacy, beneficence, and non-maleficence. An ethically sound answer as to whether an HIV-positive athlete should be allowed to participate in sports (practice and competition) should be based on the above-mentioned universally recognized moral principles.

## Mandatory HIV Testing?

As stated above, one of the basic precepts of ethical reasoning is based upon the concept of the greatest good for the greatest number of people. One way to combat the spread of HIV in sports is to require mandatory testing. This argument is prevalent and favored especially by coaches and has several positive points. If it is possible to identify those infected with HIV, it will be easier to take extra precautions to avoid transmission to other participants. On the surface, this statement seems to be legitimate. One can envision a team of trainers and health professionals present at any competition in which the infected athletes compete standing ready with bottles of bleach, rubber gloves, and towels to clean up any bodily fluid that might spill on the playing surface. Furthermore, knowledge of every athlete's HIV infection status will allow for governing bodies of sport to take steps to ban them. Would this lessen the chance of "potential" infection? Possibly, as there is the chance that HIV could be spread through bleeding contact wounds. Does this possibility warrant and justify the mandatory testing of all athletes? As with any ethical discussion, one must decide if the rules that require the testing of all athletes make rational sense. Morally, we need to be made cognizant of the idea that mandatory testing and/or banning athletes are the best actions for the insured safety of the majority of people.

The argument for HIV testing of all athletes participating in contact sports is based on the conviction that every remote chance of HIV spread through blood contact needs to be eliminated. It is assumed that this information would be useful in controlling the spread of HIV, whether this includes preventing the HIV-positive athletes from participation in the sporting competition. Certain branches of the US armed services require testing for all communicable diseases every eight months; federal convicted prisoners are strip-searched and subjected to mandatory testing for HIV; several state boxing commissions require mandatory testing for all professional boxers; then why should athletes participating in contact sport not be tested for HIV? The advocates for testing argue further that an oral test developed to detect HIV, i.e., Epitope, rather than a blood test, makes the HIV testing easier and cost effective (Epitope, Inc., 1995).

What is overlooked in the pro-HIV-testing argument is the potential inaccuracy of these tests with regard to false-positive and false-negative results. A joint position statement by the *American Medical Society for Sports Medicine* and the *American Academy of Sports Medicine* clearly objects to random HIV testing:

> *Massive screening in low-prevalence populations leads to a higher rate of false-positive tests resulting in undue duress, counseling, and complex follow-up evaluation. Most importantly, any testing program, no matter how widespread, is not justifiable precisely because it fails to further diminish the 'too low to qualify' risk of blood-borne pathogen transmission in sport. Other factors, including overwhelming costs, as well as legal and ethical considerations of mandatory testing for populations that may include minors, further suggest that there is no rational basis for supporting blood-borne pathogen test in sports (emphasis added by authors). (American Medical Society for Sports Medicine and the American Academy of Sports Medicine, 1995, 514)*

Mandatory testing is a "cruel punishment" unless there is substantial justification for doing so. Is mandatory testing in the best interest of most people? Although theoretically it would protect competitors from the possible spread of HIV in the sport setting, it would also place an enormous emotional burden on the athlete who tests false-positive.

Although there has been no specific study conducted about the percentage of athletes infected with HIV, one study of 18-24-year-olds conducted in 1990 indicated a 0.08% prevalence of HIV infection (McGrew et al., 1993). That is, of every one thousand athletes tested, approximately 0.8 were infected with HIV. The number "discovered" through a mandatory testing of athletes may be even lower, as those known to be infected may not choose to play sports. However, it can be argued that while dealing with a false-positive reading on an HIV test may be traumatic to the tested athlete, it is certainly beneficial if another person can be prevented from contracting the virus while in athletic competition. This is certainly a valid justification if there is legitimate reason to believe that HIV is spread through contact sport.

Those who promote the testing of all athletes who compete in "bloody" sports would argue from the beneficence point of view. Namely, by identifying the infected athletes human welfare is promoted and further harm is prevented to those who may become infected during the athletic contest end practice session. If there are legitimate reasons to believe that the infected athlete poses a threat to the health and welfare of the non-infected athlete, then under the principles of both non-maleficence and beneficence the HIV-infected athlete must be banned. However, in reality this is not the case. As stated previously, there are no documented cases of HIV transmission through sports yet. "Given the actual nature of contact and blood exposure in sport, the risk of HIV transmission in the athletic setting seems to be infinitely small and below any threshold that we can actually quantify" (McGrew, et al., 1993). If the potential for transmission cannot be measured, how can one justify mandatory testing and subsequently banning athletes? However, there does exist in sport the theoretical possibility for HIV to be transmitted. No authority has said that it cannot or will not ever occur.

One can easily go through the activities of our daily lives that pose infinitely greater health risks than competing against HIV-infected athletes. In the same way that knowledge of infection will limit possible spread, not getting into a car will limit the possibility of dying in a traffic accident. Human beings are constantly required to weigh the potential of harm against the good that may result from a given action and then to take reasonable steps to minimize those risks. For most, the good that comes from using an automobile outweighs the harm of the possible accident. People must take reasonable precautions like wearing seat belts, buying cars with airbags, and completing regular vehicle maintenance to reduce the possibility of accidents and injuries. Likewise, the potential for harm in competing against an HIV-infected athlete is so small that one cannot logically promote the mandatory testing of all athletes. But, unlike the car scenario, mandatory testing athletes for HIV is not a reasonable precaution and subsequent banning from sport, if the HIV test is positive, will cause more harm than good. Several studies have shown that people infected with HIV benefit from exercising and being involved in sport, both at the physical as well as the psychological level (Ciccolo, et al., 2004; Florijn, Voelker and Valley, 1995). Thus, it is of greater benefit to the HIV-positive people/ athletes to continue their participation in sport and not be eliminated due to a positive HIV test result, particularly since the chance of contracting HIV through sport, even contact sports, is very remote, if the proper precautions are adhered to. Hence, educating people in the world of sports about the actual risk of HIV infection as well as following proper guidelines to prevent the spread of HIV should be of major concern, but not mandatory testing. Although it is possible that there may occur a documented transmission of HIV through sport in the near future, given the facts currently available, mandatory testing of athletes for HIV stirs up an irrational fear of a falsely existing danger of HIV transmission through sport.

## Conclusion

The risk of transmission of HIV in the sport setting is extremely low if there is proper education and compliance with the universal precautions and clean-up procedures. McGrew, et al., (1993) surveyed NCAA institutions and found considerable laxity in the practice of universal precautions by sport personnel. Lack of regular education programs and posted infection control policy were also cited as ongoing problems. Twenty years later, this issue is not of as great concern among the general public any more, although the health risks today still stay the same.

Obviously, most sports governing bodies in the US are being overly cautious when it comes to prevention: risk reduction through exclusion of the injured athlete. It can be concluded that their policies of risk reduction outweigh the individual athlete's right to participation in a sporting event. Furthermore, one must be aware that the rational decision-making process may be clouded by personal biases. Homophobic attitudes and fear of contagion, despite minimal risk, may override rational moral reasoning. By disclosing the status of the HIV athlete, professionals in the exercise, sport and health arena may not be certain if they are preventing further harm, removing the threat of harm or actually causing harm. What becomes the greater good: exercising confidence or protecting others who feel that they have a right to know about all possible risks involved in athletic participation? There will be a great deal of pressure from parents and others involved to be warned about potential dangers; however, the principles of autonomy and informed consent are equally strong legal and moral restraints to publicize the HIV status of athletes.

Based on the absence of documented HIV transmission and the very low probability of transmission in the sport settings, the *World Health Organization* and the *World Federation of Sports Medicine* have recommended the position that there is no reason to deny participation in sport to the HIV-positive athletes (World Health Organization, 2010). This position has also been adopted by other sport organizations such as the NCAA and the NFL in the mid 1990s.

If the decision is to allow all athletes to participate regardless of their HIV status, the policy pertaining to testing of athletes is irrelevant. However, if the decision is that the HIV-positive athlete should be denied participation in sport, as it is with competitive boxing (in several states), this raises a whole set of questions regarding mandatory testing of all athletes and potential problems with HIV tests including accuracy and costs. It has been established that adapting universal precautions in dealing with body fluids greatly minimizes the risk of HIV transmission. Based on these reasons, the need for mandatory testing of all athletes for possible HIV infection is unfounded and not recommended.

The "Joint Position Statement" by the *American Medical Society for Sports Medicine* and the *American Academy of Sports Medicine* (1995) clearly states that infection with HIV alone is insufficient grounds to prevent participation of the HIV-positive athlete. The *National Athletic Trainers' Association* policies and "Code of Ethics" from 1995 already stated explicitly that it is unethical to discriminate on the basis of medical conditions, including infection with HIV. Hence, when health and sport professionals are asked to develop policies to protect athletes from contracting HIV through sports, it is imperative that they base their decision on moral reasoning and facts rather than fiction.

While the risk of transmission of HIV in sports in minimal, it is necessary to educate all athletes (professionals and amateurs) about risk reduction and risk elimination in non-sports settings where all of the infections currently occur. This calls for a focused, well-coordinated, sustained action on the part of the athletes, policy makers, athletic organizations, institutions of higher learning, coaches, athletic trainers, and others associated with sport.

## References

American Academy of Pediatrics (1992). American Academy of Pediatrics Policy Statement: Human Immunodeficiency Virus Acquired Immunodeficiency Syndrome (AIDS) in the Athletic Setting. *The Physician and Sports Medicine, 20* (5),189-191.

American Medical Society for Sports Medicine and American Academy of Sports Medicine (1995). Human Immunodeficiency Virus (HIV) and Other Blood-Borne Pathogens in Sports – Joint Position Statement by the American Medical Society for Sports Medicine (AMSSM) and the American Academy of Sports Medicine (AASM). *The American Journal of Sports Medicine, 23,* 510-514.

Brown L.S, Phillips, R.Y, Brown, C.L., Knowlan C., Castle L., & Mover J. (1994). HIV/AIDS Policies and Sports: The National Football League. *Medicine and Science in Sports And Exercise, 26,* 403-407.

Calabrese L.H., Haupt H., Hartman L. & Strauss R. (1993). HIV and Sports – What is the risk? *The Physician and Sports Medicine, 21* (6), 173-180.

Centers for Disease Control (1994). HIV Counseling, Testing and Referral: Standards and Guidelines. Atlanta, GA: US Department of Health and Human Services, Public Health Service.

Centers for Disease Control and Prevention (2010). CDC Revises HIV Infection Estimates. HIV/AIDS Prevention. www.avert.org/worldstats.

Ciccolo, J., Jowers, E. & Bartholomew, J. (2004). The Benefits of Exercise Training for Quality of Life in HIV/AIDS in the Post-HAART Era. *Sports Medicine, 34*(8), 487-499.

Davey, R. T., Goldschmidt, R. H., & Sande , M. A. (1996). Anti-HIV Therapy in 1996. *Patient Care, 55-72.*

Epitope, Inc. (1995). *OraSure HIV-1: Oral Specimen Collection Device.* Beaverton, OR: Epitope.

Florijn Y., Voelker K., Valley E. (1995). Sport und HIV Infektion. In Bundesministerium für Gesundheit, *Sport und HIV-Infektion Handbuch.* (pp. 123-175). Baden-Baden, Germany: Nomos.

Legg., J.J. & Minkoff., H. S. (1996). Vertical Transmission: Now Preventable. *Patient Care,* 160-163

Levy, J.A. (1993). The Transmission of HIV and Factors Influencing Progression to AIDS. *The American Journal of Medicine, 95* (7), 86 -100.

McGrew, C., Dick, R., Schneidwind, K. & Gikas, P. (1993). Survey of NCAA Institutions Concerning HIV/AIDS Policies and Universal Precaution. *Medicine and Science in Sports and Exercise, 25,* 917-921.

National Athletic Trainers Association (1995). Blood-borne Pathogens Guidelines for Athletic Trainers. *Journal of Athletic Training, 30,* 203-204

National Institute of Allergy and Infectious Diseases (1994). HIV Infection and AIDS. Bethesda, MD: US Department of Health and Human Services, Public Health Service December, p.2. Philadelphia Department of Health (1996). AIDS Surveillance Quarterly Update: Cases Reported Through June 30, 1996. Philadelphia: PDH, AIDS Coordinating Office. Seltzer, D. (1993). Educating Athletes on HIV Disease and AIDS. *The Physician and Sportmedicine., 21* (1), 109-115.

Sankaran, G.; Volkwein, K. & D. Bonsall (Eds.) (1999). *HIV/AIDS and Sport: Issues, Impact, and Challenges.* Champaign, IL: Human Kinetics.

World Health Organization, in Collaboration with the International Federation of Sports Medicine (2010). *Consensus Statement from Consultation on AIDS and Sports.* Geneva, Switzerland: WHO.

## CHAPTER 5:

# YOUTH INVOLVEMENT IN SPORT – FITNESS – PHYSICAL ACTIVITY

### International Position Statement on Physical Education

- *Physical education develops physical competence so that children can move efficiently, effectively and safely and understand what they are doing. The outcome, physical literacy, is an essential basis for their full development and achievement.*

- *Physical education in school is the most effective and inclusive means of providing all children, whatever their ability/disability, sex, age, cultural, race/ethnicity, religious or social background, with the skills, attitudes, values, knowledge and understanding for lifelong participation in physical activity and sport.*

- *[Physical education] is the only school subject whose primary focus is on the body, physical activity, physical development and health; and helps children to develop the patterns of and interest in physical activity, which are essential for healthy development and which lay the foundations for adult healthy lifestyles.*

- *[Involvement in physical education, sport, and fitness] contributes to children's confidence and self-esteem; enhances social development by preparing children to cope with competition, winning and losing; and cooperation and collaboration. It is increasingly being used as a tool in development, including recovery from trauma and conflict, and encouragement for school attendance and retention. (ICSSPE, 2010)*

- *More people participate in sport during their youth than at any other time in their lives. Although for many young boys and girls sport involvement is limited to informal neighborhood play, an increasing number of North American youth participate in highly organized athletic competitions. Indeed, youth sports are now a $5 billion industry. (Sage & Eitzen 2012)*

- *By encouraging regular physical activity, you can help your child develop healthy lifestyle habits that will last into adulthood. ... To encourage regular physical activity among young children and foster long-lasting positive change, the U.S. Department of Health and Human Services' Centers for Disease Control and Prevention (CDC) created the VERB campaign to encourage youth to be physically active. The VERB Play Without Borders campaign encourages your child to try different kinds of play form around the world. ... The website 60play.com provides you with ideas for the entire family to get active, and find local places to pursue physical activities. (CDC, 2004)*

There is no doubt that children need to be physically active on a daily basis. It is an important regulator of the development process for physical, social, emotional and moral learning, as well as promoting health and fitness. Children also learn about rules and equal treatment of others, which will help them in later life. High self-esteem helps in making positive decisions, both morally and realistically. In addition, physical activity is very important for brain development. The question is how much and what kind of physical activity, sport and fitness is good for them? The vast array of offerings in the sport and fitness industry and declining mandated physical education programs leave parents with mixed messages and sometimes confusion regarding what to choose for their children. What is the role of the parents or better what should their role be? Research has shown that 85% of parents put too much pressure on winning; 9% of parents never even encourage their children to participate in sports; and 85% of parents criticize the individuals running youth sport programs (National Council of Youth Sport, 2010).

Children partake in sports and physical activity mainly to have fun, do something they are good at, stay in shape, and play as part of a team. Although the parents play a critical role in their children's participation in sports and physical activity (they are the ones to sign the kids up or motivate them to be involved), they could also be the biggest negative influence in their children's sporting involvement by overemphasizing winning, having unrealistic expectations, coaching their own child, and pampering the child too much.

Millions of kids around the globe – from preschoolers to teens – are climbing into uniforms every year, following coach's orders, sweating to win. Is all this organized and supervised activity good? Families' attitudes show that there are benefits – it is fun, and it teaches confidence and fitness. On the other hand, parents and their children are not blind to shortcomings such as sleepless nights, high pressure to win and injuries. In addition, studies conducted by the President's Council on Physical Fitness attest that fitness among youth is not improving and, in some important areas, is declining. This dilemma, which crosses national borders, culminates in the consensus that while sports programs produce some superbly conditioned youngsters, many more are unfit. A new school of thought says sport and fitness are not necessarily the same thing and that more time should be spent educating children about fitness and physical activity rather than competitive sports.

In this chapter, three critical issues related to children's involvement in sport and physical activity are analyzed. First, the social and moral development through sport and physical activity will be spelled out, stressing all major benefits for children being physically active throughout their childhood and later life. Second, the increasing problems associated with an overemphasis of competitive sports – nationally and internationally – will be described, stressing possible solutions to making the children's involvement a positive and satisfying one. And third, the national decline of physical education programs offered in North American schools is analyzed with its detrimental consequences for the future of our children and a call for change.

## Issue 1

## Social and Moral Development through Sport and Physical Activity

The development of social and moral behaviors starts in early childhood and manifests itself throughout people's youth. Physical play is a very important part of growing up and "serves as a strong regulator of the developmental process" (Ewing, 2003). Physical play can be chasing games, rough housing, wrestling, or practicing all kinds of physical skills, such as jumping, throwing, catching and striking. These activities teach young children important lessons in how to interact with other people, whether young or old, boys or girls. Unfortunately, fathers are still much more engaged in physical play with their boys than with their daughters, unless the fathers have only girls. If the latter is the case, these fathers often see the need to get the girls involved as well. And often they become the strongest proponents of girls' involvement in physical activity and sports throughout the girls' upbringing. Mothers are often in charge of getting the girls physically involved, and they will do much more of that if they have experienced the benefits of the involvement in sports and physical activity at a young age themselves.

Physical play during infancy and early childhood is central to the development of social, emotional, and moral competence. Researchers have found that "children who engage in more play with their parents, particularly with parents who are sensitive and responsive to the child, exhibit greater enjoyment during the play sessions and were more popular with their peers" (MacDonald, 1988). Children learn early on to become more aware of their own emotions and learn to monitor and regulate their own emotional responses. They watch their parents' behaviors, their smiles and laughs or frowns and disengagements of the activities, and they will copy such behaviors. If children want the fun to continue, they will engage in the behaviors that please the other so that play continues. They also learn that there are limits to rough play, when someone is hurt, whether that is physically or emotionally, which results in the termination of the activity. Through these early activities with parents and peers, children learn appropriate behavior in the social situations of sport and physical activity (Ewing, 2003).

Later on in sport, children learn to assess their social competence, for example the ability to get along with others, through the feedback they get from their parents and coaches. At the beginning they hear only a "no" – that is not acceptable behavior. As they get older and more inquisitive, they want to know "why," and they will know what behaviors are appropriate in certain situations and which ones are not. Children will learn that rules and regulations are important to follow so that a game can take place and that everyone gets fair and equal treatment. They learn about taking turns with their teammates, sharing playing time, and valuing rules. "The learning of social competence continues as we expand our social arena and learn about different cultures" (Ewing, 2003, 1). Other cultures might stress different rules and values. If and when we expand ourselves, adaptations to different situations in life are a constant in the social learning process.

Sport participation can further help children to develop self-esteem. This is a very important social competence, as it provides the prerequisites to judge oneself, one's self-worth and one's abilities to be capable, significant, successful, and worthy (Coopersmith, 1067). It has been suggested that one of the biggest barriers to one's success in the classroom, as well as later on in life, is low self-esteem. And today too many children come to school and sport teams with low self-esteem. However, sports, if introduced the right way, can greatly help to develop this important competency early in life. The importance of enhanced self-esteem cannot be overlooked, and it can be fostered through the pride and joy children experience as their physical skills improve. As long as their skills are improving, children will feel good about themselves. However, when they are not doing as well as their parents or coaches expect them to, they feel shame and disappointment. Here it is critical that the adults provide supportive feedback, interpreting the failure to the child. "Children need to be taught that a mistake is not synonymous with failure. Rather a mistake means a new strategy, more practice, and/or greater effort is needed to succeed at the task" (Ewing, 2003, 2).

However, the role of positive feedback is not as simple as avoiding negative responses. Coaches and parents have to learn that it is pertinent to the young person to know specifically what part of the action or performance was not correct and specific ways how to improve it. It is simply not enough to say "good job" as positive feedback; what is needed is a detailed description, such as "good job in using both of your hands at the same time catching that ball." And if a movement needs improvement, what was lacking and how to change it also has to be spelled out exactly. Thus, the quality of feedback is critical to the children's development of self-esteem and perceptions of competence. Rather than the quantity of feedback, the instructional content needs to be stressed in helping the children to develop skills and perceived physical as well as social competence.

Research has shown a significant relationship between physical competence, interpersonal skills, and peer acceptance (Weiss & Duncan, 1992). Boys and girls who believed that they were physically competent in sport were rated as having higher physical competence by their teachers, were more popular with their peers, and were competent in social relationships. Furthermore, a study published in the journal Neuroscience (2003) confirms that exercise increases the chemical BDNF (brain-derived neurotrophic factor) in the brain that controls learning and memory. Thus, exercise also supports the development of the brain in storing and retrieving information. The stereotype of the "dumb jock" is therefore finally defeated.

Furthermore, the development of high self-esteem is critical to help youth buffer the many negative influences experienced in society today. The Women's Sport Foundation (1999) has released research showing that girls who have high self-esteem are less likely to become pregnant as teenagers and are more likely to leave an abusive relationship than girls with low self-esteem. When teenagers evaluate themselves in a positive way, they are more capable of saying "no" to drugs and gangs. High self-esteem will not guarantee that youth will make the right decisions, but it does provide a stronger basis for resisting the pressures currently existing in society.

In addition to developing a positive sense of self, involvement in sport activities can assist children in learning what is right from wrong, which is commonly referred to as moral development. For example, the moral concept of fairness lies at the heart of every sport. For youth to learn about fair play, sport activities must be designed to facilitate cooperation rather than just competition. One of the best ways to teach children about fair play is through teaching the rules of the games and abiding by the rules during competition. Furthermore, time and positions must also be shared during the early learning periods. If fair play is to be taught and learned, it is the responsibility of all those associated with the sport experience to help athletes learn and appreciate the concept of fair play (Ewing, 1997).

Parents, coaches, and officials will undermine the learning process of the concept of fair play if they are not consistent in their teaching and personal conduct. Most coaches and parents espouse the virtue of fair play until they perceive that the opponent is gaining an advantage or winning unfairly. "Parents may even chastise the coach who abides by the rules and does not win, which sends a mixed message to youth about the importance of fair play. Journalists and broadcasters have fallen into the same trap of believing that the only worthy performance was that given by the winning team regardless of whether they abide by the rules or not" (Ewing, 1997). Parents and coaches must help youth interpret the appropriateness of these behaviors in light of what is right and wrong.

In sum, children who are exposed to regular physical activities early in life will benefit in several important ways throughout their lives. In addition to becoming physically fit, and thus, preventing many negative health consequences that are due to inactivity and a sedentary lifestyle, children will also learn stress management, increased self-esteem, positive social interaction, and improved mental well-being. Educational institutions are fundamental starting points for changing the future physical activity patterns in our culture. All schools should deliver comprehensive programs that promote physical activity. Physical education curricula should provide experiences that are enjoyable, offer significant amounts of physical activity, and promote lifelong participation in physical activity (Pate, et al., 1995). Furthermore, adherence to physical activity has been shown to relate directly to convenience or participation (Foreyt & Goodrick, 1995). Thus, we must make participation in physical activity convenient for and accessible to everyone in society. "Being physically educated involves the joy and exhilaration of moving well, and experiencing the fun and freedom of any movement, even if not done well. It involves feeling whole, able, and competent as a person" (NASPE, 1999).

## References

Centers for Disease Control and Prevention (2004). VERB Play without Borders. www.verb.com

Ewing, M. (1997). Promoting Social and Moral Development Through Sports. Retrieved on-line October, 2003: http://ed-web3educ.msu.edu/ysi.

Foreyt, J. & Goodrick, G. (1995). Living Without Dieting: Motivating the Obese to Exercise and Eat Prudently. *Quest, 47*, 263-273.

NASPE (National Association for Sport and Physical Education) (1999). *Sport and Physical Education Advisory Kit II*. Reston, Virginia: NASPE Publication.

Neuroscience (2003). The Journal of the International Brain Research Organization, retrieved at: www.eurekalert.org/pub _releases/2003-09/ohs-cn092603.php

Pate, R., Pratt, M., Blair, S., Haskell, L., et al. (1995). Physical Activity and Public Health: A Recommendation from the Centers for Disease Control and Prevention and the American College of Sports Medicine. *The Journal of the American Medical Association, 273* (5), 402-407.

Sage, G. & Eitzen, S. (2013). *Sociology of North American Sport*. New York/ Oxford: Oxford University Press.

Women's Sport Foundation (1999). www.womenssportfoundation.org.

## Issue 2

# Kids, Sport and Peril – An International Dilemma

More people participate in sport during their youth (until 18 years) than at any other time of their life (Eitzen & Sage, 1993, 71). While many children's sport experiences are limited to informal neighborhood play and physical education taught in schools, an increasing number of youth participate in highly organized athletic competition. Organized youth sport programs developed after World War II in North America and Europe. Young boys were provided with organized sport activities with the aim of becoming strong, assertive, competitive men. During the '50s and '60s, these sport programs increased rapidly. Most programs were for boys between 8 and 14 years of age. Until the 1970s, girls' interest in sport was widely ignored in most countries. As a result of the women's and fitness movements, government legislation prohibited gender discrimination. The Educational Amendments Act in the United States introduced "Title IX"1 in 1972, which prohibits gender discrimination in any educational institution receiving federal funds; and the prohibition applies to sport. Today we have almost as many sport programs for girls as for boys; however, this does not mean that there are equal opportunities for girls in every instance when it comes to sport. Major shortcomings compared to the male support in sport include time and places of training, scheduled competitive events, travel support, media and newspaper coverage (see also Chapter 7).

Involvement in youth sport programs is widely encouraged by society and parents. Advocates of youth sport programs claim that they provide self-discipline, cooperation, achievement motivation, courage, persistence, and more (Eitzen & Sage, 73). According to a "Miller Lite Report on American Attitudes towards Sports," only 9% of the parents in the survey said they have never encouraged their children to participate in sports; however, 85% of the general public in the United States criticized how youth sport programs were run (p. 59). The criticism given was that too much emphasis is placed on winning and not enough on the physical and psychological development of the participants. In this analysis, I will first look at both sides of this controversial issue, the positive and negative aspects of organized youth sport programs; and secondly, I will suggest some changes in order to meet the needs of the children, which are to have fun and to gain fitness.

## Objectives and Controversies of Organized Youth Sport Programs

The positive and negative effects of youth sport programs on children are manifold and have been widely discussed in European and American scholarship. The benefits for children engaging in youth sport programs are usually ascribed to a positive development of social, physical, and psychological traits. Proponents of these programs also argue that children are given the opportunity to have fun and learn values that are important in society. The following positive arguments are presented in the literature.

### Objectives

1. Sport benefits children socially because it provides an opportunity for social interaction outside of the classroom (Boklund & Bjorklund, 1988, 197). It is an excellent way for children to make friends. Participation in organized sport programs provides children with the feeling that they are part of a group. Also, a sense of unity can be gained when the team wins and when it loses.

2. The physical benefits of practicing sport are the most obvious. It is known that on the average, young athletes grow and mature in a similar manner to non-athletes; however, there is variation in size, physique, body composition, and in maturity status associated with specific sports. Malina (1988) and others have already shown in the 1980s that a certain amount of physical activity is necessary to support normal structural growth. Those same reports have also found that exercise can increase bone width and mineralization while inactivity can decrease mineralization (Malina, 1988, 121ff). The specific benefits to children are hard to determine. It has been discovered that regular training results in an increase in lean body weight and a decrease in body fat, but what is due to exercise and what is due to natural growth is hard to specify. Involvement in organized sport programs promotes physical fitness and exercise for children, which is beneficial at a young age, and actually any age. Such activities during youth might lead to lifelong participation in sports (Boklund & Bjorklund, 1988, 197). And if one gets involved in physical activity during childhood, one is much more likely to engage in physical activity throughout life.

3. Sport also gives children the opportunity to improve and master physical skills (Trunzo, 1989, 226). It is the mastery of these skills that leads to psychological benefits for children. As children improve in physical skills, they develop confidence and pride in their abilities. Sports give children the opportunity to succeed, not by winning, but by gaining a personal sense of accomplishment. "For young children, the mere act of swimming a lap without stopping ... is enough reward. In general, they couldn't care less if their pace is less than Olympian" (Trunzo, p. 226).

4. The most important benefit ascribed to youth sport programs is the opportunity for kids to have fun. Kids basically like sports and enjoy being

involved in them. Sport enjoyment is defined as "a positive emotional response to one's sport experience that reflects feelings and/or perceptions such as pleasure, liking, and perceived fun" (Scanlan & Lewthwaite, 1988, 45). Enjoyment, though a critical aspect of the youth sport experience, is a relatively new concept or construct that has not received much research attention yet. Having fun is not the only key element in informal sports. Scanlon & Lethwaite observed a direct correlation between children's enjoyment in sport and a positive social evaluation and recognition for children's achievements by adults, regardless of the outcome of the performance (p. 46).

5. And lastly, proponents of organized youth sport programs argue that they teach children important societal values that are vital to their growth process (Beuter, 1972). Through team sports especially, children can learn that cooperation and teamwork are necessary to achieve a common goal. Understanding the concept of winning and losing is another important lesson, which can be taught through sports. The values that are taught through sport can be summarized in what the successful American football coach Vince Lombardi espoused:

> *He was a good coach because he was successful; he accumulated a lot of goods for the players who were fortunate enough to be part of his ... family. He relied on individual hard work and discipline, and instilled in his men the consciousness that they were better and must achieve according to their elite status. His manner was hard and puritanical: he drove his men to their limits, promising them 'success' in return. (Beuter, 1972, 389)*

This statement reflects how the legendary Vince Lombardi used sport to instill the values of the North American society in his men, which are: family, hard work, discipline, achievement, competition, and success – not necessarily in this order. However, it needs to be pointed out here that in other cultures, sport reflects different values.

Besides the above-mentioned apparent positive aspects attributed to sport, many scholars have pointed out the detrimental effects that involvement in organized youth sport programs will bring about for children. Critics have argued that winning is emphasized over having fun, parents and coaches expect too much from the children, and the programs can negatively affect parent-child relationships. In addition, organized youth sport programs are too stressful, physiologically as well as physically, and create the potential for dropping out from sports altogether. "It negatively affects parent-child relationships. In addition, organized youth sport programs are too stressful, physiologically as well as physically, and create the potential for dropping out from sports altogether. It is occasionally reported that children's competitive sport programs are organized, legitimized forms of child abuse, where youth are berated, humiliated, and exerted by adults to win at all costs" (Martens, 1988, 235). How are these children affected by the advancement of an adult conditioned, planned, and organized sport program during their childhood? Experts have given the following answers.

### Controversies

1. Children would never think of their own accord of subjecting themselves to organized forms of sport aimed for long-term performance. For children, having fun and being involved in the activity comes absolutely first. Most children involved in sports would rather play on a losing team than sit on the bench of a winning one; they are oblivious of competition. But because youth sport programs are deliberately set up by adults to emphasize winning and performance, children soon realize this and develop competitive attitudes. They become more concerned about playing well and winning than they do about fairness and fun; that is, they are responding to the pressures imposed onto them by parents and coaches (Coakley, 2004).

2. Because organized youth sport programs are adult controlled, these sports tend to be more serious than informal games, which are controlled by the children themselves. Organized youth sports are rule-centered with "the action, the personal involvement, and the behavior of the players being regulated by rules, which are strictly enforced by adults" and thereby restrict the individual freedom and creativity of the children (Coakley, 2004). Playing time in organized sports is also controlled by adults, and because they emphasize the outcome of the game over the process, the children with greater skills will receive more playing time. This leaves the less-skilled players, those in need of more practice, sitting on the bench. Coakley points out that the adult control of organized sport programs restricts the friendship and affection usually displayed in informal games (p. 140). The most frequent mistake made by adults is to think that children's teams are miniature versions of adult or even professional teams. They often do not realize that playing team sports requires an understanding of the meaning of strategy, which is beyond the cognitive abilities of most children under the age of twelve. This is frustrating for both adults and children because the adults wonder why the children are not performing as they have been taught and the children are trying to do their best to please their parents and coaches rather than just having fun.

3. High expectations can also lead to increased pressure from the parents and coaches onto the children, which directly affects the parent-child, as well as the coach-child relationships. When parents become too emotionally

involved, it overwhelms and causes anxiety for the children. "Overzealous parents cause a program to lose its child orientation. The activity becomes a spectator sport for adults" (Trunzo, 1989, 228). Sometimes parents even push their children into certain sports, which the children do not necessarily enjoy and would have not picked by free choice. Some children come to believe that their relationship with their parents depends on their sport involvement and performance because they only get positive feedback when they win. "If parents are not careful about the content of these unspoken messages, they can lead their children to think that being an athlete is a prerequisite to continued parental interest and concern" (Coakley, 2004, 99). A revelation of a student in my sport sociology class exemplifies this perfectly:

> I remember when I was in eighth grade, I wanted to make the basketball team because I thought it would make my dad talk to me more. I knew he "liked" my brother for his baseball and my sister for her track and basketball. I thought I had to be in a sport for him to notice me, too. (Undergraduate student, West Chester University of Pennsylvania, 2001)

Frustration in children is caused by the child trying too hard to please others, especially the parents. Adult intrusion robs the youngsters of the greatest potential of sport: the opportunity to have fun, to develop self-discipline and responsibility for their own actions.

4. Organized youth sport programs have been accused of being too stressful for children. Highly anxious children in sports have been identified as chewing their nails, displaying jitters, having staccato speech, and possessing tense facial expressions (Martens, 1988, 239). Children engaged in individual sports seem to be more anxious than those involved in team sports. It depends on the children and the sport as well as the individual situations within the sports as to whether or not the children are stressed. Causes of competitive anxiety are found in the uncertainty about the outcome of the competition and the importance attached to these outcomes. "Some coaches seem to be more skilled at making their athletes feel uncertain than they are in teaching the techniques of sport" (Martens, p. 241). Parents and coaches may also make the children feel uncertain about their social status or the importance on the team, and they forget why the children are participating in sport in the first place. It has been shown that children who have fun during their game or match, regardless of whether they win or lose, are less stressed after the contest than children who experience less fun (Scanlan & Lewthwaite, 1988, 45). Overemphasis of winning often leads to repeated perceived failure by the young athletes. They need to be taught how to set performance goals, or goals that they can control such as distance, speed, and accuracy. This can lessen competitive anxiety (Martens, p. 243).

Children handle stress very differently. Often situations occur where realistically very little additional stress, if any, is placed on the child, yet that child has been shown to be under a great deal of stress. It is not necessarily the stress being placed on the athlete but the way the athlete perceives things to be. Many children will get themselves so worked up, with help from a coach and/or parent, that if by any small fraction they do not achieve their goal, a great depression and more stress befalls them. Depression at a young age can lead to great confusion. A young athlete is defenseless against the influences of coaches and parents. After all, those are the people who have gotten the child where he/she is now and often these children's main goal has switched from that of self-gratification to pleasing others.

5. Another major drawback of competitive athletics for children is the number of injuries occurring mainly during training. "These include sprained ankles, twisted knees, fractured wrists, or a whole variety of similar types of injury" (Micheli, 1988, 280). Whether there is a greater or lesser chance of this occurring in sport situations as opposed to free play situations is very difficult to compare. However, a second type of injuries, the so-called overuse injuries, are clearly the result of repetitive training and, in the case of the injured child, the repetitive microtrauma to tissues of the extremities overstressed by training (Micheli, p. 281). These injuries do not occur in the free play situations. Children can sustain many of the same injuries as adult athletes, but they appear to have a special risk because they are still growing. This concern has resulted in an ongoing debate as to whether growing children should safely participate in contact or collision sport.

6. Organized youth sport programs also have the potential to create dropouts from sport altogether if the children are subjected to too many negative experiences. This will happen when programs ignore issues related to individual development among young people; when there is too much pressure to win, too little time to have fun and too much emphasis on training and winning (Eitzen & Sage, 1993, 80). Programs that emphasize competition and outcome over the concerns of having fun, learning skills and individual improvement are the ones that usually create these negative experiences. If the children do not feel that they are capable of doing what the coaches and parents expect and are not positively encouraged, they will quit. "Enjoyment or fun has been identified by children as a major reason for their sport participation, whereas the lack of enjoyment has been associated with children's decisions to drop out of organized sport" (Scanlan & Lewthwaite, 1988, 45). Burnout is a term that is especially applied to elite child athletes who are very successful in sport but drop out nevertheless. Children who suffer from burnout syndrome on the average have been competing for a long time and are so pressured to do well that they become bored and lose motivation

(Coakley, 2004). The burnout syndrome is more severe than dropping out simply because children who are burned out often quit sports altogether, while dropouts seem to shift to other sports, which can be interpreted as a normal trial-error sampling procedure (Burton, 1988, 245).

Other problems associated with mainly competitive sports include increased violent behaviors on and off the playing fields, especially in contact sports such as ice hockey or football. Another problem is the increased drug-use and abuse found not only in society in general but in so-called fitness activities (weight training) and sports as well. The performance-enhancing drugs frequently used among teenagers are mainly steroids (Coakley, 2004). It has been reported that 1 out of 19 high school boys take steroids trying to get bigger. These are not only the athletes, but any boy who is trying to achieve the current body ideal favored by North American society, which for men is being big and bulky/muscular.

Generally, the major criticism regarding top-level sports, which includes certain organized youth sport programs, is that they are not primarily of educational nature (see Grupe, 1988). Grupe posits that the interest lies in the self-preservation of the social system and the constant improvement of athletic achievement along with cultural, political and ideological motives. Thus, at the end of the 1980s, Grupe already noted that "children must be protected from attention-seeking parents, ambitious coaches, egotistic officials and the pressure of public expectations" (1988, 232). This has become even more urgent for today's society. We have to do away with those organized sport programs that do not allow children to be children and infringe upon their rights to being children. That does not mean that we have to eliminate organized sport programs altogether, but there is an outcry for reform. Since children obviously benefit from involvement in sport, more than they would if they were not active at all, organized sport programs for children need to focus on the educational values of sport and the individual needs of children emphasizing fun and fitness. Children can obtain numerous positive effects can be obtained through organized sport programs if they are properly organized and adapted to suit the child.

## Suggestion for Reforming Organized Youth Sport Programs

Many suggestions and proposals for reform can be found in the literature dealing with children's involvement in organized sport programs (Coakley, 2004; Martens, 1988; Burton, 1988; Eitzen & Sage, 1993; Grupe, 1988; Telama, 1988; and more). The major quest concerns changes in order to meet the needs of the children rather than those of the adults. Thus, the perceived ability of all performers needs to be evaluated in order to help children to experience consistent personal success. This proposal calls for an adjustment of the goals of youth sport programs, an adoption of new strategies and an increased effort by the administration, coaches, and parents. At its heart lies a learning experience about sport and fitness and the prevention of dropping out of sports altogether.

1. An athlete-centered philosophy must be developed wherein the personal growth of the athlete is more important than winning (Burton, 1988, 253). Such an approach will help all participants to become successful and develop positive feelings of self-worth. Parents and coaches need to be educated that the main objective of the children's involvement in sport is to reinforce this positive "competitive philosophy."

2. Rules need to be modified. Traditionally, structured organized sport lacks action and scoring. Thus, rules should be modified according to the rules children employ in informal games. Informal games foster fun and excitement through extensive action, close scores, and a high degree of personal involvement of all participants. This can be achieved by implementing handicap systems, "do overs," position rotation, altering the number of players on the field, and more. Numerous opportunities to affirm friendship with teammates and opponents are also given during informal games. There are many more opportunities provided for low-ability participants to meet their abilities and the uncertainty of the outcome when scores are close, which makes competition more fun and exciting for performers at all ability levels. Any strategy that fosters higher personal involvement increases the excitement and enjoyment, as well as the performers' perceived ability (Burton, 1988; Coakley, 2004; Sage & Eitzen, 2013).

3. An effective coaching education program needs to be implemented nationwide, which helps coaches to adapt an athlete-centered coaching philosophy that meets the needs of all children regardless of skill level (see Martens' *American Coaching Effectiveness Program*, 1988; check also website of *The Institute for the Study of Youth Sports*, 2012). Performance goals should be set for all participants that emphasize success as "surpassing personal performance standards rather than exceeding the performance standards of others" (Burton, 1988, 260). This performance approach should be used in the correction of skills, as well as the rewarding of goal achievements. Athletes should also have input in team selection, training, and strategies used in competition.

4. Parents and coaches need to show support even when children are losing or performing poorly. No pressure should be put on the children to perform well. Parents also need to limit their personal involvement so that children do not believe that their participation in sport is most important in their relationship with their parents.

5. Early specialization in only one sport should be prohibited in order to avoid over-use injuries. It is not necessary for children to start training for one particular sport very early. It is sufficient that they are engaged in sport within a framework that allows them to gain the positive experiences discussed earlier and insights of competition in general in order to learn to handle success and defeat. Concentration on one sport should not keep the child from enjoying a variety of play and movement experiences.

6. Organized sport programs must be geared toward the total development of the child: physical education, growth, and health. Fun and enjoyment in sport must be maintained. Achievement and records are not the ultimate meaning of sport; it is the enrichment that sport can offer, fulfillment of life, and self-perfection that accompanies high achievement (Grupe, 1988, 231).

In sum, organized youth sport programs are worth the effort, if they benefit the children; that is, if they provide opportunities to develop physical, social and communicative skills, self-confidence, friendship, fun and enjoyment, as well as fitness. In general, involvement in competitive sports can be a very positive influence on a child's development. A healthy physical development goes hand in hand with a well-rounded education. Too much pressure from parents and coaches needs to be eliminated through the proposed changes. After all, children have some rights as well, and they include fun and enjoyment of physical activity as well as acting like children rather than miniature adults. Thus, several years ago, the Bill of Rights for Young Athletes was established, which stressed the children's needs over those of overzealous parents and coaches.

---

**Bill of Rights For Young Athletes** (see *The Institute for the Study of Youth Sport*)

1. Right to participate in sports.
2. Right to participate at a level commensurate with each child's maturity and ability.
3. Right to have qualified adult leadership.
4. Right to play as a child and not as an adult.
5. Right of children to share in the leadership and decision-making of their sport participation.
6. Right to participate in safe and healthy environments.
7. Right to proper preparation for participation in sports.
8. Right to an equal opportunity to strive for success.
9. Right to be treated with dignity.
10. Right to have fun in sports.

---

Children's interests must come first. If the above changes were to come about, more children would participate in sports, the dropout rate would lower and participation in sports would be filled with many more positive experiences. If children's obvious interest in sports can be maintained, there will be a greater chance for lifelong involvement in sports and exercise. This could lead to a major improvement of the fitness level among the nations.

*The Institute for the Study of Youth Sports* provides useful information regarding what parents can do to help create positive experiences for children when they are involved in sports. The key issue here is to emphasize FUN and enjoy participation in sport. Further strategies include:

- creating a climate that emphasizes learning and improvement
- maintaining realistic expectations
- supporting your child
- supporting your coach
- supporting the competitive spirit (the emphasis here is not to win, but rather to compete against another individual or team, so that everyone is pushed toward greater levels of excellence, excellence that could not otherwise be achieved without the opponent)
- managing your emotions

Regardless of the sport, parents can play a positive role in their children's athletic experiences by considering the welfare of their children first, considering the opponent as someone else's child, and placing themselves in the shoes of coaches and officials. The following strategies are recommended by the *Institute for the Study of Youth Sports* (2013) for parents who want to help their children to play well in any sport:

- Avoid getting involved in on-court disagreements if possible.
- Avoid boosting your child's confidence pre-match by telling her she will win. Instead tell her she will play well and remind her of the reasons why.
- Avoid comparisons and stop talking about the draw.
- Avoid nagging and allowing your nerves to stress the player.
- Avoid emotional reactions in the stands.

Although many parents are interested and eager to coach their own children in a sport they love, this is not necessarily a good idea because children often cannot differentiate between the role of the parent and that of the coach "played" by the same person. However, American youth sport programs heavily rely on parental involvement at this level. There is a lot of research focusing on how this could be a successful rather than a detrimental strategy not only for the player but for the whole family. In essence, the focus of any for-play, sport, fitness or physical activity for children needs to be FUN so that the experience will be positive and encouraging to the children so that they continue throughout their lives.

# References

Boklund, B. & Bjorklund, D. (1988). Getting Into the Team Spirit. *Parents Magazine*, June, 197.

Brown, E. & Branta, C. (Eds.). (1988). *Competitive Sports for Children and Youth. An Overview of Research and Issues.* Champaign, Illinois: Human Kinetics.

Burton, D. (1988). The Dropout Dilemma in Youth Sports: Documenting the Problem and Identifying Solutions. In: R. Malina (Ed.) *Young Athletes. Biological, Psychological, and Educational Perspectives* (pp.245-266). Champaign, Illinois: Human Kinetics.

Coakley, J. (2004). *Sport in Society. Issues and Controversies.* St. Louis/ Toronto/ Boston/Los Altos: Times Mirror/Mosby.

Grupe, O. (1988). Top-Level Sports for Children From an Educational Viewpoint. In R. Malina (Ed.) *Young Athletes. Biological, Psychological, and Educational Perspectives* (pp. 223-234). Champaign, Illinois: Human Kinetics.

Howell, R. (1982). *Her Story in Sport: A Historical Anthology of Women in Sport.* New York: West Point. *The Institute for the Study of Youth Sports* (2013). www.edwp.educ.msu.edu/isys.

Magill, R. & Ash, M. & Smoll, F. (Eds.) (1982). *Children in Sport.* Champaign, Illinois: Human Kinetics.

Malina, R. (1988). Biological Maturity Status of Young Athletes. In: R. Malina (Ed.) *Young Athletes. Biological, Psychological, and Educational Perspectives* (pp. 121-140). Champaign, Illinois: Human Kinetics.

Martens, R. (1988). Competitive Anxiety in Children's Sports. In: R.Malina (Ed.) *Young Athletes. Biological, Psychological, and Educational Perspectives* (pp. 235-244). Champaign, Illinois: Human Kinetics.

Martens, R. & V. Seefeldt (Eds.) (1979). *Guidelines for Children's Sports.* Washington, D.C. American Alliance for Health, Physical Education, Recreation and Dance.

Micheii, L. (1988). The Incidence of Injuries in Children's Sports: A Medical Perspective. In: E. Brown & C. Branta (Eds.) *Competitive Sports for Children* (pp. 279-284). Champaign, Illinois: Human Kinetics.

Miller Lite Report on American Attitudes Towards Sports (1993). Milwaukee, Wisconsin: Miller Brewing Company

Sage, G. & Eitzen, S. (2013). *Sociology of North American Sport.* New York, Oxford: Oxford University Press.

Scanlan, T. & Lewthwaite, R. (1988). From Stress to Enjoyment: Parental and Coach Influences on Young Participants. In: E. Brown & C. Branta (Eds.) *Competitive Sports for Children and Youth* (pp. 41-48). Champaign, Illinois: Human Kinetics.

Telama, R. (1988). Sports In and Out of School. In: R. Malina (Ed.) *Young Athletes. Biological, Psychological, and Educational Perspectives* (pp. 205-222). Champaign, Illinois: Human Kinetics.

Trunzo, C. (1989). Choosing a Sports Program for Your Child. *Working Woman,* September, 226-228.

## Issue 3

# The Detrimental Decline of Mandated Physical Education in the United States

*(by Matthew Cummiskey)*

## Introduction

"It was the best of times, it was the worst of times; it was the age of wisdom, it was the age of foolishness; ... we had everything before us, we had nothing before us" (Dickens, 2010). This quotation by Charles Dickens metaphorically represents the current state of school-based physical education in the United States. On one hand, there are a multitude of benefits ascribed to physical activity and physical education. However, on the other hand, physical education (PE) has not seen a corresponding increase in mandated instructional time or status; in fact, physical education programs are being reduced or eliminated (McCullick, 2012).

These reductions are ongoing despite the fact that physical education has rightfully focused more attention on promoting lifetime physical activity and fitness (Graham, Holt-Hale & Parker, 2007). Physical education is not synonymous with team sports; in fact, the new message is more inclusive, stating that "there is something for everyone" (Burgeson, 2004, 29). Quality physical education is increasingly seen as the basis for healthy and active lifestyles, thereby promoting success in future endeavors (Burgeson, 2004). According to the *U.S. Department of Health and Human Services* (2008), regular physical activity, the type afforded by regular on-going physical education, promotes a robust cardiovascular system, decreases body fat and strengthens muscles and bones, all while lessening the likelihood of heart disease, type II diabetes, high blood pressure, and osteoporosis.

According to the National Association for Sport and Physical Education's position statement, titled "Physical Education is Critical to Educating the Whole Child" (2011b), students' performance in schools improves when they are both physically and mentally healthy. Active students miss fewer classes, behave better, engage in less risky behavior, concentrate better and score higher on standardized tests. Likewise, the International Council of Sport Science and Physical Education (2010) released a statement supporting the need for on-going quality physical education that was supported by the International and Paralympic Olympic Committees, the United Nations (UN) Educational, Scientific and Cultural Organization and the UN Office on Sport for

Development and Peace. The statement of support identified physical education as the most effective means for promoting lifetime physical activity, that it is the only school subject focused on the entire person including the body, health, social development, coping with competition, cooperation, and collaboration.

Other researchers have also shown that physical education improves student attendance, engagement in class, and motivation to learn while reducing behavioral problems (Pellegrini, Huberty & Jones, 1995; Strong, et al., 2005). One of the most powerful and increasingly explored topics is the link between physical education, physical activity, and academic achievement. Several studies have reported a positive correlation between physical fitness and academic achievement (California Department of Education, 2005; Texas Education Agency, 2009; Centers for Disease Control and Prevention (CDC), 2010a). Texas was the first state to mandate a statewide physical fitness test and the results were conclusive. According to their state senator, "This data confirms what we have always thought to be true – that there is a strong correlation between a student's fitness and their scholastic success ...We need to move forward on this issue as if lives depend on it – because they do!" (Texas Education Agency, 2009, 2). According to the CDC, 14 studies found a positive link between physical education and academic achievement and/or behavior and increased time in physical education did not come at the expense of achievement in other subjects.

Physical education can also play a critical role in combatting the increasing waistlines of children and adults. According to a 2012 article in the *Journal of the American Medical Association,* 16.9% of children and adolescents between the ages of two and nineteen were not just overweight, but were obese. Although the rise in the obesity rate has diminished recently, it continues to increase at a slower rate. Among adults, no state in the US has an obesity rate below 20%; and in fact, 12 states have a percentage greater than 30%. The economic costs of obesity are staggering – $147 billion in 2008 (Finkelstein, Trogdon, Cohen & Dietz, 2009). Dividing that figure by the Census population in 2008 (303 million), $485 was spent per person to treat obesity – the figure per taxpayer is even higher. This study also found that it costs an additional $1,427 per year to treat an obese person versus one of normal weight.

This issue will present an overview of the instructional mandates for physical education in the USA and will analyze the factors that contribute from the outside and from within to the increase or decrease of instructional time of physical education nationwide.

## Instructional Mandates for Physical Education

Despite the aforementioned evidence supporting the need for ongoing, regular, and frequent physical education in public schools, there exists great variability in the mandated amount of instructional time throughout the United States. The federal government does not require physical education to be taught in any of the nation's schools; instead that responsibility is delegated to the states (National Association for Sport and Physical Education [NASPE] & American Heart Association [AHA], 2012). AAHPERD (American Alliance for Health, Physical Education, Recreation and Dance) recommends that all elementary students engage in a minimum of 150 minutes of PE per week and that middle and high school students accrue 225 minutes per week (NASPE, 2011b). These recommendations are supported by the Centers for Disease Control and Prevention as well as the National Association of State Boards of Education. However, few states and/or districts meet these recommended guidelines. To examine the current amount of mandated physical education instructional time as well as trends over time, three source documents will be considered: the *Youth Risk Behavior Surveillance* (CDC), the *School Health Policies and Programs Study* (CDC) and the *Shape of the Nation Report* (NASPE & American Heart Association).

The *Youth Risk Behavior Survey* (Grunbaum, et al., 2004) provides limited data regarding physical education but does address whether students attended physical education on one or more days in an average week and whether they attended PE class daily (Table 9). These data also delineate the variability between states and local school districts.

*Table 9: Youth Risk Behavior Surveys 1993-2011*

|      | Enrolled in PE | State Range | State Median | Local Range | Local Median |
|------|----------------|-------------|--------------|-------------|--------------|
| 1993 | 52.1           | 21.6-94.9   | 52.4         | 37.4-92.6   | 58.5         |
| 1995 | 59.6           | 26.6-93.4   | 48.2         | 33.6-89.8   | 55.9         |
| 1997 | 48.8           | 31.3-91.9   | 50.0         | 26.8-90.2   | 58.1         |
| 1999 | 56.1           | 29.1-93.3   | 46.6         | 39.1-87.7   | 50.1         |
| 2001 | 51.7           | 71.9-91.5   | 83.6         | 54.9-84.9   | 75.1         |
| 2003 | 55.7           | 27.3-93.7   | 44.9         | 32.6-88     | 48.1         |
| 2005 | 54.2           | 25.2-94.2   | 48.9         | 27.9-85.8   | 45.9         |
| 2007 | 53.6           | 28.4-90.8   | 41.7         | 29.3-78.9   | 44.3         |
| 2009 | 56.4           | 29.1-92.0   | 43.8         | 35.5-81.1   | 47.2         |
| 2011 | 51.8           | 32.8-91.3   | 46.2         | 31.7-79.5   | 47.0         |

*Note: All numbers are percentages*

The overall percentage enrolled in PE reflects little change and was not statistically significant according to a trends analysis conducted by the CDC. Although there were reductions in both the state and local medians, the changes were not statistically significant.

Since 1987, AAHPERD has published the Shape of the Nation Report principally examining state guidelines for physical education (NASPE & AHA, 2012). Determining instructional trends and mandates over time proved problematic however, due to limitations in what data states provided, variability in terms of what data AAHPERD requested, and the fact AAHPERD was not able to provide reports older than 2001. Since 2006, the number of states that mandate physical has improved at all three school levels (Table 10).

Table 10: States Mandating Physical Education

| | Number of States in 2012 | Percentage | Number of States in 2006 | Percentage |
|---|---|---|---|---|
| Elementary | 43 | 84.3 | 36 | 70.6 |
| Middle School | 41 | 80.4 | 33 | 64.7 |
| High School | 44 | 86.3 | 42 | 82.4 |

Note: The District of Columbia is considered a state

The number of states that mandate a minimum number of minutes in physical education has also improved since 2006 at the elementary and middle school level (Table 11).

Table 11: States Mandating a Minimum Number of Minutes in Physical Education

| | Number of States in 2012 | Percentage | Number of States in 2006 | Percentage |
|---|---|---|---|---|
| Elementary | 16 | 31.4 | 11 | 21.6 |
| Middle School | 18 | 35.3 | 7 | 13.7 |
| High School | Not available | | 10 | 19.6 |

Note: The District of Columbia is considered a state

For states mandating an instructional minimum, that number was compared to the recommended 150 minutes in elementary school and 225 minutes per week in middle and high school (Table 12).

Table 12: Mandated Minutes Per Week

| Elementary (n=16) | | | Middle School (n=14) | | | High School (n=10) | | |
|---|---|---|---|---|---|---|---|---|
| # of Minutes | No. | Percentage | # of Minutes | No. | Percentage | # of Minutes | No. | Percentage |
| 0-29 | 0 | 0 | 0-44 | 1 | 7.1 | 0-44 | 1 | 10 |
| 30-59 | 4 | 25.0 | 45-89 | 4 | 28.6 | 45-89 | 1 | 10 |
| 60-89 | 3 | 18.8 | 90-134 | 3 | 21.4 | 90-134 | 3 | 30 |
| 90-119 | 5 | 31.3 | 135-179 | 2 | 14.3 | 135-179 | 1 | 10 |
| 120-149 | 1 | 6.3 | 180-224 | 1 | 7.1 | 180-224 | 1 | 10 |
| =>150 | 3 | 18.8 | =>225 | 3 | 21.4 | =>225 | 3 | 30 |

Three states (5.9%), New Jersey, Louisiana, and Florida, meet the recommended 150 minutes per week of elementary PE, and three states (5.9%), Montana, West Virginia, and Utah, meet the recommended 225 minutes per week of middle school PE. Likewise, three states meet the recommended amount of PE in high school. Therefore, the recommended amount was only state-mandated in nine of the possible 153 school levels (5.9%). The actual number is even lower due to the number of states approving "loopholes" for physical education (NASPE & AHA, 2012). For example, students in several states can substitute Junior Reserve Officer Training Corps (JROTC), interscholastic sports, marching band, or community sports for physical education credit. Waivers may be granted for health, physical disability, religious beliefs, or early graduation. The number of states allowing substitutions and waivers has increased since the 2006 Shape of the Nation Report. In 2012, 33 states allowed for substitutions and 28 for waivers compared to 27 and 18 respectively in 2006. The 2001 report did not disaggregate substitutions and waivers.

The CDC also publishes data related to physical education instructional time courtesy of the School Health Policies and Programs Study (SHPPS), available every six years (Lee, Burgeson, Fulton, Spain, 2007). Between SHPPS 2000 (Burgeson, Wechsler, Brener, Young & Spain, 2001) and SHPPS 2006, the number of states and districts mandating that schools teach physical education increased in all school levels. The increase was most pronounced in kindergarten and throughout middle school and high school (Table 13). Across all secondary grades, the percentage at least doubled. In 8.6% of elementary schools, 13.3% of middle schools and 38.8% of high schools (15.6% overall), physical education was required but not linked to specific grades.

Table 13: Percentage Requiring Physical Education to Be Taught by Grade Level

| Grade | % of Schools – SHPPS 2000 | % of Schools – SHPPS 2006 | Grade | % of Schools – SHPPS 2000 | % of Schools – SHPPS 2006 |
|-------|---------------------------|---------------------------|-------|---------------------------|---------------------------|
| K | 39.7 | 49.7 | 7 | 26.2 | 67.1 |
| 1 | 50.6 | 57.2 | 8 | 25.1 | 65.5 |
| 2 | 50.5 | 57.7 | 9 | 13.3 | 55.3 |
| 3 | 51.3 | 58.0 | 10 | 9.5 | 33.2 |
| 4 | 51.5 | 58.2 | 11 | 5.8 | 20.2 |
| 5 | 50.4 | 61.1 | 12 | 5.4 | 20.4 |
| 6 | 32.2 | 68.1 | | | |

The most recent SHPPS also collected data for the first time on whether states and local school districts require local schools to provide a minimum amount of time for physical education such as minutes per week, hours per quarter, or hours per year (Lee, Burgeson, Fulton, Spain, 2007). For elemetary school, 36.0% of states and 75.8% of local school districts require a minimum amount of physical education compared to 37.3% and 76.0% for middle school and 58.0% and 81.0% for high schools.

A long-standing goal of the *Healthy People Reports* issued by the CDC is to increase the amount of daily physical education throughout the United States (U.S. Department of Health and Human Services [USDHHS], 2010 or *HealthyPeople*.gov, 2013). The drive for daily physical education is closely tied to the recommended number of minutes per week: 30 minutes of physical education per day at the elementary level equals 150 minutes per week and 45 minutes per day at the secondary level equals 225 minutes per week. Healthy People 2020 identified that the nation will increase the proportion of both public and private schools that require daily PE for all students. In 2006, only 3.8% of elementary students, 7.9% of middle school students, and 2.1% of high school students attended physical education daily for an entire school year. In 2000, those percentages were higher: 8.0%, 6.4% and 5.8% respectively. The percentage for middle school improved slightly, whereas the percentage for elementary and high schools more than halved. Therefore, contrary to the goal, the percentage of daily physical education has mostly decreased.

The data presented by the *Youth Risk Behavior Surveys, Shape of the Nation Reports*, and the *School Health Policies and Programs Study* presents a complex picture of the instructional mandates for physical education in the United States. On one hand, the percentage of students enrolled in PE has increased, as has the number of states and districts mandating PE by school level and grade, and the number of states mandating a minimum amount of instructional time.

On the other hand, the number of states permitting substitutions and waivers has increased dramatically, and the overall amount of daily physical education has declined.

Unfortunately, there is no way to accurately determine how much physical education an average 3rd grader in Connecticut receives versus another 3rd grader in Montana. Quite often, the amount of mandated physical education is determined at the local level and not the state, reflecting the decentralized nature of education in the United States. States and districts establish policies requiring physical education but typically not a specific amount. Even when states or districts set clear policies, substitutions and waivers alter the equation.

## External Factors Affecting Mandated Physical Education Instructional Time

There are many forces outside the auspices of physical education that impact instructional time. Perhaps the greatest is the interplay of state guidelines versus local ones (NASPE & AHA, 2012). Some states set guidelines, such as what subjects will be offered, how many credits earned or how many minutes accrued but still leave many decisions to local agencies; a concept identified as "hybrid control." Other states opt for "local control," meaning almost all educational decisions are determined at the local level, not the state level.

Pennsylvania is an example of a hybrid control state. Planned instruction in physical education must be provided to every student in every grade during elementary and middle school and every student during high school (The Pennsylvania Code, n.d.). The language of the mandate is important; note how the high school requirement does not say for how long. A school district could provide physical education to every student for one week or four years, and both would meet the requirement. Pennsylvania does not mandate a specific number of minutes; instead it focuses on the standards. Instruction must be aligned with academic standards and school districts must create an assessment system that measures the degree to which the standards are being achieved. An important but little noticed distinction in the Pennsylvania code states that "elementary education teachers are qualified to teach art, music, health, including AIDS and other health issues, and physical education within a grade-by-grade (K-6) self contained elementary school." In essence, the laws allow for traditional elementary classroom teachers to teach physical education and other subjects. Recently, the school district of Upper Darby voted to eliminate all "special" teachers due to budgetary constraints and instead have the classroom teachers teach those subjects. This change is permissible under Pennsylvania state law.

Like Pennsylvania, Iowa mandates that physical education be taught but does not specify a minimum number of hours (McCullick, Baker, Tomporowksi, Templin, Lux & Issac, 2012). Instead, the state requires 30 minutes of physical activity in grades K-5, a requirement that could be fulfilled by recess. Since many students are not physically active during recess (Lee, Burgeson, Fulton, Spain, 2007), is the requirement still met? Like Pennsylvania, the requirements are subject to a considerable degree of autonomy from local school districts. In Wisconsin, elementary schools must engage in physical education at least three times per week but again there is no set number of required minutes or hours. Elementary classroom teachers may conduct up to one-third of physical education instruction under the supervision of PE specialists. Nebraska is an example of a local control state, where local teachers and administrators are charged with providing an appropriate amount of instruction in each subject area (McCullick, Baker, Tomporowksi, Templin, Lux & Issac, 2012). The state statutes identify that "the schedule is sufficiently flexible to encourage teachers and students to address emergent needs and topics ... The elementary school has a representative weekly schedule for each classroom teacher encompassing experiences in ... Physical Education." If a school or districts finds there is an "emergent need" to improve math scores, then physical education and other subjects may be summarily reduced.

The lack of specific mandates and requirements in the state statutes has proven problematic for physical education due to the large degree of interpretation afforded to administrators (McCullick, Baker, Tomporowksi, Templin, Lux & Issac, 2012). As noted earlier, a school district may offer physical education one day or every day in a school year and still meet the requirement. If an individual, group or organization chooses to challenge a school district's interpretation of the statutes, the likelihood of success is low (2012). The courts generally side with states or local districts as part of a general deference toward those entities in curriculum-related matters. The courts are more inclined to challenge statutes related to educational opportunity, financing and students with disabilities, but not curriculum (American Law Reports 4th, 2010).

In light of these facts, physical education should be mindful of the quote "the best offense is a good defense." It is imperative that physical educators and other professionals advocate for clear language and binding statutes thereby increasing the likelihood that statutes will be interpreted consistently and more favorably toward physical education (USDHHS, 2010). Once statutes are written they are difficult to unwind. For example, the author petitioned the Pennsylvania Department of Education regarding the procedures for filing a complaint relating to the Upper Darby School District and as yet has received no reply.

Another major factor affecting physical education instructional time is state and local budgets (Stancill, 2012). Due to the recent economic slowdown tax credits and tax-rate reductions, many states were left with budget deficits. According to the Pennsylvania Office of the Budget, the total allotment for education decreased from approximately from $10.4 billion in 2010-2011 to $9.6 billion in 2011-2012 (2013). This translated into thousands of dollars at the local level that school districts were forced to cut or make-up. For example, the 2010-2011 state funding for the Philadelphia City School District was $1.278 billion but for 2011-2012, the amount was $989 million (Pennsylvania State Education Association, 2013). The total reduction was 22.5% of its budget. In a separate article, the Pennsylvania State Education Association (2013) noted that the "budget ax" has fallen disproportionly on physical education, art, music, libraries and sports. In a recent survey by the same organization, 58% of school districts cited reducing physical education, art, music, electives and AP courses in response to tighter budgets. Francesca Zavacky, senior program manager for AAHPERD, stated that instructional time for physical education is being reduced in the face of tight budgets (Stancill, 2012). She went on to say that since most states lack definitive policies requiring physical education, it is easier to cut during challenging economic conditions. The lack of available resources leaves nearly every facet of education (subject areas, teachers, administrators) competing against one another for available funding (McCullick, Baker, Tomporowksi, Templin, Lux & Issac, 2012). In the end, each area must justify its funding or face potential reductions.

One particularly powerful way to justify a subject's place in the curriculum is through test scores, particularly the high stakes variety mandated by the Act (NCLB, 2001). Administrators face pressure to meet adequate yearly progress that is principally tied to testing in reading, writing, mathematics, and science (Doolittle, 2007). In fact, NCLB legislation designates that those subjects are part of the core, a moniker not extended to physical education. As a result, instructional time in physical education has been reallocated to other subjects (American Pediatric Association, 2013). The public school curriculum is becoming increasingly stratified with tested subjects toward the top and non-test subjects toward the bottom (Lux, 2010). A debate in Texas encapsulated many of these sentiments as legislators considered eliminating high school physical education in order to "better spend" the money and time elsewhere (Rhea, 2009, 4).

Since interpretations of state education laws are flexible, school administrators (school boards, principals, etc.) have an large effect on physical education. This can be problematic in cases where principals are unaware of appropriate practices and what constitutes quality physical education (Helion, 2009). Too often, administrators negatively view physical education through the lens of their experience in schools and not best practice. They are more likely to have negative expectations and focus more on how a teacher manages a class than being educated in the physical arena (Rhea, 2009). Class size is sometimes increased to the point that student learning becomes a challenge (Hennessy, 2005). According to the 2006 SHPPS report, 36% of the schools that required physical education had a maximum allowable teacher-to-student ratio, the median maximum being 29.6 (Lee, Burgeson, Fulton, Spain, 2007). Physical educators are sometimes forced to accommodate the loss of their teaching facility due to school functions such as a blood drive or school play (Lux, 2010). The implicit message therein is that PE is not important. Administrators can also have a positive effect on physical education – particularly where the program is strong or there is a district level coordinator. According to the most recent SHPPS report, 62.2% of districts have and 45.7% require that a trained professional oversee and coordinate physical education (Lee, Burgeson, Fulton, Spain, 2007).

The interplay of these external factors has had a cumulative effect on physical education known as marginalization – physical education is low in status and lacks appropriate respect from the educational community (Stroot & Ko, 2006). According to Blankenship and Coleman (2009), marginalization from outside the field has promoted the idea that physical educators are not real teachers. MacDonald (1995) reported that many physical education teachers feel isolated, have limited access to professional resources and struggle to overcome preconceptions. These outcomes can have real consequences for physical education in terms of resource allocation, teacher-to-student ratios and scheduling. In some cases, marginalization leads to a self-fulfilling prophecy where teachers conform to poor practices because that is what is expected. Perhaps the greatest slight is the fact that physical education, despite all its benefits for students and the school community, is not a core subject, whereas language arts, mathematics, science, foreign language, civics and government, economics, arts, history, and geography are identified as such (Gambescia, 2006). The news is not all negative however, 27% of physical educators reported increased support from parents (Roslow Research Group, 2009), and a report by the CDC (2010b) found that 54-84% of parents regarded physical education as important as other subjects depending on the subject being compared. Nearly 95% of parents stated that physical education should be a required part of the school day for all students (NASPE, 2003). Finally, over 90% of parents supported more physical education in schools (Harvard School of Public Health, 2003).

## Internal Factors Affecting Mandated Physical Education Instructional Time

The April 2011 issue of *JOPERD* asked respondents "What are the most effective and ineffective ways of advocating for physical education and physical activity?

(p.53) A theme that emerged in the responses was first building a quality program in the gym. In essence, "Don't ask for publicity or favors until you've taken care of your own house." Therefore, it is important to ask what is the current state of physical education in the United States. Is the profession "worthy" of additional instructional time in order to promote lifetime physical activity and fitness, to imbue students with the countless benefits that come from being physically active? Like the issue of state mandates, the issue of instructional quality is complex and affected by a broad range of issues. Certainly there are exceptional programs but also abysmal ones. That leads to the obvious question of why there is such a large spectrum of quality, often within the same district and in some cases within the same school.

Multiple researchers have found a pattern in that the quality of physical education diminishes over time; the best programs are generally to be found in elementary schools (Fredricks & Eccles, 2002; Jacobs, Lanza, Osgood, Eccles, & Wigfield, 2002). According to Rhea (2009), elementary and middle school programs have improved over the years by emphasizing the acquisition of movement and sport skills. Teachers at these levels created not only an active classroom but a learning-focused classroom as well. Unfortunately in high school, there is generally less emphasis on educating students compared to simply being active, and thus, there are lower expectations for performance. This trend has exacerbated to the point that some physical education teacher education (PETE) programs report having difficulty placing teacher candidates in quality programs (Beyer, 2008).

The socialization of new teachers impacts the quality of instruction, particularly in high schools and to some extent in middle schools due to the larger number of teachers (Blankenship & Coleman, 2003). Socialization was defined by Lortie (1975) as an experience "that happens to people as they move through a series of structured experiences and internal the subculture of the group" (p.61). The impact of socialization depends on many factors, one of which is the size of the school – new teachers are simply outnumbered. According to Helion (2009), socialization is

> evident in far too many programs to be ignored. New teachers come in ready and willing to work hard, only to be told that their work ethic is reflecting badly on their veteran colleagues, so they had better 'tone it down.' They are told to forget what they learned in school, because that stuff does not work in 'real life.' They are told that they are working too hard... (They) are told, 'We don't do things that way here.' This statement often comes along with the implication that they will not be here long if they do not conform. Team teaching of large classes that becomes more a case of team monitoring or officiating too often results

157

from this lack of professionalism. The fall-back position for many new teachers becomes that of 'go along to get along' (p.5).

What often happens in mid-sized to large programs is new teachers join a large staff and become socialized into poor practices. A few years later, a new teacher arrives and the same process begins again; the end result being no net difference in a program over time. It takes either a critical mass of quality teachers hired in close proximity or singular teachers hired separately with the ethics and "stamina" to do what is right and keep the interest of students foremost in their mind and practices.

One of the appropriate practices that should be employed is student assessment aligned to the standards (NASPE, 2009b). In the current environment of high-stakes testing, it is imperative that physical educators use assessment data to document student learning. Any discipline that cannot demonstrate measureable outcomes resulting from instruction is vulnerable to being reduced or eliminated entirely (Rink, 1999). Unfortunately, the existing assessment culture is dominated by attendance, effort, behavior and timeliness (Collier, 2011). According to the most recent SHPPS report, schools reported using the following factors: level of participation (95.8%); attitude (89.3%); appropriate attire (69.4%); attendance (56.9%); skill improvement (53.7%); skill level (49.3%); fitness scores (45.9%); knowledge tests (45.7%); self-management skills (39.7%); and physical activity outside of school (11.8%). In order to be as respected as other subjects, assessment practices must be aligned. Does the science teacher factor attitude, attire, and attendance into course grades; if not, neither should physical educators. In 2007, Doolittle highlighted Victor High School as a model for appropriate use of assessment. A course syllabus describes exactly how students will be graded – 60% on physical skills, 20% on cognitive written quizzes, and 20% on daily participation as measured on a four-point rubric. As physical educators incorporate more learning-focused assessment like those at Victor High School, inappropriate practices, such as "rolling out the ball," will be reduced because they are incompatible with a proper assessment (Wirszyla, 2002). As teachers improve their ability to accurately document student learning, the marginalization of the profession should be reduced (Collier, 2011).

Resistance to assessment has proven particularly strong among teachers in the psychomotor domain due to the fact that students have different skill levels (Henninger and Carlson, 2011). This is ironic considering that the psychomotor domain is the heart and soul of physical education and what distinguishes the subject from others. True, some students have little aptitude for tennis as an example, but so too do other students have little aptitude for the Pythagorean formula in mathematics or the periodic table in chemistry. Yet those subjects, despite wide variations in aptitude, assess. So too should physical education.

The problem is that some administrators and parents accepted the idea that physical education inherently biases the less athletic. As a result, some schools do not incorporate physical education into student grade point averages (GPA) (Table 14).

Table 14: States Mandating PE Included in GPA

|  | n= | Percentage |
|---|---|---|
| 2012 | 26 | 53.1 |
| 2006 | 22 | 43.1 |
| 2001 | 30 | 58.9 |

Note: The District of Columbia is considered a state

This result not only makes students less accountable but also reinforces the marginalized status of physical education. When done properly, assessment can motivate students to learn and clarify expectations in terms of performance (James, Griffin, & France, 2005).

Sheehy (2011) claimed that physical educators fail to communicate the importance of skillfulness. This oversight feeds into the misconception that physical education is physical activity. AAHPERD (2006b) cautioned that the purposes of physical education, acquiring motor skills, exploring sports and rules, and promoting lifelong fitness cannot be met purely by physical activity or recess. Recently, the American Pediatric Association (2013) stated that "physical education is an academic discipline," and recess should not come at the expense of physical education. How many students, parents and administrators would consider physical education an academic discipline? Therein lies part of the problem. According to James (2011):

> While NASPE and several states have clearly articulated standards that have helped professionals identify what students should know and be able to do in physical education, by the end of each educational level (i.e., elementary school, middle school, and high school), there is little consensus in regard to curricular focal points at specific grade levels within the larger educational levels.

These variations create large instructional variations and an unclear sense of purpose. According to Doolittle (2007), many high school physical education programs look like they did 20 years ago, and the field has not specifically addressed the issues of expectations – what students should know and be able to do at specific grades.

In contrast, other fields have explicitly described content at each educational level (James, 2011). For example, the *Common Core State Standards for Mathematics* delineate in great detail what knowledge and skills student will acquire in grades 1-8 and then divides high school into numbers and quantities, algebra, functions, modeling, geometry and finally statistics and probability (National Governors Association Center for Best Practices, 2010). No so much model exists in physical education where most content, aside from movement skills at the elementary level, can be taught in any grade. Basketball is commonly taught starting in second or third grade and continues throughout high school. When should basketball instruction begin, when should it end, and what should a student be able to do by the 5th grade, by the 8th grade and by 10th grade? There is no agreement on these questions, and therefore if students do not meet the prescribed levels of performance, there is little consequence for the student or the teacher for that matter. There is also little agreement on what activities should be taught – are rugby and tchoukball acceptable curricular options? There is no consensus with the result being that both appropriate and inappropriate activities are commonplace. For example, 58.9% of elementary schools play duck-duck-goose and 55.0% play king-of-the-hill (Lee, Burgeson, Fulton, Spain, 2007). In all school levels, 68.1% play dodgeball and 81.8% play kickball, despite a specific position statement from AAHPERD stating that dodgeball is an inappropriate practice (2006a).

Although physical education cannot point to a specific body of knowledge all students should acquire, it has rightfully been shifting its focus from traditional team sports to lifetime activities and fitness (Ennis, 2010). The goal is to promote active, healthy adults. Many programs have added yoga, pilates, badminton, golf, swing dance, and other lifetime-oriented activities to the curriculum. The problem is that not enough programs have modernized their offerings. According to the Roslow Research Group (2009), the top ten activities taught in physical education were basketball (93% of schools), personal fitness (88%), volleyball (88%), jump rope (86%), soccer (83%), baseball or softball (75%), football (74%), dance (70%), ultimate or other disc sports (69%) and hockey (64%). Note how seven of the ten activities were team oriented. Contrast those activities versus the top activities by total participants in 2011 among people seven years of age and older: exercise walking (97.1 million), exercising with equipment (55.5), swimming (46.0), camping (42.8), aerobic exercise (42.0), bicycle riding (39.1), hiking (39.1), running/jogging (38.7), bowling (34.9) and working out at a club (34.5) (National Sporting Goods Association, 2011). Not one of the top ten activities is a team sport, and in fact basketball is the first one listed in the thirteenth position. Every school subject is preparing K-12 learners to be successful adults. How can physical education make a similar claim when there is such a fundamental misalignment between the content being taught and its usefulness to adults?

On some level, K-12 students know physical education can and should do better. Students' perceptions of physical education, like overall program quality, decline over time (Subramaniam & Silverman, 2007). The increasingly less positive perceptions are more pronounced among girls, and by the time students are in high school, their average attitudes vary from neutral to slightly negative – this is in marked contrast to the generally positive attitudes among elementary students. Students, like quality programming, can be the greatest advocates for physical education. However, there are four principal aspects of curriculum students react negatively toward: 1) repetitive content; 2) lack of learning; 3) lack of relevance; and 4) and over-reliance on competitive team sports (Bernstein, Phillips, & Silverman, 2011). Due to these factors, physical educators turn many students against us. There is an old expression that the student who hated PE the most becomes the school board president, principal or some other authority position. As reported earlier, parents are thankfully supportive of PE. According to France and colleagues (2005), 79.3% of parents stated their child's PE grade was as important as other subjects, and 84% had positive perceptions of physical education (NASPE, 2002). So even though Sheehy (2011) contends that parents generally view PE as a meaningless experience, most parents support it. Perhaps parents recognize the importance of physical education and activity and, despite its shortcomings, are willing to provide some latitude and support while the profession works to improve overall quality.

There are other internal or "self-inflicted" factors that affect physical education program quality. Some physical educators emphasize coaching at the expense of instructional quality collaboration with colleagues, a problem that is more acute in middle and high schools (Wirszyla, 2002). Not all physical educators have a certification or degree in physical education – this policy varies considerably by state. According to the 2006 SHPPS, 94.9% of elementary PE teachers had an undergraduate degree, of those 64.4% majored in physical education (Lee, Burgeson, Fulton, & Spain, 2007). Among middle and high school teachers, 97.6% had a degree, of those 71.6% majored in physical education.

## Increasing Mandated Instructional Time in the United States

Nationally, there has not been a dramatic increase or decrease in the amount of mandated physical education instructional time. The largest variations occur within individual states and school districts as a result of legislation and/or budget cuts. Some states, such as Virginia and Florida, are actively trying to increase the amount of physical education. Regardless of these efforts, it is clear that mandated instructional time falls substantially below the 150 and 225 minutes recommended by AAHPERD, the CDC, the AHA and other groups.

Since the federal government does not address physical education, it is the providence of states and individual grassroots efforts within states to affect change. Considering the unhealthy habits of today's students, there has never been a better opportunity to convince the public of the necessity of physical education (Grabner, 2012). Fortunately, many of the shortcomings of physical education are internally generated and "easier" to amend. The external factors affecting physical education are more complex but concerted efforts can prove meaningful.

Creating change is often debated in terms of top-down versus bottom-up approaches. Top down allows experts to assess the situation and make recommendations for change (Wirszyla, 2002). However, change from the top often has less teacher buy-in and has proven less effective due to not considering the opinions and circumstances of teachers on the ground (Grabner, 2012). Bottom up change occurs through a multitude of individual and group efforts on the part of teachers, parents, PETE faculty and physical education coordinators. Change is more likely to be practical and real-world based. At a recent meeting of PETE faculty from most physical education degree granting institutions in Pennsylvania, the topic of stemming job losses and improving overall quality of instruction was debated. Several in attendance noted that 20 years earlier the same topics were discussed and several bottom-up strategies were employed (Wentzel, 2012). Unfortunately, those interventions had little effect; it was agreed that such efforts should be continued and expanded to include top-down strategies. Affecting change is not an either-or question; rather, it is a thoughtful combination of the two approaches that may prove most effectual.

In terms of top-down interventions, physical education should continue and expand efforts at the national level, particularly in light of the *Let's Move Campaign* championed by US First Lady Michelle Obama. In 2004, the Child Nutrition and WIC Reauthorization Act was passed, which required schools to implement a school wellness policy (Graber, Woods, & O'Connor, 2012). The act principally improved lunchroom nutrition and recess allocations but did not result in substantive changes to physical education. The law is generally reauthorized every five years; for the next iteration, physical education should push strenuously for schools to require the AAHPERD recommended amount of physical education.

Physical education should strive to be part of the academic core in all states. For example, in Ohio, physical education is part of the academic core whereas in Pennsylvania, it is not (Ohio Department of Education, n.d.). Being part of the academic core would increase both the status of physical education and its teachers while also improving its position in relation to other subjects (Gambescia, 2006). In addition, core subject teachers must be highly qualified and therefore hold not only a bachelor's degree but full certification in their respective teaching area. As noted earlier, only two in three physical educators majored in physical education (Lee, Burgeson, Fulton & Spain, 2007).

Physical education should build its own version of the Common Core State Standards, which specifically list what knowledge, skills and disposition students should acquire in each grade, much like mathematics and English language arts currently do. The physical education common core standards should list what activities and assessments are permissible and, in doing so, build a common base of knowledge that truly represents what students should know and be able to do. A common core would not be as formulaic as a national curriculum but would make evaluative judgments about what is and what is not appropriate to teach and assess. For physical education to be respected, it must stand for a specific body of knowledge. Education has traditionally been seen as a matter of local control but creating national competencies improves accountability and allows educators to find gaps in their instruction (Beyer, 2008).

According to Collier (2011), the current standards-based, high-stakes testing environment requires measurable and distinct learning outcomes, the very kind afforded by the Common Core. Once those are established either nationally or within states, it becomes easier to craft state assessments for physical education. The assessments could be administered at the conclusion of elementary and middle school and upon final graduation in high school. They could be combined with health education or remain separate entities. Such an approach is analogous to "fighting fire with fire." For years, physical education has been marginalized and cut at the expense of test scores. Having its own high-stakes exam would provide data, improve the status of PE and drive more consistent instruction. Perhaps most critically, it would improve accountability for administrators and other people who determine physical education instructional allotments. There would be pressure to maintain favorable scores and improve deficient ones through professional development; in either case, reducing physical education time could result in a negative consequence. Statewide assessments would also improve accountability for teachers by demonstrating which ones are emphasizing learning and which ones are merely "rolling out the ball."

Creating change from the bottom-up is equally as instrumental as top-down reform. As noted earlier, change must begin from within and that means building consistently high-quality programs on a school-by-school basis (Sheehy, 2011). Once that happens, it is imperative that physical educators tell others, particularly administrators and parents. Advocacy in physical education has been a well-discussed topic, including such outlets as bulletin boards, newsletters, open houses, webpages, email blasts, parent/child activity nights, parent play days (bring a parent to PE), themed school dances and interactive homework to name a few (Henninger & Carlson, 2011; Lux, 2010). Physical educators should look the part of professional educators and become involved in "academic" matters, such as IEP meetings or writing across the curriculum, while also taking the lead in the school wellness policies. Advocacy also entails meeting with state and national legislators about the importance of quality PE (Grabner, 2012).

Professional development is another tenet of successful reform. It is imperative that it be ongoing, frequent and content specific (Armour & Yelling, 2007). Too often professional development is not relevant to physical education, infrequent and not aligned with previous experiences. Physical education-specific professional development opportunities include national, regional and state conventions, the Program Improvement in Physical Education workshop series (PIPEline) and webinars.

Prusak, et al., (2010) noted that district physical education coordinators improve overall program quality. They help create and enforce district-wide curriculums while also providing more frequent professional development. According to Wirszyla (2002), they improve accountability for existing teachers, enhance university-level collaborations, and help sequence the curriculum through the grade levels to reduce overlap. Clearly there are several advantages to district-level PE coordinators although in tight budgetary times, their numbers have been reduced with the result being a more fragmented approach to physical education.

## Conclusion

Data provided through SHPPS, YRBS and *Shape of the Nation Report* reveal a complex picture of mandated instructional time in the United States. Nationally, there have not been dramatic changes to the overall mandated instructional time whereas for states and local districts there has been. Some of the factors affecting instructional time are external to physical education whereas others are internal. Regardless of their origin, it is important that people in the field of physical education find ways to counteract them and increase mandated physical education to the levels recommended by AAHPERD. Traditionally these efforts have been bottom up in nature; however, there has been an increase in top-down approaches particularly through legislative action. Future efforts must focus on collecting data regarding how students are benefiting from physical education and in doing so increase the accountability of teachers. These so-called "surveillance systems" (Siedentop, 2009, S168) will in time provide the critical evidence that students in physical education are meeting the standards. Without evidence, physical education cannot stand on its own two feet. As changes unfold, it is important to remember that major shifts in instructional practices do not happen overnight (Patton & Griffin, 2008) but through concerted effort from the "bottom" and the "top," differences will begin to be felt where it matters most – in the lives of students.

# References

American Academy of Pediatrics (2012). *The crucial role of recess in schools.* Elk Grove Village, IL: Author. DOI: 10.1542/peds.2012-2993

American Law Reports 4th § 1, 1139 (2010).

Armour, K. M. & Yelling, M. (2007). Effective professional development for physical education teachers: The role of informal, collaborative learning. *Journal of Teaching in Physical Education, 26,* 177–200.

Bernstein, E., Phillips, S. & Silverman, S. (2011). Attitudes and perceptions of middle school students toward competitive activities in physical education. *Journal of Teaching in Physical Education, 30,* 69-83.

Beyer, R. (2008). Restructuring the secondary physical education curriculum to meet new challenges. *Journal of Physical Education, Recreation and Dance, 79*(9), 27-32.

Blankenship, B. T. & Coleman, M. M. (2009). An examination of "washout" and workplace conditions of beginning physical education teachers. *The Physical Educator, 66*(2), 97-111.

Burgeson C. R., Wechsler H., Brener N. D., Young J. C. & Spain C. G. (2001). Physical education and activity: Results from the School Health Policies and Programs Study. *Journal of School Health, 71*(7), 279-293.

Burgeson, C. R. (2004). Physical education's critical role in educating the whole child & reducing childhood obesity. *The State Education Standard, 5*(2), 27–32.

California Department of Education (2005). *A study of the relationship between physical fitness and academic achievement in California using 2004 test results.* Sacramento, CA: Author.

Child Nutrition and WIC Reauthorization Act of 2004, Pub. L. No. 108-265, § 204, 118 Stat. 729 (2004).

Collier, D. (2011). Increasing the value of physical education: The role of assessment. *Journal of Physical Education, Recreation and Dance, 82*(7), 38-41.

Dickens, D. (2010). *A tale of two cities.* Mineola, NY: Dover Publications.

Doolittle, S. (2007). Is the extinction of high school physical education inevitable? *Journal of Physical Education, Recreation and Dance, 78*(4), 7-9.

Ennis, C. (2010). On their own: Preparing students for a lifetime. *Journal of Physical Education, Recreation & Dance, 81*(5), 17-22.

Finkelstein, E. A., Trogdon, J. G., Cohen, J. W. & Dietz, W. (2009). Annual medical spending attributable to obesity: Payer- and service-specific estimates. *Health Affairs, 28*(5), 822-831.

France, T. J., Moosbrugger, M. & Brockmeyer, G. (2011). Increasing the value of physical education in schools and communities. *Journal of Physical Education, Recreation and Dance, 82(7)*, 48-51.

Fredricks, J. A. & Eccles, J. S. (2002). Children's competence and value beliefs from childhood through adolescence: Growth trajectories in two male-sex-types domains. *Developmental Psychology, 38*, 519–533.

Gambescia, S. F. (2006). Health education and physical education are core academic subjects. *Health Promotion Practices, 7(4)*, 369-371.

Graber, K. C., Woods, A. M. & O'Connor, J. A. (2012). Impact of wellness legislation on comprehensive school health programs. *Journal of Teaching in Physical Education, 31*, 163-181.

Grabner, K. C. (2012). Maximizing legislative opportunities for school physical education reform. *Journal of Physical Education, Recreation and Dance, 83(7)*, 4-6.

Graham, G., Holt-Hale, S. A., & Parker, M. (2007). *Children moving: A reflective approach to teaching physical education.* New York, NY: McGraw-Hill.

Grunbaum, J. A., Kann, L., Kinchen, S., Ross, J., Hawkins, J., Lowry, R. & Collins, J. (2004). Youth risk behavior surveillance – United States, 2003. *Morbidity and Mortality Weekly Report, 53(2)*, 1-96.

Harvard School of Public Health (2003). *Obesity as a public health issue: A look at solutions.* Boston, MA: Author.

Healthy People 2020 (2012). Physical Activity . Retrieved from http://www.healthypeople.gov/2020/topicsobjectives2020/objectiveslist.aspx?topicId=33

Helion, J. (2009). Professional responsibility. T*he Journal of Physical Education, Recreation & Dance. 80(6)*, 5-6, 62.

Hennessy, B. (2005). Supersizing classes is not healthy. California Association for Health, P*hysical Education, Recreation, and Dance Journal, 67(4)*, 8-11.

Henninger, M. (2007). Lifers and troopers: Urban physical education teachers who stay. *Journal of Teaching in Physical Education, 26,* 125-144.

International Council on Sport Science and Physical Education (2010). International Position Statement on Physical Education. Berlin, Germany: Author.

Jacobs, J. E., Lanza, S., Osgood, D. W., Eccles, J. S. & Wigfield, A. (2002). Changes in children's self-competence and values: Gender and domain differences across grade one through twelve. *Child Development, 73,* 509–527.

James, A. R. (2011). Introduction. *Journal of Physical Education, Recreation and Dance, 82(6)*, 15-16.

James, A. R., Griffin, L. L., & France, T. (2005). Perceptions of assessment in elementary physical education: A case study. *The Physical Educator, 62(2)*, 85-95.

Lee S. M., Burgeson C. R., Fulton J. E. & Spain C.G. (2007). Physical education and physical activity: Results from the School Health Policies and Programs Study 2006. *Journal of School Health, 77,* 435-463.

Lortie, D. C. (1975). *Schoolteacher: A sociological study.* Chicago, IL: University of Chicago Press.

Lux, K. M. (2010). How to raise the status of physical education at your school. *Journal of Physical Education, Recreation and Dance, 81*(8), 40-42, 56.

Macdonald, D. (1995). The role of proletarianization in physical education teacher attrition. *Research Quarterly for Exercise and Sport, 66*(2), 129-141.

McCullick, B., Baker, T., Tomporowski, P., Templin, T.,, Lux, K., & Isaac, T. (2012). An analysis of state physical education policies. *Journal of Teaching in Physical Education, 31,* 200-210.

National Association for Sport and Physical Education (2002). Adults'/ teen's attitudes toward physical activity and physical education. Reston, VA: Author.

National Association for Sport and Physical Education (2003). *Parents' views of children's health and fitness: A summary of results.* Reston, VA: Author.

National Association for Sport and Physical Education (2006a). *Position on dodgeball in physical education.* Reston, VA: Author.

National Association for Sport and Physical Education (2006b). *Recess for elementary school Students.* Reston, VA: Author.

National Association for Sport and Physical Education (2009). *Appropriate instructional practice guidelines for high school physical education.* Reston, VA: Author.

National Association for Sport and Physical Education (2011b). *Physical education is critical to educating the whole child.* Reston, VA: Author.

National Association for Sport and Physical Education & American Heart Association. (2012). *2012 Shape of the nation report: Status of physical education in the USA.* Reston, VA: American Alliance for Health, Physical Education, Recreation and Dance.

National Governors Association Center for Best Practices, Council of Chief State School Officers. (2010). *Common core state standards for mathematics.* Washington DC: Author.

National Sporting Goods Association (2011). *2011 sports participation – Ranked by total participation.* Mount Prospect, IL: Author.

No Child Left Behind, 115 Stat. 1425 (2001).

Ohio Department of Education (n.d.). *Graduation requirements: Ohio core.* Retrieved from http://www.ode.state.oh.us/GD/Templates/Pages/ODE/ODEPrimary.aspx?Page=2&TopicID=1696&TopicRelationID=1702

Pellegrini, A. D., Huberty, P. D., & Jones, I. (1995). The effects of recess timing on children's playground and classroom behaviors. *American Educational Research Journal. 32*(4), 845-864.

Pennsylvania Office of the Budget. Retrieved from http://www.budget.state.pa.us/portal/server.pt/community/past_budgets/4571

Pennsylvania State Education Association (2013). Retrieved from http://www.psea.org/apps/budget/budgetimpact.aspx

Pennsylvania State Education Association (2013). We stand together: The school funding crisis. Retrieved from http://www.psea.org/general.aspx?id=9686&MID=735

Rhea, D. J. (2009). The physical education deficit in high schools. *Journal of Physical Education, Recreation and Dance, 80*(5), 3-5.

Rink, J. (1999). Show me your outcomes. *Teaching Elementary Physical Education, 10*(4), 5.

Roslow Research Group. (2009). *Physical education trends in our nation's schools: A survey of practicing K-12 physical education teachers.* Port Washington, NY: Author.

Texas Education Agency. (2009). *Physically fit students more likely to do well in school, less likely to be discipline problems.* Austin, TX: Author.

Sheehy, D. A. (2011). Addressing parents' perceptions in the marginalization of physical education. *Journal of Physical Education, Recreation and Dance, 82*(7), 42- 44, 56.

Siedentop, D. L. (2009). National plan for physical activity: Education sector. *Journal of Physical Activity and Health, 6*(Suppl. 2), S168-S180.

Stancill, J. (2012, January 10). Schools pressed to do more to keep kids fit. *News Observer.* Retrieved from http://www.newsobserver.com/2012/01/10/1766290/schools-pressed-to-do-more-to.html#storylink=cpy

Strong, W., Maline, R., Blimkie, C., Daniels, S., Dishman, R., Gutin, B. & Pivarnik, J. (2005). Evidence-based physical activity for schoolage youth. *Journal of Pediatrics, 146*(6), 732-737.

Stroot, S. A., & Ko, B. (2006). *Teacher socialization and induction. In Handbook of Research in Physical Education.* Edited by D. Kirk, M. O'Sullivan & D. Macdonald. Berkeley, CA: Sage Publications.

Subramaniam, P. R. & Silverman, S. (2007). Middle school students' attitudes toward physical education. *Teaching and Teacher Education, 22*, 602-611.

Texas Education Agency News. (2009, March 9). *Physically fit students more likely to do well in school, less likely to be disciplinary problems.* Austin, TX: Author.

The Pennsylvania Code. (n.d.). *Chapter 4. Academic standards and assessment.* Retrieved from http://www.pacode.com/secure/data/022/chapter4/chap4toc.html

U.S. Centers for Disease Control and Prevention. (2010a). *Physical activity, physical education and academic performance: A review of the literature.* Atlanta, GA: U.S. Department of Health and Human Services. 2010.

U.S. Centers for Disease Control and Prevention. (2010b). *The association between school-based physical activity, including physical education, and academic performance.* Atlanta, GA: U.S. Department of Health and Human Services.

U.S. Department of Health and Human Services. (2008). *2008 Physical activity guidelines for Americans.* Washington, DC: Author.

U.S. Department of Health and Human Services. (2010). *National physical activity plan.* Washington, DC: Author.

Wirszyla, C. (2002). State-mandated curriculum change in three high school physical education programs. *Journal of Teaching in Physical Education, 22*, 4-19.

## CHAPTER 6:

# RACE/ETHNICITY AND SPORT – FITNESS – PHYSICAL ACTIVITY

### *News Headlines*

- *Vile racism raised its ugly head during a boys basketball game near Pittsburgh on Friday, when fans of a nearly all-white suburban school ran on the court in banana suits and made monkey noises to taunt the players of their rivals, who play for a school which is predominantly African-American. (www.sports.yahoo.com, Feb 8, 2012)*

- *There is discrimination and disadvantage in sport as there is in everyday life for ethnic minorities. ... There are many different barriers that people of an ethnic minority face. These include assumptions made about black and ethnic minority people, for example that all Asian girls aren't allowed to wear swimsuits. This can limit their opportunities to take up a sport. ... Or in Islam ... there are guidelines within which sports can be practiced; this entails women following their faith by not engaging in mixed gender sports and by observing a dress code. This consists of covering the hair and wearing modest clothing by covering the arms and legs. ... This can put young women off sport and physical activity and may also include early negative experiences of P.E. at schools. The negative perceptions about physical activity can last into adulthood, making it more difficult for these young women to engage in sport. (www.voices.yahoo.com/barriers-affecting-ethnic-minorities-sport-today, October 2012)*

- *The Heavy Burdens of Black College Athletes. Graduation rates of black football and basketball athletes are consistently among the lowest in the nation. ... A culture of greed is at the root of those pitiful graduation rates. Basketball and football programs produce the most revenue in most athletic departments, which have placed a severe strain on education priorities. Take the 2010 men's Division 1 basketball tournament, in which only 31 percent of participating teams graduated at least 70 percent of their Black players. Meanwhile, 79 percent of the teams in the tournament graduated at least 70 percent of their White players. ... Amateur athletes, especially youth of color in high-revenue-producing sports ... are shamelessly exploited. (www.thecrisis.com, Summer 2010)*

- *Racism in Football – in Britain. Yet last season, barely a week went by without a controversy: Luis Suarez abused Patrice Evra on the pitch. Two people were* convicted after racist tweets. Micah Richards closed down his Twitter account after being abused. And, this week, Chelsea and England's John Terry was in court charged with a racially aggravated public order offence. ... 'You've got to show a corporate understanding of what racism and exclusion is all about, and it has to be understood and carried though by the management teams.' (www.theguardian.co.uk/football/2012)

- Jeremy Lin, an American, whose parents are from Taiwan, said he has to work harder to earn respect. ... The NBA playmaker of Chinese heritage whose rise last season sparked "Lin-sanity" worldwide, told GQ magazine in a cover story that he still feels the sting of racist attitudes. ... He feels a sense of bigotry toward him, that people see his skills as more limited because of his unique status. ... Lin felt racism slaps last season such as an ESPN website headline "Chink in the armor" after he had a poor showing on the court. (China Daily, 10/18/2012, p. 22)

In post-civil rights United States, participation in any cultural activity seems to be open to anyone regardless of their race or ethnic background, "but despite a lack of formal barriers, whites and blacks consume different forms of culture at different rates" (Goldsmith, 2003, 147). Such differences are present in various areas, such as language, approaches to education, music, hairstyles and dress preferences, as well as sports and physical activity. This chapter focuses heavily on the African-American population, as one of several the disadvantaged groups in North American society, since it represents one of the biggest minority groups currently residing in the United States with about 13 percent of the population. In addition, there is currently more research available on the topic of black involvement in sport and physical activity than on other minorities residing in the US. However, the experience of racism and prejudice is certainly not unique to this minority part of the population.

Teaching about the subject for decades, I have found that students are resisting talking about the issue for several reasons. First, race is considered a taboo topic for discussion, especially in a racially mixed setting. Second, many students, regardless of their racial group membership, have been socialized to think of the Unites States as a just society. And third, many students, particularly whites, initially deny any personal prejudice, recognizing the impact of racism on other people's lives, but failing to acknowledge its impact on their own. Therefore, some basic facts and definitions have to be spelled out first.

**Racism**, defined as a "system of advantage based on race," is a pervasive aspect of US socialization. It is virtually impossible to live in the USA without being exposed to some aspect of personal, cultural, and or institutional manifestations of racism in society. Race affects positions in the social structure, for example in the housing or job market (racial segregation), schools, socioeconomic status, and neighborhoods (Goldsmith, 2003). Some cultural differences between whites and blacks result from the socioeconomic inequality between the groups. "This probably reduces opportunities [for blacks] to swim and play soccer, and it crowds willing sports participants into the few available sports and facilities" – such as basketball and football (Goldsmith, 2003, 153).

*Prejudice*, defined as "preconceived judgment or opinion, often based on limited information," is clearly distinguished from racism. It is assumed that all of us have some kind of prejudice as a result of our upbringing; these can be positive or negative. However, it is our educational responsibility to resolve these issues and replace myth and stereotypes with accurate information. In US society, the system of advantage clearly operates to benefit whites as a group, and especially white males. We may not be blamed for what we have learned while growing up, but as adults we have the responsibility to try to identify and interrupt the cycle of oppression. It is assumed that change, both individual and institutional, is possible.

This chapter focuses on the issue of black involvement in sport and physical activity in various cultures. First, the particular sporting situation for African-Americans in the USA will be analyzed. The second issue introduces a unique African "sport," *Capoeira Angola*, an instrument of cultural resistance and survival of African tradition and values in the global community.

## Issue 1

## Racism in US Sport?

> On April 15, 1947, Jack Roosevelt Robinson stepped on the grass of Ebbets
> Field as a member of the Brooklyn Dodgers and became the first African-
> American to play in modern league baseball. The crumbling of baseball's
> wall of segregation was a harbinger of the Civil Rights movement. It
> came a year before President Harry Truman integrated the military
> and seven years before the United States Supreme Court, in its historic
> Brown v. Board of Education decision, declared school desegregation
> unconstitutional. (Sharon Robinson, New York Times, October, 2012)
> Jackie faced a lot of difficulties playing in the MLB, but Jackie kept his
> head up and fought back against racism and discrimination. He played
> ten outstanding seasons, and they won the World Championship in
> 1955. He was inducted into the National Baseball Hall of Fame in 1962.
> Jackie Robinson will always be remembered for what he did for the
> baseball world and "breaking the color barrier" in sports.

Jackie Robinson opened the door to African-Americans becoming involved in
more than just playing the game. Blacks have developed their own unique
styles and have become an integral part of the sporting culture in the USA –
haven't they? This historical overview will shed some light on the heritage of
this culture and pave the way for the much-heated debate regarding biological
versus cultural differences when it comes to the sport participation of blacks
and whites.

### Historical Development of Black Involvement in Sport and Physical Activity

There are no records of sport in the days before slavery. Generally there are
three historically distinct phases of African-American participation in sport: (1)
exclusion from sports for Blacks before the Civil War – during slavery; (2) sport
segregation according to the Jim Crow Laws after the Civil War until the 1960s;
and (3) the integration of blacks into sports since the mid-20th century (Sage,
1998, 88).

The Africans who were later to become American slaves participated in sports
such as horse racing, canoe racing, archery, foot racing, acrobatics, wrestling
and stick fights. It is often believed that some of the early American settlers'
interest in sport may have rubbed off on black slaves, but there is no real way
of knowing because there were never any records of athletic achievement by

slaves. When slavery ended, blacks began to imitate many of the "white" sports, just as the middle and lower classes of the Middle Ages had imitated the sports of the nobility.

In the late 1800s, slavery was abolished, but racism was still present through the so-called *Jim Crow Laws*, that stated that blacks and whites were separate but equal. The separation of blacks and whites penetrated nearly every area of life. These laws removed blacks from many previously integrated activities. During this period, many whites refused to play in a sporting match if a black person was on the opposing team. "Blacks were considered 'uncivilized' and should not be allowed to compete with Whites" was the assumption by many (Sage, 1998).

Examples of racism in those days included the search for the "White hope of boxing" in the early 1900s. This search was for the white man who would defeat the black boxing champion, Jack Johnson, who had won the heavyweight boxing championship in 1908. Another example of racism was present during the 1936 Olympic Games in Berlin, Germany, where Hitler wanted to showcase and prove the Arian supremacy. During these Games, Jessie Owens, one of the most accomplished track stars ever from the USA, achieved one of the greatest individual performances in the history of track and field. He won four gold medals, and Hitler left the stadium in protest. Hitler also did not stay for the presentations of these medals and refused to shake the hand of Jessie Owens because he was black.

During the times of segregation, blacks and whites had their own sport systems and teams. In the so-called "black" or "Negro" leagues, they started to compete exclusively against each other (Coakley, 2004). The same was true for college sport, where black student-athletes competed at black colleges in their own black conferences (Sage, 1998), with a few exceptions such as Jesse Owens or Jackie Robinson, who participated with whites on the same teams.

After WWII, Major League Baseball (MLB) was the first sport to accept blacks onto their teams; the legendary Jackie Robinson was the first African-American athlete on an all-white team in 1947. However, most people did not like to see this integration but their opinions remained as follows: "They've been getting along all right playing together, and they should stay where they belong in their league" (Eitzen & Sage, 1993, 324). Ten years later, there were still only 18 black players in the MLB. With the Civil Rights Movement, the situations for blacks in society and thus also in sports began to change. In addition, the increasingly profitable business of sports benefited greatly from having the best players on the team; thus, the earlier desegregation in sports was all profit-driven. White colleges began to recruit black athletes, and blacks themselves started to inquire with white rather than black colleges about possible athletic scholarships in the hopes of making it into the professional ranks after college. Subsequently, all-black sport teams and leagues folded altogether in the 1960s.

Of course, the integration of blacks into white teams was not without its problems. Blacks generally had to endure extreme hardships, which included being threatened with killings, being spat at both on and off the playing fields, racial remarks and slurs, and more (see the speech by Jackie Robinson's daughter at WCU, on tape in WCU library, 1997). At the college level, conflicts occurred about scheduling all-white teams against teams with black players. There were problems finding separate eating and hotel accommodations for the visiting players of a biracial team, and deciding when to allow Blacks to participate in intramural and varsity athletic programs.

Before the 1950s, black participation was concentrated within a few sports (e.g., baseball, basketball, and football). After the 1960s, desegregation of sports ceased for the most part; it was the hardest to change in the South, since slavery had been more prevalent in that part of the country, and people's opinions change very slowly. However, money was the main driving force behind schools' desegregation of their athletes.

Today, blacks and whites are participating in sports together. Studies have shown that boys of both racial groups participate the most in football and basketball, followed by baseball, soccer, and swimming. "Among girls in both racial groups, basketball is the most popular sport, then softball and cheerleading, followed by soccer and swimming. ... Blacks have higher participation rates than whites in basketball, football, and cheerleading ... Whites have higher participation rates than blacks in swimming, soccer, and baseball/softball" (Ogden & Hilt, 2003, 149). Why are there differences in sports preferences between whites and blacks, and why are blacks overrepresented in certain sports and underrepresented in most others?

## Black Dominance in Sport?

**Facts**
- Sports in the US have long histories of racial and ethnic exclusion and under-representation in most sports, even in high school and community programs.
- The number of black athletes has increased in team sports since WWII.
- In 2011, there were 77% African-American players in the NBA, 67% in professional football, 8.5% in Major League Baseball, and 26% in Major League Soccer.
- The other 40 men's and women's sports played in college hardly have any athletes of color.

- There is a virtual absence of black athletes in archery, auto racing, badminton, bowling, canoeing/kayaking, cycling, equestrian events, field hockey, figure skating, golf, gymnastics, hockey, figure skating, golf gymnastics, hockey, motocross, rodeo, rowing, sailing, shooting, alpine and Nordic skiing, soccer, softball, swimming, table tennis, team handball, tennis, volleyball, water polo, yachting, and many field events in track and field (Lapchick, Racial and Gender Report Card, 2001 and 2011).

Researchers in the social sciences have tried to explain why blacks dominate some sports, such as basketball and football, but are totally underrepresented in most others. Theoretical explanations range from (1) biological/genetic interpretations, to (2) psychological, and (3) sociocultural differences.

## (1) Biological/Genetic Interpretations

Biological theories assume that there are genetic differences between the races, and that these differences give blacks an edge over whites when it comes to sport competition (see Coakley, 2004; Volkwein, 1994; Sailes, 1996; Hoberman, 1997). These theorists try to prove that blacks have more red muscle fibers or better endurance, which they relate to better performance in various sports. Studies include jumping tests, tests in the motor development of black and white infants, muscular biopsies of fast and slow twitch muscle fibers, and more. However, these tests may be based on a racist hypothesis that tries to prove that there is a difference. They are expected to demonstrate support of the stereotype that European-Americans have fewer of these physical characteristics but a greater development of the intellect. And then researchers falsely conclude that there are better athletic performances overall by blacks over whites in some sports, which they justify with these biological/genetic interpretations, stating that there is a "natural difference."

Although there are differences between blacks and whites as a group, there are even more differences within a given race. So far, all of the research that has been conducted trying to relate these biological differences to better athletic performance by blacks over whites was not able to scientifically "prove" this assumption. On the contrary, this research is one more manifestation of people's racist attitudes wanting to prove that there are greater differences than similarities (Coakley, 2004; Hoberman, 1997). The fact is that there are far greater similarities among athletes per se, no matter what race, than there are differences. What makes a great athlete a great athlete is a combination of the right body type for a particular sport, opportunities and access to good facilities and coaches, as well as great dedication to the chosen sport, and a lot of *very hard work*. However, biological theorists ignore all other factors but the genetic ones when conducting their studies. Hence, this limited view does not represent the complex reality, but rather tries to convey and support a prejudiced and racist view of the world.

Further problems with these bio-scientific studies include the question "Who is black?" Racial categories are ill defined. Black sociologist Harry Edwards has asked, "Does one drop of black blood make a person fit the black category? The truth is that there is a lot of mixture!" (see Film "The Black Athlete – Fact or Fiction," 1989). For example, Tiger Woods is only one-quarter African-American, yet he is often identified as black because of how race has been defined in the United States.

Lastly, the sampling of people for these bio-genetic studies is problematic. Often, randomly superior whites are compared to randomly superior black athletes; and then the outcome is generalized and adapted for the whole population at large. At present, we do not know whether black athletes actually possess physical traits superior to those of whites. In order to avoid various forms of racial separation "scientists must know about the racial ideologies that permeate the cultures in which they live and do their research. ... If they don't do this, their research will deepen our sense of racial separateness in the world instead of deepen our knowledge about the complexity of human behavior and the full range of human genetic variations. This is a potentially dangerous way to do science" (Coakley, 2004, 296). Thus, many researchers claim that psychological and social reasons are more important in the making of a great athlete.

## (2) Psychological Interpretations

Psychological interpretations have found that African-Americans have come to believe the biological ideology that "blacks are naturally better athletes." This belief was voiced, for example, in an interview with the former black baseball player Joe Morgan: "Blacks, for physiological reasons, have better speed, quickness, and agility... I don't know why, but we are clearly superior in that way" (in Vogler & Schwartz, 1993, 111). Furthermore, when blacks are convinced that they are better in certain sports than in others, they will mainly choose to participate in these particular sports. The result is the overrepresentation of blacks in a few sports, such as basketball and football, and a total under-representation in most other sports.

The African-American subculture places a positive emphasis on the importance of physical and verbal skills. Athletic prowess, especially in black males, but also black females, is highly valued. Black athletes are folk heroes, especially in their communities, more than other accomplished African-Americans. This high level of status and recognition among their peers and the public adulation, especially as accorded to African-American basketball players, puts more pressure on black youth to succeed in sports more than any other social domain. Thus, African-Americans may perceive sport to be one of the few avenues to succeed in the highly competitive American society because their upward social mobility in the economic system is limited (Sage & Eitzen, 2013). A young African-American role model is more likely to be a sports hero than a young white male's role model. The determination and motivation dedicated to becoming successful in sport is thus far greater and more intense among black youth than it is among white adolescents in the USA.

If blacks and whites are convinced of the biological ideology, then whites would not try very hard to participate and become good in the so-called black sports, and the result would be that whites would channel their energy elsewhere. On the other hand, coming from a low socioeconomic background and seeing black sport stars made bigger than life through the media, the conviction among black youth becomes one that sports might be a secure way to achieve upward social mobility. However, the downfall is that this is a fallacy as well. Arthur Ashe stated this clearly, "[Fewer] than 900 black athletes are earning a living in sports – and not more than 1,500 overall including coaches and trainers. By comparison, there are perhaps 3 million black youth between the ages of 13 and 22 who dream of a career as an athlete. The odds are 20,000 to 1 or worse. Statistically, you have a better chance of getting hit by a meteorite in the next 10 years than getting work as an athlete" (Ashe, 1993).

## (3) Sociocultural Interpretations

Cultural studies have found that the over-representation of black athletes in selected sports is due to the over-emphasis of the importance of sport in the African-American community. Verbal and physical abilities are highly regarded qualities in black culture, which are equally reinforced by men and women. Successful athletes are the superstars, and they become the role models for many black children (Sage & Eitzen, 2013). However, this is only true for a very few sports, mainly basketball, football and baseball, that are very profitable and produce revenue in schools, universities, and the pros. In the so-called non-revenue producing sports, such as table tennis, gymnastics, diving, and others, black athletes are almost non-existent.

The explanation for the above-described phenomena is based on the socioeconomic situation of African-Americans in the USA. Since blacks are still not as visible in other prestigious job opportunities that are certainly wide open for whites, such as lawyers, doctors, engineers, professors, business owners, etc., they are gravitating into areas where the discrimination is not as fierce anymore, such as sports and the entertainment business. "Gifted black athletes will usually make out alright, but what happens to the thousands of young un-athletic children whose only heroes are sport stars? How many brilliant doctors, teachers, lawyers, poets, and artists have been lost because intelligent but uncoordinated black youths had been led to believe by a racist society that their only chance for getting ahead was to develop a thirty-foot jump shot or to run the 100 in 9.3" (Ashe, 1993)? As a result of the emphasis of certain sports in the black culture, whites are turning to other sports and employment opportunities (Volkwein, 1994).

Basketball has become an integral part of black culture; it is part of the collective identity of African-Americans, just like jazz or hip-hop because it is culturally marketed as black (Odgen & Hilt, 2003). Basketball influences black culture in the following ways: through encouragement and compulsion of black youths to pursue basketball as a sport and leisure activity; the predominance of black role models in basketball; black youths' use of basketball for self-expression and empowerment; and blacks' view of basketball as a vehicle for upward social mobility. Ogden & Hilt have noted that basketball uses expressions and empowerment as facilitators because the mass media has helped popularize the notion that blacks have used courts as sanctuaries of resistance and self-determination in oppressive and hostile inner city environments. They talk about how shoe and clothing companies portray black basketball players in pick-up games against beat-down, fenced-in playgrounds and urban decay. Some ads even have basketball players using street talk as an expression of inner city language. This study also found that African-Americans felt that playing basketball was an activity that best fit their leisure styles and preferences (Ogden & Hilt, 2003). Thus, young black males especially internalize the cultural role of basketball by incorporating basketball related apparel and paraphernalia in their own personal styles and approaches.

Young African-American males use celebrity black athletes as reference points and role models during their pre-teen years. These athletes help define their own masculinity, and inner city kids feel like these role models are successful men who can relate to their socioeconomic struggles. Basketball is seen as a means of social status for black youth, and many African-Americans believe that basketball is a vehicle for upward social mobility. Thus, basketball is perceived as the fastest way to a career in professional sports and out of an undesirable socioeconomic situation (Ogden & Hilt, 2003).

## Racial Discrimination in Sports

Many young people in the USA dream of a career as an athlete. However, the odds of becoming an athlete and making a living playing sports are very scarce. It is only one percent of all athletes at colleges and universities who will ever make it to the pros. When student-athletes focus all of their energy on becoming professional athletes rather than concentrating on getting a degree from the institution of higher education they attend, many leave the universities without a diploma in their hands. This is a particular problem for blacks participating in football and basketball, who dream of a professional career and then are not graduating (Edwards, 1988; Volkwein, 1994; Sage, 1998; Sage & Eitzen, 2013). Without a degree they are less likely to achieve upward social mobility.

Further structural constrains are that blacks are rarely found in sports that require special facilities, coaching and competition usually provided by private clubs. Many country clubs are still "white only" (no blacks or even Jews allowed). There is great under-representation of black athletes in at least 44 of the sports that are offered at colleges and universities. These include: hockey, ice skating, swimming, diving, golf, tennis, gymnastics, archery, shooting, badminton, skiing, kayaking, horseback riding, sailing, table tennis, men's volleyball, and more. In comparison, whites still participate more often in the "black sports" – football and basketball – than blacks participate in all these other "white" sports. Thus, the over-representation of blacks in these few sports is not the norm, but rather the exception. Furthermore, studies have shown that whites from the middle class more often participate in sports than all blacks together. Thus, whites, and not blacks, are still dominant in the participation of the US sport (Coakley, 2004; Sage & Eitzen, 2013).

Blacks participate in the sports that receive financial support for their living domains, including facilities, coaching, and mental support. Thus, it depends what is offered in their communities in recreational and school sport programs. Basketball and boxing are the two favorite sport activities of black youth. Sport participation that is more expensive and requires memberships in private clubs is not necessarily accessible. Many golf clubs still do not allow blacks to play on their greens. The same is true for tennis and motor sports. Although blacks dominated the sport of horseback riding as jockeys in the beginning of the 20th century, they were also excluded from this sport for the most part at the end of the 20th and the beginning of the 21st century (Sage & Eitzen, 2013; Lapchick, 2011).

Even though sport had opened its doors to the African-American population before the rest of society did in the 1960s, the integration of blacks and whites is mainly restricted to the playing fields. Research has shown that blacks and whites do not have much social contact off the playing fields. Through more social interaction between the various minority groups in society, myths and prejudices about them could be diminished; however, through the lack of contacts outside of sports, these stereotypes are often further strengthened (Coakley, 2004). Thus, racial discrimination in and through sports continues and is most visible in the two areas of (1) stacking and (2) coaching and administrative positions in the world of sport.

## (1) Stacking

Another phenomenon of discrimination in sport that often occurs is described as "stacking" by researchers, which generally means segregation by positions played in a given sport. In certain sports where blacks are dominating, not all playing positions are equally occupied by black athletes. For example, in professional baseball, black athletes are pre-dominantly found in outfield positions ("running positions"), while white athletes dominate the positions as pitcher or catcher ("thinking positions"). In football, the so-called thinking positions are also occupied by whites, such as quarterback, guard, kicker/punter or center, while the running back, wide receiver or corner back positions are played by blacks (Sage & Eitzen, 2013; Coakley, 2004).

In basketball, the phenomenon of stacking is not existent any longer, because of the high percentage of black players. In the 1950s and 1960s, blacks mainly held the center playing positions in basketball, while whites played center or point guard. The high percentage of black athletes in basketball, over 85 percent, changed this situation in the '80s and '90s, as did new strategies that have developed since. Thus, stacking has vanished in basketball, but is still existent in football and baseball. The positions where blacks are stacked require strength, speed, dynamics, and prowess – all physical characteristics; while whites are stacked in positions that require intelligence, mental stability, and independent decision-making (Lapchick, 1989). This segregation in playing positions in the sports of football and baseball are a reflection of the stereotypes still attached to blacks and whites; not only in US society, but in European societies as well.

Research has found that stacking is based on the ideology of genetic racial differences still held by coaches and managers. The belief behind stacking or "positional segregation" is that certain biological differences present an advantage to playing certain positions; and the stereotypical thinking is that "blacks are physically and whites are mentally superior." The consequences of stacking include situations wherein black and white players have come to believe themselves that they are better at playing some positions rather than others (Vogler & Schwartz, 1993). Even when black athletes enter college as quarterbacks, they often want to be trained as receivers or wide receivers in order to have better chances in the recruitment process for the pros, although we are now seeing the first African-American quarterbacks in professional football. Thus, the phenomenon of stacking is further strengthened by the players themselves, but hopefully this is gradually changing. The reality is that even in the professional ranks, the career of an athlete in so-called thinking positions is longer than in the physical positions. Subsequently, the pay in the physical positions is not only lower, but the playing career is also shorter and the pay into the player's pension fund is less (Vogler & Schwartz, 1993). Hence, stacking has many negative economic consequences for black athletes.

### (2) Coaching and Administrative Positions

At the end of active playing careers, many professional athletes hope to stay on as coaches or administrators. Especially if they do not have a diploma from a university, there are not many employment opportunities for retired athletes. Many professional athletes do not have a university degree – only 20% of professional basketball, 33% football, and 16% of professional baseball players have finished a degree in higher education (Lapchick, 1991); and today these statistics have not changed much.

Diverse statistics found in the *2011 Racial and Gender Report Card* (Lapchick) show that black athletes, although over-represented in the sports of basketball, football and baseball, are under-represented in the coaching and administrative positions in sports. Not long ago, there were no black head coaches in the NBA. In 2001, there were ten head coaches of color; ten years later, there are 30% people of color in head coaching positions versus 77% African-American players. And 36% of all professional positions in the NBA are held by people of color, including general managers and owners (7%).

In football and baseball, most black coaches are usually assisting white head coaches (Hoberman, 1997); in 2001 there were two in the NFL (10%) and six in the MLB (23%). Ten years later, there are eight head coaches of color in the NFL (22% African American coaches versus 67% African-American players) at the beginning of the 2011 season. This represents an all-time record for hiring coaches of color in the NFL. "The Rooney Rule, which requires that people of color be interviewed as part of the search process for head coaches, helped triple the number of African-American head coaches in the NFL" over the last ten years (Lapchick, 2011, 70). However, the owners of the NFL are still all white. And in baseball, the number of head coaches in 2011 are 12% for African-Americans (versus 8.5% players), 17% Latinos (versus 27% players), and 71% whites (versus 61.5% players) in Major League Baseball. There is no person of color serving in the position of CEO or team president on MLB teams (Lapchick, 2011).

As these statistics show, even affirmative action did not change much for the highest positions held in the word of sports; only in the minor-ranking jobs have people of color increasingly moved up over the years. This phenomenon is true for professional as well as university and college sports. Sport sociologists have summarized the research findings concluding that discrimination is the major factor why African-Americans and other minorities are still hardly present in head coaching and upper management positions in sports. However, over the last ten years, we have seen some changes in the right direction. With the implementation and adherence to rules such as the Rooney Rule in the NFL, we should see further improvements in the near future.

However, due to the practice of stacking, black athletes are also often overlooked when it comes to the hiring of coaches, because more athletes are hired as coaches who come from the central "thinking" or controlling playing positions. This example shows what consequences one form of disadvantage/discrimination has further down one's path. One form of discrimination will carry over into another one. Thus, the myths and misconceptions about any ethnic group in society have far-reaching consequences that are part of every aspect of one's social life, including sport.

## What can be done?

People within the world of sport and physical activity have come to acknowledge that there is still racism and discrimination in sport in the 21st century; and they have worked toward the elimination of racial disadvantage and discrimination in order to achieve better quality sport for African Americans and other ethnic minorities. The literature spells out the following aims: raising awareness of racial inequality in sport; increasing the number of black and ethnic minority decision makers in sport; improving skill and developing a positive attitude toward an active life for young black and ethnic minorities; and increasing opportunities for them.

Stereotypical thinking can be challenged through racial-awareness training and opportunities can be provided for different cultural groups to pursue their own cultural activities. This means that instead of encouraging ethnic minority groups to take part in white sports, why not give them the chance to play their own sports in North America and Europe, for example, in physical education class. An example of this is *Kabbadi*, a team sport originally from the Indian subcontinent, which is often played to stay fit. Another example is the sport of *Capoeira Angola*, which was developed by Africans in diaspora and is described in detail in the next issue of this chapter.

In order to increase the participation of ethnic groups in sport, certain barriers will have to be broken. One of these barriers is racism. There are many campaigns trying to get rid of racism in sport. One of the most popular is the *Stand up Speak up* worldwide campaign by Nike. This campaign empowers soccer fans to show their opposition to racism. The symbol of the campaign is a black & white interlocking wristband, as worn first in public by Thierry Henry at the World Player of the Year gala in Zurich in December 2004. The wristband was created as a symbol of camaraderie with the players and fans who share a determination to take positive action against racism in international football (American soccer). Nike launched high-profile TV advertising to support this campaign. Another international campaign aimed at kicking racism out of football/soccer is the *Kick it Out* campaign. This campaign is supported and funded through various international football associations. With campaigns like these being promoted by the sport's biggest role models, this has had an extremely positive effect, especially for the children and adults involved in these sports.

In North America, the NCAA, as well as the professional sporting associations, also have their own campaigns to be more inclusive and to fight discrimination and racism within their ranks. However, despite numerous reform efforts to clean up college sports, especially Division 1 football and men's basketball, the violations of NCAA rules continue with low graduation rates as well as athletes receiving illegal money from boosters (Sage & Eitzen, 2013, 127). The Knight Commission of Intercollegiate Athletics is a program created in 1989 that emphasizes the reconnection of intercollegiate sports with the educational mission of colleges and universities. However, as long as the *structure* of big-time, commercial college athletics stays intact, "a structure that is largely responsible for the pervasive corruption and abuses," hope for fundamental reform is just a dream. Any reform movement geared toward real change "should be directed at three crucial areas: the way sports are administered, the education of athletes, and the rights of athletes" (Sage & Eitzen, 2013, 128).

The professional sport leagues all have a business interest to become more diverse and foster a more inclusive culture; this is a "strategic priority critical to the continued growth of the game, strengthening ... clubs and continuing to lead through innovation" (Lapchick, 2012, 155). The formal commitments include a variety of programs directed toward diversifying employment and leadership, as well as offering urban youth initiatives, and supporting education and philanthropy, i.e., through scholarships. Furthermore, these initiatives are directed toward game and market development and community relations. Each major sport league has its own programs; however, they all state that diversity is one of their core values and an integral element in establishing their strategic initiatives (Lapchick, 2012).

## Conclusion

Why are there still cultural differences between whites and blacks? These differences have been created in complex ways; they are based on the structural inequalities between blacks and whites and by the relations between them throughout history. "In cultural forms consumed more by whites – swimming, soccer, and baseball (and by extension, opera and country/western music) – racial differences result mostly from racial inequalities in SES [socioeconomic status], neighborhoods, or some other structure (e.g., school size)" (Ogden & Hilt, 2003, 167).

Furthermore, sport as an avenue for upward social mobility for African-Americans seems to be a widely held belief by whites and blacks alike. However, more detailed investigations into the world of sport reveal that discrimination is still present there as well as in other areas of the US society. Thus, only at the surface does it look as if sport has made greater strides to overcome the injustices still suffered by blacks today. It is simply a myth that sport provides avenues for upward social mobility – that is only true for a very few. Even though blacks seem to have more opportunities in sports than in other social arenas, discrimination still continues: Blacks are admitted to lower-level occupations but are virtually excluded from positions of power and authority in the world of sport. Even though an African-American male has made it all the way to being the president of the US, that does not mean that racism and discrimination against blacks is non-existent.

It is true that a few top-level athletes can benefit from participation in sports. For example, "Magic" Johnson and Tiger Woods have gained great upward social mobility due to their involvement in sport, which they might not have achieved otherwise. And many African-American student-athletes are also benefitting from their athletic scholarships; however, this is not the norm but rather the exception. Media and advertising campaigns, however, show a different picture which presents sports as an arena where discrimination has been overcome. These campaigns have also led to the belief among the young black population that sports present great avenues for upward social mobility, when in fact education is a much more secure road to success. Black males have especially come to believe that sport is "THE way out," which then stirs all their energy and dedication in the wrong direction. Hoberman criticized this phenomenon: "that the black intelligentsia has had so little to say about the ruinous consequences of making athletic achievement the prime symbol of black creativity is in itself cause for concern" (1997, xxi).

Even if blacks would face less discrimination in sport in the near future, there are only a small number of jobs available in sports compared to the rest of the job markets in the US. However, it is very difficult to convince young black males that it would be wiser to channel their focus onto education rather than solely sports. As long as black athletes are presented as superheroes and "bigger than life," it will be very difficult to re-focus young African-American males into more lucrative and profitable careers other than sports. It is essential to teach that education is a more secure route to achieve upward social mobility than sport

– which is a myth that hinders and hurts black athletes more than whites. Sport is a reflection of society, and many more changes are needed before we can call the United States a truly fair and just society.

## References

Ashe, A. & A. Rampersad (1993). *Days of Grace*. New York, NY: Knopf.

Coakley, J. (2004). *Sport in Society – Issues and Controversies*. [8th Edition]. Boston, MA: McGraw Hill.

Edwards, H. (1988). The Single-minded Pursuit of Sports Fame and Fortune is Approaching an Institutional Triple Tragedy in Black Society. *Ebony*, August, 138-140.

Eitzen, S. & G. Sage (1993). *Sociology of North American Sport*. [6th Edition]. Dubuque: Brown Publishers.

Film (1989). The Black Athlete – Fact and Fiction. NBC News Special, November.

Goldsmith, P. (2003). Race Relations and Racial Patterns in School Sport Participation. *Sociology of Sport Journal, 20*(2), 147-177.

Hoberman, J. (1997). *Darwin's Athletes: How Sport has Damaged Black America and Preserved the Myth of Race*. Boston, New York: Houghton Mifflin Company.

Lapchick, R. (1989). Race on the College Campus. Pp. 55-71. In: Lapchick, R. & J. Slaughter (Eds.). *The Rules of the Game. Ethics in College Sport*. New York: McMillan.

Lapchick, R. (1991). *Five Minutes to Midnight: Race and Sport in the 1990s*. Lanham: Madison Books.

Lapchick, R. (2011). *Racial and Gender Report* Card. www.tidesport.org

Ogden, D. & M. Hilt (2003). Collective Identity and Basketball: An Explanation of the Decreasing Number of African-Americans on America's Baseball Diamonds. *Journal of Leisure Research, 35*(2), 213-227.

Racial and Gender Report Card (2001). Found at http://www.sportinsociety.org/

Sage, G. (1998). *Power and Ideology in American Sport*. [2nd Edition]. Champaign, IL: Human Kinetics.

Sage, G. & Eitzen, D. (2013). *Sociology of North American Sport*. New York, Oxford: Oxford University Press.

Sailes, G. (1996). An Investigation of Campus Stereotypes. Pp. 193-203. In: Lapchick, R. (Ed.). *Sport in Society*. Thousand Oaks: Sage Publications.

Vogler, C. & S. Schwartz (1993). *The Sociology of Sport*. Englewood Cliffs: Prentice-Hall.

Volkwein, K. (1994). "Schwarz-Weiß-Malerei" im nord-amerikanischen Sport. In: Alkemeyer, T. & B. Broeskamp (Eds.). *Fremdheit und Rassismus im Sport*. Dvs-Protokolle, Clausthal-Zellerfeld.

## Issue 2

# Capoeira Angola –
# A Symbol of Cultural Resistance and Survival

*(by Margaret Ottley)*

*Capoeira Angola* is fast becoming one the most unifying forces and symbols of resistance and survival for Africans in contemporary society. This phenomenal art form transcends the wisdom of the ancestors through its music, song and dance – three of the most powerful catalysts of African self-expressiveness and spirituality. The pulsating beat of Capoeira's central musical source, the berimbau (gunga, medio and viola or violinha), a bow-like percussive instrument, evokes the legacy of the past, revealing wisdom to understand the present and gain insight into the future. Capoeira Angola creates a path for present generations to rediscover their unique African heritage apart from differing social values learned from Western cultures.

Viewing the world through historic lenses affords Africans a greater understanding of their role in society as community builders and deters them from self-serving and other individualistic objectives. Greater economic, political, psychosocial, and spiritual interdependence within global African communities will inevitably lead to communal independence of all African peoples.

The concept of global growth and African liberation and unity is a macrocosm of the philosophical beliefs transmitted in the *roda*, or life circle, in which Capoeira Angola is played. The message of the roda is one of respect for one's heritage, physical and mental discipline, effort, determination, hard work and sweat, self awareness, and awareness of the dynamic structure of a rapidly changing environment. It also equips individuals with the appropriate tools and skills to stay on top of their game, developing strategic skills to easily adjust to different styles and innovative techniques. In essence, the roda of Capoeira Angola has become a safe space amidst external chaos resulting from conflicting contemporary western ideologies, attitudes, and values. The spirit of the roda teaches active practitioners to not readily succumb to these external group pressures and to continually strive for excellence in all aspects of life.

For the past two decades, Capoeira Angola has grown in popularity in countries such as Europe, Australia, Canada, and the Caribbean. In the United States of America, it is found in major cities such as New York City, Washington D.C., Philadelphia, Boston, Atlanta, and Oakland. However, its presence in today's society is a result of the courage and determination of African people in the face of centuries of colonial and postcolonial oppression. The mere survival of Capoeira Angola continues to be a cultural phenomenon.

The origins of Capoeira Angola remain obscure to researchers and capoeiristas alike. Researchers believe that in the late 1700s, Capoeira was considered a "social infirmity" by the first government of the newly established Republic of Brazil. Historian Nestor Capoeira (1995) theorized some motives behind the suppression of Capoeira Angola in 1892. He explained that the Portuguese colonizers in Brazil would not promote the practice of an art that gave Africans a sense of pride, self-confidence, cohesion, and the skill of a fearless fighter. These characteristics were contrary to the enslaved Africans' expected condition of servitude.

On December 15, 1890, Minister of Finance Ruy Barboso signed the Brazilian Penal code, which destroyed many important documents concerning slavery in an attempt to cleanse the country from an institution that had paralyzed its development for many years (Almeida, 1986). It was not until the early 1930s that Capoeira became a socially accepted national sport and became a symbol of self-expression, determination, and liberation.

The purpose of this chapter is to examine the role of the sport Capoeira Angola as an instrument of cultural resistance and survival for African people in diaspora and to highlight the invaluable contribution the art form may make to personal and social development. There are two popular forms of Capoeira, Angola and Regional. However, for the purpose of this chapter, the emphasis is placed on Capoeira Angola, the original form of Capoeira.

## Origins of Capoeira Angola

Capoeira Angola is often referred to as an African/Brazilian martial art/dance. Some researchers found that Capoeira Angola's peaceful Bantu origins made it an ideal instrument of war during African captivity and enslavement. Historically, as Africans refused to submit to the savage and brutal conditions of slavery, thousands of them escaped from the plantations and found refuge in hills and mountains. Free and organized Maroon colonies were formed in Jamaica, which were patterned by other Caribbean islands. In St. Domingue (Haiti), the genius of Toussaint l'Ouverture, leader of the slaves, defeated British troops and in 1799 was recognized by France as the country's Governor General. After Toussaint's capture and later death in France, new leaders, in particular Jean Jacques Dessalines and General Christopher, defeated Napoleon Bonaparte's French army and established the first independent, black republic.

Slaves uprisings also occurred in Grenada, Dominica, Curaçao, and St. Vincent (Sunshine, 1996). In Brazil, enslaved Africans combated the oppressive colonial power of the Portuguese during revolts and in defense of free Quilombos-African communities. The dance-fight nature of Capoeira Angola made it seemingly

187

appear as playful sparring involving style, wit, flexibility, and strategy. Music was played during Capoeira sessions not only to teach the rhythmic heart of the art but also to mask its martial power. The enslavers initially thought it was high-spirited acrobatic dancing (Mansa, 1997).

"By the mid-1940s, Capoeira had been recognized by the Brazilian government as an official sport" (Dossar, 1994). In an attempt to briefly explain the concept of the sport, sociologist and capoeiristas, Nester Capoeira (1995) identified the interconnected levels of Capoeira, which are the physical aspect, the philosophy, and the musical instruments and songs. The physical aspect relates to "the fight, the dance and the competition" (Capoeira, 1995, 30). "Only one's hands, head, and feet are allowed to touch the floor. Being swept off of one's feet and landing on one's bottom disqualifies a player" (Dossar, 1994, 87). In practice, when the game is played, players limit their strikes to using their bodies to show their opponents that they can be hit. Players learn from their masters how to acknowledge "their camaraderie as well as their opposition" (Thompson, 1988, 138).

## Theoretical Perspectives

The persistence of African cultural art forms in the African diaspora, despite centuries of suppression by colonial and postcolonial powers, symbolizes courage, resilience, and the determination of African people. White and Parham (1990) claimed that traditional scholars were unwilling to recognize the presence of African influence on the lifestyles of blacks. These scholars believed that the brutal effects of slavery, the resulting economic, legal, and political oppression forced blacks to abandon the existing traces of African culture.

Some historians believed that people of African decent, for example in the West Indies, did not maintain a substantial history of their own, nor did they retain a native civilization, language, or religion of their own (James, 1985.) James argued that even the Rastafarians resorted to the English Bible to prove that the Emperor of Ethiopia was God. However, this deprivation of authentic African culture made them an open people to a number of disparate civilizations.

Other researchers support the view that Western culture had an impact on modern Black culture, but they reject any notion that enslaved Africans were empty vessels who were acted upon, shaped, and dominated by Western culture (Nobles, 1974). White and Parham suggest that to discount the presence of the concept of the African norm is to miss the forest for the trees. African worldview signifies the individual as a thinking, acting, feeling, experiencing, knowing, dynamic being endowed with supreme life force. People are psychologically interlocked with each other in a framework that values collective survival, interdependence, and feelings of compassion, love, joy, and sensuality.

Aesthetically, African normative base reflects a unified sense of youthfulness, vitality, flair, color, playfulness, and animation in music, song, dance, and language. Additionally, the perseverance and mutual respect of our ancestors that lead to positive outcomes, cooperation and determination also stand in sharp contrast to the values and attitudes of today's young generation. Many researchers argue that youths today are losing their traditional values and ultimately their ability to successfully negotiate their way through life in ways that lead to positive outcomes and the development of a full range of choices and options (White & Parham, 1990).

It is therefore imperative that young people of African decent learn to appreciate that the traditional values suppressed by Western ideologies are the same values that contributed to the survival of African people. They must learn to take into consideration the unique characteristics of their ancient culture and know that those characteristics are the trademark for success and self-identity.

Within an Africanist sociocultural framework, it is also imperative that young people understand the factors within a dynamic social system that may contribute and/or influence the attainment of personal and communal goals. A strong sense of self will provide them with a balance between internal desires and external demands. This self-knowledge includes the extended self, ancestors, unborn, nature, and the community (White & Parham, 1990). The concept of self-knowledge serves as a determinant of attitudes and perspectives toward the importance of ancestral play, such as Capoeira Angola.

For an African, Capoeira Angola is one of life's metaphors that symbolizes self-determination, liberty, and survival of past cultural oppression. It may serve as a road map, which helps the individual toward a goal of achievement, desire, trust, and pride. These positive qualities are contradictory to the negative, hostile realities that promote the socially driven, self-destruction of Blacks in today's society. A history of slavery and racial victimization, combined with the psychic damage inflicted by systematic and religious theories of black inferiority, imposed upon blacks a historical burden that went beyond poverty and poor living conditions (James, 1963). White and Parham (1990) argued that blacks were seen as culturally deprived and required cultural enrichment. Western idealists established a subservient standard that deemed inferior any other cultural differences in values and lifestyles.

On the other hand, black culture legitimized itself in the face of geographical challenges by maintaining a rich oral tradition. Through music, song, and dance, the presence of Capoeira Angola recorded the heritage of African people and symbolizes survival, struggle, and liberation. Capoeira Angola is a metaphor for black sociocultural norms ventilating what is considered unnatural human behavior and illuminating a more holistic presence of ancestral connectivity, harmony, and rhythm.

## Nature of Rhythm

Melodies, harmonies, and rhythms reveal meanings and insights into self. One sees more ways to look at a problem, an idea, or a person. Music and rhythm seem to induce a heightened empathy for others, a sense of unity among people, and "a sensitivity for the divine" (Bonny & Savary, 1990). Rhythm is a "force" that moves from the inside out. It is a force, that helps propel individuals to explore and seek sensations, take risks, and become adventurous as they interact with their environment. Jahn (1961), a noted scholar who wrote several books on African culture, quoted philosopher Leopold Sedar Senghor, in Muntu, to capture the inseparable relationship between rhythm and culture:

> Rhythm is the architecture of being, the inner dynamic that gives it form, the pure expression of the life force. Rhythm is the vibratory shock, the force which, through our senses, grips us at the root of our being. It is expressed through corporeal and sensual means; through lines, surfaces, colors and volumes of architecture, sculpture or painting; through accents in poetry and music, through movement in dance. But, doing this, rhythm turns all these concrete things towards the light of the spirit. In the degree to which rhythm is sensuously embodied, it illuminates the spirit (Jahn, 1961, 164).

In movement forms and sports, in particular, research has shown that as an external medium music stimulates a positive effect on an individual's movement repertoire. However, to view music simply as an external stimulus used for exercise or to create and/or explore moods and emotions or to provide positive reinforcement is limiting. These activities may stimulate a sense of euphoria or create a temporary escape from the harshness of reality but may not create a more ongoing state of well-being. Simply listening or even dancing to music without a historical point of reference deprives the individual of engulfing the spirit of the music. In actuality, the individual resumes to a prior state soon after the music ceases.

In African rhythmic sense, the use of actual music is not essential to become attuned to the natural rhythm of the body. An individual's entire being is inextricably woven and organized into a fabric of rhythmic patterns. The heartbeat, breathing, and intestinal rhythms are only a few examples of the most vital functions for existence (Bartenieff & Lewis, 1982). In a musical sense, rhythm may be explained as "musical notes," which are added one after the other to form a scale. Physically, the movement of the head, the shoulders, the arms, the hips, and the legs developed one after the other, reveal the natural interdependence of the parts of the body (Bertherat & Bernstein, 1979).

This interdependence of parts is related to a sensory experience of the body. "Who we are" is reflected and manifested in our bodies. For this reason, postural characteristics and physical alignment are reflective of one's mental state. Furthermore, through the body and senses, one formulates a mental picture of reality. It is the harmonious interaction between psyche and soma that promotes conflict-free functioning and peak performance (Schoop & Mitchell, 1974).

Schoop and Mitchell (1974) also believe that the most powerful use of music is that which delves beyond the conscious merging with the unconscious and manifests itself in personal body rhythms within every individual. Through this rhythm, the body is naturally constructed to function at its maximum, and individuals would be more likely to develop their own personal style. The exploration of natural body rhythms attempts to take an in-depth journey within the self, to have individuals rediscover their natural body rhythms through holistic participation. They become aware of the sensory experience of the body, discarding defective postures and actions that they have been involuntarily executing for years (Bertherat & Bernstein, 1979).

## Self-identity and Capoeira Angola

According to dancer, choreographer, and researcher Welsh Asante (1979), individuals discover three main senses as they find integration, organization, and meaning in themselves and their social environment. First, the multiple rhythmic sense helps the individual to learn that movement and rhythm are inseparable; the more the senses are involved, the more rhythmic individuals flow. They become more in tune with tasks and others around them. Second, the holistic sense represents silence or stillness. It is as much a part of performance and rhythm as sound and movement. For example, Michael Jordan, the ex-basketball player for the Chicago Bulls, performs a jump shot that can be perceived as having a take-off, pause and execution sequence. This is a major aspect of his personalized rhythm; if that silence and stillness are broken, the rhythm is destroyed. A third sense is repetition; this is not a mere repeat of a skill in practice but the intensifying of one movement, one sequence, or the entire skill. It is not static; individuals move from one level to another – closer to her or his goal. When the skill is completely learned, they reach a sense of satisfaction.

Time is a factor in skill acquisition, but a sufficient amount of time is desirable, rather than a set amount of time regardless of progress.

## Movement Aesthetics of Capoeira Angola

Capoeira Angola movement aesthetics are further analyzed to explain the dynamic applications associated to the art. Welsh Asante (1990) and Thompson's (1974) paradigms of African movement aesthetics, such as polyrhythmic, curvilinear, multidimensional, and coolness, may be directly related to movement aesthetics found in Capoeira Angola. It is therefore not surprising that Capoeira Angola has grown in popularity amongst young people of African decent. For example, its "freedom to improvise and create openings for attack [and defend] keep the game's action fluid" (Dossar, 1994, 92) develops skills in decision-making and strategic planning. Capoeira Angola "stresses flexibility, strength, ground techniques, and the ability to confuse the opponent through feints, and malicia" (Dossar, 1992, 6). These characteristics require great cognitive and physical skill and are key alertness, reaction and movement.

## Major Characteristics of Capoeira Angola

- *Malicia:* Malicia refers to "having the ability to fool, thereby mentally and physically disarming an opponent" (Dossar, 1992). D'Aquino (1983) explained that the use of malicia is to hide one's intentions and abilities until they can be used to one's utmost advantage. In capoeira, the term "malicia" refers to a mixture of shrewdness, street-smarts, and wariness (Capoeira, 1995), which result as the sharpness of the students' games improve and their bodies learn to respond correctly to the tactics of the jogo [game], and as they become able to defend and attack with precision, power, and grace (Almeida, 1986).
- *Aus:* a Bantu word for cartwheel (Thompson, 1988). It represents personal, special and temporal awareness through movement, strategically placing oneself in a more proactive position. Situations are better assessed when viewed from various angles, and often times, from the bottom up.
- *Ginga:* a Portuguese word for the basic capoeira move; shifting the weight from the front foot to the back, then to the front again, while simultaneously holding the left arm up in defense, then the right arm, in opposition to the leg positions. A motion that involves rocking from side to side while bouncing forward and back (Thompson, 1988). The basic ginga lays a foundation for all other movements. It represents balance, style, momentum, and flow. It is the yardstick with which life's opportunities are measured, planned, and implemented.

- *Negativa:* a basic get-down defense stratagem from Kongo, one leg bent inside, the other extended forward, ready to trip up any enemy. The low gravity makes the player, momentarily almost invulnerable (Thompson, 1988).

- *Roda:* a Portuguese word for "circle" in which the game is played (Dossar, 1994). All of life's challenges and contradictions are intertwined in a universal circle or wheel. Players realize their path of consciousness, gain insight, and utilize conflict resolution and problem-solving techniques as they commune with each other.

- *Capoeiristas:* one who practices the art of Capoeira, legacies, and philosophies as a way of life.

## Implications for (Movement) Education

The rapid international growth of Capoeira Angola signifies that present generations have rediscovered its unique cultural relevance. The effects of the movement art form go far beyond its aesthetic qualities. Music, song, and dance are the media through which ancestral messages manifest themselves in the individual. The interdependence of body parts give them a sense of "Who they are" and their relations to their communities and society at large. However, it is the awaking of the sub-conscious self that is most significant. The conscious pathways deepen into the unconscious domains and manifest themselves in personal, social and cultural meanings within every individual.

The individuals' subjective experience, which emerges during improvisational play in Capoeira, is followed up with self-observation, self-reflection, and movement reproduction of significant aspects of sequences. In this way, the individual is able to organize, and thus physically master, the flood of unconscious stimuli that emerge during periods of spontaneous improvisation (Levy, 1992). The individual is then able to experience that feeling without conflict and can communicate it accurately and realistically, and other people can recognize and react to it. It is the individuals' responses that reinforce the performer's sense of reality.

The spirit of Capoeira Angola unleashes individuals' courage to pursue social and cultural goals and the determination to cope with the inequalities and injustices of existing society and persistence to restructure social institutions. The influence of social change results in political, economic, mental, and spiritual liberation of all African peoples. Capoeira Angola gives individuals a sense of belonging, community, pride, and ethnic identity. They understand the unifying strength within the phrase "there is no 'I' in 'we.'" The word "I" stands alone immersed in self-serving and group-sabotaging objectives.

Through the senses, Capoeira Angola helps individuals formulate a mental picture of reality. Postural characteristics and physical alignment of the body are reflective of one's mental state. The roda provides a forum for individuals to play a key role in their own educational and personal development. They are exposed to constant practice, feedback, peer evaluation and opportunities to vicariously model great Capoeira mestres who are always willing to dazzle enthusiastic students with their fine form and sit and share their philosophies in camaraderie.

Capoeira's social structure allows individuals the opportunity to develop at their own pace, gain confidence with every successful task accomplishment and transport themselves from a reactive mindset to having proactive focus and becoming a self-directed being. The personal meaning young capoeiristas learn in the roda is the basis of all human fulfillment and self-actualization.

# References

Almeida, B. (1986). *Capoeira: A Brazilian Art Form*. Berkeley, California: North Atlantic Books.

Bartenieff, I., & Lewis, D. (1982). *Body Movement: Coping With the Environment*. New York: Gordon and Breach.

Bertherat, T., & Bernstein, C. (1979). *The Body has Its Reasons: Anti-exercises and Self-awareness*. New York: Avon.

Bonny, H., & Savary, L. (1990). *Music & Your Mind: Listening With a New Consciousness*. Barrytown, NY: Station Hill Press.

Capoeira, N. (1995). *The Little Capoeira Book*. Berkeley, California: North Atlantic Books.

D'Aquino, I. (1983). *Capoeira Strategies for Status, Power and Identity*. Dissertation. University of Illinois. Ann Arbor, MI: UMI.

Dossar, K. (1994). *Dancing Between Two Worlds: An Aesthetics Analysis of Capoeira Angola*. Unpublished Doctoral Dissertation, Temple University, Philadelphia, PA.

Dossar, K. (1992). Capoeira Angola: Dancing between Two Worlds. *Afro-Hispanic Review, XI*, pp. 5-10.

Jahn, J. (1990). *Muntu: African Culture and the Western World*. New York, NY: Grove Press.

James, C.L. R. (1985). *At the Rendezvous of Victory*. London, England: Allison and Busby.

Levy, F. (1992). *Dance Movement Therapy*. Reston, VA: American Alliance for Health, Physical Education, Recreation and Dance.

Mansa, C. (1997, May). Capoeira Angola is. In: C. Mansa (Chair), *Working Through Differences to Achieve One Goal*. Symposium conducted at the third annual Capoeira Angola Encounter, Washington, DC.

Nobles, W. (1974). Africanity: Its role in Black Families. In: A.K. Burlew, W.C. Banks, H. P. McAdoo, & D.A. Azibo (Eds.), *African-American Psychology*. Newbury Park, CA: Sage Publication, Inc.

Schoop, T., & Mitchell, P. (1974). *Won't You Join the Dance? A Dancer's Essay Into the Treatment of Psychosis*. USA: Mayfield Publishing Co.

Sunshine, C.A. (1996). *The Caribbean: Survival, Struggle and Sovereignty*. Washington, DC: Epica.

Thompson, R.F. (1974). *African Art in Motion*. Los Angeles: University of California Press.

Thompson, R.F. (1988). Tough Guys Do Dance, *Rolling Stone*, March, 135-140.

Welsh-Asante, M., & Welsh-Asante, K. (1990). *African Culture: The Rhythms of Unity*. Westport, CT: Greenwood Press.

White, J.L., & Parham, T.A.P. (1990). *The Psychology of Blacks: An African-American Perspective*. Upper Saddle River, NJ: Prentice Hall.

## CHAPTER 7:

# GENDER AND SPORT – FITNESS – PHYSICAL ACTIVITY

*Sport is training ground where boys learn what it means to be men. ... Because sport is identified with men and masculinity, women in sport become trespassers on male territory and their access is limited or blocked entirely. (Pat Griffin, 1998) Sports is a women's issue because female sport organization empowers women, thereby inexorably changing everything. (Mariah Burton Nelson, 1994)*

The changing role of women in sport has become a more significant subject in society as a whole, since women have increasingly moved into previously male-dominated domains, such as work, sports, church, and the military. Physical and athletic abilities of women in sport and physical activity are constantly increasing; some researchers even predict that women may outperform men in certain sports in the near future. However, the issues at stake are not so much the existence of women in sport, but rather their particular role within sports. "According to many scholars, it seems that throughout history, with some exceptions, biological differences between the sexes predicted role specialization and possibly status and power differential" (Sands, 1999, 100). Early on in history, in many cultures, the female role had been relegated to the private spheres, specializing in domestic and child-rearing responsibilities. While male power had been closely related to the public spheres of life, where sports developed. In the past, "sports also produced male-only bonding that occurred outside the family and away from females" (Sands, 1999, 102).

When women finally increasingly moved into the world of sports during the latter half of the 20th century, they were not embraced with open arms. Rather they were treated, and still are often treated, as intruders in a male-only domain. Ongoing power struggles are manifested in various forms of harassment against women, such as sexual harassment. However, in order to understand the problems associated with the increased participation of women in sport over the years, an understanding of the impact of one's gender in the development of an individual as well as society at large is necessary. In this chapter, the primary focus will be on the injustices and inequities females have faced in sports and physical activity over the years. However, the picture would not be complete if such an analysis would ignore the larger social analysis of gender issues. Furthermore, it is pertinent to discuss what gender equity means and how it can be achieved. Thus, this chapter will explore the following issues regarding gender in sport and physical activity. First, it will be considered whether women's increased participation has helped to liberate or further oppress them. Second, the on-going controversies about Title IX will be explored. Third and fourth, the controversial issues of sexual harassment and abuse, as well as homophobia in sport, will be discussed.

## Issue 1

# Sport – Liberation or Oppression?

Sport, although enjoyed by millions all over the world no matter what race, gender, age, religion, physical ability, or sexual orientation, has been oppressive and liberating at the same time. Depending on the time in history, social status of people engaging in sport, and philosophy of the country and nations, sport has helped many people find enjoyment, pleasure, and relief from daily routines and problems. Furthermore, sport has aided many in the development of self-esteem as well as their general concept of being and self; however, not everyone has or has had the chance to experience the great joys of sport participation and physical activity to the same extent. Sport is also used by leaders in the world to keep people under control, as well as to promote nationalism and culturism, which is a certain philosophical view of the culture one lives in. Money and power have always had a great influence on what people engage in, and the same is true for the area of sports and physical activities.

> Male/female disparities in wealth, power, and prestige are ubiquitous social phenomena. Men are privileged throughout the occupational structure; they experience greater material rewards, a higher level of deference and esteem, and a more dominant position in the control of both their personal lives and their social activities. (Sage & Eitzen, 2013, 316).

"People like to think that sport transcends issues of money and power, and economic inequalities" (Coakley, 2009, 280). It looks like sport is open to everyone who wants to have access to it – whether it is on the playing field or in the spectator stands. After all, on television one can follow whatever is going on in sport for "free." Furthermore, many people believe that sports provide wonderful avenues for people to make money and improve their status, including their socioeconomic situation in society. However, these beliefs distract from the realities that are experienced by many where these assumptions do not hold true. In this chapter, the exclusion and inclusion of North American women in the sporting domain will be investigated based on historical and sociocultural analyses.

## Historical Account

In the United States as far back as 1790, black and white women were socially and politically active in female literary associations, anti-slavery societies, missionary groups, maternal and relief organizations, benevolent societies, and liberation and freedom organizations. In the context of these times, women were active but not involved in organized sports. Nevertheless, they were concerned with improving themselves, their health and preparing themselves for the most important role of their lives – motherhood (Sterling, 1984).

Sport, recreation and leisure were limited to the wealthy. "By the early 1880s upper-class women were joining their husbands as members of country clubs and were participating in tennis, golf, and horseback riding" (Cordes & Ibrahim, 1999). In 1888, the invention of the safety bicycle gave women an alternative to walking and bathing. Aviator Amelia Earhart wore bloomers, which set a fashion trend for women to free themselves from the requirement of having their ankles covered with long dresses. When the Turnverein movement brought gymnastics from Germany to the United States around 1880, municipalities began to open public gymnasiums, and women started to participate in gymnastics, calisthenics, swimming, basketball and volleyball. Also during this time, the public parks movement began to establish botanical gardens and beautification societies. This development led to new recreational pursuits that included women.

The establishment of the *Girls Guide* and *Girl Scouts* in 1912 also included females in some physical activity; and by 1980, the clubs had a membership of 2.9 million people (Krause, 1995). A visionary, named Luther Halsey Gulick, felt that girls needed to exercise as much as boys. In 1910, he founded the *Camp Fire Girls of America*, one of the first organizations where girls could explore nature and vigorously pursue character building through play activities. These activities for women in the early 1890s are described as a form of play, entertainment, and recreation, but not a revenue producing sport as we think of it today. *The Girls Clubs of America*, founded in 1945, was the first and only organization, which provided daily physical activity programs for girls. The National Girls' movements sought to be a significant force within the feminist movement; as an active member of the *Women's Action Alliance* it participated in forming the *National Women's Agenda* (Krause, 1995).

"Finally, when women moved increasingly into the world of sport during the latter half of the 20th century, they were not embraced with open arms. Rather they were treated, and still are treated, in many ways as intruders in a previously male-only domain" (Volkwein & Sankaran, 2002, 27). Thus, the struggle for the privilege to participate in sport has been a long hard -ought battle, with many "casualties" along the way. For example, during World War I and World War II women came to the forefront in social life. When men were called to fight in the wars, women worked in the factories and played semi-professional baseball and basketball; events that were watched and enjoyed by the masses. These women's teams travelled from state to state mostly in the West and the Midwest.

During World War II, the All-American Girls Baseball League was formed. Between 1943 and 1954 more than 600 women played a schedule of 110 to 116 games a year with nearly 1 million fans flocking to the games. Babe Didrikson dominated the Ladies Professional Golf Association (LPGA). The Women's Professional Bowling Association (WPBA) was established in 1959, and in 1950 Althea Gibson broke the color barrier in professional tennis, becoming the first African-American to compete in a Grand Slam event; the US National Tennis Championships at Forest Hills, New York. In 1957, Gibson won the women's singles title becoming the first African-American man or women to win a national Grand Slam title (Cordes & Ibrahim, 1999, 176).

When the wars were over, the women were "forced" to resume their roles as wives and mothers. Many chose to continue to play ball. College women who wanted to continue to play formed organizations like the *Girl's Athletic Associations* (GAA), the *Women's Athletic Association* (WAA), and the *Women's Recreational Association* (WRA). Through these organizations, high school and college women could continue to participate in physical activity. However, there was no budget, no equipment, no pay for coaches, and no recognition for the jobs as women's physical educators. These extracurricular activities were in addition to regular teaching job assignments. Throughout the 1930s and 1940s women had no athletic or sports teams, no scheduled competitions, and no future in sports. In fact, women were not encouraged to educate themselves in high school or college.

In the early 20th Century, American women were not allowed to vote, own property or make contracts. They were not expected to pursue higher education or to contribute to public life; in fact, they were actively discouraged from becoming anything other than housewives and hostesses or, if unmarried, dutiful daughters (Cordes & Ibrahim, 1999, 172).

At that time, education was designed to support the family and its current social structures. While men enjoyed the privilege of a college education, most women did not. Women were especially not allowed to step onto a playing field. They were relegated to participation as cheerleaders, gymnasts and dancers – as entertainers while men had established sport teams in schools and universities in which they could develop character, physical skill and other career potentials. Men played football, baseball, ran track and field, and participated in many other sports as well. Indicative of this time in sport was a saying that GOLF meant, "Gentlemen Only Ladies Forbidden." Even in education, women were believed to be unimportant. In educating a man, you educate a man. However, when educating a woman, you educate a family. And since the family is the strongest core of our civilization, it would behoove us to invest in both.

## Current Situation

Today, women's roles have changed considerably. Women have gained entry into physical activity through recreation and leisure pursuits. Much of the transformation of women's sport as we know it today was made possible through social and political struggles for equity and humanity. The introduction of gender equality through the establishment of Title IX in 1972 in the United States led to the formal creation of equal opportunity for women in educational institutions that receive federal funding.

> Title IX states: "No person in the United States shall on the basis of sex, be excluded from participation in, be denied the benefits of, or be subjected to discrimination under any education program or activity receiving Federal financial assistance" (see Issue 2). This included sport and athletics.

Prior to Title IX, women controlled women's games and athletics without financial support for facilities, uniforms for athletes, transportation to competitions, or any of the trappings of present-day programs that coaches and women athletes of today take for granted. Women scheduled their sporting events, recruited athletes, and fundraised for uniforms and transportation. They developed administrative, organizational, coaching, and leadership skills. However, since the introduction of Title IX, the situation for girls and women has changed tremendously. While female participation in sports has greatly increased over the last 40 years, athletic and coaching positions for women were severely reduced. "In 1996, only 18.5% of women's programs were administered by women and the proportion of women's coaches have declined to 47%. This is a decline of 8% from 1994 despite the growth of women's teams by 20% during the same two year period" (Cordes & Ibrahim, 1999). Although the majority of girl's teams in high school programs were coached by women as of 2011, this was not true at the college level, where we have seen a further decline of women coaches to 43% in 2010 (Sage & Eitzen, 2013, 332).

Further disturbing facts include that the percentages of African-American head coaches of women's basketball teams were less than 7%, while 50% of the student-athletes were African-American females in the three divisions of the NCAA in 2010. And another discriminatory issue revolves around the payment for services and average salaries for women coaches compared to men coaches. There remains a wide range of salary disparities between men and women's coaching jobs, among them the top salary figures for the best Division I men's basketball coaches, who had an annual salary between 3-4 million dollars in 2011, while the top women's basketball coaches' salary in the same Division ranged from 1-2 million dollars (Sage & Eitzen, 2013, 333). Hence, more men than women are now in control of women's athletics with greater salaries, better facilities, and high school and university jobs that were previously held by women. So the struggle for women being in control of women's sports continues.

In 1973, the most publicized battle between the sexes was staged in Madison Square Garden in New York between Bobby Riggs and Billy Jean King. Bobby challenged Billy Jean to play a tennis match to settle the debate, once and for all, that the worst male tennis player could overpower and beat the best woman tennis player in a match. These types of debates about men's superiority over women went on, not only in the tennis circuits, because men felt that the accommodations and salaries they made in relationship to that of the women was warranted. At this particular match between Billy Jean King and Bobby Riggs there was more at stake than just a tennis match; it was a match to establish a place for women in professional athletics. Women had been fighting for equal pay in the tennis circuits and in life. Men were getting two and three times the purse that women got at the same events, whether these were local, national, or grand slam tournaments. Men would argue that watching women was not as interesting as watching men. However, this event proved them wrong. Madison Square Garden was filled to capacity and television viewers were glued to the screen. Bets were waged as to who would win. Even the most ardent male supporter of women athletes did not believe that Bobby Riggs would lose to Billy Jean King. Tensions remained until the last point was played. Billy Jean King had defeated Bobby Riggs. Today, the purse for women in tennis is comparable to that of men playing at the same event.

Pre-Title IX through post-Title IX, women of all races, temperament, and types have been revolutionaries. Their mere presence and drive gave them recognition. Although doors were closed for women to enter the world of sports for many years, they found ways to be included nevertheless. Today we celebrate women athletes, dancers, and performers, such as Katherine Dunham, Pearl Primus, Judith Jamison, Debbie Thomas – skating; Wilma Rudolph, Lucinda Williams Adams, Florence Griffith Joyner ("Flo-Jo"), Jackie Joyner Kersey – track and field; Flo Hyman – volleyball; Venus and Serena Williams and Chanda Rubin – tennis; and gymnast Dominique Dawes (Brooks & Althouse, 1993, Ploski, & Brown 1967). The names are endless.

## Voices of the Oppressed: The African-American Female Experience

Voices of oppressed women can be heard in every corner of the United States. Donna Lopiano, director of the *Women's Sport Foundation*, wrote of her degrading experiences as a young athlete trying out for a sport on the boys' teams because she was good enough to do it (Lapchick, 1996). Similar experiences are still happening regardless of the sport. The love of the game compels athletes of every color, race, religion, and gender to play. Over time, women have had to overcome the burdens of gender, of challenging sports, and the social stigma associated with societal labels, such as "tomboy" or other sex-role stereotypes. Many grandmothers used to warn their female grandchildren: The girls that the boys play ball with in the daytime are not the same girls they take to the prom at night.

The often wrongly perceived paradox of being a female and being an athlete makes it difficult for women to overcome the social stigma and being accepted as an individual. "Flo-Jo" with her personality, style, long nails, long hair, and fancy track attire changed that image from a masculine athlete to a beautiful, feminine woman. She was able to market her image into commercials and into television shows. Even as feminine as she was, she was accused of using steroids in competitions simply because she shattered track records so convincingly. Many female athletes are still not considered feminine or attractive. For example, it was heard in the locker rooms of the tennis circuits that "Venus is no beauty" – well Venus is beautiful now. Today, media embraces both her and her sister. The diversity within American culture and multiculturalism speaks to everyone within and from the context of sport.

African-American women in sport are "double oppressed" based on race and gender. Although for almost every sport there has been an African-American present in individual and team sports (for both men and women), the media coverage for African-Americans in individual sports has not been widely covered. Individual sports by its very nature are inherently "elite." Therefore the coverage at those events will invariably focus on the most socially and economically prominent individuals participating because of the elite nature of the event. African-American athletes in individual sports are often ignored or portrayed in a negative fashion. African-American women have not had the same social restraints of sports participation as white women (Brooks & Althouse, 1993). To excel in sports is hard enough without the added burden of gender and racial discrimination. Many of the female African-American athletes had their beginnings in the *Historically Black Colleges and Universities* (HBCU) and not in predominately white educational institutions. African-American sportswomen have served as role models for their race and engendered a sense of pride and accomplishment.

Venus and Serena – together the famous African-American tennis stars' accomplishments in their time excel what few black women were able to accomplish throughout history. Althea Gibson did it; Zina Garrison, Lori McNeil, Katrina Adams, Renee Blount, and very few others were able to break through the tennis ranks and stay at the top of their game for any length of time. However, what the Williams' sisters have done is to form a union through their family ties to accomplish a monumental common goal. They have made every black person proud in sharing vicariously through their accomplishments. The Williams sisters were able to deflect the conspiratorial environment by working together as friends and sisters and ignoring all of the distractions and negative press and staying focused on the most immediate task of winning matches.

Women's athletics is now a marketing frenzy. One headline Olympic soccer team player shed her shirt and exposed her bra. "Williams Slam Sisters, Serena's soaring shots, defeating Jennifer Capriati to win the crystal racket trophy" (Scott, 2001; Wooldruff, 2001). The Euro-centric standard of beauty does not fit the images and portrayal of African-American women. The Williams sisters have evolved and created a style of beauty that is uniquely theirs but many black women can relate to. These women are able to garner major million-dollar endorsement contracts in addition to tournament checks previously only enjoyed by whites. These women are now able to extend their economic life as leaders and in careers in athletics beyond their active competitive years. They will be able to do what they want and retire from active competitions comfortably. Few white women and no African-American women have ever been able to achieve to this point.

Careers in athletics for African-American women have been few, perhaps as high school teachers and in a few black colleges and universities as teachers and athletic directors. Beyond that, careers for black women in sport was non-existent. Only recently have black women athletes like Zina Garrison, Cheryl Miller, and Cheryl Swoops had any commercial success as announcers or in advertising commercials after their competitive careers. The intellectual and academic pursuits have not been favorable toward African-Americans either. What are the drawbacks of concentrating on sports and athletics? Arthur Ashe often told young people not to focus on sport because only a few attain the gold medals, while others are lost in a sea of poverty unprepared to do anything else. Arthur Ashe and others like him recommended education over athletics as an avenue to achieve upward social mobility.

Unfortunately, for blacks, education is not the total answer. As evolution would dictate and as many have realized, economic security and a stable family life is also of critical importance. The African-American community of the past, which produced athletes like Arthur Ashe, no longer exists. The business and entrepreneurs who contributed to and supported the community have dwindled in numbers and power. The few African-American philanthropists like Bill Cosby, John H. Johnson of Johnson Publications, the former Beatrice Corporation executives, and Oprah Winfrey quietly make donations to worthy causes, some of which are youth programs.

Sport has truly been one of the only ways that African-Americans have bridged the gap to majority culture and economic independence. However, this is not necessarily true for African-American women. Sport has enabled a few superstars with multiple talents to branch into music, theatre, art and other lucrative professions. Debbie Thomas skated into the history books and later became a doctor. Althea Gibson made her name in tennis and later tried the Ladies Professional Golf Association (LPGA) tour. Dancer Katherine Dunham and pentathlon champion Jackie Joyner-Kersey returned to their hometown of East St. Louis, Illinois, to build community sports centers and develop successful youth groups and community programs.

These entrepreneurial endeavors are famous and encouraging. But more financial support and public outreach programs are needed to ensure that all girls are encouraged and are provided with the opportunity to try out various sport activities. Furthermore, the social structure, and especially the family structure for African-Americans, has to change in North America in order for young girls to receive continuous support from home, as well as school, society, and the media. The home seems to be an important indicator for achieving success in and through sports, and this factor has often been overlooked or not acknowledged in its importance.

## What can be done?

Unfortunately, racism and sexism are still alive. It is not just confined in one central location, but racism is pervasive and interwoven into the fabric of the North American life. Sport has been a medium for social change and has changed the social medium already. Sport is a reflection of our culture and society. In sport and its social interactions, one can tell the person by the way the game is played, and one can tell the soul of a culture by the games the people play. People form a link in a chain of time. Trailblazers, innovators, visionaries, all are spanning the tides. The people before lay the groundwork for the people that follow. A poem from the Napoleon Hill lectures captures what can be done (Hill, 1992):

*"An old woman, traveling a lonely highway"*

*Traveling old women came to the close of day,*
*cold and gray, to a chasm deep and wide.*
*The old woman crossed the trails in the twilight dim,*
*For the sullen stream had no fears for them,*
*But, one turned when she reached the other side*
*to build a bridge to span the Tide,*

*"Old woman," cried her fellow pilgrim near,*
*You are wasting your strength in building here,*
*Your journey will end at the close of the day,*
*and you will never again pass this way,*
*You have crossed the chasm deep and wide.*
*Why build you a bridge at even tide?*
*As the builder raised her old gray-head,*
*Good friend, on this path I have come, she said,*
*There comes after me, an unwitting youth whose feet must pass this way.*
*This stream which has been as naught to me,*
*To those fair head children may this, a pitfall be.*
*They too, must cross in the twilight dim,*
*Good friend, I am building this bridge for them.*

Every woman who has blazed the trail in sport and athletics so that others would have an opportunity to play, grow, and develop the skills necessary to become a contributing member in this society, have done more to support women, blacks and other minorities in sport than any written laws. Gender inequalities and injustice against females in sport have taken many forms. Whether they are based on some biological and psychological myths about women's participation in sport and physical activity or based on unequal opportunity for participation or unequal access to authority and power in sports, these perceptions can be changed. The true testaments are those women whose deeds were great, even if they go nameless. Instead of thinking of what has or has not been done for and to women, we need to look at the examples that have been used in the past for success and strategize to make a plan to move forward to build a more inclusive world of sport and physical activity in the 21st century.

# References

Brooks, D. & Althouse, R. (Ed.) (1993). *Racism in College Athletics: The African American Athlete's Experience.* Morgantown, West Virginia: Fitness Information Technology, Inc.

Coakley, J. J. (2009) *Sport and Society: Issues and Controversies.* St. Louis, Mo: Mosby Yearbook Inc.

Cordes, K. A. & Ibrahim, H. M. (1999). *Application in Recreation & Leisure for Today and the Future* (2nd Ed.). Boston: WCB-McGraw-Hill.

Hill, N. (1992). *Science of Personal Achievement.* Napoleon Hill Foundation, Niles, Illinois: Nightingale-Conant Corporation.

Krause, R. (1997). *Recreation and Leisure in Modern Society.* California: Addison Wesley Longman, Inc.

Lapchick, R.E. (Ed.) (1995). *Sport in Society – Equal Opportunity or Business as Usual?* London: Sage Publications.

Ploski, H. A. & Brown, R. C. (1967). *The Negro Almanac.* New York, NY: Bellwether Publishing Co., Inc.

Sage, G. & Eitzen, D. (2013). *Sociology of North American Sport.* New York, Oxford: Oxford University Press.

Scott, E.L. (Ed) (2001). Domination Divas: Venus and Serena Williams live up to the HYPE. *Tennis Week Magazine,* September.

Sterling, D. (Ed) (1984). *We Are Your Sisters. Black Women in the Nineteenth Century.* New York, NY: W.W. Norton & Co.

Volkwein-Caplan, K. & Sankaran, G. (2002). *Sexual Harassment in Sport – Issues, Impact and Challenges.* Sport, Culture and Society book series, Vol. 1. Oxford, UK: Meyer & Meyer Sport.

Woodruff, M. (Ed.) (Jan 2001). She Said, She Said. *Tennis Magazine,* New York.

Women's Sport Foundation (2010/11) website: www.womenssportfoundation.org

## Issue 2

# Equity in Sport through Title IX?

The study of gender and sport requires a deeper analysis into the equity issues that are currently debated in relation to Title IX; it requires an understanding of the impact one's gender has on the development of the individual as well as society at large. This issue will provide insight into the gender topic related to sport, including social contexts, sport socialization, achievement motivation, gender belief systems, and locker room behaviors and how these issues relate to Title IX. First, an overview of gender issues will be provided, spelling out what gender issues have been and what they are today. Then, gender and the social context as well as the role gender plays in sport socialization will be examined. Next, the role gender plays in sport achievement will be explored. This is followed by a look at how gender belief systems (acceptable expected behaviors) affect sport. Lastly, based on this analysis so far, Title IX and gender equity will be discussed, and some reflections on the current and future status of gender studies in sport will conclude this analysis.

## Gender Issues

Gender issues deal with the fair and equitable treatment of men and women. This consists of providing equal opportunities for women and men in terms of selection of careers, equal compensation for equal work, equal representation in politics, and equal distribution of family and household responsibilities. One of many areas where equality among women and men is still being contested is in the area of sport.

In the world of sport, as well as in the rest of society, gender differences came about through the popular belief that the male model (biologically) was the "correct model," and that anything that was different from the male model was, by that very difference, "wrong." Still, today, males are characterized to be the strong, rational, and active gender whereas females are characterized as the weak, irrational, and passive gender.

These differences can be characterized by one of two terms: sex differences or gender differences. *Sex differences* refer to the biologically based differences between males and females. *Gender differences* refer to the social and psychological characteristics and behaviors associated with each gender (Gill, 1992, 144). Historically, all traits (physiological or psychological) were believed to be based in biology. In light of this fact, females were traditionally thought to be psychologically different than males. Therefore, the term sex differences is the appropriate term to describe early works, while the term gender differences describes later works.

Although there is a long history of both sex and gender differences, the most impressive work of current times comes in the 1974 work of Maccoby and Jacklin. They found that despite all the research on the differences between males and females, few conclusions could be drawn. Only four areas of differences existed in their work (mobility, visual-spatial ability, verbal ability, and aggressive behavior). Later research has cast doubt on these areas of differences as being gender based and found them to be more personality-based rather than gender-based (Maccoby & Jacklin, 1974).

## Gender and Social Context

Before gender stereotypes and beliefs are analyzed, it is necessary to gain a firm understanding of gender-related behaviors. We need to understand the social context or the immediate expectations, self-perceptions and situational cues that influence any given situation. Gender-linked behaviors are dependent upon several different factors, highly flexible, and very dependent upon the make-up of the individual, as well as the influence of others through their expectations of themselves and others (Gill, 1992, 154). Social norms and belief systems, as well as each situation help to define these individual characteristics. This means that all behaviors of people are driven by or linked to what others expect of us and what we expect of ourselves. These self-expectations, however, are shaped by what our society deems as appropriate or acceptable.

Social experiences and contexts for females and males are different even when they appear to be similar; not so much because they experience the same world differently but because they experience different worlds (Gill, 1992, 155). From the 1920s to the introduction of Title IX in 1972, women's sports operated as segregated and independently of men's sports programs; they were rarely treated as equal programs. Schools that had athletic programs for female students also had an *athletic department* and a *girl's or women's athletic department*. Oftentimes, the rules of the men's games would be modified for the "less physically suited" females (e.g., six-on-six basketball, three sets in a tennis match instead of five, tees that are closer to the green than the men's tee in golf, and riding side saddle). Although these adapted rules gave women an opportunity to participate in sports, the rules did not change the way that society socialized boys and girls.

## Gender Role in Sport Socialization

In childhood, physical activity and involvement in competitive sport is mostly related to gender, with males being more involved in competitive sport than females. Boys spend more time in physical activities with their parents than girls do. Thus, girls are less likely than boys to accept that physical activities are okay. Even today, the greatest number of drop-outs from sport are teenage girls (President's Council on Physical Fitness and Sport, 2007).

The skills that are needed for successful sport skills are best developed through spontaneous unsupervised play, an activity that most girls rarely are permitted to participate in (Coakley, 2009). Parents and adults tend to closely monitor what girls do and allow boys to "run wild." This differential treatment conveys an underlying belief about what is and what is not appropriate behavior for girls and boys, and later men and women.

Stereotyping and labeling by adults and parents determines what is appropriate for a child. Even educated people today continue to believe, either consciously or subconsciously, that there are inherent differences between the sexes that make girls less suited for physical activities than boys, especially in competitive activities (Greendorfer, 1992, 207). Consequently, boys still continue to experience a more rewarding and positive (supportive) set of experiences that predispose them toward sport, while girls receive less rewarding, less consistent, less systematic, and a less supportive set of experiences that tend to turn them away from sport (Coakley, 2009).

During adolescence, the family becomes less important in a child's life and peers become more important. Peers are the people who either accept or reject their fellow adolescents. Additionally, peers determine social status within the school. Children tend to go out for the sports that their peers deem cool or acceptable. Choosing the wrong sport can have major social consequences for a teen, since peers tend to provide positive environments for sport participation for sports they like and negative environments for those sports they do not like.

In addition to being influenced by peers, teens' sport choices are influenced by their school. The school system can encourage or discourage involvement in certain sports and physical activity by promoting one sport over another. An example of this would be a middle school that promotes American football over soccer because the high school American football team is a nationally recognized team or because the soccer team might not have had a winning season yet. The middle school wants to continue to build up the winning ways of the high school instead of developing the talents of the next generation of athletes and thus "forces" athletes to select American football over soccer if they want to be successful athletes.

Sport is definitely becoming a more acceptable activity for females, although sport is not at the same level of "acceptable behavior" for females as it is for males. Numbers for participation in sport and fitness activities for girls and women have increased substantially since the 1950s. Boys, however, still frequently get the upper-hand when it comes to coaching, practice times, uniforms, and school support than do girls (Coakley, 2009; Acosta & Carpenter, 1998).

In adulthood, participation in sport is mostly determined by the activities one engaged in as a child, not by gender issues (Greendorfer, 1992, 206). It should be noted, however, that more males than females are participants as adults because they are encouraged to participate in sport as children. In light of this socialization factor, it is still more acceptable for a man to be involved in sporting activities than it is for a woman. Those women who do participate in adulthood sporting activities were raised to see sport as part of the normal or expected family activities, much like their male counterparts.

## Gender and Sport Achievement

In the past, it was found that men are more competitive than women. In sport, however, things get to be a bit more complicated. Although males are still found to be more competitive and win-oriented than females, females are found to be more goal-oriented and achievement-oriented than males (Gill, 1992, 149). An example that illustrates this point well is one that involves male and female track athletes who train together. Although both athletes run the same event, during their training sessions, the male runner constantly focused on beating his female opponent, whereas the female runner focused upon improving her form (Gill, 1992). However, researchers today have stated that other factors besides gender, such as socialization factors and social issues, may affect these orientations (competitiveness, win orientations, and goal orientations). For example, if a person grows up with a fear of success (even when they win, they get hurt or criticized for not succeeding well enough) then they will not try to succeed. Conversely, others will try to succeed because they are motivated to avoid failure (they are criticized or hurt if they do not win or if they fail). This factor may help others to possess a win-based attitude (Sage & Eitzen, 2013).

Previously, it was also found that females apparently reported lower expectations of success than did males. When looking at gender neutral or feminine tasks, however, females did not lack as much confidence (Gill 1992, 150). In other words, the better females thought they were "supposed" to do, the better they did. The same applies to males, except they reported success in masculine activities instead of feminine activities. Even with this in mind, males still predicted success more often than females did.

These gender differences take a lifetime to build and are influenced by gender role socialization, gender stereotypes, expectations of others, and sociocultural norms, as well as individual characteristics and experiences. With this in mind, boys today still seem to value sport more than girls do. Typically, boys tend to believe, more so than girls, that they are capable in sports. "Sport is consistently rated as a much more sex typed thing than math or reading ... Although physical characteristics and aptitude have some influence, the sociocultural context and socialization process seem to be the primary source of gender differences in self-perceptions" (Gill, 1992, 151).

## Gender Belief Systems and Psychological Effects

Gender belief systems encompass diverse gender stereotypes and attitudes about appropriate characteristics, roles, and behaviors. There are two general categories of gender belief systems that exist for individuals, gender schematic and gender aschematic. "Gender schematic individuals tend to interpret situations and process information according to gender stereotypes and rely on gender schema to explain and guide actions when other schema, such as ability, are more appropriate" (Gill, 1992, 152). These individuals tend to see situations in gender terms, stereotype others, and restrict their activities to conform with gender stereotypes (e.g., a girl who will not play soccer or football because it is not ladylike, or a boy who will not figure skate because it is not a manly sport). Gender aschematic individuals tend to use more appropriate and relevant schema than gender to categorize activities.

Gender schematic processing by teachers, parents, coaches, and others within the social context of sport may influence sport behaviors, just as the participant's own gender schema affects behavior. For example, if a coach /teacher or other adult criticizes a boy's interest in gymnastics or a girl's interest in American football, the child will try to conform with the adult's expectations, unless the child has a gender aschematic belief system or the support of another adult with a gender aschematic belief system. This example shows that gender influence depends not only on the gender constructs of the individual but also on the gender constructs of others and the particular situation.

In other words, how people think males and females differ is more important than how the sexes actually differ. Each gender has a different set of expectations. These expectations change (tend to become more positive) when given clear information, experience, gender-appropriate tasks, and reduced social evaluation. Gender stereotypes are pervasive, have multiple components, and hold gender beliefs about role behaviors, occupations, physical appearance and sexuality. These gender stereotypes persist despite the fact that males and females hold similar attitudes and that parents claim to encourage sport participation equally among their sons and daughters.

Males are still "expected" to play sports as children more so than girls. If they do not play sports, then something is "wrong" with them. Sports participation gives males a sense of belonging (Messner, 1993, 260). Females are not expected to play sports as much, but they are not ridiculed as much as they have been in the past for playing sports, as long as they do not cross the line into traditionally male or contact sports. Although this is changing, females are still expected to take part in sports that emphasize aesthetics or individuals more so than males. Males, on the other hand, are encouraged to participate in sports that emphasize competitive or team sports more so than females. This can be linked to other gender beliefs (e.g., that males are still believed to be better suited for physical activity than females). Sport can give females the same sense of belonging that males gain from sport.

Males tend to have a more firm, even flexible, orientation to the rules of the game. Males believe that rules are what make and keep fairness (Greendorfer, 1992, 211). Males will make ground rules or adaptations before the game begins to make things fair but refuse to change the rules once play begins. For males, the development of gender identity involves the construction of positional identities, wherein a sense of self is solidified through separation or differentiation through the rules. The masculinity of males is defined through these actions. Failure to adhere to the rules or to separate oneself from emotions on the field makes you a "wuss" or a "wimp."

Females tend to have a more pragmatic or flexible orientation to the rules of the game and are prone to make exceptions and innovations to the rules to make the game fairer, even if it means changing the rules mid-game. Females are more likely to succeed in games that focus on cooperation instead of competition or to not keep score in order to keep things fair (Greendorfer, 1992, 211). This stems from the fact that females tend to define themselves through their relationships to others. Competition, or making a comparison of worth or ability, threatens these relationships and the identities of the females associated with them.

## Locker Room Behaviors

Even more socialization differences between females and males can be seen when looking at the locker room behaviors. Although talk for both genders revolves around common interests of the players, there are notable differences. Males in their locker room mostly talk about common interests. Underlying this talk, however, is an ever-present sense of competition, both for status on the team and between the team and its opponents. Male athletes learn early to avoid public expressions of emotional caring or concern for one another because such things define them as weak or feminine (Curry, 1993, 276). This influences what men say in front of others, especially about things that define their masculinity.

In particular, males are more selective about what they say about women and their own sexual conquests. Talk about women, according to numerous studies, typically consists of talking about women as objects, talk that is very aggressive and hostile toward women. Talk about homosexuals parallels talk about women (Curry, 1993, 279). Essentially, this type of locker room talk promotes a rape culture. Yet, despite the fact that locker room talk is said to promote a rape culture, when compared to the general population of male students, the proportion of sexual assaults involving athletes (in reported cases only) is not significantly different. The only real difference in the two populations is that sexual assault cases involving athletes are reported to judicial affairs more often than non-athletes (whose cases are reported more often to rape centers or other non-hearing type boards) (Crosset, 1995, 126).

While male athletic teams provide a communal context for the celebration and realization of masculinity and male dominance, women athletes face the challenge of constructing a community within a society that alternately supports and belittles their efforts. Much of the teams' conversation, like that of men, is small talk about common interests. Generally, this small talk centers around the daily lives and activities of the athletes (e.g., movies, school, other games in their sport, pets, etc.). Women talk about men and their own relationships. Like men, women talk about sex in their locker room conversations. Unlike men, women rarely talk about men as objects. Instead, talk about sex is done in general terms, in a joking manner and is rarely about one's own experiences. Usually women use the experience of others as a vehicle to contribute to a sexual conversation (Theberge, 1995, 395). Another difference is that, in general, women accept, but rarely acknowledge the homosexuality of a teammate. Even though homophobia does exist in the world of women's athletics, women do not talk about it as violently as men.

## Title IX

In 1972, the U.S. Congress enacted what is popularly referred to as Title IX. Title IX simply states "No person in the United States shall on the basis of sex, be excluded from participation in, be denied the benefits of, or be subjected to discrimination under any education program or activity receiving Federal financial assistance" (Shaw, 1999, 7). Title IX falls under the jurisdiction of the

Office of Civil Rights in the Department of Education. The Office of Civil Rights will investigate a Title IX violation if any one of the thirteen areas appears to be out of compliance with Title IX. The areas of investigation include: participation ratio women/men; status of women as coaches; salaries; budgets for male versus female teams; travel allocations; uniforms and equipment; playing time and fields; recruitment budget; meal allowances; status of locker rooms/changing rooms; sports information; and athletic training. The Office of Civil Rights has investigated several cases dealing with Title IX compliance in the past. For example, in the last 15 years, Colorado State University, Brown University, and Indiana University of Pennsylvania (IUP) were all investigated for eliminating programs in athletics in an inequitable manner. In the case of Colorado State University (1992), the school eliminated the women's softball team for budgetary reasons without cutting any men's teams (Shaw, 1999, 9). In 1991, Brown University planned to eliminate four programs (women's volleyball, women's gymnastics, men's golf, and men's water polo). This would have taken about $62,000 from the women's budget and $16,000 from the men's budget, while keeping the percentage of athletes that were females constant. Brown justified this method as being in compliance because it was in accordance with the interested and able percentages of males and females. IUP (1993) decided to eliminate four programs to cut its budget (women's gymnastics, women's field hockey, men's soccer, and men's tennis). This action cut participation figures for women to 38% at an institution where 56% of the student body is female (Shaw, 1999, 11).

In all of these cases, the courts ruled that the institutions in question were not in compliance with Title IX. The courts did sympathize with the frustrations of trying to cut the budget and remain in compliance but stressed compliance above sympathy. Stressing compliance, schools need to offer opportunities in proportion to the population of the undergraduates (proportion of males and females) at their school, budgets need to be proportionately distributed, and a commitment to add programs 20 years ago is not an automatic guarantee for future compliance by today's standards.

As with every issue, Title IX presents both challenges and opportunities. Administratively, Title IX presents the following challenges:

- How is Title IX compliance achieved while budgets are being cut? (How do we expand without spending more money?)
- How do we explain a cut in status to a male varsity program that is full of history and status while promoting a female program to the varsity level that might be a brand new sport to the institution without a proven track record?
- How do we address the issue of American football?
- To be in compliance, we must provide opportunities based upon percentages of interest within the general population of the student body, but American

football takes up so many of the numbers of scholarships offered to males that maybe it should be considered as a separate category?

- Do we have the facilities to be equitable? If not, how do we plan to achieve equity?

Socially, Title IX presents similar issues. How to achieve Title IX compliance without upsetting alumni donations or the general public is an issue because they might see the cutting of men's programs and the addition of women's programs as an unfair practice. What these supporters need to realize is that "Title IX law restricts the ability to cut women's programs at all, unless the institution shows that sports participation is in substantial proportion to their undergraduate population or if the institution shows a continual pattern of increasing opportunities for women to participate in athletics" (Shaw, 1999, 19).

Although Title IX presents administrative and social challenges, it also brings about administrative and social opportunities. Administratively, Title IX assists in bringing about changes, such as equitable treatment of women's sports programs, because it requires similar funding to be spent on men's and women's programs. Socially, Title IX can lead to recognition as a leader in compliance with the public and attract students and funding for the institution. Also, Title IX gives schools an opportunity to build an era of champions in "new" women's sports (ice hockey, soccer, crew, team handball, synchronized swimming, etc.), as well as the recruiting advantages that are associated with championship programs.

Additionally, Title IX gives institutions the opportunity to be used as a model program, which other institutions can use as a guide or reference in dealing with Title IX issues. Conferences like the Big Ten instituted voluntary compliance goals of having 40% of all participants be women by 1997, up nearly 10% from 1992 participation figures. The University of Iowa goals exceeded that of the Big Ten by having a goal of participation of women as proportionate to undergraduate enrollment by 1997. Stanford has gone so far as to add three new sports for women (synchronized swimming, lacrosse, and water polo) and to increase support in all areas, such as support services and financial backing, from 40% in 1992 to 45% in 1997 (Shaw, 1999, 18). History has shown that these goals were set too high. Policies like these will eventually bring about equality in sport for women, if they are adhered to, which has been a big problem since the introduction of Title XI and is still ongoing.

## Gender Equity

Gender equity is often characterized as a debate between the fate of women's athletics and the economic viability and perceived potential profitability of men's athletics. Women's athletics is viewed as a threat to men's athletics, as a leach that is trying to suck the blood, or in this case money, out of the money-making men's athletics programs when in fact, very few schools make money off any of their athletics programs.

The concept of gender equity has been and continues to be debated as to what it really is. There are, however, two definitions of gender equity that seem to be used as the basis for determining if gender equity exists in any given situation – one by the NACWAA (National Association of Collegiate Women Athletics Administrators) and one by the NCAA (National Collegiate Athletic Association). The NACWAA definition assumes comparable interest levels for males and females and discounts program history as irrelevant when dealing with present needs. The NACWAA definition deals with a moral concept of gender equity. The NCAA definition deals with a legal concept of gender equity. The NCAA definition of gender equity does not offer an ideal concept of what gender equity is, rather it discusses gender equity.

Gender equity has become an issue in the media, as well as for athletic administrators. Women are covered less frequently than men in sports. When women are covered, they are often found in resting or emotional states, called "girls" even if they are in their twenties, in poses with sexual connotations, or in aspects of their non-sporting lives, more often than men (Blinde, et al., 1991, 100; Coakley, 2004). This holds true, with the exception of calling women girls, even in NCAA News. When comparing media coverage, the NCAA still covers men more often than women.

When women are covered in the media, there is always a reference to the male game like there are two institutions, basketball and women's basketball. Comments are made on things such as rule differences, difference in styles, and on the way that a female would survive in the male game (Blinde, et al., 1991, 103). Granted this is probably done because viewers might be more accustomed to the men's game. There is, however, no comparison during the men's game to the women's game to account for women who are not accustomed to the rules of the men's game because they have played and attended women's games for such a long time.

A final area of concern for gender equity is that of coaching and administration. The number of women in administration and coaching has dropped dramatically from 1972 to 1990, even in the coaching of women's teams. According to Shaw (1999) and Coakley (2004), this can be attributed to many different factors ranging from the use of the "old boys" network to a lack of qualified women coaches and administrators. In general, men tend to view a lack of women in the field of athletics as an indication that women are unable or unwilling to b like men (e.g., women are less willing to move, women fail to apply for the jobs, and time constraints on women with families) or that the women simply have "character flaws." Women, in general, tend to view the lack of women in the field of sport as a result of external factors (e.g., discrimination, the dynamics of the personnel process, etc.). The lack of women in the field of athletics as coaches or administrators probably results from a combination of all of these factors. Some women might not be in the field simply because they do not see as many women in positions of authority in departments of athletics, because men who were in charge tended to hire people who thought like they did (e.g., other men), and other numerous reasons.

## Conclusion

Even though great strides have been made toward gender equity in sports over the years, mainly in highly industrialized nations, we are still far from the total realization of this goal. Over 30 years have passed since Title IX was enacted in the United States, but many schools are just now beginning to comply. In other parts of the world, where no legislation specifically calls for gender equity in sports and athletics and where people have to rely solely on education, for example in Great Britain, the situation for women in sports does not look very rosy either. Wigmore says that in 1999 "the constraints that women face in the pursuance of sport are many" (1999, 22):

> There are the gender role constraints and the concomitant time consuming duties associated with those roles. There are the expected stereotypical behaviours and the conflict, and sanctions, that women experience when operating outside of the stereotypes. There is the masculinity of sport itself and the trivialisation and marginalisation of women's sporting achievements in the media. Unless a crisis of hegemony occurs, this situation will self perpetuate. Future generations of students will continue to see sport in a gendered and hierarchical way with women's sport at the bottom of the hierarchy. (Wigmore, 1999, 22)

This passage shows that it takes more than legislation and education to ever achieve equality in the sporting world for both women and men. It takes tremendous changes in ideological thinking patterns that are still based on hegemony rather than equality. "Hegemony is the achievement of leadership by a class or a group over the rest of society. Its views are accepted or accommodated by the society, they are not imposed by severe forces" (Wigmore, 1999, 14). Sport is still mainly viewed as a male domain where women are tolerated but have not moved into the spotlight the same as men have. This is true worldwide.

Up to this point, gender studies in sport have developed a basis for understanding the differences between females and males and has aided in the development of equitable programs. In order to remain a vital force behind sport, gender studies in general also need to incorporate socioeconomic and ethnic theories in order to determine what role gender has in and of itself and within the greater social and cultural context.

What makes sport unique in regard to gender studies is the fact that sport is one of the first popular institutions that is making an effort to provide equitable treatment for both men and women. The issues of Title IX and gender equity are difficult to tackle in the United States, especially when the sport of American football is taken into the equation. Thus, some schools want to count American football as a third gender when it comes to dealing with economic equity issues related to Title IX. Of course, if football were taken out of the equation, Title IX compliance becomes easier for schools to accomplish. On the other hand, with football in the equation, football can be used (at some schools, mainly the Big Ten) to fund more athletic opportunities for women, which in turn makes Title IX compliance easier. At the same time, this raises a "slippery slope" of sorts and raises all kinds of questions. For example, if football is an exception, why do we not count men's basketball, or men's ice hockey; or, if football is used to fund women's sports, why could not more men's sports be funded instead? The arguments pro and con are not new and are still ongoing. The website of the Women's Sport Foundation provides a nice overview (www. womenssportsfoundation.com, 2013).

As for the issue of women playing contact or traditionally male sports, we should consider the fact that most of the sports in the United States, contact or otherwise, were originally men's sports. The success of and increased participation in women's soccer, field hockey, lacrosse, rugby and basketball, for example, are proof enough that given the opportunity women will and can play any given sport, regardless of gender, and they will continue to play until they cannot play any longer.

# References

Acosta, V. & L. Carpenter (1999). *Women in Intercollegiate Sport. A Longitudinal Study – Twenty-One Year Update 1977-1998.* Department of Physical Education and Exercise Science, Brooklyn, New York 11210.

Berg, R. (1996). Women Need to Pursue Careers in Coaching or Administration. *Athletic Business 20* (11), 9.

Bird, A.M., & McCullough, J. (1977). Femininity within Social Roles as Perceived by Athletes and Nonathletes. In M. Adrian & J. Brame (Eds.), *NAGWS Research Reports 3* (pp. 57-63). Washington D.C.: American Alliance for Health, Physical Education, and Recreation Publications.

Blinde, E.M., Greendorfer, S.L., & Shanker, R.J. (1991). Differential Media Coverage of Men's and Women's Intercollegiate Basketball: Reflection of Gender Ideology. *Journal of Sport and Social Issues 15* (2), 98-114.

Bryson, L. (1993). Sport Maintenance of Masculine Hegemony. In A. Yiannakis, T.D. McIntyre, & M.J. Melnick (Eds.), *Sport Sociology: Contemporary Themes* (pp. 286-296). Dubuque, Iowa: Kendall/Hunt Publishing Company.

Coakley, J. (2009). *Sport in Society: Issues and Controversies.* Boston: Mc Graw Hill Higher Education.

Conniff, R. (2003). Title IX: Political Football. *The Nation*, March 24, 19-21.

Crosset, T.W., Benedict, JR., & McDonald, M.A. (1995). Male-Student Athletes Reported for Sexual Assault: A Survey of Campus Police Departments and Judicial Affairs Offices. *Journal of Sport and Social Issues 19* (2), 126-140.

Curry, T.J. (1993). Fraternal Bonding in the Locker Room: A Pro-feminist Analysis of Talk About Competition and Women. In A. Yiannakis, T.D. McIntyre, & M.J. Melnick (Eds.), *Sport Sociology: Contemporary Themes* ( pp. 273-284). Dubuque, Iowa: Kendall/Hunt Publishing Company.

Gill, D.L. (1992). Gender and Sport Behavior. In T. S. Horn (Ed.). *Advances in Sport Psychology* (pp. 143-160). Champaign, Illinois: Human Kinetics Publishers.

Greendorfer, S.L. (1992). Sport Socialization. In T. S. Hom (Ed.), *Advances in Sport Psychology* (pp. 201-218). Champaign, Illinois: Human Kinetics Publishers.

Griffin, P. (1998). *Strong Women, Deep Closets.* Champaign, IL: Human Kinetics.

Maccoby, E. & Jacklin, C. (1974). *The Psychology of Sex Differences.* Stanford, CA: Stanford University Press.

Messner, M. (1993). Boyhood, Organized Sports, and the Construction of Masculinities. In A. Yiannakis, T.D. McIntyre, & M.J. Melnick (Eds.), *Sport Sociology: Contemporary Themes* (4th ed., pp. 259-271). Dubuque, Iowa: Kendall/Hunt Publishing Company.

Nelson, M.B. (1994). *The Stronger Women Get, the More Men Love Football.* New York: Harcourt Brace and Company.

President's Council on Physical Fitness and Sports (2007). *Physical Activity & Sport in the Lives of Girls*. University of Minnesota: The Center for Research on Girls & Women in Sport.

Sage, G. & Eitzen, S. (2013). *Sociology of North American Sport*. New York, Oxford: Oxford University Press.

Sands, R. (1999). *Sport and Culture. At Play in the Fields of Anthropology*. Needham Heights, MA: Simon & Schuster.

Shaw, P. (1999). Achieving Title IX Gender Equity in College Athletics in an Era of Fiscal Austerity. *Journal of Sport and Social Issues 19* (1), 6-27.

Shifflett, B., & Revelle, R. (1994). Gender Equity in Sports Media Coverage: A Review of the NCAA News. *Journal of Sport and Social Issues 18* (2), 144-150.

Staurowski, E.J. (1995). Examining the Roots of a Gendered Division of Labor in Intercollegiate Athletics: Insights into the Gender Equity Debate. *Journal of Sport and Social Issues 19* (1), 28-44.

Theberge, N. (1995). Gender, Sport, and the Construction of Community: A Case Study From Women's Ice Hockey. *Sociology of Sport Journal 12* (4), 389-402.

Wigmore, S. (1999). It Just Is – Isn't It? *The Bulletin of Physical Education, 35* (1), 14-22.

Women's Sport Foundation (1997). R*eport on Title IX, Athletics and the Office of Civil Rights*. East Meadow, NY: Women's Sport Foundation.

Women's Sport Foundation (2013). www.womenssportsfoundation.com

# Issue 3

## Sexual Harassment of Women in Sport

### National Figures on Sexual Harassment in the USA:

- *1 out of 4 women will be sexually harassed at some point during her academic or working life*
- *35% of female students say they experience some form of gender harassment from their instructors or professors*
- *14% of men feel they have experienced sexual harassment in the workplaces*
- *67% of men say they would feel flattered by sexual proposition from a woman, while only 17% of women say they would feel flattered by a sexual proposition from a man. (American Psychological Association, 2004)*

Sexual harassment is generally defined as unsolicited and unwanted sexual attention that a person in a position of power pays to someone in a subordinate position (Brackenridge, 1996). "Those who sexually bother others are usually seeking power over those they bother" (Tangri, et al., 1992). Such behaviors include lewd comments, pinching, touching, caressing, sexual jokes, or intimidating sexual remarks. Sexual abuse, on the other hand, is groomed or coerced collaboration in sexual and/or genital acts where the victim has been entrapped by the perpetrator. It may include exchange of privileges for sexual favors, forced sexual activity or physical violence (Brackenridge, 1996).

This section focuses mainly on sexual harassment, which is more widespread than sexual abuse and sexual assault. Also, sexual harassment is the precursor to the more severe forms of sexual misconduct. It is our hope that sexual abuse and assault can be prevented as people become more educated and concerned about the milder version of sexual dominance, which is sexual harassment. Once the public in general and the people in sport in particular accept that sexual harassment is indeed a misconduct that should no longer be excused nor tolerated, behaviors that fall into the category of sexual harassment will hopefully diminish; then sexual abuse and assault may not follow.

The most frequent scenario of behaviors that constitute sexual harassment involves powerful men and less powerful women. But same-gender harassment also occurs, as does harassment and abuse of subordinate men by women. For women athletes, sexual harassment would most likely involve such attention from male coaches or other males who might affect their careers.

## History of Sexual Harassment

Sexual harassment has existed as long as men and women, but only in recent decades have such unbalanced relationships been carefully documented and characterized as harassment. For much of history, this kind of behavior was viewed as normal, natural, and, in some situations, part of the social order. Women kept silent about it fearing retribution.

In the 1970s, with its wave of feminism, women began to assert their right to be free of such attention, and thus, the term sexual harassment was coined. Media coverage helped to bring sexual harassment to the public's attention, and two social phenomena helped bring sexual harassment to the forefront. The first was that women entered the workforce in record numbers. A second influence was the movement for equal rights for women, which contributed to a shift in the way both women and sexuality were viewed by the society.

Sexual harassment and sexual abuse (also referred to as gender violence) are not new phenomena, yet discussions and research on this topic in the context of sport are still scarce. Allegations of sexual harassment by athletes against coaches have become more prevalent since the mid-1980s, and an ever-increasing number of romantic/sexual relations between coaches and athletes have come to light. This has made the ethical behavior of coaches a prominent concern for sports administrators. In the scientific literature, investigations about the relationship between sport and gender violence is frequently reported. This research – mainly conducted in North America and Europe – has been stimulated through feminist work in sport on sexual harassment and gender relations. Research has focused primarily on professional standards, legal status, and social order on college campuses and sexual violence in the locker room.

Very few major national-level surveys of sexual harassment and abuse have been conducted. However, one study gathered data about the incidence, experience perceived fears, and safety levels among Canadian Olympians. In the Netherlands, the National Olympic Committee sponsored a qualitative investigation about harassment and abuse experienced by young male and female athletes. In Norway, the National Olympic Committee also supported a study on sexual harassment of elite female athletes (Fasting, 2000a). In England, Celia Brackenridge has been leading studies on sexual harassment and abuse at various levels, including top-level sports. In Germany, Birgit Palzkill and Michael Klein have conducted research for the German Sport Foundation (1997). And in the United States, Carol Oglesby, Michael Messner & Don Sabo (1994) have been working on this issue in conjunction with the Women's Sport Foundation (1994). Also, Karin Volkwein and associates carried out a survey on perceptions and experiences of sexual harassment among female college athletes (1997) and a comparative study of sexual harassment among female college students (Volkwein, et al., 2002). Mariah Burton-Nelson, former elite athlete and now a journalist, published two books on women and sport (1994 and 1996) that address the need for athlete/child protection. Other countries, such as Israel, Denmark, Germany, and Australia, are also engaging in research into gender violence in sport.

## Defining Sexual Harassment and Sexual Abuse

Sexual harassment and sexual abuse are two different though related phenomena. The Women Sport International Task Force (1998) defines both. Sexual harassment is unwanted, often persistent, sexual attention. It may include "written or verbal abuses or threats; sexually oriented comments; jokes, lewd comments or sexual innuendoes; taunts about body, dress, marital status, or sexuality; shouting and/or bullying; ridiculing or undermining of performance or self-respect; sexual or homophobic graffiti; practical jokes based on sex; intimidating sexual remarks, invitations or familiarity; domination of meetings, training sessions or equipment; condescending or patronizing behavior; physical contact, fondling, pinching or kissing; sex-related vandalism; offensive phone calls or photos; bullying on the basis of sex."

Sexual abuse, according to the Task Force (1998), occurs "after careful grooming of the athlete until she believes that sexual involvement with her abuser is acceptable, unavoidable, or a normal part of training or everyday behavior. It may include: exchange of rewards or privileges for sexual favors, groping, indecent exposure, rape, anal or vaginal penetration by penis, fingers or objects, forced sexual activity, sexual assault, physical or sexual violence, and incest."

Similarly, the *Women's Sport Foundation* (1994) defines sexual harassment as the unwanted imposition of sexual advances in the context of relationship of unequal power. It impairs one's access to educational resources and one's right to enjoy a healthy athletic experience. Sexual harassment is a violation of the law. The *Equal Employment Opportunity Commission* defines sexual harassment as "unwanted sexual advances, request for sexual favors, and other verbal or physical conduct of sexual nature, which are either made on a *quid pro quo* basis or create a *hostile environment*." An example of quid pro quo sexual harassment is a situation where a coach may withhold scholarships, a starting position, or playing time as a result of the athlete's refusal to submit to the coach's sexual demands. *Hostile environment* sexual harassment is a situation where the coach's crude behavior creates an environment that hinders the athlete's ability to participate in the sport. In these situations, victims feel that no one will believe them or that their scholarship will be in jeopardy.

There are parallels between sexual harassment and sexual abuse; both are discriminatory and display an abuse of unequal power between the harasser and the harassed on a personal level, as well as within the social structure, or hierarchy of power. Sexual harassment is the abuse of power in which its use relegates women to vulnerable, inferior workplace positions through sexual coercion and/or unwelcome sexual advances and/or innuendoes. Generally, the harasser occupies a position of power and authority and then abuses that power by sexually harassing the employee. In fact, only a minority of about 25 percent of cases of sexual harassment are botched seductions in which the harasser is trying to get someone to engage in sex and even fewer cases, about 5 percent, involve a bribe or threat (Brackenridge, 1995). Instead, the real underlying motive of sexual harassment seems to be men's assertion of their power.

## Risk Factors

Sexual harassment is extremely widespread. It is said to touch the lives of 40-60 percent of working women and similar proportions of female students in college and universities (Sexual Assault/Sexual Harassment – Resource and Policy Guide, 1992). Sexual harassment and abuse can occur between male and female, female and male, male and male, and female and female. However, reports of gender violence are highest between male (as the harasser) and female (as the harassed) although same-gender harassment is becoming more frequent. National figures on sexual harassment in the United States reveal that one out of four women will be sexually harassed at some point during her academic or working life. Thirty-five percent of female students say they experience some form of gender harassment from their academic instructors or professors. Official complaints of sexual harassment and sexual assault underestimate incidences of sexual violence; the National Victim's Center reported in 1992 that 84 percent of rapes go unreported. Despite the large amount of evidence of sexual harassment, students seem to pursue few complaints through official grievance procedures.

Many factors may contribute to this silence, including the individual's vulnerability, lack of assertiveness, and lack of awareness of or refusal to recognize blatant instances of sexual harassment. In some cases, the silence might be due to the failure of institutions, such as university campuses or sport clubs to publicize complaint mechanisms adequately, their reluctance to regulate the private lives and personal relationships, and gender bias inherent in their policies and procedures. Therefore, any sample based on official reports does not accurately represent the number of incidents of sexual harassment and sexual assaults.

In sport, risk of sexual harassment or sexual abuse arises from a complex interplay of factors. These include weak organizational controls within sport clubs dominating and controlling behaviors by coaches, and vulnerability, low self-esteem, and high ambition among athletes. Athletes are particularly vulnerable when they become emotionally reliant on or obsessed with their coaches who are not subject to independent monitoring.

## Effects of Sexual Harassment

Sexual harassment can devastate a person's physiological health, physical well-being, and vocational development. Women who have been harassed often change their jobs, careers, educational programs, or academic majors; female athletes who have been harassed often leave their sport. In addition, women have reported psychological and physical reactions to being harassed that are similar to other forms of stress. The American Psychological Association (APA, 1998) lists the following psychological reactions: depression; anxiety; shock; denial; anger; fear; frustration; irritability; insecurity; embarrassment; feelings of betrayal; confusion; feelings of being powerless; shame; self-consciousness; low self-esteem; guilt; self-blame; and isolation. Physiological reactions include headaches, lethargy, skin reactions, weight fluctuations, sleep disturbances, nightmares, phobias, panic reactions, and sexual problems. Career-related effects listed are decreased satisfaction, unfavorable performance evaluations, absenteeism, and withdrawal from sport.

Sexual harassment by coaches has significant effects on athletes, as it does on the institution or coach. The Women's Sport Foundation (1994) indicates that "sexual harassment claims can result in large monetary damages against the harasser and/or educational institution where the harassment took place. Accusations of harassment adversely affect the image of the institution or team and the coach's career. The potential loss of employment is great whenever sexual harassment is brought forward or when accusations are handled poorly by administrators."

## Explanations of Sexual Harassment

The literature on sexual harassment provides three models of explanations for the occurrence of sexual harassment: the natural or biological model; the organizational model; and the sociocultural model (Tangri, et al., 1992). Each of these three models may be applied to a specific sexually harassing situation; however, in most cases it is a combination of all three models that defines sexual harassment behaviors.

In brief, the natural or biological model asserts that sexual harassment is simply related to the sexual attraction between people, which is totally natural. This explanation defends that sexual harassment is not intended to hurt anyone, it is simply a natural expression of "men's stronger sex drive" or a pursuit of one individual who is attracted to another. The second organizational model asserts that sexual harassment "is the result of a certain opportunity structure created by organizational climate, hierarchy, and specific authority relations" (Tangri, et al., 1972, 90). This model may or may not take into account the various distributions of men and women in the authority structure. And the third, or sociocultural, model contends that sexual harassment reflects society at large with its differential distribution of power and status between the sexes. This model is also seen as a mechanism that supports and strengthens male dominance over women in society at large and the various workplaces academia or sports. This model further explains male motivation to maintain this differential of power and status, and the female socialization to succumb to it.

In most court cases about sexual harassment in the United States, people have used the biological model as an explanation for this behavior; and many times this positivistic (or "natural") explanation has helped to set the perpetrator free as the burden of proof has been on the victim. However, the other two models (the organizational and the sociocultural) are more complex and offer insights into the negative effects of sexual harassment in situations of unequal power, such as workplaces, the military, academia, sports, and more.

## Sexual Harassment, Sport, and the Imbalance of Power

Sexual harassment in sport might be more difficult to detect than in other life situations. The demanding schedule associated with sports puts coaches and athletes in constant contact with each other. Researchers note that a coach's primary goals are to display the sport for the fans and promote positive institutional relations. The relationship between a coach and athlete is critical for the success of the individual and the team. Coaches often try to reduce the psychological distance between themselves and their athletes in order to control them. Young and adolescent athletes might tolerate harassment by the coach more than they would put up with such behavior in other social spheres. Young athletes accept the coach as an authority figure who gives orders that extend into the private sphere of their lives. This includes control over medical treatment nutrition, injuries, social activities, and consumption of alcohol and cigarettes, as well as social and sexual activities (Lenskyj, 1992). Individual rights in sport usually take a backseat over the notion of winning and the good of the team. Several studies demonstrate that even the most assertive and independent women rarely question the coach's authority, nor do they challenge coaches' psychologically manipulative or abusive behavior (see Lenskyj, 1992; Brackenridge, 1995 and 1996; Volkwein, et al., 1997). They may fear that a rejection of their coach' sexual advances could end their athletic career.

Furthermore, many sports involve a lot of hands-on instruction. For example, both gymnastics and wrestling require close physical contact during practice between the coach and the athlete. Touching the athlete is part of the sporting experience; however, not every touch may be appropriate. Hence, the athletic situations provide an easy ground for the coach to come in close contact with the athletes. This leaves open the possibility for abuse or the coach taking advantage of the situation. The physical, technical, and social power that the coach has over the athlete provides further grounds for trespassing and possibly abusing this power. The question is whether these various interactions the coach has with the athlete can be construed as a form of sexual harassment. Many people believe that judgment about the culpability of the coach's behavior ought to be based solely on the recipient's perception. Hence, the Woman's Sport Foundation (1994) notes, "whether the harasser's behavior is deliberate and purposeful or simply has the effect of creating an offensive atmosphere does not matter. Only the outcome counts." Others believe that this standard can be unfair to the coach.

Substantial amounts of research have concluded that sexually aggressive behavior (sexual harassment and sexual assault) are usually a form of violence and not a form of sexuality, and are due to a mixture of social and psychological factors, with sociological elements also playing a major rule. Particularly in the domains of sports and athletics, social factors such as masculine hostility toward women and the imbalance in power based on status and gender are evident. It has been well documented that sexual harassment is more prevalent in institutions based on hierarchical principles with unequal distribution of power (see Sanday, 1981 and 1990).

Comparative anthropological research by Peggy Sanday (1981 and 1990) spells out other social factors that contribute to the prevalence of sexual misconduct in societies. She found that cultures that display a high level of tolerance for violence, mate dominance, and sex segregation had the highest frequency of rape, both individual and gang rape. Thus, sexual assault and sexual harassment are likely to occur in a group environment that binds men emotionally to one another and contributes to their seeing sex relations from a position of power and status, such as in the environments of the military and sports.

In the context of sports, the coach holds power over the athletes in regard to money, playing time and even team membership. Sexual harassment is more frequently perpetrated by males against females. This situation seems to be the case because men hold physical power over women, and the social structure also puts them in a superior position. Based on the ratio of men to women employed in sports, as a workplace, it appears women are prime targets for sexual harassment. Once people understand what constitutes sexual harassment, complaints over incidents of harassment occur more frequently. Currently very few sports institutions around the world have educational programs regarding sexual harassment in place.

## Body Erotics and the Media

The increasing perception of the female athlete as an erotic object is an additional problem related to gender violence in sport. This image has been hyped by the media in recent years. In top-level sport, where female athletes are becoming more dependent on managers than on coaches, marketing one's fit body has become a focus. Professional sport has become entertainment, and viewing a female body as an erotic image often becomes more important than the actual athletic performance (see Palzkill, 1993; Klein & Palzkill, 1997; Nelson, 1996).

Where sport has become a business, the primary focus becomes satisfying the interests of the sport consumers. Recent research points out that this has led to the further degradation of female athletes. In many cases, young women are dropping out of sport because of the erotically charged atmosphere, although they might not have experienced personal pressures. When women leave sport, it again becomes a male domain, where men continue to reproduce their "male authority" and dominance over women, which constitutes the breeding ground for gender violence in the first place.

## Incidences of Sexual Harassment in Sport

Sexual harassment cases vary, but they are plentiful and quite easy to locate in the newspapers, on television or the internet. In the sporting world, sexual harassment cases are found at every level, ranging from high school, private sport clubs, university athletics to professional sport and the Olympics. In most situations, the victims are female and the perpetrators are male; however, there is same gender harassment as well. Incidences have been reported involving athletes, athlete and coach, athletes and administrators/owners. Any situation where there are potential power issues involved provides grounds for sexual harassment, but that is not to say that that is the only reason behind sexual harassment allegations.

To provide the reader with a taste of what type of complaints of sexual harassment are filed, we selected ten cases at various levels of sport. The selection is at random and by no means an all-inclusive list. Also, whether the perpetrator was convicted or not does not necessarily speak for severity of the incidences. We just want to demonstrate what people complain about in order to get a better picture of what falls under sexual harassment. As women's sports grow, so do sexual harassment suits.

1. *High School:* In Hickory, North Carolina, a female basketball player at Lenoir-Rhyne High School filed a sexual harassment grievance with the school against the assistant coach. She accused the coach of initiating sexual activity and asking her not to talk about the relationship. Shannon was to swear that she would not say anything. She was removed from the team and asked to leave school by her mother until further notice. The coach declined to comment.

2. *High School:* The New Milford, Connecticut, Board of Education voted to move the high school's gymnastics team to a new facility. The decision was made one year after the owner of the facility previously used by the team was suspended by the USA Gymnastics and the US Association of Independent Gymnastics Clubs for alleged sexual misconduct with minors. The owner has not been charged yet. The move took place because the owner's alleged misconduct made the district vulnerable to possible future lawsuits.

3. *High School:* A former national track coach of the year was sentenced to three years in prison for molesting a 15-year-old male athlete. The judge ruled that there was a strong likelihood that he would continue to molest others. The family of the victim is suing the Pasadena Unified School District, alleging it covered up previous complaints about Turner.

4. *High School:* A coach was sentenced to six years in prison for molesting children under his care during the 1970s. He is banned from public parks where there are children under the age of 14. He was guilty of abusing 7 boys and one girl while serving as a soccer coach and grade school teacher in Saint Bruno, Quebec. He took advantage of the children on out-of-town soccer trips. He had been living in the home of two of the victims and began abusing one of them at the age of 12 in a relationship that lasted 9 years. A civil lawsuit was filed by the victim who is now 42 years old.

5. *University level:* A Tennessee trainer had a sexual harassment case against the Tennessee men's athletic department. She endured a series of slights, affronts, embarrassment and possibly threats. She also claimed that one of the quarterbacks "mooned" her in 1990. In 1997, they reached a settlement with the university for $300,000. The athletic department claimed that she sent mixed messages. The trainer said that sexual harassment is treated as a joke at the university.

6. *University level:* A former University of Oklahoma female soccer player filed a federal lawsuit in October of 1999 charging incidents of physical abuse and sexual exploitation while she was on scholarship with the team in 1997-1998. The suit claims that the players were subjected to violent punching

and grabbing by her former coach and two assistant coaches, and they were forced to perform simulated sex acts on videotape during an off-campus trip. She is seeking damages over $75,0000.

7. *University level:* Penn State's Assistant Football Coach Jerry Sandusky was charged with sexual harassment and abuse of his players, as well as child molestation, over many years (2011).

8. *Private Club:* In Simsbury, Connecticut, the executive director of the International Skating Center of Connecticut has been placed on paid leave pending an investigation. A 23-year-old athlete accused her coach of touching her inappropriately for five years while he coached her. The coach has denied the allegations (2000).

9. *Professional sports:* A female US national team player and a former college player of the year have accused their former coach of inappropriate behavior that included uninvited sexual comments. Her fellow athlete has accused the same coach of creating a hostile environment for her before cutting her from the team. The North Carolina soccer coach denied the allegations. Furthermore, a 20-year veteran at Syracuse was accused of massaging, fondling and propositioning two scholarship tennis players (1999).

10. *Professional sports:* A former baseball scout who is out on bail after spending five months in jail is a scout for the San Francisco Giants. Fifteen players accused the scout of sexually harassing them in 1998 while threatening to cut them from the Giant's farm team in San Pedro. The scout denied all the charges and said that he cut the players because they did not have enough talent, and he was under budget pressure from the Giants to reduce the number of players from 40 to 26. If he is convicted, he could spend up to ten years in jail. He claims that he is a victim of an extortion attempt. He claims, "I am innocent and I am not afraid to continue confronting this situation like a man until my name is cleared." He scouted big names like Sammy Sosa, Carlos Bergen, and Sandy Alomar (1998).

11. *Olympics:* In 1996, a Sri Lankan sprinter won the silver medal. She was forced to put her training on hold because of sexual harassment allegations involving unnamed officials at the Sri Lankan sports ministry. She said that stress and shock made it impossible to work, and she wanted guarantees of security claiming her life and that of her husband were under threat for failing to comply with alleged sexual demands. Her allegations were dismissed as the product of a deranged mind. The senior government minister who dismissed her case compared her to a black American youth, the clear implication that the claims of harassment were implausible.

# Educational Strategies and Training Programs

The best interest of institutions cannot be served until those working within the institution admit that a problem exists. While academia has started to recognize the harmful consequences of exposure to sexual harassment in the learning process and established guidelines and intervention programs, athletic administrators have been reluctant to recognize the problem. Thus, administrators need to formulate clear guidelines, set up educational workshops for coaches and athletes, and implement programs to combat the problem (Katz, 1995).

Research suggests that information and education on what constitutes sexual harassment is needed to prevent conflict and misunderstandings between coaches and athletes. Interventions will not only help athletes to clarify potentially ambiguous behaviors but will also assist coaches by establishing clear boundaries for appropriate interactions. Such interventions can only succeed in an environment in which athletes feel free to report instances of sexual harassment and in which their reports will be taken seriously. Due process must also be given to both athletes and coaches.

In the domain of sport, coaches, athletes, administrators, staff, and others need to be educated in order to prevent the escalation of harassment at the earliest stages possible. Educational intervention programs specifically tailored to athletes will help them to interpret potentially ambiguous behaviors. This information would also help the coach in his or her interaction with the athlete by delineating clear boundaries for appropriate interactions. The best interest of institutions will be strengthened if policies and procedures address sexual harassment issues and institutions take proactive approaches to eliminate such practices.

With the increase in cross-gender coaching (Acosta & Carpenter, 1998) extra investigative steps should be undertaken regarding coaches' backgrounds before they are hired. Furthermore, athletic departments should institute proactive policies that have already been implemented elsewhere for identifying and eliminating sexual harassment and punishing offenders (Bake-Finch, 1995; Canadian Association for the Advancement of Women and Sport and Physical Activity, 1994; Lenskyj, 1992; Parrot, et al., 1994; Wolohan, 1995). For instance, the Women's Sport Foundation (1994) notes that a strong sexual harassment policy has to include the following items:

- a definition of sexual harassment and unethical sexual/romantic relationships between coaches and athletes
- clear and simple reporting procedures
- a procedure for investigation that ensures fair and swift resolution of the complaints

- an appeal process to ensure due process to anyone receiving sanctions stemming from sexual complaints; clear sanctions and disciplinary actions to deal with substantial transgressions

The Women's Sport Foundation (2013) points out that "athletic administrators (paid or unpaid) must be proactive in dealing with harassment. The administration must take steps to insure that its own institutional environment does not promote sexual harassment." The Women's Sport Foundation has laid out steps to create an environment inhospitable to sexual harassment. Specifically, the Foundation recommends the following (www.womenssportsfoundation):

- develop a strong policy that defines and prohibits sexual harassment and sexual relations between coaches and athletes
- develop clear written guidelines and administrative procedures for addressing alleged incidents of sexual harassment
- distribute policy and procedures to each employee, coach, and athlete; incorporate that policy into administrative and student handbooks
- continue to educate staff, coaches, and athletes about the definitions, policy, reporting procedures, and sanctions

Furthermore, WomenSport International encouraged all sports organizations to:

1 Prepare and implement codes of ethics for coaches, whether they work with adults or children.
2 Foster a climate of open discussion about the issues of sexual harassment and abuse so that athletes feel confident enough to speak out.
3 Develop athlete autonomy wherever possible, including adopting coaching styles that give optimum autonomy and responsibility to athletes.
4 Become involved in coach education programs that inform and advise about the ethical and interpersonal issues of sexual harassment and abuse and about the technical aspects of physical touch in coaching the sport.
5 Adopt athlete and parent educational programs that inform and advise athletes on their rights and how to maintain their integrity and autonomy.
6 Introduce and use reporting and mediation systems for both athletes and coaches, ideally with the assistance of trained social work or counseling professionals.
7 Ensure that parents are fully informed of the whereabouts of their children at all times and are involved as fully as possible in supporting the work of coaches.
8 Adopt rigorous screening procedures for the appointment of all personnel, whether coaching staff or volunteers.
9 Be constantly vigilant and avoid complacency and expect and demand the highest standards of accountability at all levels of the sport.
10 Celebrate the good work of athletes and coaches on a regular basis.

The need for special educational programs for student-athletes and coaches about sexual harassment has yet to receive universal acceptance by athletic administrators. For example, although the National Collegiate Athletic Association (NCAA) has established workshops on drug and alcohol abuse, which are now mandatory, topics such as violence and sexual harassment are barely discussed (Volkwein, et al., 1997). Thus, it is essential that athletic departments at educational institutions implement the steps outlined above in order to combat sexual harassment.

*The Australian Sport Commission* (2000) provides the following comprehensive list of guidelines that must be developed in order to prevent and combat sexual harassment:
- Guidelines for sport and recreation organization
- Guidelines for coaches; administrators; athletes and officials
- Guidelines on addressing disability harassment and discrimination
- Guidelines on addressing homophobia and sexuality discrimination
- Guidelines on protecting children from abuse
- Awareness raising and educational seminars
- Skills training courses for Harassment Contact officers and Complaint Officers
- Educational and promotional activities (conferences, articles, media interviews)
- Consultations and advisement
- Database of harassment contact and complaints officers (by sport and by state)
- Research on athlete's perceptions of harassment
- Research on sexual abuse of athletes
- Model Member Protection Policy
- Updates/newsletter for trained officers

Education is the key to helping to combat sexual harassment in sport. It is important that every participant (player, coach, manager, or other personnel) knows what the "rules and boundaries" are for his/her chosen sport, as well as what the boundaries of appropriate behavior are considered to be for that sport. The consequences for overstepping those boundaries, where they can obtain help if he/she is subjected to sexual harassment, and what his/her options are must be made known to the person. Hence, a targeted approach to ensuring a sexual harassment-free sport environment should include the following actions: meetings to discuss and plan how sexual harassment can be averted and dealt with; developing appropriate policy; implementing procedures for dealing with complaints along with documentation of the process; conducting educational/ informative seminars; instituting skills training courses for harassment contact office staff and complaint officers; and developing proactive prevention strategies.

As research on sexual harassment continues to focus on the sporting world, there is hope that educational programs will be developed and implemented worldwide in the near future. However, it is of utmost importance that institutions establish a well-publicized anti-harassment policy and grievance procedure that effectively prevent and correct sexually harassing behavior. Everyone in the world of sport needs to be aware of the policies, and an individual has to be designated to coordinate compliance in order to encourage prompt reporting of incidences (see Chapter 6 in this book). Since many educational institutions in the United States have formulated detailed sexual harassment policies and adopted clear complaint procedures, their work can serve as a reference for other organizations that are still in need of establishing these important steps in order to prevent and combat sexual harassment.

## References

Australian Sports Commission (1998). Harassment-free Sport: Guidelines for Sport and Recreation Organisations. Belconnen: Australian Sport Commission.

American Medical Association (1998). *Strategies for the Treatment and Prevention of Sexual Assault*. www.ama-assn.org.

Acosta, R & Carpenter, L. (1998). Perceived Causes of the Declining Representation of Women Leaders in Intercollegiate Sports – 1998 Update, published at Brooklyn College: Brooklyn, NY.

American Medical Association (1998). *Diagnostic and Treatment Guidelines for the Mental Health Effects of Family Violence*. www.ama-assn.org.

American Psychological Association (1998). *Public Communications – Sexual Harassment: Myths and Realities*. www.apa.org.

Baker-Finch, S (1995). Don't Stand for Sexual Harassment. *AussieSport Action* 6(4), 16-17 (available on-line at http://www.ausport.gov.au).

Benedict, J. & A. Klein (1997). Arrest and Conviction Rates for Athletes Accused of Sexual Assault. *Sociology of Sport Journal 14*, 86-94.

Bohmer, C. & A. Parrot (1993). *Sexual Assault on Campus. The Problem and the Solution*. Lexington, MA: Lexington.

Brackenridge, C. (1991). Zwischengeschlechtliche Trainerbeziehungen: Mythos, Drama oder Krise? *Coaching Focus* (Nationale Trainerstiftung: Leeds) 16, pp. 12-14.

Brackenridge, C. (1994). Fair Play or Fair Game? Child Sexual Abuse in Sport Organizations. *International Review for the Sociology of Sport, 29*, pp. 287-299.

Brackenridge. C. (1995). Das kann hier doch gar nicht passieren. Sexuelle Belästigung und Missbrauch im Sport. In: Fair Play Initiative des deutschen Sports unter Federstiftung der Deutschen Olympischen Gesellschaft & Bundesausschuss Frauen. In Sport des DSB (eds.) *Fair Play – für Mädchen und Frauen im Sport*. Frankfurt/Main, Germany. Pp. 32-39.

Brackenridge, C. (1996). *Healthy Sport for Healthy Girls? The Role of Parents in Preventing Sexual Abuse in Sport*. Paper presented at the Pre-Olympic Scientific Congress, Dallas, USA, July.

Brackenridge, C. (1998). *Child Protection in British Sport – A Position Statement.* Cheltenham, CL, England.

Brackenridge, C. (2001) *Spoilsports: Understanding and Preventing Sexual Exploitation in Sport.* London: Routledge.

Burton-Nelson, M. (1996). *The Stronger Women Get, the More Men Love Football. Sexism and the American Culture of Sports.* New York: Harcourt Brace.

Burton-Nelson, M. (1994). *Are We Winning Yet? How Women are Changing Sports and Sports are Changing Women.* New York: Random House.

Canadian Association for the Advancement on Women and Sport and Physical Activity (1994). *Harassment in Sport: A Guide to Policies, Procedures and Resources.* Ottawa: Author.

Cense, M. (1997). *Red Card or Carte Blanche.* The Netherlands: NOC/NSF.

Chacon, P. (1994). Former Coach Pleads Guilty to Child Rape. *Boston Globe,* December 3: 14.

Cleary, J., Schmieler, C., Parascenzo, L. & Ambrosio, N. (1994). Sexual Harassment of College Students: Implications for the Campus Health Promotion. *Journal of American College Health, 43,* 3-10.

Crosset, T., Benedict, J. & McDonald, N. (1995). Male Student-Athletes Reported for Sexual Assault: A Survey of Campus Police Departments and Judicial Affairs Offices. *Journal of Sport and Social Issues,* May, 126-140.

Fasting, K. (2000). *Sexual Harassment in and outside of Sport. Forms of Sexual Harassment Experienced by Female Athletes and Non-athletes.* Paper presented at the XXVII International Congress of Psychology, July, Stockholm, Sweden.

Figone, N (1994). Teacher-Coach Role Conflict: Its Impact on Students and Student-Athletes. *Physical Educator 51,* 29-34.

Garlick, R. (1994). Male and Female Responses to Ambiguous Instructor Behaviors. *Sex Roles 30,* 135-158.

Hall, A. (1996). *Feminism and the Sporting Bodies: Essays on Theory and Practice.* Champaign, IL: Human Kinetics.

Kane, M. & Disch, L. (1993) Sexual Violence and the Reproduction or Male Power in the Locker Room: The 'Lisa Olson Incident'. *Sociology of Sport Journal, 10,* 331-352.

Katz, J. (1995). Reconstructing Masculinity in the Locker Room: The Mentors in Violence Project. *Harvard Educational Review 65,* 163-74.

Klein, M. & B. Palzkill. (1997). Präsentation von Ergebnissen der Studie Gewalt gegen Frauen und Mädchen im Sport. Vortrag auf der Tagung des Ministeriums für die Gleichstellung von Frau und Mann in NRW. *Gewalt gegen Frauen und Mädchen im Sport.* Essen, Germany.

Kirby, S. & L. Greaves (1996). *Foul Play: Sexual Harassment and Abuse in Sport.* Paper presented at the Commonwealth Gaines Conference, Victoria, BC, Canada.

Lenskyj, H. (1992a). Unsafe at Home Base: Women's Experience of Sexual Harassment in University Sport and Physical Education. *Women in Sport and Physical Activity Journal, 1,*19-33.

Lenskyj, H. (1992b). Sexual Harassment: Female Athletes' Experiences and Coaches' Responsibilities. *Science Periodical on Research and Technology in Sport 12* (6), 1-5.

Masteralexis, L. (1995). Sexual Harassment and Athletics: Legal and Policy Implications for Athletic Departments. *Journal of Sport and Social Issues,* May, 141-156.

Messner, M. & D. Sabo. (1994). *Sex, Violence, and Power in Sports: Rethinking Masculinity.* Freedom, CA: Crossing.

National Victim's Center (1992). *Rape In America.* Report to the Nation. Arlington, VA: Author. April, 23.

Palzkill, B. (1993). Koerper und Bewegungsentwicklung in Gewaltverhältnissen. Was hat Sport mit sexueller Gewalt zu tun? In: P. Giess-Stueber & I. Hartmann-Tews (Eds) *Frauen und Sport in Europa.* Sankt Augustin: Academia. Pp. 170-182.

Parrot, A.; Cummings, N.; Marchell, T.C. & Hofner, J. (1994). A Rape Awareness and Prevention Model for Male Athletes. *Journal of American College Health 42,* 179-86.

Sanday, P. (1981). The Socio-Cultural Context of Rape: A Cross-Cultural Study. *Journal of Social Issues, 37,* 5-27.

Sanday, P. (1990). *Fraternity Gang Rapes: Sex, Brotherhood, and Privilege on Campus.* New York: New York University Press.

Sexual Assault/ Sexual Harassment – Resource and Policy Guide (1992). Temple University.

Tangri, S., Burt, M. & Johnson, L. (1992). Sexual Harassment at Work: Three Explanatory Models. In: *Sexual Harassment – Confrontation and Decisions.* Buffalo, NY: Prometheus Books. Pp. 89-109.

Volkwein-Caplan, K., Schnell, F., Devlin, S., Olsen, M. & Sutera, J. (2002). Sexual Harassment of Women in Athletics vs. Academia. *Journal of Sexual Agression, 8* (2), 69-82.

Volkwein, K, Schnell F., Sherwood, D. & Livezey, A. (1997). Sexual Harassment in Sports: Perception and Experiences of Female Student Athletes. *International Review of the Sociology of Sport, 32*(3), 283-296.

Wolohan, J. (1995). Title IX and Sexual Harassment of Student Athletes. Journal of Health, Physical Education, *Recreation and Dance*, March, 52-55.

Women's Sport Foundation (1994*). An Educational Resource Kit for Athletic Administrators: Prevention of Sexual Harassment in Athletic Settings.* East Meadow, New York.

Women's Sport Foundation (1994). *An Educational Resource Kit for Athletic Administrators: Prevention of Sexual Harassment in Athletic Settings.* East Meadow, New York.

Womens Sport Foundation (2013). www.womenssportsfoundation.com

WomenSport International. (1998). *Sexual Harassment and Abuse in Sport.* [Brochure]. Cheltenham, GL, England.

## Issue 4

# Homophobia in Women's Sport

Women who do participate in sport may find their athletic skills demeaned, employment opportunities lost (Griffin, 1992), or endorsements revoked due to their perceived sexual orientation. Manifestations of homophobia in women's sport result in a preference for male coaches (Griffin, 1992). Many girls, fearful of being labeled as lesbians, choose not to participate in sports (Women's Sports Foundation, 2013). As a result of homophobia, the psychological well-being of many females who remain active in sport continues to be hindered.

Homophobia can also negatively impact the physical well-being of females. Studies show that women who are physically active have a lower incidence of osteoporosis, breast cancer, and depression, as well as higher self-esteem. In addition, girls who participate in sports have a lower frequency of teen pregnancy and higher graduation rates (Women's Sports Foundation, 2013). Given these benefits, women and girls should be encouraged to participate in sports. Rather, the homophobia-based barriers inhibit many women and girls from participating (Lenskyj, 1990), resulting in them missing out on the physical and mental benefits that sports afford. This section clarifies the issues associated with homophobia in general, considers the impact of homophobia on women in sport, discusses the psychological and physical implications of this impact, and proposes a theory of why homophobia is a critical mechanism in sport.

## History of Xenophobia and Homophobia

According to Webster's Dictionary (1988), xenophobia is the fear or hatred of strangers or foreigners. In general, it applies to the fear or hatred of people that are different. That fear and lack of knowledge or understanding of those differences make it difficult, if not impossible, to communicate in a rational way with people who are different. In such situations, the fear of these differences is covered up with overt displays of aggressive behavior toward things or people whom they fear. Aggressive behaviors are a means of communicating disapproval. Today, a more sophisticated display of these fearful behaviors are portrayed in acts of exclusion, ostracizing, violence, bigotry, selfishness, persecution, taunting, fear and mistrust, projection of self superiority, or the spreading of negative and false rumors based on stereotypes and not truth or facts (Berry, 2000).

Most people seem to love and find comfort in what is familiar conversely disliking any thing different, especially when the establishment is challenged and change might occur as a result. Change alone provides a source of discomfort and anxiety. It is the fear of the unknown, the uncertainty of events, and the unknown fluidity and direction of human relationships that is at stake. However, differences add unique contributions to the human community. Each individual contributes his/her talents to the whole and often provides what is needed in the world. Thus, negation and disapproval of differences destroys vital resources for a more diverse life.

An example of disapproval of someone different is the 1998 beating of a young man in Colorado, who was beaten to death by a group of boys because he was gay. This act of violence against this young man displays a fear of homosexuals, where the homosexual is at a distinct disadvantage and not accepted as equal. Homophobia is a fearful reaction against gays. Homophobia is an emotional reaction directed against gay men, lesbian women, transgender and transsexual individuals. The acceptance of violent behavior against homosexuals is an artificial barrier designed to identify and isolate one person or group from the majority.

Homophobia is a fairly recent phenomenon (Griffin, 1992), the term being coined in 1972 (Lock & Kleis, 1998). Homosexual behavior itself has been treated as "sport" in some cultures. For example, Japan had a highly articulated "homo-social aesthetic" that extended back to before the 1600s (Lock & Kleis, 1998). Lock and Kleis (1998) tell us that "in traditional Japanese society homosexual behavior was viewed as a diversion or hobby that was separate from one's serious procreative duties" (p. 425). This cultural environment, however, changed after 1912 due, in part, to the encroachment of Western-style homophobia (Lock & Kleis, 1998).

Research suggests that a significant portion of the population is homophobic to some degree (Lock & Kleis, 1998). Lock and Kleis (1998), summarizing historical studies, found that greater hostility toward homosexuals is predicted when the individual has a greater acceptance of traditional gender roles, religious and political conservatism, lack of known personal contact with homosexuals, and perception that their friends agree with their attitudes. In addition, the research literature suggests that males are more homophobic than females (Lock & Kleis, 1998). Lock and Kleis (1998) state that homophobic attitudes, in severe situations, are associated with narcissistic defenses maintained into adulthood, and less severe attitudes are associated with immature, neurotic, or mature defensive styles. Lock and Kleis (1998) reason that these attitudes are used to control anxieties.

In related fields, researchers found that among males, homophobia is related to masculinity, fear of femininity, subconscious homosexuality, and gender role rigidity. It was also stated that men, regardless of their sexual orientation, who describe themselves as lower in femininity and higher in assertiveness and independence were the most homophobic (Lock & Kleis, 1998). Homophobia may be linked to negative attitudes toward women and femininity. Lock and Kleis conclude that homophobia has both different functions and degrees of intensity. Homophobia can be related to anxieties about gender, gender role, gender-role conformity and, especially in males, anxieties about power, authority, and dependency (Lock & Kleis, 1998).

Cahn (1993) explored the historical relationship between lesbianism and sport. Fears of mannish female sexuality in sport are initially centered on the prospect of unbridled heterosexual desire. By the 1930s, female athletic mannishness began to be identified with heterosexual failure and unattractiveness to men. According to Cahn (1993), many physicians, physical educators, sportswriters, male athletic officials and casual observers, have stated that strenuous athletic pursuits endanger women and threaten the stability of society, as too much exercise could damage female reproductive capacity. They maintain that women athletes will become manlike and adopt masculine dress, talk, and mannerisms (Cahn, 1993). These beliefs support the traditional perception of the role of women in society. Historically, women have had to dress as men to disguise their woman-ness in order to travel freely and to pursue careers that traditionally had been earmarked for men. Writers, musicians and others had to write using the name of their husbands, fathers, brothers in order to be published.

Women, historically, have been portrayed as caring, nurturing, and expressive in nature (Oglesby, 1978). Accordingly, women are multitask-oriented, that is, they have the ability to handle many tasks at one time. For example, women have historically stayed at home to cook meals, clean the house, and raise the children. This ability to nurture and take care of a family through multitasking relieved men of helping with these duties, making it possible for men to focus on providing financially for the family. This role of women in society began to change with the eruption of World War II. Many women were forced out of the home and into the jobs their husbands held before leaving for battle. Many women found that to be successful in the work force, they had to cultivate certain traits – traits that historically have been attributed to men. These traits include being strong mentally and physically, being aggressive and demanding at times, and staying focused on a single task. As more women developed these traits, they became empowered by their ability to do "man's work." As a result of this independence, many women chose to remain in the workforce once the war ended.

Today's family structure continues to challenge traditional gender roles. More women are entering the work force and holding high-powered executive jobs, while men are becoming more involved with raising children and tending to household duties. As this occurs, we see that male and female roles are becoming blurred. However, in the world of sport, the traditional roles continue to flourish and create conflict with newer, less restrictive behavior (Oglesby, 1978).

# Implications of Homophobia on Women in Sport

The psychological barriers raised by homophobia are reflected in social behaviors and attitudes toward women and girls. Appearance is one area affected. For example, the physically fit or muscular body of an athlete is perceived as an obvious physical indicator of the sexual orientation of a female athlete. Likewise, the short hair worn by female athletes is associated with "gayness."

Socially, it becomes difficult for a female athlete to dress or wear hairstyles conducive to vigorous physical activity without risking them being taken as trademarks of sexual orientation. Likewise, socializing with groups of athletic women can be taken as lesbian fellowship. Another effect of homophobic-based social constraints is that of women not pursuing athletic careers for fear of being labeled as "gay."

For example, a woman who is serious about her coaching career and chooses to coach at a top level faces the possibility of being perceived as "gay" or "not normal," whereas, her male counterpart is considered "loyal" or "devoted" to his career. The same discrimination holds true for female physical educators. A female who chooses to take a career in athletics very seriously must consider that she could potentially suffer the effects of homophobic discrimination (Potera & Kort, 1986).

Wellman and Blinde (1997) have looked at how homophobia and the lesbian label impact the professional careers of women basketball coaches at Division I universities and its effect on their ability to recruit athletes. They found that homophobia in women's sport narrowed career choices for women and impacted decisions in the hiring of both head and assistant coaches. In terms of recruitment, questions from prospective student-athletes, parents, and high school coaches about lesbians on the coaching staff or team were common, as is the practice of using insinuations about the presence of lesbians on rival teams as a frequent negative recruitment technique. Lesbian issues were reported by some coaches as being influential in their decisions of which students to recruit (Wellman & Blinde, 1997).

Expression of homophobic discomfort takes many forms: the use of jokes; anti-gay slurs; avoiding personal behavior perceived to be gay; and avoiding association with people thought to be gay (Cohen, 1993). For the female coach, this may mean ostracism by and isolation from co-faculty in schools and colleges and/or lack of support for her team or collaborative ventures among faculty and/or students.

If a woman is gay, she may be scared away from sport by the prospect of her sexuality becoming part of the public domain (Women's Sports Foundation, 2000b). A woman's sexual orientation has not been shown to have a bearing on degree of professionalism or how well she performs her job. Yet, many people believe these two are directly related. Because of this belief, many lesbian athletes and coaches keep their sexual orientation secret or even "play straight" to protect themselves (Women's Sport Foundation, 2013).

The personal belief system is also target for homophobic discrimination. For example, women espousing feminist beliefs are often labeled as lesbian. Even tolerance is not tolerated: many believe if a woman is accepting of lesbians, she also must be a lesbian. This may lead to a self-defensive stance to prove that one is not a lesbian, which may be interpreted that one must be homophobic and therefore against lesbians. This creates a situation that appears to force sportswomen to choose between feigning gayness or a homophobic identity.

## Women Athletes' Portrayal by the Media

Sport is a microcosm of society. In sport, as in the world, there are those who prefer the company and relationships with same-sex partners. The fear of displaying that kind of affection openly has many negative repercussions for the people involved. Society in general, as well as the media, prefer to give public images of manly men and feminine women as displayed by men playing football and women doing gymnastics or dance. A few years ago, for example Anna Kournikova, who played on the Women's Professional Tennis (WPT) tour, was the heartthrob of many men and young boys because of her beauty. Even though she rarely got to the finals, won tournaments and never a grand slam, she had many lucrative commercial endorsements. She was a media darling and was on the cover of many magazines with numerous offers for modeling and acting.

Martina Navratilova, the tennis star, was one of the first women in the modern era of tennis to publicly admit that she was a homosexual. Billy Jean King had a long extensive legal battle, a "palimony" suit, in which she was sued by a woman who said she had made life commitments and promises and wanted to get paid for the time they spent together. Venus and Serena Williams, also playing Women's Professional Tennis, have worked hard on conditioning and preparing for the game, but due to the media they are also known to be interested in fashion, clothes, shopping, and designs. They have been frequent guests on television award shows and late night shows. They have now conformed to the Eurocentric image and the value of beauty in the Western world. In years past, they wore beaded hair and Afro-centric styles; now they have straightened their hair that is long and flowing.

During the 2003 French Open, reporters asked Serena what she thought of Ladies Professional Golf Association (LPGA) Annika Sorenstam's playing with the men golfers at the Professional Golf Association (PGA) Colonial Tournament and whether she wanted to do the same in tennis. Serena said, "I am not interested; I just want to play women's tennis." The reporter pressed her and asked, but what if you were tempted to play men's tennis? Serena replied, "But I am not tempted" (NBC sports coverage, 2003). Annika was interviewed by NBC in May 2003, a week before the PGA Colonial Tournament in Texas. She had just spent six months to a year conditioning and preparing for the tournament building up her body. Annika said that her husband recognized her strength and stamina and that she was not the same athlete she was a year earlier prior to the training, but she was physically much better now.

The media coverage for the tournament was enormous and the crowds that followed Annika around the Colonial that day were both supportive and non-supportive of her "playing with the boys." Many felt that she was taking an opportunity away from a male golfer. Annika's reply to this was that she needed to make a living, too. In golf, the score determines how one moves on in the tournament and not the gender. The gentlemen who played the round of golf with Annika that day said that she had gained their respect. She hit the ball straighter than most of the men but her putting fell short with a score of 74 for the round; thus, she did not make the cut to play in the tournament.

Annika is by far the best woman on the LPGA tour and has won more tournaments than anyone, male or female, including Tiger Woods. She is the first woman in 58 years to play on the men's tour. In 1945, "Babe" Didrikson Zaharias played golf with the men because at that time there was no women's golf. Change is difficult and someone has to break the ice for change. No doubt Annika has moved the game of golf to a different level. She gained the respect of the golfers worldwide. She was in the middle of the pack, not the last one and for a first time outing that is good for any golfer. She was not trying to be a man, but to raise her game, do the best she could, and compete on a level par with her skill. She was prepared to play the game but was unprepared for the scrutiny and examination that came along with the challenge.

Stigmas for female athletes continue to be pervasive in sport as well as in general life. Women are not "allowed" to excel in athletic performance without accusations and allegations of homosexuality, doping, masculine tendencies as well as aggressive and confrontational behaviors. Men, on the other hand, displaying even violent behaviors, rarely are faced with serious consequences unless criminal charges are filed in the judiciary system. Even then many of the male athletes are released of their own recognizance unless they are accused of murder. Unfair and unequal treatment often is a result of homophobic behavior exercised in the general community among both men and women.

## Explanations of Homophobia

One explanation of homophobia proposes that men encourage the widening of these psychological barriers to restrict women's experience in the world of sport (Women's Sports Foundation, 2013). This account holds that because the athletic world has historically been male dominated, men view sport as their sacred place to frolic, play, and feel uninhibited. Sport is their safe heaven to show overt public affection of hugging, kissing, and slaps on the backside as well as to be aggressive, competitive, confident, and proud. Women, therefore, are not allowed to experience sport as it attributes to men's loss of supremacy in aggressive and competitive behaviors and occupations. "Women who [are aggressive, competitive, confident, and proud] go against social norms, therefore, an effective way to prevent women from challenging these social norms is to stigmatize sport participation by women" (Cohen, 1993, p. 195). As a result of this, many women and girls choose not to participate in sports.

The media helps perpetuate the psychological stigma against women in sports as demonstrated in the examples above. Also, in a study of the 2000 Olympic Games and the coverage given to men's versus women's sports during the games, gender differences were found (Higgs & Weiller, 2004). NBC televised 86 hours of Olympic coverage; 60 hours of this coverage were randomly taped and evaluated. The taped coverage focused on the same distribution of sport activities as the televised coverage. Content analysis revealed that the commentators' use of adjectives describing men and women athletes was unbalanced. For example, in their use of descriptive factors there were 185 terms regarding strength used to describe the male athletes. Phrases such as, "strongly aggressive in rebounding," "strong passing team," "strong powerful drive to the basket," as well as, "he's a killing machine" (volleyball), and "he kills a jump serve." On the other hand, there were only 68 terms of strength used to describe the women as well as 15 terms of weakness. These phrases included, "she's a strong rebounder but her shooting skills are weak," "she powered through the pick only to throw up a weak shot," and "did she get some heat on that one; what a banger." This same study also recorded overt sexist comments such as, "he is the Michelangelo of the event" and "she is the chief fashion plate of the Olympic Games." Further, it was revealed that the personal lives of the male and female athletes were discussed in different terms. For example, about Gwen Torrence (track and field), the commentators stated that she "has a new focus in her life with her baby." For Gail Devers (track and field), the commentators made it a point to mention that she gets up early to train with her husband. In each of these cases, points of emphasis were on the family and not the athletes themselves.

Finally, it was found that the commentators focused on the appearance of the women athletes with comments such as, "she has the prettiest nails in the competition" and "she's a little too chunky for this event" (Higgs & Weiller, 1994). The size and popularity of the Olympic Games ensures a wide audience for these types of comments, adding to the psychological detriment to women in sport. Kriegh and Kane (1997) confirm these findings. They found that over the past two decades, sport media scholars have shown that female athletes are portrayed in ways that trivialize and undermine their accomplishments as highly skilled competitors, denying them power. This suggests that sports media is helping to reinforce the expectation that women and girls should conform to the traditional female roles. This, in turn, supports barriers to serious participation in sport by females.

## A Theory of Homophobia

Three themes seem to underlie and permeate the literature of women and sport (1) sport is a masculine trait; (2) women and girls cannot defend themselves, and (3) lesbianism is infectious, contagious and epidemic. Sport for women and girls is non-threatening and therefore safe when it is perceived as females play-acting maleness. Homophobia is the mechanism by which perceived play acting is maintained and serious "sportswomanship" is curtailed. The maleness of sport is pervasive throughout the literature. The adjectives used to describe participation and success in sport are masculine. This leads to the attitude that the goal of sportswomen is maleness and not accomplishment, athletic prowess or fitness.

The relative lack of concern in the literature for gay male coaches of men or women's sport or gay women's sport and gay players in male sports give the perception that males are capable of controlling the negative influences of the behaviors of gay males involved in sport. By contrast, the relative pervasive concern in the literature for lesbians in female sports suggests females are incapable of controlling the behaviors and influence of gay women in sport. Further, the relative pervasive concern that a lesbian in the league will turn the other females into lesbians presumes women and girls, in contrast to men and boys, are weak-willed and easily influenced, and unable to resist perceived recruitment overtures of women versus men.

The apparent preference to link successful female athletes with traditional female roles and attributes seems to suggest that if sport is a temporary curiosity or intrigue away from a woman's real role it is tolerated. That is, play-acting sport can be tolerated; and the play-acting is confirmed through reminders of the femininity of the play-actor. Conversely, if women are serious about pursuing athletic careers, they are subjected to serious scrutiny on all levels of their lives.

## Conclusion and Recommendation

"As girls and women engage in sports in record numbers, homophobia remains one of the impediments to athletic participation and entrance into sport-related fields. Fears of either being labeled as lesbian or 'converted' are abundant among girls and their parents" (Women's Sports Foundation, 2013). To help reverse the current tendency to discourage women's and girl's participation in sport, we need to begin portraying womanhood in terms of physical and psychological strength rather than in terms of weaknesses. We need to portray the feminine body in terms of fitness and health rather than in terms of soft, sultry, seductive and sedateness. We need to portray the female psyche as self-governing rather than vulnerable. Perhaps we need to revisit women's introduction to play and sport and be sure we are not teaching, albeit unknowingly, learned helplessness on the playground through the division of play space and games. We need to educate.

How do we educate? The Women's Sports Foundation (2013), an advocacy group for females in sports, offers a *Homophobia Resource Kit*. This is a collection of articles by authors Pat Griffin and Mariah Burton Nelson. The information regarding this kit can be obtained online at www.womenssportfoundation.org. We can also become educated by reading, asking questions, and attending forums and conferences on women in sport. The more we learn, the more we can help educate others about this topic.

In summary, although the hegemony of capitalist life is pervasive and powerful, people are the creators of their own destiny. The way a society and sport is set up does not prevent any changes or challenges to the social structure. Space for resistance and even transformation is possible. Change might not come about easy and will always take longer than one expects; however, the potential for sport to be a liberating force for all is theoretically given, if people who are under-represented and oppressed will speak out. The powers in place can never stifle the human need to play and move – and thus sport has great potential to be a liberating force and to shed the oppressive ways.

# References

Berry, W. (2003). Essays Examining Xenophobia by William W. Berry of Buffalo, New York. (http://members.aol.com/esberry/myhomepage/news.htlm)

Cahn, S. K. (1993). From the "Muscle Moll" to the "Butch" Ballplayer: Mannishness, Lesbianism, and Homophobia in U.S. Women's Sport. *Feminist Studies, 19*(2), 343-368.

Cohen, G. (Ed.). (1993). *Women in Sport: Issues and Controversies*. California: Sage Publications.

Greendorfer, S. L., & Rubinson, L. (1997). Homophobia and Heterosexism in Women's Sport and Physical Education: A Review. *Women in Sport and Physical Activity Journal, 1*(2), 189-210.

Griffin, P. (1992). Changing the Game: Homophobia, Sexism, and Lesbians in Sport. *Quest, 4*(2), 251-265.

Griffin, P. (1989). Homophobia in Physical Education. *CARPER Journal, 55*(2), 27-31.

Higgs, C., & Weiller, K. (2004). Gender Bias and the 2000 Summer Olympic Games: An Analysis of Television Coverage. *Journal of Social Issues, 18*(3), 234.

Kriegh, L. A, & Kane, M. J. (1997). A Novel Idea: Portrayals of Lesbians in Young Adult Sports Fiction. *Women in Sport and Physical Activity Journal, 6*(2), 23-62.

Lenskyj, H. (1990). Power and Play: Gender and Sexuality Issues in Sport and Physical Activity. *International Review for the Sociology of Sport, 25*(3), 235-245.

Lock, J., & Kleis, B. (1998). Japan's Journey into Homophobia. *American Journal of Psychotherapy, 52*(4), 425-436.

NBC Sports Coverage, May 26, 2003.

Oglesby, C. (1978). *Women and Sport: From Myth to Reality*. Philadelphia: Lea and Febiger.

Potera, C., & Kort, M. (1986). Are Women Coaches an Endangered Species? *Women's Sports and Fitness, 8*(9), 34-35.

Reuters (2003). "Golf: Sorenstam Highlights Gender Gap Say Athletes." *The New Zealand Herald*, May 26.

Uncle Donald's Costro Street-Gay Games: A Brief History of Gay Games. [online]. Available: http://www.backdoor.com [2000, March 19].

Webster's 9th New Collegiate Dictionary (1988). Massachusetts, Merriam Webster Inc.

Wellman, S, & Blinde, E. (1997). Homophobia in Women's Intercollegiate Basketball: Views of Women Coaches Regarding Coaching. *Women in Sport and Physical Activity Journal, 6*(2), 63-82.

Women's Sports Foundation (2013). Homophobia in Women's Sports. Online: www.womenssportfoundation.org

Women's Sports Foundation (2013). Women's Sport and Sexuality: The Myth and the Reality. Online: www.womenssportfoundation.org

# CHAPTER 8:

# (DIS-)ABILITY AND SPORT – FITNESS – PHYSICAL ACTIVITY[2]

*(with Edward Coyle, Jr.)*

Ability not Disability Counts (Lipton, 1970, 3).

## Introduction

In recent years, there has been increased interest in health promotion for the physically disabled through sports and fitness participation. In addition, we have seen tremendous growth of organized sports for the disabled and of participation by disabled people in various sports, physical activity, and fitness programs. Consequently, the contemporary growth of wheelchair sports has raised significant questions concerning the physical fitness training of wheelchair athletes. The importance of physical fitness in the areas of muscle strength, muscle endurance, cardiovascular endurance and flexibility and its significance in sports performance is well understood by physical educators and coaches. The level of competition for paraplegic athletes has increased immensely over the last forty years and is of high caliber, as witnessed in the steadily increasing performances in the Paralympic Games over the years. Consequently, the training techniques are very important.

McPherson already stated in 1979 that "each year athletes themselves seem to come up with varying training methods which have worked successfully for them. These methods are useful but it is imperative that in order for the athlete to meet his/her full potential, qualified coaching is a must, complemented by adequate facilities and research" (p. 13). Emes stated in 1981, "There is a need for further investigation into modified techniques and equipment for training" (p. 178). In 1981, "research into the physiologic response of the disabled athlete to exercise and training is in its infancy" (Stewart, 1981, 166). Good exercise programs for the disabled are still one of the most neglected areas in exercise physiology. Little is known concerning the physical capacities and exercise limits of the disabled. Those who are confined to wheelchairs are becoming more and more visible in the realm of physical activity. There is a growing and vital need on the part of both the practitioner and the clinician for reliable exercise alterations when faced with a situation involving a handicapped person.

---

2 Part of this research has been presented at the Sweducation 7th International Congress in 1997

Research has confirmed the low fitness levels of the disabled. Fitness is often poor in the disabled, and normal wheelchair use does not seem to provide adequate training stimulus. Paraplegia causes various disturbances in the injured spinal cord. Consequently, each spinal-injured person varies in fitness level, according to the location of the injury on the cord and the level of activity of the person. Therefore, in choosing physical fitness activities for the disabled, it is important to ensure that the activity chosen is not harmful to the condition.

Davis, et al., state that participation in exercise programs should be based on the results of a fitness assessment and on the level of the spinal cord lesion in those with paraplegia (2001). Studies have shown that the disabled often show poor cardio-respiratory endurance, higher body mass and more fat than sedentary able-bodied subjects unless they participate in wheelchair sports. It has been found that the atriovenus oxygen extraction at sub-maximal workloads appears to be higher in spinal cord-injured patients. These limits may be sufficient to restrict exercise capacity and $VO_2$maximum. Overall, many studies have confirmed that many wheelchair users are less fit than they could be. Hence, the outcry for proper training techniques that would improve the paraplegic athletes physical fitness is evident in order to enable them to reach qualifying levels to compete in national and international championships for their sports.

In this chapter, an overview of the history of "therapeutic exercise" and the origins of the sports for the disabled will show how much progress has been made to serve this under-privileged part of our community, and how far away we still are to fully integrate the disabled into the world of sport and physical activity.

## History of Therapeutic Exercise

Since the beginning of time, people have contracted different diseases and crippling injuries that have resulted in various types of disabilities. Doctors have always been interested in the improvement of health and fitness of disabled people. Consequently, many types of therapeutic exercises have been developed to help improve weakened muscles in an attempt to hasten convalescence and improve mental attitudes. In ancient Rome, Asclepiades recommended walking and running for dropsy. Themison recommended strenuous exercises to help cure many acute diseases. Celsus, when he was discussing hemiplegia and other paralyses, notes that a "perfect cure is rare"; gradual exercise and walking as much as possible is recommended. Galen became one of the first doctors to classify exercises according to their vigor, duration, frequency, use of apparatus, and the part of the body involved. Avencia wrote that for each organ there is an exercise, and that "if men exercised their bodies by motion and work at appropriate times, they would need neither physicians nor remedies" (Basmajian, 1981).

This coincides with our modern slogan "exercise is medicine!"
In the 16th century, Mercurialis used gymnastics as a medical intervention to cure disease. His principles for medical gymnastics were:

- Each exercise should preserve the existing healthy state.
- Exercise should be suited to each part of the body.
- Exercise should not disturb the harmony of the body.
- All healthy people should exercise regularly.
- Sick people should not be given exercise that might exacerbate existing conditions.
- Special exercises should be prescribed for convalescent patients on an individual basis.
- Persons who lead a sedentary life urgently need exercise. (Basmajian, 1981, 11-12)

Martin Luther believed in the value of exercise to keep the body strong and improve one's health. Luther said, "Music chases chagrin and melancholy; gymnastics produces a strong robust body and keeps it in a state of health. It can keep you young people from idleness, debauchery and drink" (Basmajian, 1981, 12).

Nicholas Andre in the 17th century introduced the word "orthopedic," which stresses the important therapeutic value of physical exercise and hydrotherapy. He said, "Of all the methods of alleviating and even curing many infirmities to which the body is subject, there is nothing to equal exercise." Andre further stated that exercise "acts to halt rachitic disease in children." He suggested "specific exercises and sports for reducing weight, increasing mobility and strengthening the spine" (Basmajian, 15). Later in the 17th century, Joseph-Clement Tissot began recreational therapy and adapted sport. Tissot believed that a surgeon should regard exercise as much a part of treatment as anything else he did or prescribed. And Cheyne in the 18th century included exercise in the hygienic regimen.

In 1845, J.A.L. Werner of Germany published a book discussing the anatomical and physiological principles of medical gymnastics for people suffering from various deformities (Guttman, 1976). Pehr Ling introduced system into exercise in the 19th century in the form of dosage and detailed directions. He classified starting positions and degree of activity. He labeled certain exercises specific. According to Basmajian (1981), Ling believed that physical exercise contributed to the "physical and moral perfection of the citizen."

In the 19th century, Dudley A. Sargent and R. Tait McKenzie promoted the Swedish and German systems of gymnastic exercise. They believed in a good physical education and exercise program as essential for the physical development and rehabilitation of the body. The advent of the first World War created a large increase in the restorative exercises in the many military hospitals. Great progress occurred with the use of exercise for the wounded and the paralyzed soldiers. Since each World War, greater use of restorative exercises have been utilized. Basmajian (1981) described how calisthenics and other exercises were given to patients while still bedridden, and a program of "adapted sports" was introduced, such as wheelchair basketball for paraplegics. Renewed emphasis was placed on "reconditioning exercise" to counteract the deconditioning and the "abuse of the rest" of the body.

Although this brief overview examined what the early physicians said concerning exercise and its use in the rehabilitation process, no specific guidelines were established to help one improve the individual disabled person's physical fitness level. R. Tait McKenzie helped to introduce change in the attitude of physicians toward exercise for the disabled (Ryan, 1984). This change took considerable time to develop but was encouraged by the work of Sir Ludwig Guttman in England after World War II. He demonstrated that even the most severely paralyzed quadriplegics and paraplegics who were permanently disabled were highly capable of hard, vigorous exercise and the training demands of sports. Guttman further noticed that the disabled were better off for their participation.

## History of Disabled Sport in the World

During World War II, Sir Ludwig Guttman, M.D., was asked to work at the Stoke Mandeville Hospital in Aylesbury, England. This was a difficult job as his assignment called for the complete rehabilitation (physically, psychologically, and socially) of injured soldiers. The greater majority of these soldiers were inflicted with spinal cord impairment to minor and greater extents. Many men were confined to wheelchairs. They were now called "paraplegics," which means that most were physically paralyzed from the waist down and were never able to walk again with the use of their legs. Many medical problems develop when an individual loses the ability to walk of his own accord. The paraplegics now lost a significant portion of their life expectancy due to urinary infections, bedsores, and gangrene, in addition to developing cardiovascular problems and general physiological, psychological and sociological problems. Many men, Dr. Guttman noticed, were dying within two years from the complications of paraplegia and subsequent issues.

Dr. Guttman decided to do "specialization" training with these men. He realized that in order for these men to survive they must have individualized general goals in life that are realistically attainable. He utilized the tool of sport via human movement progression to reach mental, physical, social and spiritual goals. Dr. Guttman also understood that in order for these men to live they must have as normal a life as the rest of society in spite of so-called "physical limitations and barriers" (Guttman, 1976).

In 1946, Dr. Guttman initiated a sports program for the men at the Stoke Mandeville Hospital. His patients participated in various sports in a wheelchair. He devised a medical classification system comprised of six classes from the severely inflicted, which he called class 1A, 1B, to a minor infliction class 6. Class 1 is a quadriplegic (all four extremities impaired) to class 6 (minor infliction, individual can ambulate). It is a very complex medical classification system, which today has been expanded and has become even more specific and complicated.

Dr. Guttman's intention through sport was to recondition oneself physically (rehabilitation and preventive medicine), psychologically and socially. His program began in the hospital, and as a result of the conditioning effects of his sport program, many of his patients became healthy and lived and participated in normal lives.

In 1946, at Stoke Mandeville, the English paraplegics competed against each other in wheelchair basketball and archery. In 1948, Dr. Guttman started a world championship at Stoke with 40 competitors in five sports. By 1976, Dr. Guttman began a world competition held every year at Stoke Mandeville. Every four years, there is now an Olympic competition in the country that holds the able-bodied Olympics, which is called Paralympics. And every two years there is a Pan-American competition for disabled athletes.

In Toronto, Canada in 1976, Dr. Guttman's movement involved 50 countries and 1,500 paraplegic Olympic-trained athletes, which marked the third largest sporting movement in the world. Many world records were broken at that Toronto Olympiad. A man in a wheelchair pushed 100 meters utilizing only his upper torso muscles in 17 seconds. Another paraplegic athlete pushed a mile run in under six minutes. Yet another completed the Boston Marathon (26.5 miles) in two hours and thirty minutes and finished in the top 10 finishers out of 5,000 runners. Many paraplegic swimmers are only seconds off the able-bodied Olympic swimming records. Later, one paraplegic weightlifter, weighing 125 lbs. and using a bench pressing in a supine position, utilizing only upper torso muscles lifted 396.5 lbs. (195 kilos).

As a result of Dr. Guttman's work, many paralyzed men and women in the world are given an opportunity to make something of themselves in spite of their physical situation. Through sport, they have the will to live and contribute. There are many paralyzed people in the world due to disease and injury.

251

In the United States alone, there are an estimated 22 million with some form of disability. Dr. Guttman realized early on that everyone has something special to contribute to society and should be given the chance. Due to disease and injury, many individual's opportunities are at least curtailed, if not eliminated. Through the sports that Dr. Guttman has established for the paralyzed, including track and field events, swimming events, weightlifting, archery, table tennis, fencing, pistol shooting, and more, these people now have the opportunity to strive for excellence in life. These sports provide dignity, confidence, discipline, enhancement of the quality of life, friendship, and personal gratification to the able-bodied as well as disabled people.

## Cardiorespiratory Fitness

There is a lot of information available on the physiological effects of training able-bodied people; however, the cross-sectional or longitudinal studies of disabled people are relatively few. Some of the most important findings in the literature will be summarized below. A large variation of cardiovascular fitness among paraplegic athletes has been observed. Generally, a reduced maximal oxygen intake, as well as a poor stroke volume, has been observed in many disabled athletes.

Dreisinger & Londeree (1982) found that "$VO_2$max and heart rate tend to increase linearly with power output" and "the training of the cardiovascular system is possible with improvement in maximal variables such as power output, $VO_2$, heart rate, ventilator volumes, respiratory quotient and lactic acid" (p. 32). Weiss & Beck (1973) observed that exercise helped to slow down the blood circulation in the paralyzed extremities. Furthermore, exercise supported positive changes in basic metabolism, alterations in the skeletal system and other tissues, and helped stop the progression of pathological changes and led to the reconstruction of bodily functions (p. 166). Stewart (1981) investigated the $VO_2$max in wheelchair athletes compared to able-bodied athletes. "This is due to less well-developed training techniques for the wheelchair athlete rather than a true physiological difference" (Stewart, 1981, 166).

Other studies concerning the cardiovascular system found that there are no major differences in the adaptive process of the cardiovascular system, the muscle system, or autonomic nervous system when compared to the able bodied population (Jochheim & Strokhendl, 1973). This is the primary reason why the same principles obtained from sports medicine and coaching also apply to the paraplegic. The authors further state that the best activities to help fulfill the requirements needed for good cardiovascular training are dynamic exercises, which use many muscle groups, high intensity and long performance time, such as swimming, long-distance wheelchair or bali-exerciser (p. 175).

Other studies have demonstrated that very active physically disabled adults performed standard forearm exercises at a substantially lower relative metabolic load than sedentary wheelchair users (Jackson, et al., 1978).

Asayama, et al. (1984) studied the energy expenditure of paraplegic marathon runners during the marathon and found that paraplegics have less physical fitness and they are subject to various types of activities that cause a great amount of stress to the cardiovascular system over time. He stated that "metabolic depression, decubitus ulcers, and prone skin are all complications of paraplegia." A study on elite wheelchair athletes looked at the performance in the areas of upper limb strength and cardiovascular fitness. It was found that strength and endurance training were equally important in enhancing maximal aerobic capacity. After spinal cord injury, Wicks, et al., (1983) suggested that "in addition to regular wheelchair ambulation, strength training and endurance training is important and should be encouraged in wheelchair-bound individuals" (p. 231).

During the XXI International Stoke Mandeville Games in Heidelberg, Germany, in 1972, spiroergometric and telemetric investigations were carried on 100 paralyzed athletes. Hulleman, et al., (1975) found that the "maximum oxygen uptake observed and the oxygen pulse were lower than in the non-disabled persons" (p. 121). Further studies found that the paraplegic runs a higher risk of becoming more and more incapacitated as time goes on. The results showed that "that the maximal aerobic power, the maximal work capacity and the mechanical efficiency, as well as the subject's well-being can be improved by physical training." Furthermore, "paraplegic patients can attain a respectably high maximal oxygen uptake if they train adequately." In order to keep the working capacity at the improved level, paraplegic patients should begin with a specifically designed training after the rehabilitation period has been concluded and continue indefinitely (Nilsson, et al., 1975, 56).

It was also found that swimming programs can increase fitness levels fourfold in paralyzed individuals compared to other cardiovascular fitness activities. This is extremely important since adult sedentary paraplegics who are confined to a wheelchair for years are less fit than the general sedentary population (Bar-Or, et al., 1976). They also found that the inactivity of wheelchair-bound children suffering from polio and cerebral palsy may cause an increase in body adiposity, reduced aerobic capacity and inferior lung function (p. 157).

## Muscle Endurance and Muscle Strength

Muscle strength, muscle endurance and the effect of upper-body muscularity on local blood supply are often factors that limit the wheelchair population.

Many paraplegic people are reliant upon their manually operated wheelchair for their ambulation. However, fitness to operate the wheelchair may vary greatly due to one's disability(ies), muscular strength and endurance, cardiorespiratory capacity and propulsion technique (Glaser, et al., 1979). Since wheelchair propulsion involves the relatively weak upper-body musculature, local arm fatigue rather than cardiovascular factors may limit one's ability to operate a manual wheelchair. Furthermore, muscular strength, muscular endurance and the impact of upper-body muscularity on local blood supply are often factors that limit wheelchair ambulation (Davis, et al., 1981).

Most studies conducted on the disabled have concluded that fitness levels are poor and below those of the able-bodied population. In summary, the cardiovascular endurance fitness of the spinal cord-injured person is poor; the muscle strength fitness of the spinal cord injured is poor, and the muscle endurance fitness of the spinal cord injured is poor.

## Conclusion

Today, there still exists a considerable difference of opinion in the physical conditioning systems and methods for the disabled, even within the same sport. There is a lack of stability among practitioners and coaches concerning the application of conditioning principles. There is also disagreement among scientists in reference to the application of conditioning principles. Many scientists disagree on the interpretation of the findings on human performance research.

This literature review relative to the physical fitness of spinal cord injured people shows that not many studies have been conducted on the fitness of the physically disabled. Initial studies began after World War II. In the 1970s and 1980s physical training of the paraplegic became more popular, which is due to the exposure of the International Stoke Mandeville Games and the Olympic Games for the physically disabled, known as the Paralympics. However, this research review demonstrates how important any physical activity on any level is for people with a disability. Although there is a wide range of disabilties that can inflict people, the conclusion of this research affirms that fitness can be improved on any level of ability or disability, along with psycho-social benefits!

# References

Asajama, K.; Yutaka, N.; Ogata, H.; Morita, H.; Kobama, S. & Hatado, K. (1984). Energy Expenditure of Paraplegic Marathon Runners. *Journal of YOEH, 6*(2) 121-130.

Bar-Or, O.; Inbar, O. & Spira, R. (1976). Physiological Effects of Sports Rehabilitation Programs on Cerebral Palsied and Post-poliomyelitic Adolescents. *Medicine and Science in Sports, 8*(3), 157-161.

Bamajian, J.V. (1981). *Therapeutic Exercise*, (3rd ed.). Baltimore: Williams & Wilkins.

Coyle, E. (1977). Paraplegic Sports. *Federation Internationale D'Education Physique Bulletin, 47*(3), 27-28.

Davis, G.M.; Shephard, R.J. & Jackson, R.J. (2001). Cardiorespiratory Fitness and Muscular Strength in the Lower-limb Disabled. *Canadian Journal of Applied Sport Science, 6*(4), 159-165.

Dreisinger, T.E. & Londeree, B.R. (1982). Wheelchair Exercise: A Review. *Paraplegia, 20,* 20-34.

Emes, C.G. (1981). Fitness and the Physically Disabled, A Review. *Canadian Journal of Applied Sport Science, 6*(4), 176-178.

Glaser, R.M.; Foley, D.M.; Laubach, L.L.; Sawka, M.N. & Suryaprasad, A.G. (1979). An Exercise test to Evaluate Fitness for Wheelchair Activity. *Paraplegia, 16,* 341-349.

Guttman, L. (1976). *Textbook of Sport for the Disabled.* Aylesbury, Bucks, England: HM+M Publishers.

Hulleman, K.D.; List, M.; Matthes, D.; Wiese, G. & Zika, D. (1975). Spiroergometric and Telemetric Investigations During the XXI International Stoke Mandeville Games. *Paraplegia, 13,* 109-123.

Jackson, R.W.; Beaver, D.P.; McCann, C.; Messner, D.G. & Ryan, A.J. (1978). Sport and Recreation for the Handicapped. *The Physician and Sports Medicine,* pp. 44-61.

Jochheim, K.A. & Strokhendl, H. (1973). The Value of Particular Sports of the Wheelchair Disabled in Maintaining Health of the Paraplegic. *Paragplegic, 11,* 173-178.

Nilsson, P.H.; Pruett, E. & Staff, P.H. (1975). Physical Work Capacity and the Effects of Training on Subjects with Longstanding Paraplegia. *Scandinavian Journal of Rehabilitated Medicine, 1,* 51-56.

Ryan, A.J. (1984). Another Olympics, Another Flame; Different Athletes, Different Game. *Physician and Sports Medicine, 4*(10), 133-137.

Stewart, N. (1981). The Value of Sport in the Rehabilitation of the Physically Disabled. *Canadian Journal of Applied Sport Science, 6*(4), 166-167.

Weiss, M.W. & Beck, J. (1973). Sport as Part of Therapy and Rehabilitation of Paraplegics. *Paraplegia, 11,* 166-172.

Wicks, J.R.; Oldrige, N.B., Cameron, B.J. & Jones, W.L. (1983). Arm Cranking and Wheelchair Ergometry in Spinal Cord Injured Athletes. *Medicine and Science in Sports and Exercise, 15*(3), 224-231.

## Chapter 9:

# Body Image and Sport – Fitness – Physical Activity

Body image issues and related problems, such as eating disorders, exercise disorders and steroid abuse, as well as obesity, are on the rise in highly advanced capitalist societies. The first section in this chapter traces these issues back to their historical roots and sheds light on the excesses of consumption and spectatorship at the beginning of the 21st century. The second part explores the issues associated with body image disorders, specifically eating disorders, in the world of sport. The third issue elaborates on the making of the modern body, including the effects the media has on women's body image.

## Issue 1

## The Body in the Age of Consumption and Spectatoritis

The rise of the fitness movement and the subsequent glorification of the body are embedded in a series of major sociocultural changes that date back to the 1950s. In general, a steadily rising standard of living and more free time provide the basis for the mass participation in leisure activities, tourism and fitness training programs. The commercialization of youth culture, the growing pop music business, and the flourishing beauty industry are some of the most obvious features of this general trend since the '60s.

The rise of the fitness and beauty industries points to something else beyond just job fitness or health maintenance. Philosophical anthropologists like Plessner (1975) have argued for a long time that sport helps to compensate for new deficits in the work process that result from such factors as long hours of intellectual work. However, one of the paradoxes of our times seems to be the less we need the body in terms of strength and endurance at the workplace, the more people are concerned with their fitness and their bodies.

The "heavenly body" (Penz, 1999) becomes a simplification of one's personality and "symbolic capital" to attract attention in a wide range of forms. The hyper-perfect athletic figure dominates the fashion model scene. Although the current body ideal for females is thin but muscular and that for males is big and muscular, body disorder problems are on the rise. The problems span from eating disorders and disordered eating to exercise disorders, and they seem to be worse among the athlete population.

First, a historical analysis of the importance of the body in highly industrialized nations and its anthropological implications during the last century will shed light on the body issues we are facing in the 21st century. Second, a philosophical view will advance the discussion of the controversial issues associated with a distorted body image, such as eating disorders, overeating and exercise disorders. Third, current body image issues as well as possible solutions will be presented, especially as they pertain to physical and health educators as well as coaches. It becomes pertinent that all teachers, parents, and friends also need to be more aware and help prevent the problems associated with the body in this age of consumption and spectatoritis.

## Historical Account of the Body Image and Current Ideal

Body image is often misunderstood as the way in which someone visually sees one's body – as if looking in a mirror. Instead, body image refers to the *mental image* a person has of the physical appearance of the body, including attitudes and feelings concerning the body (Rucinski, 1989). What does North American society accept as the ideal body? The answer to this question has changed greatly over the past two centuries.

During the 19th century, interest in sports grew tremendously in America. Men entered into the realm of competitive physical sport first and found that physical activity was a good way to maintain one's virility and athletic manhood. However, a problem arose when women began to stream into educational institutions with the introduction of Title IX in 1972, the work force, political reform movement, and sports participation, all of which were areas of male domination. The entrance of the female athlete into a male-dominated sector of society made her a potentially disruptive character to the expected norm because sport had been preserved as a domain of male competition in which masculinity was asserted. Women who entered into sport were seen as bordering between the ideals of femininity and masculinity, as well as a threat to the traditional gender roles of the strong male and weak dependent woman. Thus, women who became involved in sport needed to take a "cautious" approach, or they risked being viewed as manly.

Nineteenth century science categorized women as the inferior sex and attributed this primarily to their reproductive system, mood swings and fluctuating menstrual cycles. Ever since this assertion, it has been an uphill battle for women's acceptance in sport society. At the same time, the traditional body image of the female was changing from that of a softer, weaker, more voluptuous figure, to one of a leaner, athletic, more assertive woman. The changes in women's social function were followed by changes in the acceptable body type as well.

Physical education programs were designed with women in mind. However, they were only accepted for involvement in more feminine, aesthetically pleasing and recreational types of physical activity. Sports for women were seen as a means of strengthening elite social ties and were not to be taken seriously.

As 20th century sport evolved, the "athletic girl" became more accepted in athletic society. However, the focus changed to an emphasis on feminine beauty and sexuality. For example, a publication called "To Reduce Flesh" stated that "The charm of a well proportioned figure is not to be overestimated, and it is one which almost any woman can possess by the expenditure of systematic effort, acquiring incidentally good health with her good figure" (Cahn, 1994). Dudley Sargent stated that "good form in figure and good form in motion ... tend to inspire admiration in the opposite sex and therefore play an important part in what is termed sexual selection" (Cahn, 1994). Thus, it is obvious that the focus for women in sport was geared more toward femininity, sexuality, and physical appearance, while men in sport were more respected for their strength, masculinity and physical prowess.

Even today, at the beginning of the 21st century, the media continues to reduce female athletes to mere sexual attributes. At the same time, male athletes have found great success and acceptance in sport society. This is not to say that male athletes are completely free of struggles with body image and acceptance issues, but rather that it is a much larger problem for females. This problem should be considered in light of our recent cultural development. We are living in a culture that adores youth and commercializes it at the same time. The fitness movement is only one example of this commercialization process; other examples are pop culture and the flourishing beauty industry. One of the major paradoxes in our time is the fact that the less we need the body in strength and endurance, to make a living for example, the more people are concerned with their bodies. The more Western societies age, the more we become concerned with staying young. As a result, physical prowess, vitality and flexibility, health and longevity are the targets of today's consumer society (Penz, 1999). People identify with their bodies and their looks; the body becomes a choice for self-expression and may be even more important than one's occupation. The wish to distinguish oneself through a muscular, fit and healthy appearance is the main reason for the fitness boom and other activities in vogue, such as the current yoga trend. "Beauty and fitness become expressions of the inner self," and with that, the body becomes a commodity for women and men. We find that even the poor do everything to wear certain clothes and sneakers in order to keep up with what Penz calls the "aestheticism of people's life" (Penz, 1999).

The most effective means to attract attention in highly industrialized societies is through beauty, which is proven by the rising demand for cosmetic surgery and cosmetic products for women *and* men. This trend differs from the traditional roles of men being the breadwinners and women being the homemakers. In order to be considered attractive today, one needs to work on one's body, which now becomes "body work." Penz describes the "heavenly body" people aspire to as one in which the "inner self is reflected." The ideal body is that of the perfect athletic figure that dominates the model scene as well as the androgynous look with bare heads or no forms. The androgynous look is not gender binding anymore, and there are only slight differences between the perfect look for women and men. The flourishing trend of body decorations for both sexes, such as piercing, tattoos, and more; or the hyper-feminization of sex, which includes enormous plastic breasts, is another testimony to the often-unhealthy search for the perfect body.

In sum, physical fitness or being involved in sports has become the main feature of today's concept of beauty. In fact, fitness and beauty have become the prominent features of the late capitalist consumer culture of the 21st century. How does this movement affect the individual? It is obvious that women's bodies have been under scrutiny for more than the past century, and it is no wonder that females struggle with so many body image issues in our society today. However, men are not exempt from this development any longer either. The easiest way to determine if someone is suffering from gender and body image stereotypes is to ask the following questions: What do you say to yourself when you see an obese person walking down the street, as compared to a thin, athletic person? Which person is more acceptable in our society? Of course, most people more readily accept the thin athletic person. We have come to associate thinness with success and popularity. It is no wonder that society has become obsessed with the pursuit of thinness by any means possible. However, at the same time, we are faced with the epidemic rise of overweight and obese people in our country. A healthy middle seems to be missing.

## Philosophical Implications of the Body Image

The German philosopher Helmut Plessner is not the first to describe the Western paradigm of the mind-dody dualism. This concept goes back to the Greek philosophers and culminated in the thinking of the Frankfurt School writers in the '60s. Herbert Marcuse, one of the Frankfurt School writers, describes the discrepancy of "people without a soul" in his famous book "The One-Dimensional Man." Here, Marcuse critiqued the way people live in highly industrialized nations, where materialistic desires over-shadow any other needs a person might have. At the end of the 20th century and beginning of the 21st century, we can conclude that Marcuse's description only touched the tip of the iceberg. People today are not only concerned about material goods, but their bodies have become a material phenomenon as well. Hence, people in highly industrialized nations have a body that is used for consumption in its various forms, whether it is fitness activities or overeating. People still *are* their bodies, *but having a body* and *being a body* have become two distinct notions. Plessner (1941) states that "man has and is a body, thus creating a cleavage in his existence."

"Having a body" that can be consumed, which is used and abused, seems to dominate the sport and fitness scene with disordered body images, eating disorders, obesity, and over exercising. In a domain such as sport and fitness activities, where humans want to master the body, perfect it by any means, and maximize its performance by any cost, the body becomes a commodity. *Having* a body becomes the most important part of one's existence; while *being* a body, and all the needs that go along with it are standing on the sideline of this great show. However, we ought not to forget, that according to Plessner, a human being "always and conjointly is a living body (head, trunk, extremities, with all that these contain) – even if he is convinced of his immortal soul, which somehow exists 'therein' – and has this living body as the physical thing" (Plessner, 1970, 35). If we forget that *being* a body is equally important to *having* a body – and the two cannot be separated from each other – we will come to the realization that this unity of having and being a body, as paradoxical as it may seem at times, is the essence of our being. Separating the two will lead to distorted images of ourselves, as well as our bodies. And this notion further fosters the distorted body images so many people in advanced industrial societies, such as the US, suffer from in the new millennium.

## Current Body Image Issues

There are many issues evolving around the body and body image today; the following selection provides a broad overview of the most common and well-researched topics. Generally, a distorted body image can result in various eating disorders, such as anorexia nervosa and bulimia; however, it can also be responsible for the increased number of overeaters in our country, leading to an alarming rise of obesity. On the other end of the spectrum are the exercise addicts and steroid abusers who try to maintain or build a body that is unattainable for most people.

### A. Distorted Body Image and Eating Disorders

Distorted body image is a common characteristic of eating disorders. Although they have existed for centuries, eating disorders did not come into focus as a dangerous disease until the past 40 years. In the time of Caesar, the Romans used to overeat at banquets and then throw up in a vomitorium so that they could return to the party and continue to indulge (McCormak, 2000). Men were respected for their large appetites and large figures. Fasting and starvation practices were also respected when holy men and women participated. These were the roots of eating disorders such as bulimia and anorexia. Today, we live in a society where there is more food available to us and less need to be physically active than any other time. In countries where food is limited, the body ideal is still rather voluptuous, representing the wealth of the person and family. In Africa, for example, young women will be sent to a "fattening hut" for one or two weeks prior to their weddings so that they can gain some extra weight to make their future husbands happy. However, in highly industrialized nations, we see the paradox of the body not being needed for earning a living, and at the same time the body becomes most important for achieving social status, adornment, and acceptance in society. With mottos such as "thin is in," as well as other advertising campaigns focusing on the body as a separate entity, it becomes very difficult for women and men to stay healthy and trim because so many of our social events and celebrations involve food, which is often processed or junk food.

Eating disorders seem to be even more prominent in the world of sports. Some of the most commonly affected sports that are plagued by eating disorders include gymnastics, dance, swimming, wrestling, track and field, field hockey, volleyball, endurance events, softball, and tennis. However, it is important to understand that eating disorders do not discriminate. They can affect anyone at any time, and we must be very cautious to identify and treat the problem. The two most common eating disorders are bulimia (about 20% women and 10% men are affected in the USA) and anorexia nervosa (about 25-30% women and 15-20% men are affected). And these numbers are still on the rise (see website of the Centers for Disease Control and Prevention, 2013).

*Bulimia nervosa* involves compulsive eating, followed by purging through self-induced vomiting, laxatives, diuretics, dieting, fasting, or exercise. This is followed by guilt and depression, which leads to resolutions to stop the binge-purge behavior. When those resolutions are broken, depression follows in a vicious cycle. The binge-purge cycle is usually done in private, and can progress from once a week to multiple times per day. Bulimia is dangerous to one's health because it can lead to cardiac arrest or kidney failure, not to mention other physical problems, such as swollen glands, tooth decay, psychological changes, and weight fluctuations (Rader, 2000).

*Anorexia nervosa* is characterized by an obsessive pursuit of thinness, in which persons deliberately starve themselves. Anorexia also can be fatal to the victim, aside from causing malnutrition, amenorrhea, psychological problems, and destruction of the body's organs. Many athletes start out with anorexic behavior, and upon needing food to compete, turn to bulimia due to feelings of guilt, thus overeating. The athlete sees the food as the enemy, which they can control, while the rest of their life is spinning out of control. Finally, the compulsive overeater is also characterized as eating disordered because of their inability to control food intake and repeated attempts to lose weight. Depression and guilt over food and body image are the main foci of the compulsive overeaters. Although less common in athletes, compulsive overeating may occur after a loss in competition, and then be followed by a cycle of bulimia. All eating disorders are extremely dangerous, and they need to be treated in order to prevent both physical and psychological problems, as well as death.

Athletes develop eating disorders for many reasons. There is always some underlying cause for distorted body image that the athlete cannot consciously control. Therefore, they feel that the only thing they can control on a daily basis is food intake. The eating disorder is a survival mechanism to help the individual cope with everyday life. Sometimes, athletes use anorexia to subconsciously punish themselves because they feel that they do not deserve to eat until they win. They may also feel that they are no good unless they weigh an unreasonably low weight. Coaches, peer athletes, and the media are often the cause for "weight ideals." An unrealistic standard is set for the athlete, and the only way to achieve it is through dangerous practices such as eating disorders. A typical scenario would be that of an aspiring gymnast who is tormented by anorexia and bulimia as she begins training with a new coach at the Olympic level. The gymnast's ultimate goal is to make it to the Olympics, and she will do anything to get there. With added pressure from coaches and parents who push her through the hard training and rigorous hours, the gymnast's support network crumbles, her eating behavior continues to change for the worse, and no one realizes that the gymnast is in trouble. Potentially, the worst-case scenario for the gymnast is death, and the least is bodily damage or loss of a career. This is a characteristic development of an eating disorder, in which pressures build on the athlete until they crack. At the same time, the athlete and the role models involved are in extreme denial until something horrible happens to the athlete's health. The bottom line is that eating disorders are dangerous, and our society and especially the world of sport need to be more aware of the problem and more willing to confront the problem when it arises.

The findings of multiple studies done with elite athletes led to the conclusion that most of those athletes plagued by eating disorders use their addiction as a means to achieve the ideals set by society. This issue will be further described in issue two of this chapter. Other reasons for involvement in eating disorders include striving for perfection and the desire to be number one, approval-seeking tendencies of the individuals, performance anxiety, and unhealthy behaviors displayed by coaches or fitness instructors.

## B. Exercise Addiction and Steroid Abuse

One of the most common problems related to eating disorders is exercise addiction. This negative addiction can easily be referred to as an "old dog with a new trick" because excess exercise takes the form of purging to control weight. The addict simply replaces one addiction with another, and this addiction is just as dangerous as the others. When a person exercises for hours a day, gets sick and injured, continues exercising, loses all social ties with family and friends, puts off other activities just to exercise, and feels unhappy every time he or she cannot exercise, there is a definite exercise addiction. Unfortunately, it is sometimes difficult for the friends and family of the exercise addict to realize that there is a problem because exercise is generally viewed as a healthy habit. Dobbins (2008) states, "There is no doubt that exercise can be a healthy activity, but when exercise takes on a life of its own, it can become as addictive in many ways as cigarettes, alcohol or drugs. Addiction occurs when you lose control, when you are so dependent on your workouts that you can't stop the activity even if you want to." Even though the exercise addict may seem to many outsiders as one who is well adjusted and striving for a goal, the person is actually very much out of control. The constant exercise is a means for people to feel that they are in control of their lives, their environment, and their weight. However, the addicts are usually doing an incredible amount of damage to their body. A lot of runners end up having nerve damage in their lower body because of continuous pounding on hard surfaces, and many exercise addicts become accustomed to using large amounts of anti-inflammatory drugs and pain killers in order to get through their workouts.

Furthermore, the pressure to achieve abnormal goals regarding appearance may encourage female athletes to engage in unhealthy and self-destructive behaviors, such as the use of anabolic steroids along with their exercise addiction. Female bodybuilders are likely to suffer from eating disorders and body image disorders in a newly categorized manner – the "eating disorder/ bodybuilder type" or ED/BT (Mann, February, 2000). The ED/BT is a form of eating disorder and exercise addiction that is marked by very high-protein, high calorie, and low-fat diets eaten at regularly scheduled intervals. The athletes also often suffer from muscle dysmorphia.

Other common problems for exercise addicts include nutritional deficiency, stress fractures, tendonitis, shin splints, arthritis, bleeding feet, and osteoporosis. The most common problem for female athletes is the development of the female-athlete triad (Eichner, 2007). Because of the high number of disordered eating habits and over-exercising, secondary problems of amenorrhea and osteoporosis occur in many females. A lack of nutrient intake, combined with over-exercising causes hormonal imbalances and broken bones in women as young as twenty years old. In fact, many women in their early twenties have the bone density of seventy-year-old women.

## C. Obesity

Compulsive overeaters are also characterized as "eating disordered" because of their inability to control their food intake and repeated attempts to lose weight. Depression and guilt over food and body image are the main focus of compulsive overeaters. Why are Americans so overweight? Americans are now the fattest people on earth. (Actually a handful of South Sea islanders still outweigh them, but they are gaining.) Seven out of every 10 – and fully a quarter of US children – are now overweight; that is two thirds of the nation. The Centers for Disease Control and Prevention (2013) estimate that 65-70% of Americans are overweight and 35.7% are obese. These statistics are even more disturbing when compared to the numbers thirty years ago. In 1980, only 32% of the US population was considered overweight and 15% were obese. Many experts agree that obesity does not just appear in adults but has its roots in childhood. Since 1970, the proportion of American children who are overweight has doubled, a rate of increase that suggests the fattening of America has a specific history, as well as a biology. The journalist Greg Critser attempts to reconstruct that history in his book Fat Land (2003). How did America get to be so fat?

There are multiple factors in our advanced capitalist society that have contributed to the fattening of American people since the 1970s. As described earlier in Chapter 4, during the last two decades, Americans began to eat on average an additional 200 calories more per day. The physiologist Hill states that "getting fat today is less an aberration than a normal response to the American environment." The advancements in technology and a more and more sedentary lifestyle are only the most obvious developments that have contributed to the fattening of the nation. Other reasons include economic and marketing strategies where small, medium and large portions are now replaced by single gigantic servings: Big Gulp, Big Mac, jumbo fries. Supersize it! Research has found that people presented with larger portions will eat up to 30 percent more than they otherwise would. Thus, the unintended consequences of cheap and abundant food are foremost the leading cause for the epidemic of obesity in this country. And the sad response by our society is the accommodation of obese people by introducing bigger seats in restaurants as well as larger clothing sizes. Less amusing is what this additional weight is doing to the health of people: the American diet has led to an epidemic of Type 2 diabetes, which now afflicts millions of children as well as adults, and costs America's health system billions of dollars a year. The exponential increase in children who are overweight will only continue to challenge our society's health care system because these overweight children will become overweight or obese adults with an increase in future health problems (Salbe & Ravussin, 2000).

## Possible Solutions

President George W. Bush defined the described situation as the "era of personal responsibility," and not a public problem. However, public as well as personal solutions to these rising epidemics are needed. When it comes to body image problems, especially for women, it appears that hardly anyone can attain the body ideals proposed by the media. Thus, we need to educate people to accept different body types and images and intervene at an early age. The message to convey should be that exercise is most important for one's health rather than beauty and looks, which seems to be the number one reason cited by young people who engage in physical activity. Public policy, along with financial support for the implementation of intervention programs, is necessary, as are mandatory daily physical education programs in all American schools.

*What can physical/health educators and coaches do to help?*

Examples from the literature include:
- Compassion and understanding.
- More wellness information should be infused into the curriculum. This is not only beneficial to overweight and obese children, but would be valuable information for any child.
- Mandatory, daily physical education, as well as health classes, need to address the problems.
- Physical fitness and physical education programs should use a health-related philosophy rather than the traditional, competitive approach.
- Adventure-based games and outdoor education activities are advised due to the fact that these activities can be successful individual explorations into a child's abilities, which can augment students' self-esteem.
- Introduce new and motivating physical activities into the PE curriculum, such as biking, hiking, or snowshoe expeditions.
- Provide individualized assessment.
- Model appropriate attitudes/behaviors: if you stress physical activity in your curriculum, then you must participate in physical activity as well.
- Physical educators, exercise leaders and coaches should develop and implement new models of sport and physical activity that can compel the participation of non-athletic and /or non-active girls and boys.

## Summary and Conclusion

New and alarming statistics regarding the dangers of obesity and a lack of exercise are emerging every day. At the same time, we are seeing an increase in eating and exercise disorders. The health predicament that obesity especially presents to our nation and the world is disturbing. However, the psychological barriers that the obese face are more disconcerting and may be responsible for the rising prevalence in excess weight. Also, the lifestyle and technological advances of modern (or postmodern) America have contributed to the sedentary lifestyle so many people live. There is increased awareness about fitness activities and their health benefits, but the ethos of the era is not conducive to following up on these many warnings Americans are bombarded with daily. There is no easy solution to the problem. As long as the country only blames the individual for their shortcomings in not exercising enough and not eating right, the situation is not going to change soon. Public policy is needed, along with a deflated focus/concern on body image, and a mandate for daily physical education in all schools.

Prevention of these problems is the key factor for educators, parents, coaches, trainers, and health care professionals. Besides the "practical tips" one can find in the literature on how to intervene at a young age in order to avoid the problems and vicious cycles of a distorted body image, overeating, or eating and exercise disorders, it is important to focus on a different approach. In order to address these problems at the roots we need a revised ethic for sport and physical activity. Therefore, changes in thinking about the winning-at-all-costs attitude, as well as a promotion of an "Eastern ideal" with a holistic approach to the human body might be most beneficial along with daily physical activity in the combat of these problems.

## References

Cahnman, W. (1968). The Stigma of Obesity. *Sociological Quarterly, 9*, 283-299.

Centers for Disease Control & Prevention (2013). www.cdc.com/Obesity Statistics

Centers for Disease Control & Prevention (2001, September 12). *Obesity and Overweight: A Public Health Epidemic.* Retrieved April 28, 2002 from http://www.cdc.gov/nccdphp/dnpa/obesity/epidemic.htm

Critser, G. (2003). *Fat Land. How Americans Became the Fattest People in the World.* Boston: Houghton Mifflin Company.

Falkner, N., French, S., Jerffery, R., Neumark-Sztainer, D., Sherwood, N. & Morton, N. (1999). Mistreatment Due to Weight: Prevalence and Sources of Perceived Mistreatment in Women and Men. *Obesity Research, 7*, 572-576.

Marcus, B. & L. Forsyth (2003). Motivating People to be Physically Active. In: S. Blair (Ed.) *Physical Activity Intervention Series.* Champaign, Illinois: Human Kinetics.

Penz, O. (1999). Fit for the Looks: Heavenly Bodies. In: Volkwein, K. (Ed.) *Fitness as Cultural Phenomenon.* Münster/Germany: Waxmann Verlag.

Plessner, H. (1941). *Laughing and Crying: A Study of Border Situations of Human Behavior.* Oxford, England: Netherlands.

Salbe, A. & Ravussin, E. (2000). The Determinants of Obesity. P. 79 In: C. Bouchard (Ed.) *Physical Activity and Obesity.* Champaign, IL: Human Kinetics.

## Issue 2

# *Eating Disorders in the World of Sport*

There is no doubt that disordered eating is at epidemic levels in the United States. Up to 24 million people of all ages and genders suffer from eating disorders (anorexia, bulimia, and binge eating disorder) in the US. Eating disorders have the highest mortality rate of any mental illness. According to Craw, et al., (2009) the mortality rate for anorexia is 4%, for bulimia 3.9%, and for other eating disorders 5.2%. Eating disorders are more widespread among adolescents and college-aged females, although they are also on the rise for males. According to the *National Association of Anorexia Nervosa and Associated Disorders* (2013), 95% of those with eating disorders are between the ages of 12 and 26, and 25% of college-aged women engage in binging and purging as a weight management technique. At the beginning of the 21st century, 11% of high school seniors suffered from eating disorders, and 91% of those were females (Rader, 2000). In the world of sport, judged sports show a prevalence of eating disorders as high as 13%, compared to about 3% in refereed sports. A significantly higher rate of eating disorders was found in elite athletes (20%) than in the female control group (10%). Female aesthetic sports, such as gymnastics, ballet, and figure skating, are found to be the highest risk for eating disorders (www.anad.org, 2013).

Many well-known gymnasts have lived lives that were plagued by problems with disordered eating: Nadia Comaneci suffered from bulimia; Cathy Rigby twice went into cardiac arrest due to her disorder; Kristie Phillips was driven to a suicide attempt; and Christy Henrich unfortunately died due to bulimia (Cuniberti, 1994). These tragedies shed light on the problem and opened the door for other gymnasts to come forward and confess their problems. The late Princess Diana admitted to suffering from bulimia for many years and well-known singer Karen Carpenter died from her battle with anorexia. Although they were not athletes, these examples show that eating disorders do not discriminate; anyone can become a victim. The US Public Health Service speculates that over 60 million Americans suffer from some type of dysfunctional eating habits (Rader, 2000), 700,000 to one million kids nationwide suffer from eating disorders (Cuniberti, 1994), and 19-30% of college-aged women display bulimic behavior (Rader, 2000). All of these numbers are staggering. Eating disorders are not just a hidden problem anymore. They are dangerous diseases that deserve attention. Unfortunately, the pressure on female athletes to succeed is extremely high, and in aesthetically emphasized sports like gymnastics, the occurrence of eating disorders is very high.

The purpose of this issue is to shed some light on the controversies associated with distorted body image, such as eating disorders and exercise addiction.

Women and men are affected differently; however, both genders battle with the detrimental consequences of disordered eating in the world of sport. Furthermore, the influence of the media in supporting distorted views of body image is not to be underestimated. After a thorough investigation of the above-mentioned issues, solutions for the future will be discussed. Coaches, teachers, parents, and friends need to be more aware and help prevent these problems.

## Cultural View on Body Image

At a young age, children learn and grow from their experiences with different role models. Parents, teachers, coaches, athletes, peers and others can have great influence on a child's perceptions of reality and growth because expectations from those role models are set very early in life. One of the most influential role models for a young person is the coach because athletes admire, respect, and trust that the coach will not do them wrong. According to *The Eating Disorders Digest* (Rosen, 1989), there is a 95% cooperation rate for athletes with coaches, and athletes are wonderful to work with because they do anything the coach tells them to do. This implicit faith in one person's judgment is dangerous when that person may be a bad role model. As little as one negative experience, such as criticism in the locker room, can mold an athlete's body image and perceptions in either a positive or negative way. Therefore, it is extremely important that role models be aware of their actions and that the experiences with their athletes are positive.

Our society is dominated by visual images on television and in magazines, which portray men in tough, masculine roles, and women in softer, feminine roles. Because of this, there have been many negative messages given to girls who become involved in sports. Duncan (1990) studied sports photographs and sexual differences between men and women in the 1984 and 1988 Olympics. The study showed that photos highlighted the sexual differences between men and women and emphasized the masculine and feminine socially constructed traits. There were many images of men in dominating positions over women, and women in inferior positions. Women were photographed in sexually suggestive poses, and athletes such as Katarina Witt and Florence Griffith Joyner, were extremely popular in photos because of their glamour and sex appeal. It has been noted that focusing on female differences is a political strategy that places women in positions of weakness. This entire concept eliminates respect for women as athletes, and sets the standard that women should not try to compete with men.

Furthermore, professional athletes are often featured in a *Sports Illustrated Swimsuit Issue* (Deford, 2011), portrayed in numerous sexy outfits and poses that have nothing to do with their sports. For example, when professional tennis player Anna Kournikova was featured in the year 2000, despite the fact that she has never won a WTA title, public fascination with this young tennis player skyrocketed because of her sex appeal. It is no wonder that women have had such great struggles with body image and unrealistic attitudes toward winning. Today, women feel like they have to do whatever they can to find acceptance or win in a man's world, even if their sexuality is exploited. The new mottos in sport have become "thin is in" and "win at all cost" in order to be the best.

## Eating Disorders and Sport

Coaches, parents and athletes should be aware of the common symptoms of eating disorders as described earlier in this chapter. The long list includes: thoughts about "feeling fat" and fear of gaining weight; feelings of loss of control when eating; feeling that one's weight determines self-esteem; body image obsession; guilt or shame after eating; repeated attempts at dieting; eating large amounts of food in a short amount of time; self-consciousness about eating; sneaking food; lying about eating habits; strict dieting; fasting; restrictive eating; self-induced vomiting; laxative and/or diuretic abuse; compulsive exercise; eating to relieve stress or depression; eating when not hungry; eating sensibly in front of others and then making up for it when alone; depression; low body weight; menstrual irregularities; gastrointestinal complaints; and embarrassment about one's weight (Radnor, 2000).

Numerous studies have been completed on eating disorders with respect to the average population. However, in regard to sport, those studies investigating athletes with eating disorders over the last thirty years will be summarized here. It is also important to realize that some of those athletes who are plagued by eating disorders use their addiction as a means to achieve the ideals set by society. Rosen (1989) studied wrestlers in the US and found that the two methods that contributed most to their eating disorders were dehydration and caloric restriction. Of those who chose to use dehydration techniques, 5% used diuretics and 11% used vomiting. One half of the wrestlers who were studied indicated that their coach advised them to use those methods. The wrestlers who chose caloric restriction were fasting for at least two days prior to a meet in order to achieve "weight," and then in the two days following, they consumed up to 11,000 calories. Both of these weight control techniques are extremely dangerous, as well as indicative of eating disorder behavior. Rosen (1989) also studied pathogenic weight control behaviors involved in eating disorders and found that 32% of world-class athletes use them on a regular basis (25% diet pills, 16% laxatives, 14% vomit, 45% combination of methods). The athletes practicing these techniques were 74% of gymnasts, 47% of distance runners,

50% of field hockey players and 25% of softball, volleyball, track, and tennis players. All of these figures are shocking, and they help to prove the prevalence of a problem in our athletes. Although this study is over twenty years old, sadly, the current number of eating disorders within the athletic community has not improved nor has the number of eating disorders in the general population.

Rucinski (1989) studied competitive US national ice skaters to determine whether there is a relationship between body image and dietary intake. An Eating Attitude Test (EAT) was administered, in which a score of 30+ was considered within anorexic range. The female skaters scored an average of 29.3 + 15 (range 4-54) and the males scored an average of 10 + 5.7 (range 3-22). It was discovered that 48% of the females fell within anorexic range, while 0% of the males fell within this range. The findings showed that the pressure on male skaters for thinness does not compare with the pressure on female skaters. Our culture pressures females to have thin bodies. Competitive skaters need nutrition education. Low caloric intakes of females in this study are consistent with dancers and athletes in other studies. The results demonstrated even back then that athletic programs should implement careful diet planning, nutrition education, and dietetic counseling to their athletes.

In 1992, Taub and Benson examined weight concerns and eating disorder prevalence in adolescent swimmers, instead of collegiate or professional swimmers in the US. They found that although female swimmers had more desire to be thin than males, neither male nor female adolescent swimmer were particularly susceptible to eating disorders or dangerous weight control techniques. The two factors that were attributed to the lack of disordered eating were the young age of the participants and the non-competitive nature of the sport. They found less win-at-all-cost behavior from the coaches and a different attitude toward the athletes. The sport was still treated as a fun activity at the younger age level. In comparison, elite athletes are expected to give everything they can to succeed and sacrifice everything to achieve their goals and dreams. The attitude toward winning and sport makes a significant difference in the outcome of behaviors.

Perfectionism and the desire to be number one may become problems among amateur athletes who are pushed to excel in a sport that they are not well suited to play. Mann (May, 2000) sited a preliminary study of 25 elite female athletes, age 19-28. Those who expressed the greatest amount of concern over mistakes made during play, doubts over actions, and overall anxiety were more at risk for developing depression, anxiety and eating disorders. Unfortunately elite athletes seem to have perfectionist and approval-seeking tendencies, which may lead to health problems. An anonymous 29-year-old Los Angeles resident spent 8 years playing competitive volleyball. Mann (May, 2000) quotes the athlete, "I was afraid to fail, and I would get really uptight and anxious about my performance before a game. Sometimes this type of anxiety helped me to win, and other times it just gave me permission to beat myself up for a mistake I made during a game." This athlete's method of dealing with performance anxiety led to severe depression and an eating disorder, which took years of therapy to recover. Perfectionism can be a good motivating force for some athletes, and it can be very bad for others. The key is finding a balance of perfectionism for athletes to succeed.

A study concerning the prevalence of eating disorders in US NCAA programs (Dick, 1991) involved a survey of 803 member institutions. Of the 803 institutions, 491 responded to the survey, 313 (64%) indicated that at least one case of an eating disorder had occurred in the last year at their institution, and 872 positive reports were submitted from the 313 institutions. Out of the 872 positive reports, 810 (93%) were submitted from women's sports and 62 (7%) were from men's sports. This study is extremely important because it shows the prevalence of eating disorders that occur in sport, as well as the overwhelming difference in occurrence in women's sports compared to men's sports. It is of great concern that the difference is so large, so there must be some underlying sociological reason why women athletes in American society are plagued by these diseases. It is the responsibility of physical educators to help stop this ongoing battle and make things better for female athletes.

In 1995, USA Gymnastics had over 50,000 registered female athletes, most of them adolescents. Therefore, they created a task force in an attempt to understand female athlete triad syndrome. Unfortunately, young gymnasts as well as runners are very susceptible to this disorder. An unpublished survey of elite gymnasts and their mothers (Technique, 1995) indicated that 28% of the gymnasts surveyed had eating disorder problems, and out of 42 NCAA gymnastics programs surveyed, 62% of collegiate gymnasts have engaged in disordered eating practices. These numbers are staggering, which is why the USA gymnastics task force was created. If these athletes are not helped, a large number of young women will suffer lifetime effects of osteoporosis and hormonal imbalance.

Elite female athletes in 35 Norwegian sport programs were studied by Little (1992). It was discovered that 18% of their athletes suffered from some type of eating disorder, compared to 5% of females in their general population. One Norwegian coach was quoted as saying, "Serious women athletes do not have menstrual cycles. You just aren't serious enough if you still have a period" (Little, 1992). This quote exemplifies the attitude that many coaches and trainers have toward female athletes. A female with a regular menstrual cycle is viewed as somewhat weak and inferior when compared to her male counterpart. Therefore, the belief is that if she loses her body fat and lowers her weight, she will be able to compete on a man's level. Because Norway is more advanced in women's sports than most other countries, there is great concern that the development of women's sports in other countries will also exacerbate the eating disorder problems in those countries.

In order for an athlete to remain at the top of her game, she has to stay in shape, and this is often accomplished in the off-season by attending different types of fitness classes. Some of the role models who teach fitness classes, however, may not always exhibit healthy behaviors themselves. To determine how prevalent unhealthy behavior is in the fitness community, Thompson and Sargent (2000) examined eating disorders, eating attitudes, negative body image and obligatory exercise among group fitness instructors in the US. Out of the 377 fitness instructors who participated, 21% noted that they had perceived or been told they had an eating disorder in the past, and the average age of onset for their disease was 20.84 years. The majority, 80.3%, reported having the disorder prior to teaching fitness, 6.1% developed an eating disorder the first year of teaching, and 9.1% developed the disorder after their first year of teaching fitness. When examining body dissatisfaction, 42.9% of the instructors wanted to be thinner than their current size.

These results bring the following questions to mind: did the instructors with a prior eating disorder start teaching to help recover from the disorder or was teaching fitness another means of purging through exercise? Are women who are overly concerned about their appearance drawn to the fitness profession? Physical activity and the fitness profession can socially play a key role in the development of healthy behaviors as well as unhealthy behaviors such as eating disorders. For this reason, fitness instructors should be aware that their own possible distorted body image issues could unconsciously transfer to the perception of their clients.

## Male Body Image Disorders and Sport

Although the primary focus has been on female athletes, there are also many males who suffer from disordered eating and exercise addiction. Fortunately, the number of afflicted males is much lower. The number of men with significant symptoms of eating disorders may be greater than originally believed. Goode (2000) cites a study from the University of Toronto, in which 10,000 residents of Ontario participated. One out of six people who qualified for a diagnosis of anorexia were male. This number is "substantially greater than the 1:10 previously reported in eating disorder programs" (Goode, 2000). Aside from male wrestlers, runners, and gymnasts who feel that they may need to lose weight, there is a group of males who feel that they need to become bigger to be better – the body builders and some track and field athletes.

Men, just like women, can suffer from poor body image, but while anorexia and bulimia affect some men in the average population, male athletes can also experience body image disorders in which they suffer from the opposite symptoms. The mantra for this population is "big to win" and "harder is better." Methods of training, excess training, and an obsession with physical appearance are the focus for many body builders. The quest for bigger muscles becomes obsessive and is known as muscle or body dysmorphia (Fillon, 2000), or in athletic circles, it is sometimes called "reverse anorexia" or "bigorexia." Training regimens and the gym become the whole basis for their identity and self-esteem, and they employ many unhealthy techniques for losing and gaining weight during training.

According to the *American Academy of Orthopedic Surgeons* (Mann, April, 2010), an estimated 500,000 young athletes use steroids to improve their athletic performance. Steroids have been shown to increase muscle mass, but they can cause serious and life-threatening complications. Even though there are numerous negative side effects to steroid use, many athletes choose to take their chances with steroids in order to reach the unreasonable goals they have set for themselves. This is apparent from the number of athletes who tested positive for steroid use at the last several Olympics. They suffered the consequences of losing their Olympic privileges and/or medals.

The characteristics of muscle dysmorphia include a preoccupation with having a lean and muscular body, spending long hours lifting weights along with excessive attention to one's diet, an impaired social and professional life, an insistence on working out and dieting when one's well-being is in danger, and being overly concerned about being too small or not muscular enough (Fillon, 2000). It is the socialization of the males and females in the US that has led to the attitude that males must be bigger and females must be smaller or leaner to earn respect.

The *American Journal of Psychology* published a study in which 200 college-aged men from the United States, Austria and France surveyed a stack of pictures portraying various male body types (Fillon, 2000). In all three countries, the men chose an ideal body that was, on average, 28 pounds more muscular than their own bodies, and they guessed that women would prefer a male body 30 pounds more muscular than their own. Harrison Pope, M.D., psychiatry professor at Harvard Medical School, concludes that "Men in the US and Europe seem to think that women want them to be much more muscular than women actually want them to be" (Fillon, 2000). This statement demonstrates that the pressure on males to be "perfect" is great enough to distort their body image, and it causes men to engage in abnormal behavior. From anorexia to body dysmorphia, destructive behavior exists in the male population. McCormak (2009) reports that between 1997 and 2007, the number of men undergoing liposuction, especially to reduce "love-handles," tripled, and men were having silicone implants inserted into their calves and chests to simulate larger muscles. Because of poor body image and body dysmorphia, these types of behavior have become significant issues for men in our society.

## The Influence of the Media

Lumpkin and Williams (1997) studied featured articles in *Sports Illustrated* from 1954 to 1997 and found that 90.8% of the articles were dedicated to the lives and sporting achievements of males. The written descriptors that were used in articles about female athletes also used blatantly sexist terms. They also found that while the role of female athletes has changed, the stereotypical portrayal of females did not change. Women were shown in recreational rather than competitive situations. They were featured in individual and dual activities associated with the upper classes only, and sports for women appeared to be more of a sexual than an athletic activity. Out of 3,723 articles studied, males were featured in 3,178, females were featured in 280, and 40 articles featured both males and females. Although these numbers are not current, this study demonstrates the differences the media and, thus, society places on men and women's roles in sports. Perhaps this study should be performed again to see if the results have changed, and if so, how much. *Sports Illustrated* is the most widely read sports magazine in the United States, and the majority of readers are white males. The ironic thing about this, however, is that the most widely sold issue of the magazine is the annual swimsuit issue that focuses on the scantily clad female bodies of supermodels such as Tyra Banks, Heidi Klum, and Rebecca Romijn. One might question whether this issue has anything to do with sport or women's advancement in sports. If a female athlete who suffers from body image issues were to look at the swimsuit issue of *Sports Illustrated*, she would not likely experience an increase in her self-esteem. Fortunately, the magazine (*Sports Illustrated*, 2000) has recently featured some "real athletes" in the swimsuit issue. Ben and Julie Crenshaw (golf), Glen and Christina Rice (basketball), Ricky Williams (football), and Evander Holyfield (boxing) were featured as famous sports figures and their spouses in swimwear attire. Regardless of the magazine's attempt to use "real people" of sport, the swimwear photos do not help young athletes develop a positive self-image.

Besides magazines, there are other media and public sporting events in the United States that use the sexuality of women to promote sports. At any given football or basketball game, there are many women on the sidelines who are cheerleaders and dancers for the team. Women are portrayed as sexual objects during half-time events, contests and commercials. Again, one might question what this has to do with sports for women. These types of events only help to further the problem with eating disorders, exercise addiction and low self-esteem in women because they portray women as mere sexual objects. Until modern society starts to take women seriously, this will not change. The gains have been small thus far, but there are many suggestions for change in the future.

Examples of women's sport and fitness magazines that can be seen on the newsstand include *Shape* and *Muscle and Fitness Hers*. These types of publications open up more opportunities for female athletes to receive media attention. There have also been several attempts at new professional women's sports teams such as the ABL (American Basketball League), the WNBA (Women's National Basketball Association), and the WPVA (Women's Professional Volleyball Association), which have helped women to gain recognition in professional sports. This also allows more opportunity for young women to develop female sport role models and have new goals to shoot for while growing up.

*Sports Illustrated* had also run a magazine just for women called *Sport Illustrated Women* from 1997-2002. It was discontinued because of the downturn in the advertising economy. Since then, the website for *Sports Illustrated* (SportsIllustrated.com) has created a Women's Sports page that is dedicated to women's college and professional sports. While some might say that the majority of women who are featured on the cover of the magazine are ice-skaters, tennis players and track and field athletes, women's recognition in sport is definitely starting to take steps in the right direction. Other suggestions for the future include the continued development of women's sporting events and women-only health clubs, as well as education and a positive, supportive atmosphere in order to boost women's self-esteem and combat unproven or unhealthy practices.

## Solutions and Prevention

Durrett (1997) makes several suggestions to combat eating disorders in sport, which emphasize starting to work with young girls before puberty begins. She believes that positive physical activity at a young age can make a huge difference in development, and activities such as girls' fitness classes, activity camps, after-school workshops, and parent-child activities can make a big difference. There are also many mentor groups, such as *Big Brothers and Sisters* and *Girls in Motion*, which work with developing adolescents to provide good role models and positive activity at a young age. All of these are good suggestions, and they could actually make a world of difference for some young kids.

Many sports' governing bodies, such as the American Volleyball Coaches Association, USA Gymnastics, and USA Swimming have created educational materials for coaches and athletes to minimize the incidence of eating disorder development (Mosley, 1997). While there are many negative effects of sport on body image, one must also realize that there are benefits to the athlete as well. Sport participation can increase self-esteem, confidence and body image if the athlete is taught in a positive manner. Other benefits include increased energy levels, lower blood sugar levels, decreased blood pressure, increased happiness, better socialization skills, discipline, teamwork, time management, and an increased ability to deal with pressure. The key to achieving such benefits for an athlete is the balance of a healthy lifestyle with their sports participation.

Teachers, parents and coaches can be taught to understand how their words and actions can seriously affect the development of a young person in either a positive or negative way. One negative comment to a young girl concerning her weight or appearance can harm her in ways that are unknown until problems develop. Because women have been struggling for so long for acceptance in our society, women feel that they have to prove themselves every day. Not only does this affect females in sport, but also women in everyday situations. Eating disorders do not discriminate against race, color, gender, or socioeconomic status. However, they are more common in young females, especially athletes. Therefore, it is important to focus on giving young girls some kind of positive physical activity and encouragement at a young age. It is also important not to emphasize perfection and/or winning.

Educators must emphasize fun, fitness, health and self-esteem. Statements such as "You're too thin," "You would be a better athlete if you were thinner," and "You look so much better now that you lost weight" are all damaging and hurtful in their own ways. The wrong message is given to the person on the receiving end of the comment. Instead, a better way to approach someone is with kindness and compassion. If you believe that a person may have an eating disorder, it is best to get them professional help immediately. During the healing process, "willpower alone does not work because it is a disease." (Rader, 2000) Approaching the person with compassion and understanding, without being confrontational, will get the best result. For example you could say, "I see that you are losing some weight, and I'm a little concerned for your health. Maybe we could talk, and you could let me help you out." The final outcome is very dependent upon the actions of the people involved and the seriousness of the disorder, so it is usually best to ask for the advice of the professional.

Prevention of the occurrence of these problems is the key factor for educators, parents, coaches, trainers, and health care professionals, and efforts should be made to ensure that all levels of gymnasts have an environment that leads to positive self-esteem. Instead of having the "thin is in" and "win at all cost" attitudes, there are several suggestions may begin the prevention process. Eichner, et al., (1997) suggest that role models and educators emphasize physical and mental health, encourage changes in thinking about winning at all cost, promote healthy eating habits for successful performance, emphasize strength and stamina and de-emphasize body weight and size, address misconceptions about weight, diets, and performance, encourage the acceptance of sexual maturation and development during puberty, and encourage discussions about menstruation and eating patterns with a confidential person. Suggestions have also been made to promote an athlete's bill of rights, provide role models to help athletes develop self-esteem, develop a system for retired athletes who have issues with adjustment to a "normal life," provide nutritionists and sport psychologists for athletes to communicate with, and provide a mentor system of former athletes for current elite athletes to learn from. If these suggestions are implemented in the family, school, and training centers, many athletes may avoid having problems with eating disorders, exercise addiction, and physical deterioration at a young age. However, once an eating disorder develops, the athlete will have to deal with it for the rest of their life because food is the "substance" that cannot be avoided. An alcoholic can learn to abstain from alcohol and live a normal life, whereas the person with an eating disorder needs to eat in order to live. Preventing eating disorders and helping athletes to have a positive body image is the ultimate goal.

## References

Cahn, S.K. (1994). Coming on Strong: Gender and Sexuality in Twentieth-Century Women's Sport. *The Free Press.*

Crow. S.J., Peterson, C.B., Swanson, S.A., Raymond, N.C., Specker, S., Eckert, E.D., Mitchell, J.E. (2009). Increased Mortality in Bulimia Nervosa and Other Eating Disorders. *American Journal of Psychiatry 166,* 1342-1346.

Cuniberti, B. (1994). Let's Let Gymnasts Grow Up, *The Kansas City Star.*

Deford, F. (2010). Advantage Kournikova, *Sports Illustrated,* June.

Dick, R.W. (1991). Eating Disorders in NCAA Athletic Programs, Athletic Training, *JNATA, 26,* 136-140.

Dobbins, B. (1988). Exercise Addicts, Reprinted by Rader Institute with permission from *Muscle and Fitness Magazine,* September.

Duncan, M.C. (1990). Sports Photographs and Sexual Difference: Images of Women and Men in the 1984 and 1988 Olympic Games, *Sociology of Sport Journal,* 7(1), 22-43.

Durrett, A. (1997). Helping Girls Help Themselves, *IDEA Today,* September.

Eichner, R., Johnson, M., Loucks, A., & Steen, S. (1997). The Female Athlete Triad, *Sports Science Exchange,* G.S.S.I., 8 (1), 1-4.

Fillon, M. (2000). *Bigger Muscles Won't Necessarily Attract – Women and Men's Preoccupation with Body Size Can Lead to Disorde*r, WebMD Medical News, August.

Goode, E. (2000). Men and Health. Thinner: The Male Battle with Anorexia, *The New York Times*, June.

Little, L. (1992). Elite Female Athletes Plagued by Eating Disorders, *The Medical Post*, July.

Lumpkin, A. & Williams, L.D. (1997). An Analysis of Sports Illustrated Featured Articles, 1954-1987, *Sociology of Sport Journal, 8* (1), 16-32.

Mann, D. (2010). Female Elite Athletes at Risk for Depression, Anxiety. Same Traits That Enable Women to Excel May Cause Problems, *WebMD Medical News*, May.

Mann, D. (2000). Pressure to Perform Takes Its Toll on Emotional Health of Young Athletes, *WebMD Medical News*, April.

Mann, D. (2000). Steroid Use, Eating Disorders Are Common Among Female Bodybuilders, *WebMD Medical News,* February.

McCormak, S. (2009). During the Height of the Roman Empire, *The Daily Bulletin*, Ontario, Canada, August.

Mosley, B.F. (1997). Striking the Balance, Technique, 17 (7), (Reprinted from *Women's Sports & Fitness,* May).

National Association of Anorexia Nervosa and Associated Disorders (2013). www.anad.org. *National Surveys.*

Rader, W.C. The Rader Institute for the Treatment of Eating Disorders, Promotional and Informational Literature, USA, 2000.

Rosen, L.W. (1989). Athletes and Eating Disorders, *The Eating Disorders Digest, 2* (2), 1-3.

Rucinski, A. (1989). Relationship of Body Image and Dietary Intake of Competitive Ice Skaters, *Journal of the American Dietetic Association, 89* (1), 98-99.

Sports Illustrated (2000). *The Swimsuit Issue.* Reviewed on SportsIllustrated.com.

Taub, D.E. & Benson, R.A. (1992). Weight Concerns, Weight Control Techniques, and Eating Disorders Among Adolescent Competitive Swimmers: The Effect of Gender, *Sociology of Sport Journal, 9* (1), 76-86.

Technique (1992). Task Force on USA Gymnastics Response to the Female Athlete Triad, September.

Thompson, S.H. & Sargent, R.G. (2000). Facing Eating Disorders in the Fitness Community, *IDEA Source*, May.

## Issue 3

### The Effect of the Media on the Making of the Modern Body

Society's strict standards of beauty have played a large role in how women have viewed their bodies throughout the centuries (Crook, 1992). The media has equated thinness and beauty as being synonymous with achieving total happiness (Shemek, et al., 1998). However, many women do not realize that the pictures they see may be airbrushed and therefore these images are not attainable. This constant striving for thinness has brought about many dieting and weight loss issues. In recent years, women have turned to various physical activities trying to achieve a certain body ideal that is considered beautiful in modern times. The following overview focuses on the current status of research relating to body image, exercise, and eating disorders as it pertains to women, and how it has evolved from the 18th century to the present day. Changes that have influenced the way Western women currently view their bodies as beauty or beast are presented.

### Historical Overview of the Making of the Female Body

The structure of the "ideal" female body has evolved over the years to what it is today. Throughout the ages, women have scrutinized themselves and gone to great extremes to alter their bodies to fit society's current standards of beauty. They have continually striven to emulate the ideals of society in order to gain social acceptance and admiration.

In 18th-century pre-revolutionary France, women's clothes were not made to be functional but rather to be admired. The clothing was made of heavy materials and the shoes were made for display. This made walking extremely difficult (Crook, 1992, 28). In the 1830s, some Victorian women became self-conscious about their appearances by the age of fifteen. This is the approximate age that the first menstrual period occurs, which marks the onset of womanhood. During the 19th century, society focused more on spirituality than on physical matters; however, the young, white, wealthy women of the upper classes were preoccupied by the size and shape of certain body parts. They continually scrutinized their hands, feet, and waist sizes because large and robust features were a sign of indelicacy, which were characteristics associated with a lower class. In contrast to the present, however, women were encouraged to focus on character rather than on their looks, which was considered to be far more important than beauty. Women were taught by their mothers to focus on improving themselves from within (Brumberg, 1997, xx).

Weight did not become a critical part of the female identity until the 1900s. The sexual revolution of the 1920s provided women the chance to break away from the old traditional rules that had been forced upon them. The "flapper" look of the 1920s revealed an expression of youth and class that displayed the body with an image that was sexually appealing (Woloch, 1984). Women were no longer forced to hide their sexuality and began to show their arms and legs (Brumberg, 1997). The onset of the first Miss America Pageant in 1921 set the stage for a new spirit of exhibitionism. During the 1920s, women for the first time began to make a conscious effort to lower their weight by dieting and exercising; they also gave up being confined by the corset (Brumberg, 1997). During the 1950s, the ideal female body was a thin waist, full, pointed breasts, and long legs in high heels. In the 1960s, women were encouraged to exercise as an incentive for improving their looks while reaping the health benefits. From 1960 to 1979, there was a trend toward non-curvaceousness, with bust and hip measurements decreasing (Markula, 1995). In the 1970s, women participated in light aerobic activities such as jogging, tennis, calisthenics, and aerobics. The ideal body was depicted as slender and shapely with soft curves, and muscle was seen as unfeminine and unattractive (Crook, 1992). In the 1980s, muscles became a central part of the ideal body, and in the 1990s, the trend toward a muscular, lean body continued. The ideal body structure is determined by the current "trends," which are exemplified by the media (Shemek, et al., 1998).

Advanced capitalist society has placed unrealistic expectations on what is deemed as a "culturally acceptable" body for women. This standard strongly influences the way in which women view their bodies. Many women have a distorted body image and misconstrued ideas of what is considered to be "attractive," as previously defined. Women who fit society's ideal are admired and therefore have greater feelings of acceptance in society. Women who do not live up to the ideals of society are not accepted, and they are plagued with negative feelings toward the appearance of their bodies, and thus, their self-worth (Crook, 1992). Many studies of normal, as well as eating disordered, individuals have shown that a large percentage of women are unhappy with their bodies and are extremely preoccupied with being thin. Furthermore, it has been shown that dissatisfaction with body image is extremely common among many women of all ages, and that this phenomenon is so widespread that it is actually considered "normal" (Imm & Pruitt, 1991).

## The Effect of the Media on Women's Body Image

Throughout the ages, the media has been at the forefront of epitomizing the cultural standard of beauty. Young women of the 1920s were more likely to be influenced by the media, specifically through newspapers and magazines, than by their peers (Woloch, 1984). The 1958 June issue of *Life* magazine carried an advertisement directed at "Chubbettes" that offered clothing styles that were made to help overweight girls look slimmer. The clothing came with a "free" pamphlet that provided parents with advice on how to deal with the ridicule that fat girls often receive. Advertisements seen in the 1990s used marketing strategies that played on female insecurities in order to sell their products (Brumberg, 1997).

The media continues to depict beautiful, slender women as symbols of prestige, happiness, love, and success. The emergence of the slender body type has become a beauty standard that is exemplified in the media. The pressure to conform to these standards has "forced" women to become obsessed with diet and exercise (Olson, et al., 2006). The media has assumed the role of the cultural gatekeeper by setting the precedent of beauty standards through the use of gaunt, unrealistic appearing women, who are depicted as icons of beauty, which all women should strive to follow. Television and movie characters are super-thin and fall into harmful stereotypes. This also applies to cartoon characters, such as Disney's Pocahontas and the Little Mermaid, as well as the Barbie doll, who are all portrayed with large breasts, tiny waists, and long slender legs (Elvin, 1998). The messages aimed at girls and women through the mass media have caused many to be dissatisfied with their bodies and an overwhelming desire to become thin (Turner, et al., 1997). This portrayal is particularly harmful to young impressionable girls because they see the images of thin women on television and in magazines and begin to compare their own bodies only to realize that they do not fit into this beauty stereotype.

However, the media uses airbrushed and retouched photos, as well as special camera angles and body doubles, that contribute to the unrealistic portrayal of the body. Even women who are slightly below the normal healthy body weight are not satisfied with the shape of their bodies. The focus of advertising campaigns that center on women is to depict an image that will attain the same look as the models when using the company's product. Polished images of beautiful, thin models are often accompanied with advice on how readers can attain the look of the models (Markula, 2005). This is the media's way of inviting women to make a body change so that they can feel better about themselves. However, this constant striving to become thinner and more appealing can have a negative effect on a woman's self image, especially when she finds that she is unable to transform her body into the "perfect body" as portrayed through the media.

Today's women continue to compare themselves to models and many are unable to accept that the images they see are not attainable for a vast majority. This unrealistic ideal is reinforced daily on television and on the pages of women's magazines. The constant bombardment of the media leaves many women feeling dissatisfied with their own bodies, and this in turn can lead them into the direction of unhealthy eating habits and excessive exercise. The media has lured its audience into the trap of becoming fixated on the weight loss and weight gains of celebrities like Oprah Winfrey and Delta Burke. This cycle continues to feed the insecurities of women who are particularly vulnerable to body image issues (Reece, 1999).

Turner, et al., (1995) performed research on the feelings of college women after viewing fashion magazines depicting thin models. They hypothesized that women would become more dissatisfied with their bodies after looking through the magazines. The randomly selected subjects were divided into two groups with one group viewing fashion magazines, and the other control group viewing news-type magazines without the presence of fashion models. The results showed that those who read the fashion magazines wanted to weigh less and were also more dissatisfied with their bodies. These results remained consistent with the trends that women are bombarded with media images throughout childhood and adolescence, with an emphasis on physical appearance prevalent in television programs and advertisements aimed at children. As children progress into adolescence, idealistic views of women are displayed in the teen magazines that emphasize fashion, beauty, and stereotypical female roles (Turner, et al., 1997).

Another example of the media's role in exemplifying body image is seen through the depiction of Playboy models and Miss America pageant contestants. For example, in 1960, the average weight of a Playboy model was 92% of the population mean. By 1978, the weight dropped to 78% of the average population mean. This decrease has continued with each issue showing skinnier models with flawless "picture perfect" bodies. The same trend is also illustrated among the Miss America contestants. Prior to 1978, the average weight of the contestants was 88% of the population mean, and by 1978, this weight dropped to 85%. During the period of 1979 to 1988, 69% of Playboy models and 60% of Miss America contestants had an average weight that was 15% or more below the expected weight for their height. This raises implications for women who may be at risk for developing eating disorders, which are prevalent among women with body weight that is 15% below the recommended weight (Turner, et al., 1997).

The media has bombarded the public with an influx of exercise gadgets, health products, workout videos, and weight loss "cure all" magic pills. It is not clear as to whether this is an increasing trend toward health and fitness or a continual preoccupation with physical appearance. However, these products promise quick results that may not be attainable for the consumers. This cycle of dieting can lead many to failure, because there is no quick easy way to achieve lasting weight loss results (Smith, et al., 1998).

## Weight Loss Issues Today

Americans share a common quest for losing weight. The media bombards consumers with products to enhance one's body through the use of weight loss and beauty products. This further reinforces the underlying point that depicts thin as "beautiful" and the assumption that the two are synonymous. Thus, the central focus of Americans tends to focus on weight loss and achieving quick results.

On the whole, Americans have become increasingly overweight. This is due in part to readily available "fast food" and the lack of time to exercise. It is estimated that 40% of women and 25% of men are attempting to lose weight. Americans spend about 30 billion dollars a year on products to help them lose weight, yet they are heavier now than ever before. Chronic weight fluctuation is also at an all-time high. The primary reason most people give for losing weight is to improve personal appearance, rather than a concern for health.

Obesity is the second leading cause of preventable death; therefore, there is a need for people to lose weight in order to improve their health. A relationship exists between ideal body weight and mortality rate. The average American is associated with having the lowest mortality rate. However, there is a weight loss paradox that suggests that in some instances losing weight can be detrimental to one's health. This is mainly true regarding diet drugs and tactics that involve rapid weight loss in a short amount of time. Low-carbohydrate diets, like the Atkins and the Zone diets, have been popular since the 1960s. These low-carbohydrate diets cause an increase in total serum cholesterol and the levels of circulating blood lipids. This can cause weight fluctuations that can be detrimental to the body because it can cause changes in blood pressure and increase the incidence of type II Diabetes (Gaesser, 1999).

## Body Somatotypes

The "ideal body" has evolved over time with the changing perceptions of body types. Body types can be classified according to somatotype, which is the physical classification of the human body that is subdivided into endomorph, mesomorph, and ectomorph (Skinner, 1993). The endomorph is characterized as round and soft with a "pear shaped" non-muscular build. The mesomorph is a square body with hard, rugged musculature, a slender waist, large bones, thick muscles, and broad shoulders. The ectomorph is a lean, frail body with small bones, thin muscles, and narrow shoulders. The negative perceptions of the ectomorphic body type have changed within the last fifty years. In the 1940s, women of this body type were perceived negatively as socially withdrawn and submissive, but today this body structure along with the slight muscle tone of the mesomorph is portrayed as the ideal. Most women are a combination of at least two of these body types (Skinner, 1993).

Researchers use somatotype categorization to determine how individuals view their own bodies. Subjects are presented with a scale of different body sizes and shapes, and they are asked to choose the body type that is representative of their own body as well as a drawing that represents their ideal body size. This technique allows researchers to measure perceived body image by comparing the drawing that is chosen to the actual body type. The degree of body image dissatisfaction is the difference between the ideal body size, the actual body size, and the perceived body size as exhibited in anorexic and bulimic women (Skinner, 1993).

## The Formation of Body Image

Body image is a mental representation of the body that gradually evolves as the body develops and changes over time (Sobral & Vasconcelos, 1996). Body image is an individual's concept of his or her personal appearance. It is affected by intrinsic and extrinsic variables, which interact to affect the individual's psychological well-being (Smith, et al., 1998, 727). Although this image may be realistic or unrealistic, it is derived from self-observation and observations of others, as well as emotions, memories, fantasies, and experiences (Mosby, 1998, 1350). A psychological test known as a "body cathexis" has shown that there is a correlation between the individual's sense of self and the level of satisfaction with different body parts (Brumberg, 1997, xxiv).

In Western culture, women tend to be more dissatisfied with their bodies than men, although men tend to want to be more muscular. Most women actually "hate" their hips, thighs, and buttocks, which contributes to the way they form their self-identity. Adolescent girls are particularly at risk for developing a negative body image at a young age (Brumberg, 1997, xxiv).

Another type of disorder that plagues women is known as Body Dysmorphic Disorder (BDD). This disorder is characterized by an extreme preoccupation with how the body looks and is characterized. This causes the individual to constantly worry and have emotional stress associated with a negative body image. People suffering from this disorder worry about every part of their body and how it looks to others. This behavior, if not treated, will eventually overtake the person's life and have a negative effect on his or her relationship with others. BDD is said to affect about 2% of the population, and it is difficult to diagnose because people who suffer from this disorder are in a state of denial and are not willing to recognize that they have a problem. This causes them to be secretive and shameful (Phillips, 1996).

Self-image is developed through external and objective attributes, as well as subjective representations of physical appearance and perception of the body. Body image plays a large part in defining the identity of a person as well as who one chooses to interact with, marry, and what type of career to pursue (Garner & Kearney-Cooke, 1996). Researchers have suggested that there is a major difference between perceived body image and ideal body image. This difference can lead to low self-esteem, high social anxiety, and may also become a precursor to developing an eating disorder (Smith, et al., 1998).

The average body size of the idealized woman has become progressively thinner from the 1950s to the present day and body fat percentages have stabilized at about 13% to 19% below what is considered to be the average healthy body weight. Current body image ideals have shifted from the frail, waif-like images of the 1960s toward a thin, mesomorphic yet athletic physique. This is portrayed in all aspects of the media with females shown as underweight with an overall toned appearance. Small hips and thighs with broad shoulders and muscular arms characterize the "new ideal body" (Bailey, et al., 1995). A study performed by Bailey, Goldberg, Dallal, Koff, and Lenart (1995) involved administering an athletic image scale to women with different shaded representations of body structures. These pictures portrayed various body structures of women and also included a component of muscularity. Women were asked to select the drawing that closely represented their own bodies as well as the body that they perceived as ideal. The subjects were divided into athletes and non-athletes, and both groups selected the athletic images as the ideal. These results show that the women were more influenced by the media's current depiction of the ideal body rather than by their participation in the sport.

Thinness has become equated with attractiveness and has become synonymous with success and socioeconomic status. A study conducted by Demarest and Langer (1996) examined perceptions of body weight by women and men, as well as what they thought what the opposite sex would find the most attractive. Subjects were given shaded drawings, asked to select the size that closely represented their own body size, and asked to select the size that they would like to be. The level of dissatisfaction was measured by taking the difference between the two. Subjects also were asked to select the image they thought would be the most appealing to the opposite sex. The male and female subjects were classified as underweight, average, and overweight. The subjects most satisfied with their bodies were average-sized men and underweight women. The subjects most dissatisfied with their bodies were average weight women, overweight women, underweight men, and overweight men. Women guessed that men would prefer a smaller sized figure than they actually did, and men guessed that women would select a larger, more muscular image than they actually did. The results show the difference in perception of body weight between men and women. Therefore, self-perception is dependent upon the person's status relative to the norms of society (Demarest & Langer, 1996.)

## Women and Body Image

Women have been "at war" with their bodies for decades. Women are continually bombarded with images of fitness and thinness in the media, and therefore, have become more obsessed with dieting and body weight than men. The difference between how women really look and how they think they should look causes mixed feelings. Many women have difficulty knowing what size they are because their mental image of their body is extremely different from their physical body. It is estimated that 40% of American women are trying to lose weight (Olson, et al., 1996). Women diet by severely restricting their calories in order to obtain a slender body rather than accepting the natural dimensions of their own bodies (Markula, 2005). The influences of the print and visual media and also opinions of other women have a profound effect on the weight behaviors of women. Many women are extremely dissatisfied with their bodies and this can lead to low self-esteem and even depression (Turner, et al., 1997).

Self-esteem is defined as an evaluation of the "self concept," and a negative appraisal of the self is significant, which can be detrimental (Smith, 1996). Studies on body image dissatisfaction have shown that women are more dissatisfied with their bodies than men (Bailey, et al., 1995; Demarest & Langer, 1996; Garner, 1997). Many postmenopausal women suffer from Social Physique Anxiety (SPA), wherein women are extremely anxious and uncomfortable with others observing their bodies. This causes women to abstain from exercise because they are uncomfortable with what others may be thinking about their bodies. SPA is seen more commonly with women who have body fat percentages greater than 37%. The factors associated with SPA are a sedentary lifestyle, high body fat percentage, and a greater percent of body fat distributed in the upper body. The individual suffering from SPA may need medical intervention in order to break the cycle of depression and anxiety and begin a program that will lead them down the road to a healthier lifestyle (Randsell, et al., 1998).

Women who are in the military succumb to increased pressures above and beyond those of civilian females. They have the responsibility of holding extremely physical jobs and competing in mandatory weight and physical fitness assessment tests. They are forced to maintain a high level of fitness without having the time to make fitness and nutritional choices on their own

A study performed by Lauder, et al., (1999) researched this issue and administered questionnaires to 443 enlisted females regarding their eating behaviors. The results of the study showed that there was a 2% increased prevalence of eating disorders among military females than civilian females. The study revealed that 6% of the women surveyed showed signs of an eating disorder.

Many body image studies have excluded the population of African-American women because of previous assumptions that there was a higher acceptance of larger shapes that would therefore protect these women from eating disorders (Williamson, 1998). African-American women suffer from more obesity-related diseases than white women. In comparing body image concerns, African-American women report less social pressure with regard to their body weight than white women (Wilfley, et al., 1996).

Measurement scales used to determine body weight classification may not be consistent for both races. Previous studies used body mass index (BMI) scales, however, these scales are based on the assumption that the standard body fits into the white middle class category (Ofosu, et al., 1998). This causes African-American women to be labeled as overweight more frequently than European American women. African-American women have 48.6% of their population overweight in comparison to 32.1% of European American woman (Ofosu, et al., 1998). This is mainly due to a difference in bone size and muscle mass rather than height, thus making it difficult to compare body weights among and between different ethnic populations.

Socioeconomic status also plays an important role in the prevalence of body image-related issues. Many African-American women who are still at the poor end of the working class are subjected to higher levels of stress and are more likely to be obese. Often these women consume excess food to comfort themselves through lonely, unhappy times because food provides a relatively inexpensive outlet. They are more likely to turn to food rather than alcohol or drugs since it allows them to remain functional as a wife, mother and/or employee (Williamson, 1998). African-American women may be at a lower risk for eating disorders, but there is a need for further research to determine the environments that contribute to unhealthy eating behaviors. This can be done through assessing the African-American women's personal struggle with weight, food and body image (Williamson, 1998).

## Adolescents and Body Image

In the 20th century, the body has become the central focus and personal project of American girls. This priority makes young women growing up in the present day vastly different from their Victorian counterparts. Many girls worry about the size and shape of their bodies because they believe that how they look is the ultimate expression of what defines them emotionally (Brumberg, 1997). Many teens spend much time, money, and energy on improving their looks. This constant focus on the body hinders the individual's ability to form relationships and develop character (Crook, 1992, 14). The onset of puberty during the initial years of adolescence forces young women to cope with physical maturation as well as the pressures and emotions that accompany this transcendence into womanhood. Menarche presently occurs around the age of twelve (in some girls even as early as age six to eight), whereas in the 1900s, girls did not begin menstruating until age fifteen or sixteen. This is due in part to a healthier living environment and better healthcare. However, this newer age of maturity does not include an accelerated ability to make judgments, and it may leave young women vulnerable to psychological and social problems.

Adolescent women begin to focus on the shape and appearance of their bodies as a primary expression of their individual beauty. The body becomes the central focus as something to be adorned with clothing and personal grooming items with special attention given to skin and hair. Young women are in a constant fight for attaining individuality while desperately trying to conform to the "norms" of society with the body as the central focus (Brumberg, 1997).

Adolescent females are discouraged from intentionally developing muscles before the age of ten. Therefore, they are steered away from activities that will develop muscle mass. There is a transition that occurs between the ages of eight and twelve wherein females are encouraged to participate in activities that are more "feminine" in nature. Discouraging females from experiencing a wide range of physical activities can predispose them to osteoporosis, eating disorders, inadequate muscle mass, and possibly depression (Smith, 1996).

Dieting for weight loss became popular among girls in the 1920s (Brumberg, 1997). It was seen as an episodic phase teenagers went through that was often brought on as a competition between two average-sized girls to see who would be the first to look "less fat." By the 1950s, persistent dieting became more prevalent among young women as they struggled with their peer identity and peer relationships. Research (Brumberg, 1997) shows that dieting habits are common in girls as young as nine, and this practice continues to increase through the teenage years. The risk of developing an eating disorder is eight times greater among dieting fifteen-year-old girls than their non-dieting female counterparts (Garner & Kearney-Cooke, 1996). A 1986 study of ten-year-old girls found that 81% of these girls had dieted at least once (Melin, Scully, & Irwin, 1986). Childhood teasing was shown to have lasting repercussions on the way that adult women viewed their bodies.

Many children are considered to be obese, according to recommended standard guidelines. Sisson, et al., (1997) performed an assessment using skinfold body fat testing that found that 67% of boys and 39% of girls were obese. Prior to assessment, the children were asked to assess whether or not they considered themselves to be overweight. A higher percentage of girls estimated that they were overweight than the boys. Parents of these children also were asked whether or not their children were overweight, and they also were more accurate at the perception of their daughters being overweight than their sons. In addition, the study found that children, as well as parents, were not aware of the importance of exercise as part of a healthy lifestyle for preventing obesity. The parents tended to be more critical regarding their overweight daughters, which may set the precedence for body image issues later in life (Sisson, et al., 1997). Studies on body image dissatisfaction have shown that women are more dissatisfied with their bodies than men. Women are primarily motivated to exercise to lose weight and enhance their physical appearance (Smith, et al., 1998).

## Athletes, Body Image and Eating Disorders

Athletes who are involved in sports that emphasize leanness are at an increased risk for developing eating disorders (Garner & Kearney-Cooke, 1996). These sports include gymnastics, figure skating, ballet, weightlifting, and running. The incidence of eating disorders found among female athletes has been reported as being much higher than in the general population of females (Lauder, et al., 1999). Subjectively scored sports such as gymnastics, dance, figure skating, and diving rely on body aesthetics as a primary means for determining the success of the participants. Of the sports where the appearance of the body is the primary focus, 23% of the athletes have a higher drive for thinness than anorexics who are not athletes (Olson, et al., 1996). Endurance sports such as cross country running, cycling, and cross-country skiing require a low body weight for enhancing performance.

Sports that necessitate weight categories, such as rowing, martial arts, and wrestling, cause athletes to indulge in extreme behaviors, which can lead to eating disorders (Drinkwater, et al., 1997). Dale and Landers (1999) observed the practices involved in "making weight" among middle and high school wrestlers to determine if the behaviors put these individuals at risk for having bulimia. Some of the weight loss tactics are dehydration, self-induced vomiting, laxatives, diuretics, excessive exercise, and fasting, all of which are characteristics of anorexia and bulimia. The purpose of their study was to examine the context in which the behavior took place and to determine if the wrestlers were using the weight loss tactics solely during their competitive season or whether their behavior was pathological. The results showed that these behaviors found during the season, which put the wrestlers "at risk" for bulimia, did not carry over into the off season (Dale & Landers, 1999).

Female athletes believe that if they are thinner they will look and perform better in their sport. This obsessive behavior causes the cycle of restricting calories and fasting in order to lose a few pounds or "make weight" for a competition (Agostini, et al., 1993). Female athletes who develop eating disorders have certain biological and psychological traits and are strongly influenced by societal pressures (Lauder, et al., 1999). Athletes with eating disorders may be unable to perform at their full capacity, and they may be at an increased risk for fatigue, weakness, lightheadedness, and/or irregular heartbeats.

## The Female Athlete Triad

Many female athletes have a distorted image of what it is to be "in shape." They are influenced by internal and external pressures to be "healthy" and "thin." Healthy, however, does not necessarily translate into being thin, and some athletes may be putting themselves in danger. They are willing to push the limits of excessive exercise while severely decreasing their caloric intake, which in turn contributes to the female athlete triad. For some women, there is a constant battle, which occurs from within that forces them to try to live up to the impossible expectations of the media, peers, coaches, and parents.

The female athlete triad was first described in 1992 as the three interrelated components of eating disorders, amenorrhea, and osteoporosis (Agostini, et al., 1993). Amenorrhea is irregular menses that can lead to osteoporosis and infertility problems. It can be caused by excessive exercise, low body weight, low body fat, poor nutrition, and/or hormonal changes. Exercise-associated amenorrhea (EAA) is the absence of menstruation, starting at the age of sixteen, in a girl with secondary sex characteristics, and the absence of three or more consecutive menstrual cycles (Agostini, et al., 1993). This can occur as a result of excessive physical training (Eichner, et al., 1997). Osteoporosis is characterized by low bone mass and structural deterioration of bony tissue. The best defense against this disease is to build strong bones early in life. This can be accomplished through strength training exercise, which has shown to strengthen the bone by stimulating the muscle to increase calcium production. Overloading the bones and the muscles through weight-bearing activities and progressive resistance training will cause the bones and muscles to increase in strength. Women affected by anorexia have been shown to have bone density that is 20% less than healthy women (Smith, 1996).

Characteristics of the triad include sporadic eating, dieting, binging, purging, and starvation. However, caloric deficit in lieu of excessive exercise leads to unnecessary weight loss. These disordered eating behaviors are psychological and caused by low self-esteem and a distorted body image, which fuels a female's obsession to be thinner.

## Eating Disorders and Body Image

As spelled out earlier, eating disorders are psychological and physiological problems related to food intake and are generally characterized as being gender specific, predominantly affecting females. They are associated with a negative body image. Women may have feelings of fatness that may serve as a catalyst causing them to resort to drastic dieting practices that involve severely restricting the calories they consume. There are also many abnormal eating behaviors that do not fit into the category of clinically diagnosed eating disorders but which may still prove detrimental to the health of the individual (Lauder, et al., 1999). Women who habitually monitor their food consumption are said to have a "normative obsession," the fear of becoming fat characterized by maintaining their weight within an eight-pound range. Their self-esteem becomes dependent on whether they are at the top or the bottom of this range (Brumberg, 1997). Many women attempt to become thinner by dieting, which often leads to the development of an eating disorder.

The incidence of eating disorders has increased significantly since the 1960s, due to social and cultural pressures to conform to the "norms" of society (Garner & Kearney-Cooke, 1996). The National Institute of Mental Health (NIMH) estimates that 3% of American women in the United States will develop either anorexia or bulimia (Fontenot & Raso, 1998). In 2001, the Centers for Disease Control and Prevention reported that 44% of high school girls polled stated that they have tried to lose weight. Among these girls, 80% utilized exercise regimens, 21% had taken diet pills, and 14% had vomited in order to control their weight (www.cdc.com). Many of these women were faced with the same pressures that athletes encounter of maintaining a certain weight and excelling physically. This constant focus on weight can lead to the development of an eating disorder, such as anorexia nervosa or bulimia (Lauder, et al., 1999), which were described in detail in the previous issue.

## Excessive Exercise and Body Image

Many women are primarily motivated to exercise for the purpose of losing weight, toning muscles, and enhancing their physical appearance (Smith, et al., 1998). Exercise actually may be a precursor to eating disorders in susceptible individuals (Imm & Pruitt, 1991). The line between what is considered "acceptable" and what is considered "excessive" is often difficult to determine. The American College of Sports Medicine recommends that an individual exercise aerobically for 15-60 minutes three to five days per week. Therefore, an individual who is greatly surpassing this amount of exercise may be within the bounds of excessive exercise (Imm & Pruitt, 1991). Research (Imm & Pruitt, 1991) shows that there is a psychological link between excessive exercise and severe dieting. Exercise causes the body to release endorphins. A study performed on animals found that excessive exercise was induced as a result of food deprivation (Epling, Pierce & Stefan, 1983). Excessive exercise, however, needs to be evaluated separately because exercise may be an end in itself, and dieting may only be a means of enhancing the performance (Davis & Fox, 1993).

An activity disorder is an inclusive category. This encompasses both excessive exercise and the eating disorder, with the distinction that the eating disordered individual is concerned with physical attractiveness, whereas, the excessive exercising individual is concerned with physical effectiveness. The common similarity between the two compulsive behaviors is a need for obsessive control. The individuals suffering from these behaviors exhibit a narcissistic behavior that causes them to become completely obsessed with their bodies. The anorexics focus on how the body looks, and the excessive exerciser focuses on how the body performs. There is a crossover, however, between the two extreme behaviors that causes the individuals to exhibit both extremes.

The study on excessive exercise and weight preoccupation conducted by Davis and Fox (1993) found that women who were extremely preoccupied with their weight and also very active were at a higher risk for developing an eating disorder than those women who displayed only one of the excessive behaviors. They also found distinct differences between the anorexics and the excessive exercisers (Davis & Fox, 1993). The excessive exercisers were more dissatisfied with their bodies, whereas the anorexics were highly dissatisfied with their bodies. Therefore, each of the extreme behaviors was responsible for the excessive behavior, both with exercise and dieting. Previous studies have shown that exercising women are more concerned with the shape and size of their bodies than non-exercising women (Davis & Fox, 1993; Olson, et al., 1996). Exercise is a strong component of health and well-being, and this has caused researchers to look at what factors motivate people to exercise. A clearer understanding of this motivation will allow health professionals to recognize warning signs for excessive exercise and eating disorders (Smith, et al., 1998).

The study completed by Imm and Pruitt (1991) analyzed the relationship between high-frequency exercise and body shape satisfaction. They found that women of "normal" body weight body fat percentage did not have an eating disorder, but those who exceeded the recommended amount of exercise were more dissatisfied with the shape of their bodies than those who exercised moderately. They also hypothesized that the high-frequency exercisers (8 or more hours per week) would be more likely to exercise when they were ill or injured than the moderate exercisers (3.5 hours). Their results confirmed the hypothesis with the high-frequency exercisers being more dissatisfied with their bodies despite the fact that they were lighter and lost more weight than the moderately exercising group. The high-frequency exercisers cited their reason for exercising to be primarily for weight control. This study suggested that they may never reach a body shape that lives up to their own standards of satisfaction. This also suggests that perception of their body is quite different from the actual reality of their physical appearance. Women with these characteristics are at risk for developing psychological problems such as low self-esteem (Imm & Pruitt, 1991).

The onset of a new exercise program may cause an initial weight loss, which serves as reinforcement for the behavior. Exercise produces a stress on the body, which causes the secretion of endorphins into the bloodstream. An individual who is an excessive exerciser becomes dependent on the endorphins. The individual realizes that increasing the amount of exercise will lead to an increase in the amount of weight loss. This cycle becomes dangerous when the exercise becomes excessive and leads to an unhealthy weight loss, which may serve as the catalyst that pushes the individual toward starvation and the development of an eating disorder (Davis & Fox, 1993). This is often the case with athletes who participate in sports where there is a strong correlation between body weight and performance.

## The New Ideal Body Image

The "ultra-thin" and "ultra-muscular" body types have been replaced by the new ideal in the 21st century, which is a curvy-athletic shape. Although, this image represents an attainable goal for women that is healthy and strong, it also brings about a challenge for women to lose weight and gain more muscle (Brandt, 2005). Women's Sports and Fitness Magazine surveyed people across the country by showing them four pictures that represented different body sizes: a super-skinny supermodel, a curvy-fit actress, a toned athlete, and a muscle-toned fitness competitor. The curvy-fit body won out, especially among the men; however, women were more likely to choose the toned athletic body type. This choice shows that women are gravitating toward the toned athletic look (Fleming, 2009).

Women need to become more informed so that they make healthy decisions when altering their bodies. The relationship between caloric intake and exercise is that weight loss is achieved by attaining a caloric deficit. This must be done, however, through a balance of healthy eating, aerobic exercise, and strength training. The combination of these factors will help the individual to achieve lasting results, which will help to improve self-confidence.

Education and awareness are essential to helping women and men recognize that they need to be comfortable with their bodies in order to combat the effects of negative body image. Furthermore, strategies have to be developed to help teachers to foster a lifestyle in their students that includes healthy diets and exercise plans. In return, all of these efforts might help young people develop a positive body image.

## References

Agostini, R., Drinkwater, B., Nattiv, A., & Yeager, K.K. (1993). The Female Athlete Triad: Disordered Eating, Osteoporosis. *Medicine and Science in Sports and Exercise, 25,* 775-777

Bailey, E.B., Dallal, G.E., Golberg, J.P., & Lenart, E.B. (1995). Current and Ideal Physique Choices in Exercising and Non-exercising College Women From a Pilot Athletic Image Scale. *Perceptual and Motor Skills, 81,* 831-848.

Brandt, M. (2005). Pumping Irony: Thin Meets Gym. *Newsweek*, October 23, 126(17), 88.

Brumberg, J.J. (1997). *The Body Project.* New York, NY: Random House.

Crook, M. (1992). *The Body Image Trap.* Washington: Self-Counsel Press.

Dale, K.S. & Landers, D. M. (1999). Weight Control in Wrestling: Eating Disorder or Disordered Eating? *Medicine and Science in Sports and Exercise, 31*(8), 1382-1389.

Davis, C. & Fox, J. (1993). Excessive Exercise and Weight Preoccupation in Women. *Addictive Behaviors, 18,* 201-211.

Demarest, J. & Langer, E. (1996). Perception of Body Shape by Underweight, Average and Overweight Men and Women. *Perceptual and Motor Skills, 83,* 569-570.

Drinkwater, B., Johnson, M., Loucks, A., Otis, & C.L., Wilmore, J. (1997). ACSM Position Stand on the Female Athlete Triad. *Medicine and Science in Sports and Exercise, 29*(5), i-ix.

Eichner, E.R., Johnson, M., Loucks, A.B. & Steen, S.N. (1997). The Female Athlete Triad. *Sports Science Exchange Roundtable, 8*(1), 327-328.

Elvin, J. (1998). Speaking Out Against Malnourished Bodies. *Insight on the News, 14,* 34.

Epling, W.F., Pierce, W.D. & Stefan, L. (1983). A Theory of Activity-Based Anorexia. *International Journal of Eating Disorders, 3,* 27-43.

Fleming, A.T. (2009). The New Ideal: What Makes a Body Beautiful? *Women's Sports and Fitness, 7*(2), 72.

Gaesser, G.A. (1999). Thinness and Weight Loss: Beneficial or Detrimental to Longevity? *Medicine and Science in Sports and Exercise, 31*(8), 1118-1125.

Garner, D.M. (1997). The 1997 Body Image Survey Results. *Psychology Today, 30,* 30.

Garner, D.M. & Kearney-Cooke, A. (1996). Body Image Survey 1996. *Psychology Today, 29,* 55-63.

Imm, P.S. (1989). *Exercise Habits and Perceptions of Body Image in Female Exercisers.* Paper presented at the fourth annual IDEA conference, Los Angeles, CA.

Imm, P.S., & Pruitt, J. (1991). Body Shape Satisfaction in Female Exercisers and Nonexercisers. *Women and Health, 17*(4), 87-95.

Lauder, T.D., Williams, M.V., Cambell, C.S., Davis, G.D. & Sherma, R.A. (1999). Abnormal Eating Behavior in Military Women. *Medicine and Science in Sports and Exercise, 31*(9), 1265-1271.

Lenart, E.B, Bailey, E.B., Dallal, G.E., & Golberg, J.P. (1995). Current and Ideal Physique Choices in Exercising and Non-exercising College Women From a Pilot Athletic Image Scale. *Perceptual and Motor Skills, 81,* 831-848.

Markula, P. (2005). Firm but Shapely, Fit but Sexy, Strong but Thin: The Postmodern Aerobicizing Female Bodies. *Sociology of Sport Journal, 12,* 424-453.

Mosby's Medical Nursing and Allied Health Dictionary (1998), Edition 5, 1350.

Melin, L.M., Scully, S., & Irwin, C.E. (1986). *Disordered Eating Characteristics in Preadolescent Girls.* Presentation at the Meeting of the American Dietetic Association, Las Vegas.

Ofosu, H.B., Lafreniere, K.D. & Senn, C.Y. (1998). Body Image Perception Among Women of African Descent: A Normative Context? *Feminism and Psychology, 8* (3), 303-323.

Olson, M.S., Willingford, H.N., Richards, L.A., Brown, J.A. & Pugh, S. (2006). Self-reports on the Eating Disorder Inventory by Female Aerobic Instructors. *Perceptual and Motor Skills, 82,* 1051-1058.

Phillips, K.A. (1996). *The Broken Mirror: Understanding and Treating Body Dysmorphic Disorder.* New York, NY: Oxford University Press.

Randsell, L. B., Wells, C.L., Manore, M.M., Swan, P.D. & Corbin, C.D. (1998). Social Physique Anxiety in Postmenopausal Women. *Journal of Women and Aging, 10* (3), 19-40.

Reece, G. (1999). Form: An Opinion. *Women's Sport and Fitness,* January, 2, 54.

Roche, A.F., Heymsfield, S.B. & Lohman, T.G. (1996). *Human Body Composition.* Champaign, IL: Human Kinetics.

Schlosberg, S. (1998). Exercising out of Control. *Shape, 17* (7), 104-109.

Shemek, J, Rabak-Wagener, J. & Kelly-Vance, L. (1998). The Effect of Media Analysis on Attitudes and Behaviors Regarding Body Image Among College Students. *Journal of American College Health, 12,* 72-79.

Sisson, B.A., Franco, S.M., Carlin, W.M., & Mitchell, C.K. (1997). Body fat Analysis and Perception of Body Image. *Clinical Pediatrics, 36* (7), 415-419.

Skinner, J.S.(1993). *Exercise Testing and Exercise Prescription for Special Cases.* Media, PA: Williams and Wilkins.

Smith, B.L., Handley, P. & Eldredge, D.A.(1998). Sex Differences in Exercise Motivation and Body-Image Satisfaction Among College Students. *Perceptual and Motor Skills, 86,* 723-732.

Smith, B.L. (1996). Strong Minded Women: Transcending Traditional Beliefs About Attractiveness, Strength and Health. *American Fitness,* Nov-Dec, 14 (6), 24-32.

Sobral, F. & Vasconcelos, O. (1996). Perceived Somatotype as Indicator of Accuracy of Body Image, a Method Using Somatotype Attitudinal Distance. *Perceptual and Motor Skills, 82,* 1107-1110.

Turner, S.L., Hamilton, H., Jacobs, M, Angood, L.M. & Dwyer, D.H. (1997). The Influence of Fashion Magazines on the Body Image Satisfaction of College Women: an Exploratory Analysis. *Adolescence, 32,* 603-613.

Wilfley, D.E., Schreiber, G.B., Pike, K.M., Striegel-Moore, R.H., Wright, D.J. & Rodin, J. (1996). Eating Disturbance and Body Image: A Comparison of a Community Sample of Adult Black and White Women. *International Journal of Eating Disorders, 20* (4), 377-387.

Williamson, L. (1998). Eating Disorders and the Cultural Forces Behind the Drive for Thinness: Are African Women Really Protected? *Social Work and Health Care, 28* (1), 61-73.

Woloch, N. (1984). *Women and the American Experience* (pp. 400-403). New York, NY: Alfred A. Knopf, Inc.

# CHAPTER 10:

# SPORT, RELIGION AND POLITICS

Throughout history there have been strong links between sport and religion, as well as sport and politics. In fact, sport has never existed independent of these connections in any social or cultural setting. However, there have been many changes since the beginning of sports. In this chapter, the relations of sport to politics and religion will be spelled out as they have been and still exist during the latter part of the 20th and the beginning of the 21st centuries. First, the influences of politics on sport will be analyzed by looking at the unique situation of sport in unified Germany. And second, the influences of religion on sport and vice versa are examined in the US context.

## Issue 1

## Sport in Unified Germany

The night the Berlin Wall came down, November 9, 1989, marked the beginning of a new era for the formerly divided Germany. The landmark event gave rise to a new social and political order based on social-democratic principles (as it was in West Germany). In unified Germany, there is no more room for Marxist-Leninist ideology (as it was in East Germany). With the fall of socialism, the East German superb top-level sport system had to fall as well because it was directly tied to the political structure of its government. East German sport science then was placed under the authority of the West German Sports Federation.

The purpose of this manuscript is to analyze how politics influences and directs sport as exemplified in the German unification process. The current status of sport, physical education, and higher education in unified Germany and its most apparent problems will be discussed. First, the two different sport systems as they existed in former East and West Germany will be described, taking the historical development into account. Second, the changes that happened after the unification will be spelled out as well as the most apparent problems German sport was faced with after the fall of the wall. The analysis concludes with a look to the future of sport in unified Germany.

## Historical Development

After World War II, Germany was divided into two countries: East Germany or the GDR (German Democratic Republic), controlled by the Soviet Union; and West

Germany or the FRG (Federal Republic of Germany), controlled by Great Britain, France, and the United States. In regard to sports, East Germany founded the so-called German Sports Board (*Deutscher Turn and Sportbund*, hereafter DTSB) in 1948 as its central umbrella institution. In 1950, West Germany founded its own sport organization, the German Sports Association (*Deutscher Sportbund*, hereafter DSB). The National Olympic Committee (NOC) for West Germany was established in 1949. The East Germans established their own NOC in 1951, but it did not receive official accreditation by the International Olympic Committee (IOC) until 1965.

Germany, as a former belligerent nation, had not been allowed to participate in the 1948 Olympics in London. However, when the Eastern NOC agreed in May 1951 to go with one German Olympic team to the Olympics in Oslo and Helsinki the next year, they were severely reprimanded by Walter Ulbricht chairman of the Central Committee of the Socialist Party of the GDR. They were told not to do so before the official recognition of the NOC of the GDR by the IOC. However, since this official accreditation for the East German NOC did not come before October 1965, West Germany alone could go to the 1952 Olympics. In 1955, the NOC of the GDR was "provisionally" accredited by the IOC but able to participate in the future Olympics only on a joint team composed of East and West Germans. This dictate held for the 1956 Olympic in Melbourne, 1960 in Rome, and 1964 in Tokyo – a period of almost 10 years. In 1965, the IOC decided that the two German NOCs had equal status.

From one Olympiad to the next, the GDR members of the Joint Olympic Team of both Germanys became stronger and stronger. And so it happened that the East German athletes won more medals at the 1964 Olympics in Tokyo than the West German colleagues; which continued to be the case in all following Olympic Games. From 1968 onward, two German teams competed, at first with the same uniforms and emblems. In 1972, the two teams were marked by different uniforms and emblems. This continued until the 1992 Olympic Games, when there was again one German team. On November 17, 1990, the NOC of the GDR ceased to exist; that same day, the former NOC of West Germany was enlarged by representatives from the East. Thus, one NOC for Germany was formed.

Before the fall of the wall, the GDR sport was administered by organization entirely dependent upon the Socialist Unity Party. Sport was regulated and steered from the party center and for the benefit of mainly top-level sport. To prove the superiority of the communist system, enormous sums of money were poured into sports. This was done at the expense of sports and physical education in the community, or sport for all. The party and its apparatus regulated the sphere of sports into such a state of perfection that the successes of the GDR seemed almost miraculous. The secret to their success was the early selection of sport talents among children at the age of 4 or 5 years, the systematic training of these youngsters in the children and Youth Sport Schools, the continuation of very regimented training practices in sport clubs subsidized and controlled by the police, the army, and the government, as well as the now well-established doping practices, even among teenage athletes. Only individual sports, such as track and field, gymnastics, and swimming, which had a chance to bring numerous gold medals home and thus would contribute to the glory of the communist system, received excessive support. Team sports, such as soccer, traditional favorites with East and West Germans, received little official support in the GDR.

The total control of top-level athletics in the GDR turned East German athletes into servants for their country. Today, these athletes revealed that they lived a very sheltered and privileged life, disconnected from the harsh reality of the average East German. The psychological hurdles of unification were experienced to an extreme degree by these athletes because they previously belonged to a privileged class in the communist system. Consequently, after the destruction of the wall, GDR sport fell into a sort of vacuum. The prerogative of the Socialist Party was abolished, the ideological orientation was gone, and the GDR sport suddenly lost its steering center.

Quite differently from the GDR, FRG sports were and still are based on a federal system; that is to say, every federal state is guaranteed autonomy to regulate its own culture and its sports (e.g., sport and physical education in state institutions and the "sport for all" movement). The federal government only has the responsibility for top-level athletics, which represents Germany on the national and international level. Sport in the democratic West was geared more toward leisure and fitness pursuits. The principal aim of the sport movement in the West was the implementation of the motto "sport for all" in the 1950s, which included children, women, and the elderly, as well as the physically and mentally handicapped.

In comparison to the support that East German top-level sport received, sport funding in the FRG was relatively small and insignificant. Top-level athletics in the FRG did not receive special funding until 1967, when Josef Neckerman, a wealthy businessman and equestrian gold medalist, established a financial aid fund for elite athletes, providing an average of about 400 US dollars a month for the individual. West German athletes could not live on these small stipends. In addition, their future after sports had not been looked after by the state. Thus, the West German athletes were, in most cases, self-determined individuals who did not necessarily identify with their country's ideological infrastructure through their participation in top-level athletics. For West German athletes, there was no meaningful analogy that linked the superiority of their social system with superior sporting achievements.

In contrast to the FRG, which spent about $70 million per year, the GDR pumped $2 billion into sport each year from the centralized government, which came to about 0.8 percent of government spending (twice as much, as they used to admit). Due to an extensive system of finding and cultivating talent in children's sport schools as well as the expertise and the number of coaches, trainers, and sport scientists whose careers were devoted to the enhancement of athletic performance, the former GDR produced (for the size of the country) a relatively high number of top-level athletes. There was one coach for every 2-3 athletes, whereas in the FRG the ratio was one coach for every 20 athletes (Tedeschi, 1991). The primary difference between the GDR and the FRG was the amount of money given to top-level athletics, a discrepancy based on the different underlying philosophies about the function of top-level athletics in the context of the development of a country.

## Sport in Unified Germany

When contracts for the reunification were developed, the home minister of Germany was naturally reluctant to preserve a sports system filled from top to bottom with obedient socialists. But at the last moment, the West wanted to keep the East German "gold medal forge." And so it happened that the three major sport research institutes, the *Research Institute for Physical Culture and Sport* in Leipzig, the *"Doping Laboratory"* in Kreischa, and the *Institute for the Development of Sport Equipment* in Berlin were kept (Kölner Stadtanzeiger, 1990), guaranteeing their existence by incorporating the three institutions in the official reunification contract. All the other East German sport institutions were given up, left to the discretion of the five new federal states. East German sport schools were closed, 85 percent of the 4,000 East German coaches left, 35 Olympic training centers were eliminated, and many athletes left for the West (Tedeschi, 1991). From a political point of view, this was the only reasonable thing to do. However, in regard to top-level sport, this decision marked the end of the gold medal harvests. The major problems for sport in unified Germany will be analyzed below relative to the three following issues: the development of sport science; the search for a new identity in a unified sport system; and the well-known doping issue.

## Development of Sport Science

There is no doubt that some sport scientists from East Germany had been among the leading scholars in their field in the world for quite some time, especially in the medical and natural science sub-disciplines of sport science. Their sole focus was the improvement of top-level sports. The secret of their success was the direct application of their knowledge to the practice of sport. The world-famous Research Institute for Physical Culture and Sport (*Forschungsinstitut für Körperkultur und Sport*, hereafter FKS) in Leipzig was the centralized and independent research institute for sport sciences in the GDR with a staff of more than 600 members researching 15 different sports (Deutsche Vereinigung fuer Sportwissenschaft, 1990). Social scientists were hired to develop educational programs for the indoctrination of the athletes with their ideology. Some of the research projects undertaken were, for example, to develop anabolics that would slow down the aging process of the brain or to increase the motivation of athletes by sending electronic streams through the brain. Blood doping was another one of many highly debated secret research projects. Secrecy was achieved by either locking the information in sealed safes or shredding it in institutionally owned paper shredders.

The existence of the FKS was not known by many people in the GDR and its research was top secret. These scientists did not share any of their research outcomes whenever they attended research conferences, which did not happen too often, but they collected research information in the field of sports from all over the world. Because there was no sharing of research information and freedom of research never existed, the East German scientists were not as far advanced on certain issues as their Western counterparts. However, their direct application of the research findings along with their close network of all sport scientists and their central organization were the key to their success in producing an enormous output of top-level performance in sport.

The counterpart of the FKS in the West was and is the Federal Institute of Sport Science (*Bundesinstitut für Sportwissenschaft*, hereafter BISp) in Cologne, which coordinates the research in the area of sport science but does not carry out research projects. The research itself is done by scholars at universities, in addition to their teaching obligations. Today, the BISp in Cologne continues to exist as it did before unification. However, it now also receives research proposals from sport scientists at universities situated in the former GDR. Furthermore, the staff of the BISp was strongly involved in the problem of reshaping and governing the former FKS.

The newly formed government had decided to restructure the FKS and to make it, if possible, a so-called An-Institut, a part of the former German University for Body Culture (*Deutsche Hochschule für Körperkultur*, or DHfK), which was remodeled into the sport science faculty of the University of Leipzig. This implies that there are now about 100 scientists, a fifth of its former staff who, without teaching obligations, continue to conduct research on top-level performance in sport. With this move, the politicians and the committee for top-level athletics of the German Sport Federation (*Bundesausschuss für Leistungssport*, or BAL) hoped to ensure a continuation of the world-class achievements in sports for which the East Germans were so famous. We now know that this hope was shattered because the unified German Olympic team has not performed nearly at the same level as the former East German athletes had done in the past.

Sport science scholars, especially those who form the 65 sport science institutes at German universities feared that this development might eventually undermine the "sport for all" focus because the IAT receives independent funding from the government. It was resisted because it undermines the motto of the newly revised German constitution (Article 39, paragraph 2; see *Zeitschrift fuer Fragen,* 1990), where autonomy, freedom of research, pluralism, and competition shall be the standard decision-making factors.

## Identity Crisis in the Unified German Sport System

The identity crisis that resulted in the unified sport system was a product of a complex political and socioeconomic dynamic. It concerned changes to athletes, sport scientists, and sport club activities. Each of these is considered below.

### (1) Search for a New Identity for the Athletes

After the GDR athletes were allowed free travel, something they had not known for 28 years, many tried to become professionals in the West. Their top coaches followed apace. When there were no positions in West Germany for them, they went to other countries, such as Italy, Austria, Holland, England, and even Australia (*Es werden Wunder geschehen,* 1997). However, many former East German athletes found themselves experiencing identity crises because it was very difficult to adapt to the new situation. They had problems getting used to their newly won freedom. All their life they had been told what to do; in the training, of course, and even in their personal life, everything was regulated for them. Suddenly, they had to make decisions on their own rather than following orders. Their reaction was fear and uncertainty about the future, which distracted them from their tremendous motivation. Under the old system, they did not have to worry about their well-being, even after sports, because athletes were taken care of by the government. After quitting sport, they used to receive retirement money and a job as well. The GDR had a superb system for athletes as long as they contributed to represent the superiority of their social system. But as persons, the athletes often lacked the abilities to think on their own, make decisions, and be creative. Their system turned out great sport machines but prevented the individual athlete from becoming a responsible and mature individual. Former East German athletes in unified Germany did not and do not receive the same financial support as in the past. They had to find a job support themselves, and they only received a small stipend from an organization called *Deutsche Sporthilfe*. About 5,000 athletes receive sports aid in unified Germany today, of which 2,962 are from the former GDR.

### (2) Search for a New Identity for the Sport Scientists

East German academic institutions and their scholars also suffered an identity crisis. At the beginning of 1990, most of the academic institutions of the former GDR looked for partners in the FRG as they had to be reformed in light of the new situation. At the same time, they tried to market and sell their expertise in the field of top-level sports. Many academicians from the East turned around, trying to whitewash their former publications under the communist system. But almost no university offered them a position in West Germany; it was easier for them to get a position in foreign countries. For example, East German doping experts as well as their most successful coaches were hired by such countries as China in the hope of transforming or continuing the "East German sport wonder." In unified Germany, however, the former East German sport scientists, as well as the sport officials, had to go through a twofold screening process: a professional and a political evaluation. Many were forced to leave the university or take an early retirement due to their past political involvement (*Es werden Wunder*, 1991).

### (3) Search for a Rich Identity for Sport Club Activities

After the fall of the wall, the interest in sport among the East German population drastically dwindled. Only 50 percent of those who used to regularly participate in physical activity continued doing so. Thus, directly after the fall of the wall, the number of sport participants decreased to only 7% of East Germans compared to about 30% of Westerners. Also, for a variety of reasons, sport in East Germany lost many spectators. People turned their back on the former privileged elite athletes, the ticket prices for sport events went up, many top-level athletes left the country, and most of all, the economic situation in the five new states in the former GDR was devastating; and it still is not up to par with West Germany. Even today unemployment is higher in the East (about 15-18 percent) than in the West (about 10 percent), and the salaries in the East are still only 85 percent of what the Westerners earn. The high unemployment rate has led to increased frustration and aggression, which is reflected in the appearance of more widespread hooliganism. In addition, the 35,000 sport facilities in the former GDR totally deteriorated (*Ostdeutsche Kommunen*, 1991). However, the communities had no money for repairs, and the federal government generally is only responsible for facilities serving top-level athletics. Because of the financial burdens the five new states were facing, the German Sport Federation developed a new "Golden Plan East" (*Goldener Plan Ost*), which provided guidelines for the rebuilding and renewal of sport facilities in the former GDR. The money for this was to come partly from the federal government, from the five new states, and from the communities. It was hoped that the sport clubs in East Germany would receive money from taxation of lottery games, such as Toto and Lotto, as do the sport clubs in the West (*Ostdeutsche Kommunen*, 1991). Until East Germans have equal access and support to sport, the production of top-level athletes will be in serious doubt.

## The Doping Controversy

The disclosure of doping in the GDR elite sports and the fact that the doping lab in Kreischa had not prevented but continuously applied, tested, and even improved doping shocked the German sporting public after the German unification. The amount of drug use in the former GDR seemed to have greatly exceeded all suppositions. It is reported that athletes were often forced by their coaches to take the drugs, or they were told that the pills they were swallowing were vitamins or other harmless substances. Before entering into any competition in the West, GDR athletes were checked in Kreischa to see whether they were "clean" or not before departure.

After the fall of the wall, day after day, leading newspapers disclosed new doping cases in the East: "Doping in GDR Swimming," "Systematic Doping for Decades in Kreischa," "324 Cases of Doping in the GDR," and so on. Brigitte Berendonk's (1991) book *Doping Dokumente – Von der Forschung zum Betrug (Doping Documents – From Research to Cheating)* reveals more shocking news about the doping practices among virtually all top-level athletes in the former GDR, who are listed by names. The headline of another article reads "Death or Male Formation" and tells how doped female athletes often walked a thin line between death and becoming increasingly "masculine." In some cases of famous sprinters, such as Bärbel Woeckel and Marita Koch, it was found that their anabolic steroid intake was almost twice as high than that of Ben Johnson when he was stripped of his gold medal. Even teenage female athletes as young as 14 years old took anabolics, which slowed down or even stopped their female development and at the same time created stronger athletes that would better serve their country by gaining athletic glory. Negative side effects, such as liver damage, severe acne, male genital formations, facial hair, and psychological formations, did not deter the trainers, doctors, scientists, coaches, and athletes from encouraging these life-threatening practices. Also, documents revealing experiments testing various combinations of drugs on teenagers being trained at state-run sport schools were found. To give high dosages of male hormones to teenage girls was "legal" practice under the East German system, whereas in the West this was and is considered a medical crime. The athletes had to sign papers swearing secrecy. If athletes refused to take the drugs or if their bodies did not tolerate them, they were thrown out of the sport schools and the training programs.

The athletes' doping plans were researched and programmed for each individual several years in advance, usually in a 4-year Olympic cycle. Twelve days before major sporting events, the athletes would restrain from taking drugs orally but would continue with injections until hours before the events. This practice, as well as checkups in Kreischa, saved most East German athletes from ever testing positive during international doping controls. Those who tested positive back home were simply restricted from traveling to the sporting events. In many ways, doping in the GDR was organized along the lines of a top-secret military strategy. Doping plans were kept locked in safes and coded so that, to a novice, they looked like very complicated computer output. Although East Germans were not alone and doping practices continue in international sports, their doping experiments displayed an unusual lack of respect toward both their athletes and the ethos of sport. The protocols of the research documents read like the ones found in some of the most inhumane experiments of the SS or other doctors of the Third Reich.

After the unification of Germany, Berlin investigators were now interrogating the East German scientists who administered the doping programs. The FKS in Leipzig claimed that all doping research was stopped immediately after the collapse of the communist government. Still, the revelations raised concerns that German sport teams in the future would secretly adopt some of the East German doping practices. Officials of the German Sport Association vehemently denied such plans, although we now know that many top athletes in the West have also been practicing doping on a more individualized basis as a regular part of their training routine since 1978 (Berendonk, 1991), and that was and still is the case in many countries in the world (e.g., China, Canada, USA, and others). Berendonk suspected in 1991 that doping would continue to be a regular part of top-level athletics in the future and that a new infrastructure of doping "experts" would be developed. She was fearful that doping practices would be kept under greater secrecy and that we would see regular monitoring by the laboratories in Kreischa and Cologne before major sporting events to prevent athletes from testing positive (p. 294). However, this is just one rather jaundiced view. The German Sport Federation installed three commissions to shed light on the doping issue and to prevent future abuses. However, many athletes, coaches, and sport scientists only received minimal punishment and small fines. This is not a great deterrent for future usage of doping in the sporting world. And we know that these practices are still continuing and even on the rise at the international levels.

## Looking into the Future

The East German sport system was a highly centralized apparatus and in no way a model for a democratic polity. Sport was used as a political tool to promote communist ideology. The athlete, a dehumanized tool within the sport system, was respected and supported only if he or she was successful. A politically governed sport has no place in unified Germany. One East German Olympic gold medalist, Juergen May, noted, "If one wants to copy the East German top-level sport, one has to copy the social order of the German Democratic Republic as well" (quoted in Voigt, 1975, 86). Thus, sport in unified Germany was in urgent need of a new political meaning as well as a new ethical foundation.

The unification of Germany was a good occasion to re-examine the Eastern as well as the so-called Western approach to sport and physical education and to redefine what sport should be in modern industrial times. A sole focus on the effectiveness of performance should never be used as the criterion for the evaluation of a sport system. Athletic success can be measured many ways. A humanistic sport system that looks to fair competition on a level playing field is only the beginning of a new direction (Haag, 1990). In all our striving for excellence in sports, we need to be careful not to look at athletes as machines. Too often, there is the tendency in top-level sports and applied sports science to treat athletes in terms of their body parts or sporting achievements rather than a human being as a whole. A cooperative approach in research among scientists from varied disciplines is a good idea as long as it is not misused for the good of the system rather than the individual. We have to separate ourselves from "the ends justifying the means" approach.

At the end of the 20th century, Germans had the unique historic chance to give new meaning to sport: to provide a higher status of sport in society in general, to restructure top-level sport by eliminating doping and other exploitative and dehumanizing practices, and to raise the quality of life for all people by implementing the "sport for all" program that includes children, the disabled and the elderly in the promotion of recreational sport and physical activity. It remains to be seen whether these unique chances for sport in unified Germany will make a difference in the right direction. It is not fair to blame those who dismantled the East German sports system: "There are more important things than sport at the moment. People are free now to do what they like" (Tedeschi, 1991, 50). However, unified Germany needs a clean sport and physical education system, since it plays an important role in educating all people – women and men, young and old, healthy and sick, able and disabled – about the benefits of sports. Such a sport system includes not only top-level athletics in the form of professional sports, but should also provide opportunities for physical activity to be part of every individuals' every day lived experiences.

# References

Berendonk, B. (1991). *Doping Dokumente. Von der Forschung zum Betrug.* Berlin: Heidelberg; New York: Springer Verlag.

Deutsche Vereinigung für Sportwissenschaft. (1990). *Informationen,* 2 and 10.

Es werden Wunder geschehen. (1991). *Der Spiegel, 41,* 252-258.

Haag, H. (1990). ISCPES-News. *International Journal of Physical Education, 27*(3), 43-46.

Ostdeutsche Kommunen werden Eigentümer der Sportanlagen. (1991). DSB *Deutscher Sportbund Presse.* Pp. 13-14.

Puzzlespiel der Sporthilfe bei Adressensuche. *Frankfurter Allgemeine Zeitung,* January, 19.

Sport Institute bleiben bestehen.(1990). *Kölner Stadtanzeiger,* October, 4.

Tedeschi, B. (1991). The High Price of Freedom. Will a Reunified Germany Continue to Dominate the International Sports Scene? *Women's Sports and Fitness,* January/February.

Voigt, D. (1975). *Soziologie in der DDR: Eine exemplarische Untersuchung.* Köln: Verlag Wissenschaft und Politik.

Zeitschritt für Fragen der DDR and der Deutschlandpolitik. (1990, Oktober). Deutschland Archiv, 3, 8, and 12.

## Issue 2

# Sport as New Religion

The new religion of sport in the modern world is constituted by the religious practices of its followers. The practices range from athlete worship to body worship. Sports are organized and dramatized in a religious way, even though it cannot be regarded as the highest form of religion. Sport is a form of "godliness," whereby the human spirit seeks to be "perfect."

Sport and religion, two seemingly opposing fields of study and practice, serve similar functions and purposes in people's lives. This factor becomes even more apparent in highly industrialized societies with their tendencies of turning away from "traditional meaning providers," such as the church, to a secularized view or explanation of the world.

> *Our repertoire of significant national, religious, and mythological symbol has been seriously drained of its potency. We are living at a time ... when all the once regnant world systems that have sustained (also, distorted) Western intellectual life from theologies to ideologies, are taken to be in severe collapse. This leads to a mood of skepticism, an agnosticism of judgment, sometime a world-weary nihilism in which even the most conventional minds bring question both distinction of value and the value of distinctions. (Postman 1992, 179)*

The shift to modernity that is characterized by Weber at the end of the 19 century as the collapse of religious authority and the rise of a rationalized bureaucratic social order with increased specialization is still important at the end of the 20th century. Many scholars, including Berman (1982) and Postman (1992) would argue that modernity does not necessarily entail more happiness for people but rather a loss of control over nature, which is prevalent in the occurrence and increase of health problems such as heart disease, cancer, and AIDS. The advance of the technological age have a dark foresight that "the uncontrolled growth technology destroys the vital sources of our humanity. It creates a culture without a moral foundation. It undermines certain mental processes and social relation that make human life worth living" (Postman, 1992, xii).

Responses to the loss and disappointments of modern culture started appear in North America first in the 1960s in the arts and a variety of leftwing politics. Turning to sport can be characterized as one of the major response people use to cope with the changes in society; other reactions include taking drugs, abusing alcohol and more. The furor of sport, including the fitness movement, can be described as a reaction by the general public to disengage from the negative effects of life in modern culture. This reaction is an attempt by individuals to counterbalance the deficiencies of the modern era. Postman argues that people are turning away from traditional values and longing for a new order that provides meaning to their lives: "Having drained many of their traditional symbols, [people] resort, somewhat pitifully, to sporting yellow ribbons as a mean of symbolizing their fealty to a cause" (1992, 180).

The idea of people having lost traditional values and shifting to sport is also spelled out somewhat cynically by von Soosten (1995). Today, it seems to be possible to declare everything as sport, and sport means everything. Thus, sport has penetrated into all spheres of social life, especially in the USA. Sport can be declared the new religion at the end of the 20th and the beginning of the 21st centuries. Why are people turning toward sport, leaving traditional religions behind? Undoubtedly, television has had a major effect on this development; it therefore can be declared the "medium for sport as a religion" (Aitken, 1992). But other factors of life in complex societies are of equal importance, including the following:

- more personal and free time has leisure sport replacing work as central focus;
- people no longer feel a puritan ethic against games and amusement;
- sport gives support to the idea that (the deeply installed North American values of) achievement, success, hard work, and discipline are ways to godliness;
- and modern human beings are to take charge of their own destiny (see Aitkett, 1992).

A general shift of values in modern societies certainly supports the rise of sport as a new religion. In the following pages, I will first analyze what value changes were conducive to the rise of sport, and second, how sport is manifesting itself as a new religion in the USA.

## Value Changes and the Rise of Sport

As noted in Chapter 3, values have changed extensively over the last 50 years. There has been a general shift away from more socially oriented values, such as equality or national security, to personal values, such as freedom, comfort, and excitement (Inglehard, 1985). Klages, et al., (1992) attribute this to the process of individualization and the changed living conditions in highly industrialized societies. Value change is therefore not as much a shift as an expansion, which results in "value pluralism" (Tetlock, 1986). Traditional value orientations do not vanish; they are extended. Generally, the "old" achievement ethic is losing its significance. Post-industrialized society is attributed by Klages, et al., as one with decreasing achievement ethics, increasing expectations of the state, and an increased orientation and interest in leisure activities, especially in the area of sports (1992, 10ff).

Reasons for value change can be attributed to the increasing process of secularization after the Second World War, the rise in the standard of living as well as consumption, the relative freedom of choice of behavior and action, increased mobility, expansion of the educational system, ecological problems, changes in family structures, extended use and influence of mass media, and more (Digel, 1986, 25-29). Politics, economics, and personal values are all inextricably linked. Thus, values and social development influence each other. That is, when society changes its goals, institutions and values change as well. This development directs the behavior and action of individuals and groups. Values and their ranking are shaped by cultural and historical context. Physical activities and sports in many pre-industrial societies were linked to religious rituals; however, in modern societies, especially in the United States, sport has now replaced religion in many people's lives. Evidence of this phenomenon will be described below.

## The Sacred in Sport

Sport in ancient Greece began as a religious rite to please the gods for fertility, rain, and healing of the sick. Over time, these influences were transformed through secularization. Modern athletes worship production and achievement (Hoffman, 1992) as well as their bodies; however, the trend is toward seeing sport religiously again and using the Christian religion to further its advances through sport. Especially in North American society, the use of religion (Christianity) by sport for its own benefits can be observed like an experiment in a test tube (see examples below). But in contrast to the beginning of time where sport served religion, religion today is used in the service of sport leading to the replacement of religion with sport. This point will be illustrated in a threefold manner:

(I) Athletes often talk about sport as a way to open mind and soul. Sport today is using and absorbing religion for its own benefits.
(2) Joggers claim they find religion on the roads not in church. Running is perceived as proof of the existence of God.
(3) Fitness pursuits embody religious body symbolism.

### (1) Sport Uses Religion

There is a religious phenomenon sweeping the country [USA] that is called 'sport.' Glamorous cathedrals are built to conduct the worship of its followers. These cathedrals are commonly referred to as stadiums – a new and modern term that indicates the changes in the modern world. The worship usually takes place on Sundays.... (Olson, 1989, 213).

Even though sport and religion may not be thought of as being linked, there has been much crossover and interaction between the two entities in recent years. This has been especially true for Christianity and athletics in the USA, which can be easily viewed by turning on the television to the professional or college games. Athletes kneel in prayer in the end zone after scoring a touchdown, or they give tribute to Jesus Christ in post-game interviews. Such behaviors are mainly witnessed in games such as football and basketball, which may also reflect the class and/or politics of the coaches and others involved in the sports. An intriguing question for further investigation on this issue is whether religiosity varies with particular sports.

Prayer is often used by athletes and coaches to cope with the uncertainty that is always present in athletics. "Lord, I want to win, and I want us to have the opportunity to glorify your name" (Kinsolving, 1993, A-4). By praying before the game, athletes are able to get rid of their anxiety, thus allowing them to focus on the contest and ultimately to perform better. Many professional teams hold weekly chapel services for the players, and numerous college teams do the same (Prebish, 1984). Another use of prayer by the sporting world is to help prepare athletes for the contest ahead. One might wonder why coaches use prayer rather than a pep talk. Football teams gather in the locker room to recite a prayer together before they step on the playing field. This type of togetherness helps to bring the athletes closer, building team unity and giving them a "we" feeling (Coakley, 2004). While praying, athletes and coaches turn to a higher authority that requests obedience but also takes the burden – the pressure to win – of their shoulders. If the athletes later "fail" to win, there is some assurance that it was not solely their responsibility. Hoffman cynically remarks that "pre-game piety usually runs in the direct proportions to the importance of the contest, the anticipated size of the audience and the probability that participation will suffer pain and injury" (1985, 67).

Finally, athletes have used religion to sanctify the behavior of the athletes and the contests. The presumption is that if something as sacred as religion can be linked with athletics, then athletics must be a worthwhile pursuit and not just aimless frivolity. Athletes spend hours of time in preparation for contests and this time investment essentially produces nothing beneficial to society other than entertainment. In order for the athletes to feel that their profession has meaning and worth, many have decided to use their athletic talents to proselytize others. The desire to use the visibility of athletic prowess for Christian witness has become institutionalized in organizations such as the *Institute for Athletic Perfection* or *Muscular Christians*. A few of the most recognized organizations are the *Fellowship of Christian Athletes, Athletes in Action, and Professional Athletes Outreach* (Coakley, 2004). The reasons these organizations have combined with athletics are because they have recognized the tremendous influence athletes have on people and the importance that athletics plays in American society.

### (2) Running as a Religious Experience

> There is also the phenomenon of the born-again runner. Akin to the born-again Christian, the individual, often middle-aged, who might have been active athletically in youth but then lapsed into sinful ways: eating too much, drinking too much, cavorting with wicked women (or scandalous men), is allowing the body to deteriorate... (e.g., occluded coronary arteries)... Like born-again Christians, these individuals are often the most active proselytizers of others, attempting to convert the non-believers into practitioners of their new-found sport/faith under the theory that if it feels this good to me, everybody else should be doing it too. 'Now I know what it feels like to be a born-again Baptist,' comments one 35-year-old female runner of the Jewish faith. 'I try to convert my non-running friends' (Higdon, 1992, 77).

Running is the most important activity in an increasing number of people's lives. These individuals are mainly from the middle class and are between 20 and 45 years of age. Running races and the preparation for future events become their worship, especially as these activities take place on Sunday mornings:

> Running is ... a purifying activity that often dominates their weekends with races and preparations for future races, becoming their Sabbath, taking over their Sunday mornings, the traditional time when at least the Christian majority in the United States attends church (Higdon, 1992, 77).

Many people have turned away from the overemphasis of competitive sports toward running in order to achieve harmony and peace with oneself and the surrounding, while others are turning to running in a highly competitive way. However, many devoted runners refer to the activity with religious terminology; some runners even claim that they experience God as they run.

> *By taking long solitary runs* I have found that one is able to get in touch with the inner-voice, the soul, and the outside world *falls* away, ... , a *different world* forms before the eyes, the heart begins to beat faster, the lungs cry out for more oxygen, and the mind thinks about ... life in general, or maybe poetry or a song that's stuck in the *brain, and the longer the run* goes on, the quickening of the pulse, the closer it becomes to a ... *religious experience, and stress and* worries melt away .... The

journey into getting physically fit *is a journey into getting to know oneself* (Student Report, 1995).

Running with its system of beliefs and practices as well as its set of ethical values can be considered a form of religion: taking care of one's body is a way of serving God's will. Running gives meaning to people's lives; they feel devotion toward a real sense of purpose, and being with nature allows them to contemplate God. Higdon goes so far as to equate Jesus' going to the mountains to fast for 40 days to create awareness of his own being with the 40 days the runner needs to adapt to an exercise program and the 40 minutes of continual running to experience the runner's high (1992, 79). When runners are interviewed about their experiences, they claim that running offers a new perspective on life, a belonging. They also experience surroundings that reflect God's glory, and they put coming events into a spiritual perspective:

> There is a difference between a traditional religion and running.... When one believes in a religion and in God, it is a belief in something outside of oneself, in a way an abandoning of power to something outside. On the contrary, a belief in running, 'the new religion,' is a belief in oneself, in one's power, in one's ability for improve discipline and to take charge of one's own life. ... running has strengthened my own religious ... beliefs (Higdon, 1992, 79).

### (3) Fitness and Body Worship

> Physical fitness and health ... describe painful experiences, tasteless foods, and none of life's simple pleasures. These words to me are a religion with the gym as my church, the weights as my bible, and exercise as my daily worship (Student Report, 1995).

Sport represents a form of contemporary embodiment. It makes people think about their bodies, while some think about religion. The whole field of body-related cultural production and consumption, even beyond sport, represents a form of body worship. The symbolic power that arises in this field is responsible to a large degree for promoting, as well as asserting, the social recognition of body ideals. Concepts of the "best self" and the "best body" replace ideals of a "beautiful soul" (Rittner, 1991). The worship and concern for the soul has shifted to worship of and concern for the body. Alkemeyer and Broeskamp (1996) claim that "the aesthetic modeling of the body through sport, influenced by the mass media and attributable to social and economic pressures of highly industrialized societies, is perhaps most obvious in body building and body-styling." Driven by an ever-growing leisure industry, as well as by the disappointment and reluctance to carry on with consumption, new waves of body cult, fitness and health follow one another in rapid succession. The focus on the here and now in consumer culture seeks perfection and fulfillment through body worship: the focus of tomorrow and concerns for the soul lose significance.

The body has always been highly contested terrain for a broad spectrum of theological and ritual practices. Previously, people engaged in ascetic practices for purification to get in closer contact with the deity; today, they diet and practice abstinence (no smoking, no drinking, no fatty foods, etc.) to achieve certain beauty ideals. Modern ascetic practices related to the body cult promise eternal youth, happiness, well-being, beauty, and health. This can only be achieved trough self-control, discipline, dieting, and exercising, or so it is claimed. Healing and modeling of the body is practiced for reasons related to the body itself – promoting health and prolonging life. The hope for a better tomorrow – the promise of the Christian religion – has lost its significance. Rittner (1991) characterizes this process by explaining that the concepts of the soul are losing their significance, while the body emerges to be of primary concern for people in modern society. The "best body" is perceived to guarantee happiness here and now; the hope and belief in a brighter tomorrow is gradually fading away (Rittner, 1991).

## Conclusion

Despite their seemingly diverse natures, the intertwined nature of sport and religion has become increasingly deeper during the 20th century in the United States. Many Christian denominations have realized the strongholds sport has on American society and have been able to justify the goodness of athletics for the Christian – quite in contrast to the Puritan disrespect of sport during Colonial times and the 19th century (Freeman, 1992). The Puritanical influence, wherein sports were condemned by the church, scarcely resides anymore. In contrast religion (primarily Christianity) has formed a union with sport.

Religion and sport share many important characteristics, which set an excellent stage for sport to qualify as a new religion. Sport shares a certain organizational structure with traditional religions, including ceremonies, rituals, heroes, symbols, myth, chant songs, and more. In addition, people in sport, much like in religion, participate through self-denial, and they are confronted with daily human living, aging, dying, failure, betrayal, guilt, and more. Another important characteristic the new religion, namely sport, shares with its traditional counterparts, is the loyalty its followers express – especially the devotion and sense of belonging, as well as the meaning that is provided to people's lives through and by sport lifts up sport from the trenches and places it in the higher spheres of religion. The "living faith" that is presented by the followers of sport in the modern world rests in the heart of reality, and thus, is a living attribute to their devotion and conviction.

## References

Aitken, B. (1997). Sport, Religion and Human Well-Being, in: S. Hoffman (Ed.). *Sport and Religion.* Pp. 237-244. Champaign, IL: Human Kinetics.

Alkmeyer, T. & Broeskamp. B. (1996). Strangerhood and Racism in Sport. In: *Sport Science Review: Changing Values in Sport, 5* (2), 30-52.

Berman, M. (1982). *All That's Solid Melts in the Air.* New York: Columbia University Press.

Coakley, J. (2004). *Sport in Society: Issues and Controversies.* Boston: McGraw Hill.

Digel, H. (1986), Uber den Wandel der Werte in Gesellschaft, Freizeit und Sport. Pp. 14-43. In: K. Heinenmann, H. Becker (Eds.). *Die Zukunft des Sports.* Schorndorf: Hofmann.

Higdon, H. (1992). Is Running a Religious Experience? In: S. Hoffman (Ed.), *Sport and Religion.* Champaign, IL: Human Kinetics.

Hoffman, J. (1985). Evangelism and the Revitalization of Religious Ritual in Sport. *Arete, 2,* 63-87.

Hoffman, S. (Ed.) (1992). Sport and Religion. Champaign, IL: Human Kinetics.

Inglehart, R. (1985). Aggregate Stability and Individual Flux in Mass Belief Systems: The Level of Analysis Paradox. *American Political Science Review, 79,* 97-116.

Kinsolving, C. (1993). Second Coming Prepared Bills' Quarterback for Big Comeback. *Intelligencer Journal, January 9,* A-4.

Klages, H.; Hippler, H.-J.; Herbert, W. (1992). *Werte und Wandel. Ergebnisse und Methoden einer Forschungstradition.* Frankfurt, New York: Campus Verlag.

Olson, R. (1989). *Winning is the Only Thing.* Baltimore: The John Hopkins University Press.

Postman, N. (1992). *Technopoly. The Surrender of Culture to Technology.* New York: Vintage Books.

Prebish, C. (1984). "Heavenly Father, Devine Goalie": Sport and Religion. *Antioch Review, 42* (3), 306-318.

Rittner, V. (1991). + und Zivilisierung. Pp. 512-527. In: G. Jüttemann, M. Sonntag, C. Wulf (Eds.). *Die Seele. Ihre Geschichte im Abendland.* Weinheim: Psychologie Verlags Union.

von Soosten, J. (1995). *Die Tränen des Andreas Müller.* Unpublished Manuscript.

Student Reports (1995). *Fitness for Life Class,* West Chester University, PA. Fall Semester.

Tetlock, P. (1986). A Value Pluralism Model of Ideological Reasoning. *Journal of Personality and Social Psychology, 50* (4), 819-827.

Weber, M. (1956). *Wirtschaft und Gesellschaft.* Tübingen.

# ALL TITLES
# FROM THIS SERIES

392 p., b/w, paperback

5 3/4" x 8 1/4"

ISBN: 9781841263380

$ 24.95 US/$ 49.95 AUS/

£ 19.95 UK/€ 24.95

Nick T. Pappas

## THE DARK SIDE OF
## SPORTS

The present work was written for athlet

coaches, managers and administrato

sports fans, educators, and students

address the rampant sexual deviancy c

aggression occurring within many athl

cultures. The book will also be an add

on in courses such as sociology of sp

sports psychology, women's studies, c

sociology.

Physical activities, fitness, and sports can be considered cultural practice

reflecting multiple meanings. The "Sport, Culture and Society" series deal

with issues intersecting sport, physical activity, health, aging, and culture

Karin Volkwein-Caplan/Gopal Sankaran

SEXUAL HARASSMENT IN SPORT

Impact, Issues and Challenges

128 p., b/w, paperback, 5 3/4" x 8 1/4"
ISBN: 9781841260594
$ 17.95 US/$ 29.95 AUS/£ 12.95 UK/€ 18.90

Earle F. Zeigler

SOCIO-CULTURAL FOUNDATIONS OF PHYSICAL
EDUCATION AND EDUCATIONAL SPORT

358 p., b/w, 12 illus., paperback, 5 3/4" x 8 1/4"
ISBN: 9781841260938
$ 19.95 US/$ 32.95 AUS/£ 14.95 UK/€ 18.90

James Skinner/Keith Gilbert/Allan Edwards (eds.)

SOME LIKE IT HOT

The Beach as a Cultural Dimension

206 p., b/w, 5 illus., paperback, 5 3/4" x 8 1/4"
ISBN: 9781841260983
$ 19.95 US/$ 32.95 AUS/£ 14.95 UK/€ 18.90

Marion Keim

NATION BUILDING AT PLAY

Sport as a Tool for Social Integration in Post-apartheid
South Africa

226 p., b/w, 69 illus., paperback, 5 3/4" x 8 1/4"
ISBN: 9781841260990
$ 19.95 US/$ 32.95 AUS/£ 14.95 UK/€ 18.90

concerns. The focus of the series is interdisciplinary, ground-breaking work that draws on different disciplines and theoretical approaches, such as sociology, philosophy, cultural anthropology, history, cultural studies, feminist studies, post-modernism, or critical theory.

Keith Gilbert (ed.)
SEXUALITY, SPORT AND THE CULTURE OF RISK

196 p., b/w, paperback, 5 3/4" x 8 1/4"
ISBN: 9781841261485
$ 19.95 US/$ 32.95 AUS/£ 14.95 UK/€ 18.90

William James Hoverd
WORKING OUT MY SALVATION

The Contemporary Gym and the Promise of

'Self' Transformation

112 p., b/w, 2 illus., paperback 5 3/4" x 8 1/4"
ISBN: 9781841261607
$ 17.95 US/$ 32.95 AUS/£ 12.95 UK/€ 18.95

Heather Sheridan, Leslie A. Howe & Keith Thompson (eds.)

SPORTING REFLECTIONS

Some Philosophical Perspectives

192 p., b/w, 2 photos, paperback 5 3/4" x 8 1/4"
ISBN: 9781841261829
$ 19.95 US/$ 32.95 AUS/£ 14.95 UK/€ 18.95

**MEYER & MEYER
Sports GmbH**
Von-Coels-Str. 390
52080 Aachen
Germany

Telephone    0049 - 2 41 - 9 58 10 - 13
Fax    0049 - 2 41 - 9 58 10 - 10
E-Mail    sales@m-m-sports.com
E-Books    www.m-m-sports.com

These books are also available online and at your local book store.

**MEYER
& MEYER
SPORT**